Bigelow's
Computer Repair
Toolkit

Related Titles

Troubleshooting and Repairing Computer Monitors, 2nd edition,
by Stephen Bigelow
Troubleshooting and Repairing Computer Printers, 2nd edition,
by Stephen Bigelow
Troubleshooting and Repairing Solid TV's, 3rd edition,
by Homer Davidson
Troubleshooting and Repairing Audio Equipment, 3rd edition,
by Homer Davidson
Troubleshooting and Repairing Camcorders, 2nd edition,
by Homer Davidson
Troubleshooting and Repairing Compact Disc Players, 3rd edition,
by Homer Davidson
*Troubleshooting, Maintaining, and Repairing Personal Computers:
A Technician's Guide,* by Stephen Bigelow
Troubleshooting and Repairing PCs: Beyond the Basics, 3rd edition,
by Michael Hordeski

Bigelow's
Computer Repair
Toolkit

Stephen J. Bigelow

McGraw-Hill

New York San Francisco Washington, D.C. Auckland Bogotá
Caracas Lisbon London Madrid Mexico City Milan
Montreal New Delhi San Juan Singapore
Sydney Tokyo Toronto

Library of Congress Cataloging-in-Publication Data

Bigelow, Stephen J.
    Bigelow's computer repair toolkit / Stephen J. Bigelow.
        p.   cm.
    Includes index.
    ISBN 0-07-912979-X (hard)
    1. IBM-compatible computers—Maintenance and repair.   2. Utilities
(Computer programs)   I. Title.
TK7889.I26B54   1997
621.39'16—dc21   96-29780
                                                           CIP

McGraw-Hill

A Division of The McGraw·Hill Companies

1 2 3 4 5 6 7 8 9 0   DOC/DOC   9 0 2 1 0 9 8 7

P/N 005802-4
PART OF
ISBN 0-07-912979-X

The sponsoring editor for this book was Scott Grillo, the editing supervisors were Fred Bernardi, and Paul R. Sobel, and the production supervisor was Pamela A. Pelton. It was set in ITC Century Light by McGraw-Hill's Professional Book Group composition unit, Hightstown, N.J.

Printed and bound by R. R. Donnelley & Sons Company.

The following trademarks and servicemarks may appear in this book. Every effort has been made to cover each appropriate reference. All other trademarks and servicemarks remain the property of their respective owners. *IBM* is a trademark of International Business Machines; *MS-DOS*, Windows, and Windows 95 are trademarks of Microsoft Corporation; *The PC Toolbox* is a trademark of Dynamic Learning Systems; *i86, i286, i386, i486, Pentium,* and *Intel* are trademarks of Intel Corporation; *CompuServe* is a trademark of CompuServe Incorporated; *AOL* and *America Online* are trademarks of America Online Incorporated.

McGraw-Hill books are available at special quantity discounts to use as premiums and sales promotions, or for use in corporate training programs. For more information, please write to the Director of Special Sales, McGraw-Hill, 11 West 19th Street, New York, NY 10011. Or contact your local bookstore.

This book is printed on recycled, acid-free paper containing a minimum of 50% recycled, de-inked fiber.

Disclaimer and Cautions

It is IMPORTANT that you read and understand the following information. Please read it carefully!

Repairing personal computers and their peripherals involves some amount of personal risk. Use **extreme** caution when working with ac and high-voltage power sources. If you are uncomfortable following the procedures or using the software that is outlined in this book, **do not attempt it.** Refer your service to qualified service personnel.

Neither the author, publisher, nor anyone directly or indirectly connected with the publication of this book shall make any warranty, either expressed or implied, with regard to this material, including but not limited to the implied warranties of quality, merchantability, and fitness for any particular purpose. Further, neither the author, publisher, nor anyone directly or indirectly connected with the publication of this book shall be liable for errors or omissions contained herein, or for incidental or consequential damages, injuries, or financial or material losses resulting from the use or inability to use the material contained herein. This material is provided *as is*, and the reader bears all responsibilities connected with its use.

Software Disclaimer

The software presented in this book and provided on the accompanying media is provided *as is*. Neither the author, publisher, nor anyone directly or indirectly connected with the publication of this book shall make any warranty or guarantee as to the performance of the software enclosed. You understand that computer software may not work on all PC platforms or configurations. Further, use of software by a particular author should not be constructed as an endorsement of that author or their software. Dealing with software authors directly should be the same as making any other mail order purchase–let the buyer beware.

Virus/Error Disclaimer

Every piece of software on the enclosed media has been checked for computer viruses and found virus-free prior to publication. However, you are **strongly advised** check for viruses using your own anti-virus tools prior to executing any new piece of software for the first time. If a computer virus is detected, *do not* execute the infected program–instead, erase the infected program from your system. Neither the author, publisher, nor anyone directly or indirectly connected with the publication of this book shall be liable for any incidental or consequential damages, injuries, or financial or material losses resulting from the occurance of computer viruses or software programming errors in any program on the enclosed media.

Data Disclaimer

You are **strongly advised** to perform a full system backup (i.e. copying the entire contents of all system hard drives to tape or other suitable media) before using any of the software included with this book. Neither the author, publisher, nor anyone directly or indirectly connected with the publication of this book shall be liable for any incidental or consequential damages, injuries, or financial or material losses resulting from the loss of data while using any program on the enclosed media.

Contents

Preface *xv*

Acknowledgments *xvii*

Notices *xix*

1 Shareware reference *1*
Software tools *1*
    Diagnostics vs. utilities *2*
    Larger vs. smaller *3*
    Windows vs. DOS *4*
    Commercial software vs. shareware *4*
The shareware concept *5*
    An issue of distribution *5*
    The idea of shareware *6*
    Problems with shareware *6*
    The ASP: a mark of quality *8*
The DLS Diagnostic CD *8*
    The CD and file compression *9*
    Installing the software *10*
    Registering the shareware *13*
    MONITORS and PRINTERS *13*
    Caring for the DLS Diagnostic CD *13*
The DLS bulletin board *14*

2 General PC hardware tools *15*
Benchmarking utilities *15*
    JCBENCH.EXE *17*

BIOS ID/reporting utilities   *19*
    BIOS.ZIP   *19*
    BIOSR11.ZIP   *21*
    PCM140.EXE   *24*
    READBI.EXE   *26*
    SHOWS174.ZIP   *30*
Burn-in/stress tests   *32*
    486TST.ZIP   *33*
CMOS utilities   *35*
    CMOS.ZIP   *36*
    CMOSRAM2.ZIP   *38*
CPU utilities   *41*
    MAXSPEED.EXE   *41*
    SRXTEST.EXE   *43*
General system tests   *44*
    ASQ0315.ZIP   *44*
    CHECK136.ZIP   *48*
    CONF810E.ZIP   *51*
    FIXCLOCK.ZIP   *54*
    OVERHEAD.ZIP   *57*
    RESOUR11.ZIP   *58*
    RITM25.ZIP   *61*
    SNOOP330.ZIP   *65*
    SPC.ZIP   *69*
    SYSCHK40.ZIP   *73*
    SYSINF.ZIP   *77*
I/O, IRQ, and DMA tests   *78*
    CHKIO.ZIP   *79*
    IRQINFO.ZIP   *81*
    PORT11.ZIP   *84*
    SPYDOS.ZIP   *86*
    SWAPIRQ.ZIP   *88*
Memory/cache tests   *91*
    486TEST.ZIP   *91*
    CACHECHK.ZIP   *93*
    MEMSCAN.ZIP   *96*
    RAMMAP.ZIP   *98*
    SHADTEST.ZIP   *100*

viii

3 Video tools *103*

Video ID/BIOS tools *104*
ATMEM10.ZIP *104*
IS_VID.EXE *106*
PSV10.ZIP *108*

Screen and palette tools *114*
HISCAN.ZIP *114*
PALU15.ZIP *117*
PSPS30.ZIP *119*
VGAHUE.ZIP *122*

Alignment tools and diagnostics *124*
CNVRGE.ZIP *124*
CRTAT2.ZIP *126*
VIDEO.EXE *128*
VIDEOT.ZIP *131*
VIDSPD40.ZIP *134*

4 Printer and parallel port tools *137*

Parallel port utilities *138*
PARAMO.ZIP *138*
EZSET.ZIP *141*

Printing utilities *143*
LASMAN.ZIP *144*
PRINTGF.ZIP *146*
PRNTGL.ZIP *151*
ZC33.ZIP *155*

Printer maintenance utilities *158*
LASERTST.ZIP *158*
LZC26.ZIP *159*
PRN-TEST.ZIP *161*

5 Modem and communication tools *163*

Port/data analyzers *164*
BBX201.ZIP *164*
COMPRT25.ZIP *166*
COMRESET.ZIP *169*
COMTAP21.ZIP *171*

COMTEST.ZIP *173*
CTSSPU22.EXE *176*
SIMTRM.ZIP *182*
UARTTS.ZIP *185*
Modem utilities *186*
LISTEN10.ZIP *186*

6 Drive tools *189*
General drive tools *190*
DAAG310.ZIP *191*
DATA_REC.ZIP *194*
DDARP_13.ZIP *197*
DISKUTIL.ZIP *200*
DKI191.ZIP *203*
SREP.ZIP *207*
Floppy drive tools *208*
AUTOTEST.ZIP *208*
CHKDRV.ZIP *210*
CLEAN4.ZIP *212*
DFR.ZIP *214*
Hard drive tools *215*
BOOTRX.ZIP *216*
CSCTEST2.ZIP *217*
DUGIDE.ZIP *219*
FIPS10.ZIP *220*
HDCP.ZIP *226*
HDINFO.ZIP *229*
IDATA.ZIP *231*
PARTITV1.ZIP *232*
CD-ROM drive tools *236*
CDCP10.ZIP *236*
CDQCK120.ZIP *238*
CDSPEED.ZIP *242*
CDTA.ZIP *245*
DA7.ZIP *247*

7 General support tools *250*
Backup utilities and organizers *250*
BACKEE28.ZIP *252*

        CF537D.ZIP   *256*
        DCF49.ZIP   *259*
        DUP59.EXE   *263*
        SUPDIR10.ZIP   *267*
Boot managers   *270*
        BOOTSY.ZIP   *271*
        CCS103.ZIP   *273*
Editors   *276*
        HW16V210.ZIP   *276*
        RAVED.ZIP   *279*
        XEV43.ZIP   *282*
Input devices   *285*
        CALJOY22.ZIP   *285*
        JOY2.EXE   *287*
        SCODE22.ZIP   *289*
        STKVGA31.ZIP   *291*
        TMTX.EXE   *292*
Reference works   *295*
        CARDG2.ZIP   *295*
        LOCATO.ZIP   *298*
        THEREF43.ZIP   *300*
Sound utilities   *302*
        SBBEEP.ZIP   *302*
        SNDST.ZIP   *303*
Speed utilities   *306*
        SLO23.ZIP   *306*
System security   *308*
        GUARD.ZIP   *308*
        RWARD2.ZIP   *313*

8 MONITORS: the commercial version   *315*

All about MONITORS 2.01   *315*
        Unlocking your copy of MONITORS   *315*
Using MONITORS   *316*
        Testing your video adapter   *317*
        Choosing video test modes   *319*
        Color bars   *321*
        Convergence test (crosshatch)   *322*
        Convergence test (dots)   *322*

Linearity test   *323*
Phase test   *324*
Focus test   *324*
The purity tests   *325*
Blank raster test   *325*
High-voltage test   *326*
Monitor burn-In   *326*
When trouble occurs   *327*
Check the screen mode   *327*
When problems persist   *327*
Making MONITORS better   *328*

9 PRINTERS: the commercial version   *329*

All about PRINTERS   *329*
Unlocking your copy of PRINTERS   *330*
Selecting the printer   *332*
Selecting the port   *332*
Manual codes   *349*
Print intensity   *351*
Help mode   *351*
Tutor mode   *351*
Running the impact tests   *351*
Preliminary setup information   *352*
Carriage transport test   *353*
Paper transport test   *353*
Paper walk test   *354*
Print head test   *355*
Clean rollers   *356*
Print Test Page   *357*
Running the ink jet tests   *357*
Preliminary setup information   *359*
Carriage transport test   *359*
Paper transport test   *353*
Paper walk test   *354*
Print head test   *355*
Clean rollers   *356*
Print Test Page   *357*
Running the ink jet tests   *357*
Preliminary setup information   *359*

Carriage transport test *359*
Paper transport test *359*
Paper walk test *360*
Print head test *360*
Clean rollers *361*
Print Test Page *361*
Running the laser/LED tests *362*
Preliminary setup information *362*
Toner test *362*
Corona test *363*
Drum and roller test *365*
Fuser test *366*
Transport test *366*
Print Test Page *367*
About PRINTERS *362*
Quitting PRINTERS *369*
Making PRINTERS better *369*

A Shareware Author Contacts *371*

B Using the Dynamic Learning Systems BBS *389*

Index *393*

Preface

In the early days of PC repair, the computer was built from large numbers of slow, basic logic components. The expense of the computer made it economically feasible to use logic probes and oscilloscopes to track down logic errors–then replace the defective component. Today, however, PC troubleshooting is an endeavor that demands efficiency. Time is money, and the faster a technician tracks down and corrects a problem, the better. The classical troubleshooting tools of yesterday have been replaced by diagnostic programs that can put almost any PC sub-system through its paces, measure its performance, and report on its status in a matter of minutes. Still other programs can be used to enhance the PC's operation, or support particular applications.

Commercial diagnostics and utilities remain at the forefront of PC repair, but the growth of "shareware" as a distribution channel, combined with a wealth of technically savvy programmers around the world, has given rise to many different, highly specialized, software tools which are adept at testing the PC and its peripherals. This book is the first to bring together over 100 shareware and public domain diagnostics and utilities onto a single disk; the *DLS Diagnostic CD*. With the CD and this book to guide them, technicians finally have a "Swiss army knife" of tools to aid their troubleshooting or upgrades.

The book is divided into 9 chapters. The first chapter explains the shareware concept, and shows readers how to use the DLS Diagnostic CD. Each piece of shareware is highlighted over the next six chapters; Chapter 2 covers general PC hardware tools, Chapter 3 covers video systems, Chapter 4 deals with printers and parallel port tools, Chapter 5 provides modem and communication tools, Chapter 6 explains drive tools, and Chapter 7 offers a number of general support tools. There are also two commercial diagnostics included on the CD; MONITORS is covered in Chapter 8, and PRINTERS is discussed in Chapter 9.

I am always looking for new software tools to enhance future editions of the book and CD, so if you have good-quality shareware diagnostics available (or know the location of some good archives), feel free to pass the information along:

Dynamic Learning Systems
PO Box 282
Jefferson, MA 01522-0282 U.S.A.
Fax: 508-829-6819
BBS: 508-829-6706
E-mail: sbigelow@cerfnet.com
WWW: http://www.dlspubs.com/

Stephen J. Bigelow

Acknowledgments

Developing and testing computer software is, at its best, a difficult and challenging task. I cannot, therefore, allow this book to go to press without acknowledging the effort and vision of each software author and organization whose work appears herein. The software presented in this book represents countless hours of research, programming, debugging, and development work.

Abri Technologies, Inc.; Air System Technologies, Inc.; Derek Altamirano; A.N.D. Technologies; John De Armond; Joerg H. Arnu; Eric Balkan; Rich Belgard; Jesse Bize; BreakPoint Software; Michael Bruss; Harry P. Calevas; Computer Tyme; Bernd Cordes; Corporate Systems Center (CSC); Cottonwood Software; Philippe Duby; Bob Eyer; Robert Falbo; FBN Productions; FoleyHi-Tech Systems; Tobin Fricke; Les Gainous; Travis Gebhardt; Shane Gilbert; Uwe Gissemann; GMH Code; Paul Griffith; Rick Hardy; Michael Holin; Harold Holmes; Bill Holt; Scott Alan Hoopes; Rick Horowitz; Wolfgang Heck; Stephen Jenkins; John Jerrim; Markus Klama; Chang Ping Lee; Steve Leonard; Randy MacLean; Marcor Enterprises; Jean-Georges Marcotte; Irving Maron; Charles F. Martin; Maxim Computers; McAdams Associates; Doug Merrett; Micro Firmware Inc.; MicroMetric; MicroSystems Development, Inc.; Morton Utilities; Thomas Mosteller; Dave Murray; Kevin Noble; No Preservatives Software; Open Systems Resources (OSR), Inc.; Jack A. Orman; Paladin Software, Inc.; Douglas S. Parman; James B. Penny; Ray Polczynski; Paul Postuma; Qualitas, Inc.; Ravitz Software Inc.; T. Roscoe; Ed Ross; Brian Ryan; Hans Salvisberg; Arno Schaefer; Kok Hong Soh; Spacebook Consulting; Randy Stack; Barry St. John; Robert Stuntz; Patrick Swayne; Tech Assist, Inc.; TechStaff Corp.; Brent Turner; Charles Vachon; Ray Van Tassle; Vias and Associates; Peter Volpa; Chet Williams; and Zittware.

Notices

The following trademarked names may appear in this book. Every effort has been made to cover each appropriate reference. All other trademarked names remain the property of their respective owners.

IBM is a trademark of International Business Machines.

MS-DOS, Windows, and Windows 95 are trademarks of Microsoft Corporation.

The PC Toolbox is a trademark of Dynamic Learning Systems.

i86, i286, i386, i486, Pentium, and Intel are trademarks of Intel Corporation.

CompuServe is a trademark of CompuServe Incorporated.

AOL and America Online are trademarks of America Online Incorporated.

Shareware reference

Computer troubleshooting generally consists of four steps: defining your symptoms, identifying and isolating the problem area, repairing or replacing the defective assembly (or component), and retesting the system. If the problem remains, you must go back to step one and start again. For a technician, it is particularly important to identify a problem as quickly and accurately as possible. The longer it takes to identify a fault, the more expensive the repair will be for the customer. Accurately identifying a problem also ensures that only the defective assemblies are replaced, which saves time and money (not to mention frustration).

Unfortunately, identifying the problem area is not always as easy and direct as it might seem. Modern PCs use an incredibly diverse array of complex components and software. For example, the computer on your workbench right now probably uses at least ten major assemblies and components—a motherboard, CPU, memory, hard drive, floppy drive, CD-ROM drive, sound board, drive controller, power supply, and video adapter—all of which are probably made by several different manufacturers. When you realize that the BIOS and operating system software must work with all of this hardware and that new hardware is constantly being introduced, you can understand that there is an almost limitless potential for problems. As a consequence, there is no single "troubleshooting chart" or "swap list" to get you out of trouble.

Software tools

To identify a problem, a technician must be able to "see inside" the computer in order to learn which functions are working and which ones are not. By understanding the adapter board or components responsible for the defective function, you can then determine where the problem lies. If you have any background in electronics, you have probably learned about some common troubleshooting tools such as multimeters, oscilloscopes, and logic probes. In fact, you probably have these hardware tools on your workbench right now. In actual practice, however, such hardware tools are not terribly effective for computer troubleshooting. The reason is that technicians often lack any original signal information to compare with the results from such test instruments.

To overcome the limitations of hardware test instruments, computer technicians have grown to depend on software tools. Software provides several unique advantages over test instruments. First, software is fast; rather than spending hours examining each voltage level and logic signal in a circuit, software can exercise complete computer functions and report on its success or failure in just a few seconds. Second, software can interact with a computer by setting different modes of operation within the computer hardware itself—an impossible task for a simple voltmeter or oscilloscope. Third, software is relatively inexpensive; good, full-featured commercial diagnostics are priced about the same as a good multimeter.

Diagnostics vs. utilities

One of the most effective means of studying an ailing PC is by using diagnostics—test programs that exercise specific functions (or groups of functions). The program code in a diagnostic can perform many different functions, but its typical operation is to read status data from register locations that are standard in the PC, then translate that status data into meaningful information that can be displayed through text or graphics. For example, a diagnostic might report a faulty hard drive, memory address, motherboard function, or communication port. Add-on cards (e.g., video capture boards) typically come with their own specific diagnostic tailored specifically for the related hardware.

Unlike a diagnostic, which is used to test specific hardware, a utility is designed to modify or control the operation of a PC or enhance the system's operation. For example, a hard drive caching program, partition table manager, or hex disk file editor would all be considered utilities. The CD contained in this book provides a selection of both diagnostics and utilities. While you might be able to glean a little diagnostic information from a utility (e.g., a hard drive cache will not initialize, possibly suggesting a fault in memory), such information will usually be quite vague, so the utility is typically followed up by a diagnostic to confirm the problem.

Larger vs. smaller

How big and complicated should a diagnostic be? This is a question that software designers continue to debate. Some programmers use the "less is more" approach, which usually results in a large number of small, simple DOS diagnostics—each performing a specific function (or set of functions). Other programmers use the "all or nothing" philosophy, which tries to create an all-inclusive, sophisticated program that can test everything (this is most prevalent in commercial diagnostics).

Ultimately, the choice of diagnostic will depend on just how closely the particular program suits your needs. If you perform a lot of basic testing on various areas of a PC, a general-purpose diagnostic might fill your need. If you find yourself dealing mostly with a few specific problem areas, you might get more results from specific diagnostics. When selecting a diagnostic, there are some important factors to consider:

How usable is the program? This is perhaps the truest measure of a program's worth. If you find yourself reaching for the program disk regularly, it's probably something you need. On the other hand, a program that you turn to only occasionally is probably not worth a lot to you.

How accurate is the program? The great diversity of hardware (and its rapid development) means that some programs will not read your hardware accurately; this is as true for commercial software as it is for shareware. Incorrect CPU and clock-speed identification are two typical examples of this problem. A program that does not provide accurate information will probably sit unused.

How often is the program updated? This also relates to a program's accuracy. Regular updates and program patches usually suggest current, reliable software. Since major new generations of computer hardware are appearing every 18 to 24 months, it is reasonable to expect a major diagnostic revision to appear around that same time frame. In actual practice, most technicians use a mix of general-purpose and task-specific diagnostics. For example, you might "standardize" on one or two general system diagnostics, and supplement that with a series of drive, memory, soundboard, or SCSI diagnostics—depending on what gives you the most trouble. One of the advantages of this book's CD is that it offers you a mix of programs to choose from.

3

Windows vs. DOS

Another important debate among diagnostic and utility programmers is using DOS as opposed to Windows 3.*xx* or Windows 95. There are two factors that make Windows-based diagnostics particularly troublesome. First, Windows makes much more extensive use of a PC's resources than DOS (that is the nature of Windows). As a result, the simple fact that Windows boots at all eliminates the possibility of serious, catastrophic faults, so anything that a Windows-based "diagnostic" could possibly report would be minor. Second, Windows makes extensive use of disk swapping and temporary files. If a Windows-based diagnostic were to trigger a system failure, it would likely leave unwanted (perhaps even corrupted) files. This weakness is particularly strong in the permanent swap file (PSF) of Windows 3.*xx* and in the Registry of Windows 95. If either of these key system files were corrupted, Windows would fail to start until the damaged file was repaired.

By comparison, booting to the DOS command line is much less demanding on a system. It requires only a little conventional memory, almost no video resources, and few (if any) drivers. Your diagnostics can then examine each respective subsystem of the PC without risking file corruption or otherwise interfering with the operation of Windows. If you have a choice in the matter, DOS diagnostics are often the preferred tools for system testing. If your system is set to boot to Windows 95, you can press F8 when the "Starting Windows 95" message appears, then select option 5, which will boot to the command prompt (MS-DOS 7.0).

Commercial software vs. shareware

Another question to plague the diagnostic industry is whether commercial software or "alternative-distribution" software such as shareware is better. This is a complicated question; there is no absolute answer, but there are some practical solutions. First, diagnostics are not terribly complex pieces of software. Often more time and effort is put into the user interface than into the actual diagnostic routines. As a result, "shrink-wrap" commercial software tends to have more features and a slicker (though not necessarily better) user interface, along with a printed manual. Alternative-distribution software, when written by a technically savvy programmer, is every bit as effective as commercial software. However, since such software is usually programmed by one or two people on a shoestring budget, it often lacks the "bells and whistles" found in commercial products. There is rarely a printed manual, though most products provide very thorough documentation in a disk file. You will find excellent diagnostics in both commercial software and alternative software.

The shareware concept

You've now seen the word *shareware* used several times in this chapter, so I should probably discuss exactly what shareware is and how it relates to commercial software. If you already understand the shareware concept, feel free to skip this section. Otherwise, this information will probably be very helpful to you.

An issue of distribution

When you think of diagnostic software, most people tend to think of fancy shrink-wrapped boxes lining store shelves. This is commercial software sold through distributors. Commercial software begins when a bright group of programmers start a small company to write software, but they don't have the marketing or merchandising know-how to get their product into the retail channel. Instead, they sell (more specifically, license) their brilliant product to a major software publishing house, who puts its own name on it, puts it in its own fancy box, and has the clout to get it into the hands of retailers. Retail distributors buy a volume of the product from the publisher (usually at a deep discount) and puts it on their store shelves. The publisher then pays the original authors a royalty from the volume sales to distributors.

As you might imagine from this scenario, the people who actually write the software you buy receive only a fraction of the price you pay at the store; the software publishers and retailers usually make the real money. An even more important problem with commercial distribution is that there is only a finite amount of shelf space to go around, and no distributor stocks everything. For example, a distributor might choose to carry two or three diagnostics, not 25 or 30. As a result, a lot of very good products never really get the attention they deserve because the people pushing the product just don't have enough clout with distributors to gain a foothold on their shelves. As a technician, you are denied a real selection of products.

Another serious problem with commercial distribution is that you rarely (if ever) have an opportunity to try a diagnostic (or any other program) before you buy it. The back of the box might look pretty, but it hardly ever reveals the "true" product. How many times have you stood in a store trying to decide between two or three similar products, then taken your choice home only to be disappointed? Trying to bring the product back is another challenge entirely. Many software retailers simply will not accept a product return once the box has been opened, and you find yourself out a bundle of money you can barely afford for a product that you can barely use. It is a system that is not fair to software buyers.

The idea of shareware

The shareware concept is a means of product distribution that allows a vast number of software products to be offered on a "try before you buy" basis. Software writers develop a shareware version of their product, which is then distributed freely through bulletin boards, online services such as CompuServe or the Internet, or even on diskettes passed between friends. If you like the software and plan to use it, you register the software with the author. Registration usually involves sending a fee to the author, although some shareware requires only that you send in your name and mailing address (referred to as *postcard-ware*), or is complete in its shareware form and no exchange of money is needed (known as *$0 shareware*). When you register a product, you will typically receive benefits such as an updated version of the product, a printed manual, free technical support, or some other combination of benefits. The advantage of shareware is that anyone can put his or her program into distribution—and be assured of a huge distribution network—for virtually no cost.

The important things to remember about shareware is that it is *not* free, it is *not* public domain, and it is *not* a demo version of some shrink-wrapped product. It is fully functional, copyrighted software that commands a purchase price. Once you have a shareware product, you may try the product for a certain period of time (typically 30 days). After that time, you must register the product (which is the purchase price) or cease using it. A shareware product is always marked as such in the startup screen and disk documentation.

Problems with shareware

Shareware is largely regarded as one of the most important developments in the software industry and many new companies, such as Netscape, Apogee Games, PKWare, and McAfee Associates, have gone commercial as a result of their product's growth as shareware. A vast number of other smaller software companies, like MVP Software, are marketing their products quite successfully where they would never have had a chance through commercial channels.

As you venture into the shareware world, however, there are some potential pitfalls to beware of. First, there is a strong potential for shareware abuse, which is when people make productive use of shareware but refuse to pay for it. This is a great "gray area" of shareware because there is no real way to regulate distribution. Shareware works only when authors receive their registration fees. This in turn allows them to develop even better software.

Software authors have several available tactics to encourage registration. The most common tool is "limited functionality," where a program is functional but limited in its capability. For example, a shareware strategy game I recently found would allow you to use only small- and medium-sized play fields and provided no customized features, but played exactly the same as the registered version, which allowed for large play fields and included the added features. In other words, shareware authors might provide you with enough functionality to make the product useful and productive, but not enough functionality to allow you to do everything you want to. Other incentives are offering a printed manual—which can be very important for lengthy documentation—and technical support.

Another problem some people have with shareware is the inconsistent use of benefits; no two products are alike, and there is no established standard of what you get when you register a product. Some shareware authors provide a wealth of benefits, while others simply send you a registered version on disk. When you decide to register a product, always look at the shareware documentation to see what the benefits are.

Finally, many people are frustrated by the way shareware authors seem to come and go. Remember that most shareware authors work either from home or from a small office where they've hung out their shingle. If the registrations don't come in, they wind up fading into oblivion—leaving their shareware product unsupported on BBS libraries and online forums all over the world. It's disappointing to find a handy shareware product, spend time evaluating it, fill out the registration form, and send in your money—only to get the registration returned unopened a few weeks later. As a rule, if you find a shareware

7

1-1 *The ASP logo.*

product you like, look for the most recent shareware version available before registering it.

The ASP: a mark of quality

For the shareware industry to survive and grow, quality products must be developed. While any enthusiastic programmer can put out a product and call it shareware, most reputable shareware authors and BBS distributors are members of the Association of Shareware Professionals (ASP). ASP members' shareware meets additional quality standards beyond ordinary shareware. Members' programs must be fully functional (not crippled, demonstration, or out-of-date versions). Their program documentation must be complete and must clearly state the registration fee and the benefits received at registration. ASP members must provide free mail or telephone support for a minimum of three months after registration. Members must also meet other guidelines that help to ensure that users receive good value for their money and are dealt with professionally. ASP representatives check each product to be sure it meets their quality standards before the author can include the ASP logo (Figure 1-1). Finally, the ASP also provides an ombudsman program to assist in resolving disputes between authors and users.

For more information on the ASP or to contact the ASP ombudsman, write to:

ASP
545 Grover Road
Muskegon, MI 49442-9427

or fax them at 616-788-2765. You can also contact the ombudsman on CompuServe by sending an electronic mail message to 70007,3536.

The DLS Diagnostic CD

Now that you understand the idea of shareware, we can finally turn our attention to the CD that accompanies this book. The DLS Diagnostic CD contains over 100 shareware and public-domain diagnostic programs and PC utilities that have been assembled from some of the finest shareware authors in the world. Whether you are a novice attempting to check your PC's configuration for the first time or an experienced technician trying to manipulate a partition on your customer's hard drive, you'll find an extensive selection of software for testing, troubleshooting, and mastering the PC. The rest of the chapters in this book examine each product in detail and explain how to get the most benefit from each one.

The DLS Diagnostic CD is arranged as a series of subdirectories, where each subdirectory holds an entire product compressed as a single file. Each product resides in its own subdirectory, so once you know the product you are interested in you can quickly locate the product and install it on your hard drive or a floppy disk.

The CD and file compression

The DLS Diagnostic CD is intended to serve as an archive rather than a working medium, so each of the programs have been compressed. To use a program on the CD, you must decompress and install it to your hard drive or a floppy disk. This part of the chapter covers some general guidelines for using the programs on your CD. You might wonder why all the programs are compressed, when they would easily have fit on and could work (in many cases) directly from the CD. There are several important reasons for this:

☐ Programs generally run very poorly from slow media such as a CD. Most of the programs on this CD run much better from a floppy disk and even better from a hard drive.

☐ Data files can't be written to a CD. Some of the diagnostic programs on this CD require that data files be written while the program is running. Since you can't write to an ordinary CD, those programs would not be usable.

☐ Compression conserves space. Compressed files are smaller and easier to work with than the individual files of an uncompressed product. Using compression allowed me to use a minimum amount of space on the CD, which reserves room for expansion in future editions of this book.

☐ Many authors prohibit the distribution of their products in an uncompressed form. Gathering up all the program files into a single compressed file helps ensure that the original shareware program has not been tampered with.

☐ Some products need to be installed. Even if the individual program files were uncompressed, some of the products on the CD need to have an installation routine run in order to organize, sort, and initialize the program files properly, so those programs would not be executable from the CD.

☐ You won't always have a working CD-ROM drive available. Even if I designed the DLS Diagnostic CD to run each product directly (and successfully) from the CD itself, you would need a working CD-ROM drive on the PC you intend to troubleshoot. This is not always possible—especially when working with older PCs.

Installing the software

Installing software from the CD to your hard disk or floppy drive is not a difficult process, but you need to pay attention to detail. The process typically involves copying, decompressing, virus checking, and then installing.

1. Insert the CD in your CD-ROM drive. Obviously, you need a PC with a working CD-ROM drive in order to install any files from the CD.

2. Decide whether you intend to install the CD program to your hard drive (step 2a) or a floppy diskette (step 2b). Keep in mind that a few of the utilities on your CD are too big to fit on a floppy disk in their fully expanded form. The description of each program in this book will warn you how much space is required.

2a. Prepare a subdirectory on your hard disk. You should never install new software to your hard drive's root directory, so prepare a new directory for the program using the DOS MD command. For example, suppose you want to install the IRQ diagnostic utility from CTS, Inc. called IRQINFO.ZIP to your hard drive. You can create a new directory from your DOS prompt with the following command:

C:\> md irqinfo <Enter>

Then switch to the newly created directory using the DOS CD command:

C:\> cd\irqinfo <Enter>

The computer will respond with your new directory as part of the command prompt:

C:\IRQINFO\>

2b. Prepare a subdirectory on your floppy disk. In most cases, you will be installing only a single product to a floppy disk, so you generally do not need to concern yourself with creating subdirectories on a floppy disk unless you intend to place more than one product on the diskette. Insert a blank, formatted floppy disk into drive A: and switch to the A: drive by typing:

C:\> A: <Enter>

The floppy drive LED will light for a moment and the computer will respond with a new prompt:

A:\>

Now use the DOS MD command to make a new directory for your product:

A:\> md irqinfo <Enter>

Next, switch to the subdirectory you just created using the DOS CD command:

A:\> cd\irqinfo <Enter>

The computer will respond with your new directory as part of the command prompt:

A:\IRQINFO\>

3. Copy the desired program file from the CD to either your hard drive (step 3a) or a floppy disk (step 3b). Suppose you still want to use that IRQ diagnostic utility from CTS, Inc. called IRQINFO.ZIP. You will find the product in its own subdirectory on the CD called IRQINFO.

3a. If you are copying from the CD to a directory on the hard drive, make sure you are in the desired directory on the hard drive and type:

C:\IRQINFO\> copy d:\irqinfo\irqinfo.zip c: <Enter>

This will copy the IRQINFO.ZIP file from the CD in drive D: to your current directory (the IRQINFO directory), which you just created on drive C:. Of course, if your CD-ROM and hard drive use different drive letters, be sure to substitute those letters in place of D: and C:.

3b. If you are copying from the CD to a floppy disk, make sure you are in the desired directory on the floppy disk and type:

A:\IRQINFO\> copy d:\irqinfo\irqinfo.zip a: <enter>

or, if there is no subdirectory on the floppy disk, simply type:

A:\> copy d:\irqinfo\irqinfo.zip a: <Enter>

This will copy the IRQINFO.ZIP file from the CD in drive D: to your current directory (the IRQINFO directory), which you just created on drive A:. If you did not create a subdirectory on drive A:, just copy the compressed file to the root directory of A:. Of course, if your CD-ROM and floppy drive use different drive letters, be sure to substitute those letters in place of D: and A:.

4. Decompress the software. Now that you have copied the program to wherever you need it, you must decompress the file. Compressed software is usually in one of two forms, an archive file (such as a .ZIP or .ARJ file) or a self-extracting file (with a .EXE extension). The type of file will slightly effect the process of decompression. You must decompress an archive file with a utility such as PKUNZIP.EXE (step 4a), while a self-extracting file will decompress itself when it is executed (step 4b).

4a. If you must decompress an archive file, use the PKUNZIP.EXE utility (in the root directory of the CD, or available from the DLS BBS at 508-829-6706). To use PKUNZIP from the CD directly, try a command such as:

C:\IRQINFO\> d:\pkunzip irqinfo <Enter>

This will use PKUNZIP from the root directory of your CD to decompress the IRQINFO file into the current (IRQINFO) subdirectory. If your CD-ROM drive uses a drive letter other than D:, be sure to substitute that letter. If you have trouble running PKUNZIP from the CD directly, copy it to the root directory of your hard drive first, then run it like the command above; just substitute the drive letter of your hard drive for D:.

4b. Execute the self-extracting file. For compressed files with an .EXE extension, you need only type the name of the file to start the decompression process. Suppose that the IRQINFO.ZIP file was actually named IRQINFO.EXE. Once you're in the right subdirectory, simply type:

C:\IRQINFO\> irqinfo <Enter>

The file will then decompress (or extract) into its constituent files.

5. Check the files for viruses. Although all the files on your DLS Diagnostic CD have been checked for viruses, you should always make it a point to inspect the decompressed files before executing any new program for the first time. Always employ this standard operating precaution with any program you get. Use tools such as Norton Anti-Virus, Microsoft's MSAV, or any of the virus tools from McAfee Associates (http://www.mcafee.com/) to check your program files. If you are placing the diagnostics on floppy disks in order to take them from PC to PC, be sure to write-protect the floppy to inhibit the transfer of viruses from other machines.

6. Install the program files if necessary. Once you decompress the program files, you should be able to run the diagnostic or utility from that point. However, you will need to configure some program files through an installation or setup routine before using the program. You can tell if this is the case by looking at the files you just decompressed; if any of the files are named INSTALL.EXE (or SETUP.EXE), you might need to execute that program first to prepare the diagnostic or utility. Installation routines are especially common for programs designed to operate under Windows or Windows 95.

Registering the shareware

Several of the shareware products on your CD are essentially free, but most request a contribution of anywhere from a few dollars to $40 or more. Now I am hardly suggesting that you run right out and register everything on the CD. The whole point of shareware is that you can try these products for free to see if they will serve your needs. Chances are that you will try most (if not all) of these programs at one time or another, but you will probably find only a few that you can really use. These few programs are the ones you should register. Don't panic; you have plenty of time to try everything!

13

MONITORS and PRINTERS

In addition to over 100 shareware and public-domain products, The DLS Diagnostic CD also contains two commercial diagnostics from Dynamic Learning Systems: MONITORS, a video board/computer monitor diagnostic and alignment program, and PRINTERS, a comprehensive diagnostic designed to aid the test of impact, ink jet, and laser printers. You can find complete details about both of these products in Chapters 8 and 9. These commercial products are complete and are compressed on the CD with a password. When you call, fax, or mail your order to Dynamic Learning Systems, you will get a serial number that will unlock the programs. Each program is $20.00 (U.S.). Check the order form at the back of this book for more information.

Caring for the DLS Diagnostic CD

Whether you install several programs of interest and store the CD for a prolonged period or keep the CD on hand for regular use, you should make it a point to protect the CD. Like any CD, there are few hard and fast rules governing its care, but there are some particular points to keep in mind. First, keep the CD in a jewel case—one

of those clear plastic boxes that audio CDs come in. If you don't
have any jewel cases handy, you can buy them at computer stores
such as CompUSA or Computer City.

If you handle the CD carefully and keep it in a jewel case, you
should be able to enjoy a long working life from the media. If
you need to clean dust or debris from the CD, use soft, lint-free
wipes to gently wipe the disk from hub to edge; never wipe in a circular motion around the CD's circumference because any
scratches can then leave the disk unreadable.

The DLS bulletin board

Chances are that you'll eventually want to look for diagnostics beyond your CD. If you can't wait until the next edition of this book,
you can always search for the latest diagnostics on the DLS bulletin board service (BBS), which specializes in PC diagnostics and
small-business utilities. You can access the BBS by dialing
508-829-6706 with your modem set to 8 data bits, no parity bit,
and one-stop bits (known as 8/N/1) up to 28.8 Kbps. You can get
more specific information on the DLS BBS in Appendix B.

14

General PC hardware tools 2

As a technician, you will frequently need to check the configuration of a system, test the system's overall operation, and optimize the system performance. You will also need tools to test the PC's major processing elements, such as the CPU, memory, cache, and other crucial areas of the motherboard. This chapter covers diagnostics that are designed for general-purpose PC testing, as well as tools for specifically testing your computer's core processing system. These programs are listed in Table 2-1.

Important It is impossible to test these programs on every possible configuration of PC hardware. If you cannot get the program to run (or encounter unexpected results), contact the program's author for more information.

System backup It is highly recommended that you perform a complete system backup before attempting to use system diagnostics and utilities. In the event that system errors or unexpected program results accidentally damage your programs or data, a backup will allow you restore your information quickly and easily.

Virus warning As a general operating procedure, you should never attempt to run a new program without checking it for viruses first. Decompress the program(s), then run your virus checker. If a virus is detected, take all necessary steps to neutralize it.

Benchmarking utilities

As personal computers continue to advance, it is often useful to measure their performance against established standards as well as co.mpeting computers. Benchmarks serve as a foundation for that measurement. There are many different types of benchmarks available today in both commercial and shareware form, but you must be careful to use benchmarks evenly between systems; variations in PC setups, drivers, and TSRs can all effect the accuracy of a benchmark's report.

Benchmarking utilities

JCBENCH.EXE   PC benchmarking utility

BIOS ID/reporting utilities

BIOS.ZIP   BIOS reporter utility
BIOSR11.ZIP   BIOS reporter utility
PCM140.EXE   POST Code Master
READBI.ZIP   BIOS date reader
SHOWS174.ZIP   BIOS ID utility

Burn-in/stress tests

486TST.ZIP   486 system stress tester

CMOS utilities

CMOS.ZIP   CMOS backup/restore utility
CMOSRAM2.ZIP   CMOS backup/restore utility

CPU utilities

MAXSPEED.EXE   CPU Speed test utility
SRXTEST.EXE   Test 386 for Cyrix 486 upgrade

General system tests

ASQ0315.ZIP   System analyzer
CHECK136.ZIP   Command-line PC diagnostic
CONF810E.ZIP   PC configuration utility
FIXCLOCK.ZIP   Clock adjustment utility
OVERHEAD.ZIP   Calculate TSR
RESOUR11.ZIP   Free system resources utility
RITM25.ZIP   Clock correction utility
SNOOP330.ZIP   System inspection/diagnostic
SPC.ZIP   PC snapshot utility
SYSCHK40.ZIP   System inspection/diagnostic
SYSINF.ZIP   System information utility

I/O, IRQ, and DMA tests

CHKIO.ZIP   Check I/O port utility
IRQINFO.ZIP   Identify IRQs
PORT11.ZIP   I/O port testing tool
SPYDOS.ZIP   Real-time interrupt analyzer
SWAPIRQ.ZIP   Redirect IRQ utility

Memory/cache tests

486TEST.ZIP   Memory write performance test
CACHECHK.ZIP   Memory/Cache test utility
MEMSCAN.ZIP   Memory scan utility
RAMMAP.ZIP   Memory display utility
SHADTEST.ZIP   Shadow RAM test utility

16

JCBENCH.EXE

Like the rebellious hot-rodders of years gone by, computer users are often in love with the idea of speed; the faster a PC performs, the more they like it. It has been difficult, however, to measure computer speed in a reliable, consistent manner in order to compare it with quoted standards or other PC models. JC-Bench v.4.00 (Table 2-2) provides technicians with a tool that finally allows the fair end equitable evaluation of different PCs.

■ Table 2-2 JCBENCH fact sheet

Program name:	JC-Bench
Executable File:	JCBENCH4.EXE
Purpose:	A computer speed testing program
Version:	4.00
Operating system:	MS-DOS 5.0 or later
Compressed file:	JCBENCH.EXE (self-extracting)
Author:	Jesse Bize
Address:	15 Yerba Buena Ave.
	San Francisco, CA 94127
ASP member:	No
Registration:	$10
Special notes:	Requires a clean boot of the PC for best results

Installation and configuration

JC-Bench is best run on a system that has been booted "clean"—with no drivers or TSRs running. You can boot your system with a blank bootable disk. If you do not have a bootable floppy for the program, you can boot clean under MS-DOS 5.0 to 6.22 by hitting <F5> when the message "Starting MS-DOS" appears. Under Windows 95, you can boot clean by hitting <Shift>–<F5> when "Starting Windows 95" appears. Unfortunately, the program must be run from the hard drive rather than from the bootable floppy disk.

Before you can use the program, JC-Bench must write a configuration file to your C:\DOS directory. This can make things a bit clumsy because the program *must* be run from that directory. You will obtain the best results by switching to the C:\DOS directory, then copying (or decompressing) the JC-Bench program files there. You can then run CONFIG, which identifies your program as a shareware or registered version. If you specify the program as Unregistered, the configuration file will be written to C:\DOS and you can then start JCBENCH4. If you have the registration codes to unlock all the program features (issued when you register the product), enter the codes through the CONFIG program.

Operation

JC-Bench focuses its testing on three areas of the PC: the CPU, video, and hard disk. The screen will keep you updated as the testing progresses (Figure 2-1). Testing is automatic and, once the program starts, no interaction is needed from the user. After the test is complete, you will see a bar graph display comparing the numerical performance of your particular system against several other "standard" PC types.

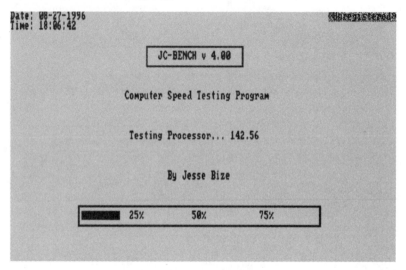

■ 2-1 *The initial working screen for JC-BENCH.*

It is also possible to run certain parts of the test by using command-line options such as:

JCBENCH4-CPU Runs only CPU Test

JCBENCH4-VIDEO Runs only Video Test

JCBENCH4-HDISK Runs only HDisk Test

JCBENCH4-CONFIG Configures the program

JCBENCH4-HELP Provides help

Performance

JC-Bench might encounter problems with some Windows video accelerator cards. Under DOS, some Windows video architectures are known to be rather slow, which could yield false (or misleading) readings for your video system. Generally speaking, an unexpectedly slow video performance number with a Windows video accelerator board probably means a false reading.

Registration

If you continue to use JC-Bench beyond a reasonable evaluation period, you must register it with the program author. Registration for JC-Bench is $10. (Please note that all prices listed in this book are in U.S. dollars, unless otherwise specified.) When you register, you will receive codes (entered under CONFIG) that will enhance the bar graph display and disable the program's registration screens. Registration also provides you with technical support for the product. You can also register the product online through CompuServe, GO SWREG. The file ID number is 11238.

Summary

JC-Bench is a simple and inexpensive PC benchmarking tool that can be especially handy if you build or configure a large number of PCs. The program effectively requires at least partial installation to your C:\DOS directory, however, which might prove inconvenient for testing a large volume of PCs. Your best strategy might be to keep the self-extracting archive (JCBENCH.EXE) on a clean, bootable disk, extract the program to your C:\DOS directory, run CONFIG to configure the program as shareware (and again later to register the program), then run JCBENCH4 to use the utility.

BIOS ID/reporting utilities

BIOS has an important impact on a system's operation, but incompatibilities, bugs, and obsolete versions of BIOS can present problems when you attempt to upgrade a system, and these problems can require troubleshooting. Unfortunately, one of the first steps in dealing with a BIOS issue is to find as much information as possible (i.e., BIOS maker, date, and so on). The following utilities will help you make the best use of BIOS.

BIOS.ZIP

Often one of the most important criteria in determining the need for a BIOS upgrade is the age of the current BIOS. This information is usually locked away within the BIOS IC itself. The BIOS utility BIOS.ZIP (Table 2-3) provides you with a quick and easy way to extract the BIOS date. The main advantage is that you need not close your applications and reboot the PC in order to find the BIOS date.

■ Table 2-3 BIOS fact sheet

Program name:	BIOS
Executable file:	BIOS.EXE
Purpose:	A BIOS date reader utility
Version:	Unknown
Operating system:	MS-DOS
Compressed file:	BIOS.ZIP (archive)
Author:	John Boshears
ASP member:	Unknown
Registration:	None ($0)
Special notes:	None

Installation and configuration

No particular installation procedures are required. You can copy the utility onto a floppy disk or hard drive, decompress the archive file with PKUNZIP, then run the BIOS.EXE program. When the program runs, it merely returns the BIOS date and terminates. The BIOS.EXE program is extremely simple and does not need to be configured.

Operation and performance

Using the BIOS.EXE utility takes a grand total of five seconds. After you type BIOS and press <Enter>, the program shows the BIOS date on the monitor and the program terminates. You can re-run BIOS.EXE if necessary, but you shouldn't need to run the program more than once for any system you're working on. BIOS.EXE is extremely quick, and there are absolutely no frills. The only output generated by the program is a single sentence indicating the BIOS date.

Registration

Although the program carries the author's name and copyright, no registration is required. This type of program is often referred to as *freeware* (or $0 shareware). Conversely, there are no benefits or technical support available for the program, and no accompanying documentation.

Summary

BIOS.EXE is a simple tool for determining your BIOS date— nothing more. Unfortunately, you will need to use other tools if you need additional information, such as the BIOS maker or revision numbers.

BIOSR11.ZIP

The BIOS data area (BDA) holds the PC's operating characteristics. This includes information such as whether or not floppy drives are present, which video mode conditions are set, and what keyboard parameters are invoked. Technicians can use the BIOS Reporter utility (Table 2-4) to examine the PC's hardware states at the address and bit level, as well as the memory that composes the BDA, without having to run a complete diagnostic. BIOSR presents a selection of drive flags, video flags, keyboard flags, and other miscellaneous equipment.

■ Table 2-4 BIOSR fact sheet

Program name:	BIOS Data Area Reader
Executable file:	BIOSR.EXE
Purpose:	A BIOS data area (BDA) information utility
Version:	1.1
Operating system:	MS-DOS
Compressed file:	BIOSR11.ZIP (archive)
Author:	Paul Postuma
Address:	16 Fullyer Drive
	Quispamsis, NB E2G 1Y7
	Canada
ASP member:	Yes
Registration:	None ($0)
Special notes:	None

Installation and configuration

There are no special installation considerations for BIOSR. You can copy the archive file to a floppy disk or subdirectory on your hard drive, then decompress the archive with PKUNZIP to reveal the only executable file: BIOSR.EXE. You can then run the program directly; no further setup or configuration steps are required. Although the program is designed to be run from DOS, it has been tested to run from a DOS window under Windows 95.

BIOSR can either be run from the command line like any utility or be installed as a TSR. To run the program from your command line, simply type BIOSR once the archive file is decompressed, and the main screen will appear as shown in Figure 2-2. If you prefer, you can load BIOSR as a 12KB TSR, which you activate with a <left Shift>–<Ctrl>–<B> combination. If the display is in a DOS text mode, the main screen will pop up. To load BIOSR into memory, use BIOSR L. To remove the utility from memory later, use BIOSR U. Make sure to remove any TSRs loaded after BIOSR before attempting to unload BIOSR (remove the TSRs in reverse order of loading).

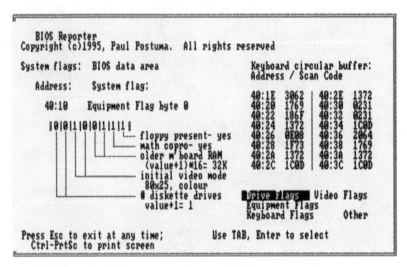

■ **2-2** *The Drive Flags display from BIOSR.*

Operation

The main screen illustrates the byte at the specified address. Each bit corresponds to a particular hardware state (e.g., whether or not a floppy drive is present) and the program reports on the meaning of each bit. For the example in Figure 2-2, you can see that bit 3 is set (1) at address 40:10h. If you follow the table down to the right, you will see that this corresponds to an initial video mode of 80 × 25 (the typical DOS video mode). On the right side of the display, a keyboard circular buffer keeps track of the most recent scan codes generated by each keystroke. Note that each address presents four hexadecimal digits; the first two digits form a "make code" and the second two digits are the "break code." This corresponds to the press and release of each button.

By default, BIOS Reporter presents a series of system flags, but there are also data displays for drive flags, video flags, equipment flags, and keyboard flags. You can select which information you want to view by pressing the <Tab> key to highlight your selection, then pressing <Enter>. An Other selection displays processing, drive, and POST address information, as shown in Figure 2-3. You can return to previous menus by highlighting the Main Menu selection and pressing <Enter>. Press <Esc> to exit the program. If you have a printer connected to your system, you can print the report pages.

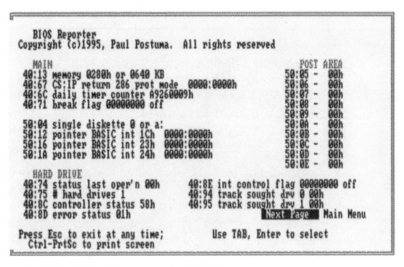

■ **2-3** *The Other data page in BIOSR.*

Performance

Operation is quick and simple. Aside from the initial load of the program, there is no disk access. There is also no significant demand on video hardware or system memory. While BIOS Reporter is a handy tool for peeking into the inner workings of your BIOS data area, it does not show all the BIOS data available in the BDA; in particular, the PS/2 BIOS is incompletely supported, and proprietary NEC diskette-related information is not presented.

Registration

Although the program carries the author's name and copyright, no registration is required for the use of BIOS (often referred to as freeware or $0 shareware. Conversely, there are no benefits or technical support available for the program and accompanying documentation is very light. However, the author does provide contact information for comments and user feedback.

Summary

Although intended primarily for programmers, BIOS Reporter is a free, straightforward tool that allows technicians to review important parts of the BIOS data area in order to determine key hardware settings that were set during initialization and operation.

PCM140.EXE

When the PC starts, the Power On Self Test (or POST) executes a series of tests in order to check the motherboard and other hardware. As each test is completed, the POST routine typically sends a completion or status code (called a POST code) to an I/O register. The codes sent to this register (usually I/O port 80h) can be displayed in hexadecimal form on a simple "POST code reader"— a board that can be plugged into any ISA slot. If there is a problem with the PC that might halt the initialization process, the last code to be displayed will tell you where the problem is. The problem is either in the code presented or in the next step, which might not have been completed.

For a technician, the problem is often knowing exactly what each code means for every possible BIOS maker. This is not an easy task, and even the manuals that accompany POST code readers do not cover every possible code or manufacturer. POST Code Master (Table 2-5) is a reference utility that allows you to cross-reference suspicious POST codes by BIOS manufacturer.

■ **Table 2-5 PCM140 fact sheet**

Program name:	POST Code Master
Executable file:	PCM140.EXE
Purpose:	A POST code cross-reference utility
Version:	1.40
Operating system:	MS-DOS 3.3 or later
Compressed file:	None (no compression used in distribution)
Author:	MicroSystems Development
Address:	4100 Moorpark Ave., Suite 104
	San Jose, CA 95117
Phone:	408-296-4000
ASP Member:	No
Registration:	$59, which includes POST board and latest software
Special notes:	Can work in conjunction with a POST board

Installation and configuration

No installation is required at all for POST Code Master. It is an uncompressed .EXE file (PCM140.EXE) and can be copied directly to a floppy disk or your hard drive. As a stand-alone executable file, you might even be able to run it from your CD. To run the program, simply type PCM140. There are no configuration requirements in order to make the shareware program work.

Operation

The entire program runs in the main display, as shown in Figure 2-4. It is separated into several major areas: the BIOS Manufacturer window, the POST Code window, the Beep Code window, and the Code Explanation window. The first step in finding the meaning of a POST code is to select the proper BIOS manufacturer. Use the left and right arrows to move the active box until the BIOS Manufacturer window is highlighted, then use the up and down arrows to scroll through the list of manufacturers until you see the correct manufacturer and BIOS version. Next, use the right arrow to move to the POST Code window, then use the up and down arrows to scroll through the possible codes until you find the last code displayed on your POST board. As you are scrolling through the POST codes, keep an eye on the Beep Codes window; if there is a beep code that corresponds to the currently selected POST code, the beep code will show up in that window. When you reach the last displayed POST code, its definition will be displayed in the POST Code Explanation window.

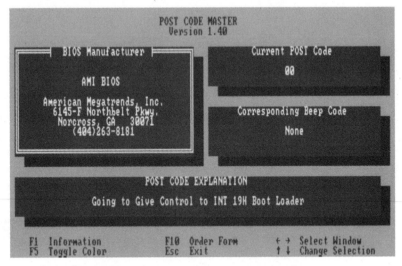

■ **2-4** *A typical POST code cross-reference from PCM140.*

If you want more information on the program, hit <F1> to display a small information window. If you want to register your copy of PCM, press <F10> for an order form. You can use the <F5> key to adjust the color scheme in the main display. You can exit the program at any time by pressing the <Esc> key.

Performance

Since POST Code Master is a single self-contained .EXE file, there is no disk access other than the initial loading. Once the program is running, you can shift from manufacturer to code number and back again with simple directional keystrokes. The shareware version of POST Code Master, however, is limited in the number of POST versions that it covers. Shareware version 1.40 covers POST codes from AMI, Award, C&T, Compaq, IBM, Microid Research, Phoenix Technologies, and Quadtel—but it might not carry POST codes for the very latest BIOS versions.

Registration

Ideally, POST Code Master is sold as part of a set: software and a hardware POST reader card. When you register the shareware ($59), you will receive the POST reader card as well as the latest version of the software. No other registration benefits are listed or implied, but the level of technical support provided by MicroSystems Development to registered users is considered to be good.

Summary

If you perform any level of PC troubleshooting, this is a good overall reference utility to help you find the meaning of those obscure POST codes. If you don't have a POST reader of your own yet, POST Code Master is probably your best, most economical opportunity to purchase one.

READBI.EXE

The ability to use hard drives in your PC is directly related to your BIOS. Specifically, the BIOS must be able to understand the drive type (i.e., the number of cylinders, heads, sectors per track, and so on). Drive types are specified in CMOS. If you've ever scrolled through a list of drive types before, you can see that there is a proliferation of types—each of which must be accounted for in BIOS. To keep the number of drive types from becoming unwieldy, BIOS makers implemented a User Defined drive type, which lets you enter drive-specific geometry to support virtually any drive. Unfortunately, not all BIOS supports the User Defined drive type, and if you need to put an odd drive on a system without that type of drive (and no User Defined type), you're basically stuck.

One way around this problem is to "burn" a new BIOS with the drive type you intend to use entered into the BIOS drive table. As you might expect, this is not a difficult process; some PROMS, a

PROM burner, and a knowledge of the BIOS drive table are really all that's required. While some highly experienced technicians will modify BIOS for their own customers, there are only a few individuals in the world who provide such services publicly. Fortunately, Markus Klama's GETBIOS utility (Table 2-6) allows you to copy your BIOS and send the file to him. He will make the changes to the BIOS table, burn a new EPROM for your PC, and send the new BIOS IC back to you.

■ Table 2-6 READBI fact sheet

Program name:	Record BIOS Utility
Executable file:	GETBIOS.EXE
Purpose:	A BIOS IC-to-disk file program
Version:	Unknown
Operating system:	MS-DOS 3.3 or later
Compressed file:	READBI.EXE (self-extracting)
Author:	Markus Klama
Address:	Carl-Maria-von-Weber Weg 8
	82538 Geretsried
	Germany
CompuServe:	100115,2167
ASP member:	No
Registration:	None for software; payment is for BIOS IC burning services only
Special notes:	You must understand the new drive parameters exactly and be proficient at installing new BIOS ICs.

Installation and configuration

The GETBIOS.EXE program must be run from a cleanly booted computer (no drivers or TSRs loaded). For best results, you should create a bootable floppy disk, then copy the READBI.EXE self-extracting archive to it. Switch to the floppy drive that now contains READBI.EXE and run the self-extracting program. When you run READBI from the floppy disk, the GETBIOS.EXE program, its documentation, and the BIOS order form will self-extract onto the floppy disk itself. This way, you can boot the system clean from your new floppy disk, then run GETBIOS.EXE directly from the floppy.

One point to consider when setting up GETBIOS is that your BIOS should *not* be "shadowed" to RAM (BIOS shadowing must be deactivated). Before booting the system with your bootable floppy disk, you might have to enter the system's CMOS setup and disable any BIOS shadowing. At that point, you can boot the system again with your bootable disk in the drive. If BIOS shadowing remains enabled, the GETBIOS program will not calculate the BIOS checksum correctly, and the copy process will fail.

The GETBIOS program does not require any particular configuration settings; it simply reads your BIOS contents and copies them to a disk file. As long as the system is booted clean and BIOS shadowing is disabled, the program should do its job properly. However, if the program reports a copy failure for any other reason, you might have to redirect the program's output to another file with a command such as the following:

A:\> GETBIOS > RESULT.LOG <Enter>

Operation and performance

The actual GETBIOS process is fully automatic and should require no user input. Once the program has copied your BIOS file to the disk, you will see a file called ROMBIOS.DAT on the disk. If you choose to run GETBIOS from a hard drive subdirectory, the ROMBIOS.DAT file will be placed in that subdirectory. You can also recognize the file by its length—either 32768 or 65536 bytes, depending on how large your BIOS is. Once the copy process is complete, the program will terminate.

One interesting aspect of GETBIOS.EXE is its level of "intelligence." It checks for a variety of factors that can prevent successful copying (e.g., if Windows is running, if memory managers are in use, or if the BIOS is shadowed). This comprehensive checking ensures that you copy only valid BIOS data to the disk file.

Once the BIOS file has been copied, you need to fill out some important system information in the accompanying order-form file, ORDER.FRM. The file is standard ASCII text, so you can load it into any text editor like DOS EDIT or Windows WordPad. Complete the order form (be especially careful when completing the drive type information).

Next, you need to send money. You're not paying for the GETBIOS program, but rather for the cost of a new BIOS IC and modifying the BIOS code. According to the documentation with READBI, the prices are relatively reasonable:

☐ New BIOS ICs $10.00 per piece

☐ Making the drive table changes and burning the new IC $10.00

☐ Additional changes for each new drive type $1.00

☐ Return shipping and handling $10.00

Let's say you need to add one new disk type to your BIOS, and your system is using a single BIOS IC. Once you have the ROM-BIOS.DAT and ORDER.FRM files ready, you will need $10 for the IC, $10 for the coding changes and burning the new IC, and $10 for return shipment: a total check of $30. If you need to add several additional drive types to your BIOS at the same time, add $1 for each additional type.

Your best method of transaction is to mail a disk with your BIOS and order-form files, along with your check or money order, directly to the program author. If you have any questions about such a transaction, you can contact Mr. Klama via e-mail.

Registration

As you probably realize by now, you're not really registering your READBI software; rather, you're using the software free and paying for a service. However, there are some other important points to keep in mind:

☐ Since this process involves international mail, it could take up to several weeks to receive your new BIOS IC(s). Your customer might not be able to wait that long.

☐ There is no guarantee that the BIOS file you send can be patched at all. If it is not possible to patch the BIOS file, you will not be charged.

☐ Watch your copyrights! BIOS is copyrighted software—no matter how old it is. That means you don't own the BIOS code. By the letter of international copyright law, it is illegal to copy your BIOS. From a practical standpoint, however, few BIOS makers will fuss if you modify the BIOS on your own system for your own purposes (or have your customer's BIOS modified for them alone). The time you will really have problems is if you try to duplicate and sell the modified BIOS code commercially. *Don't do it.*

☐ By all means, keep the original BIOS IC(s). If the patched BIOS IC(s) fail to work for any reason, you can always reinstall the original IC(s).

Summary

When upgrading or repairing older PCs, you might need to use a hard drive that is not supported by the drive types available in the system's BIOS. The solution is normally to upgrade your BIOS. Unfortunately, BIOS updates might no longer be available for older systems. When this happens, one of your only alternatives is to "patch" the BIOS with your desired drive type. It is not uncommon for skilled technicians to patch their own BIOS, but the READBI package provides you with this specialized service without the hassle of patching the BIOS yourself.

SHOWS174.ZIP

In the push to reduce costs and improve system performance, motherboards have employed the use of *chipsets*, groups of highly integrated ICs that work together to provide the major functions needed by the motherboard. Not only does this reduce the overall number of ICs needed on the motherboard (reducing size and power consumption), it allows each IC to be optimized for peak performance. To determine the capabilities (and limitations) of a motherboard, it is often necessary to identify the chipset being used. While you might be able to determine this from looking at the chipset elements themselves, it is much more effective to use a diagnostic that can detect and identify the chipset for you. The Show System Chipset utility (Table 2-7) from MicroFirmware is designed to help identify older chipset types.

■ **Table 2-7 SHOWS174 fact sheet**

Program name:	Show System Chipset
Executable file:	SHOWSET.EXE
Purpose:	A utility that indicates the motherboard chipset in use
Version:	1.74
Operating system:	MS-DOS 3.3 or later
Compressed file:	SHOWS174.ZIP (archive)
Author:	MicroFirmware, Inc.
Address:	330 W. Gray Street
	Norman, OK 73069-7111
Phone:	405-321-8333
URL:	http://www.firmware.com/
ASP member:	No
Registration:	None; freely distributed
Special notes:	Boot the system clean to DOS only.

Installation and configuration

To achieve the best accuracy, MicroFirmware suggests that SHOWSET be run during a clean boot of the PC. You should therefore create a bootable system disk and copy the SHOWS174 archive file to your floppy. You can then switch to the drive containing your floppy and run a decompression utility such as PKUN-ZIP. This will decompress the archive file to the floppy disk. Once the archive is decompressed, you can reboot the PC from your bootable floppy, then run the SHOWSET utility from the A: prompt. No specialized configuration is needed to operate the program once it is decompressed.

Operation

Once you run the SHOWSET.EXE utility, operation is almost automatic. The program is somewhat intelligent; it will detect memory managers and other memory utilities that will interfere with chipset detection. If the system is booted clean, SHOWSET will simply provide some last-minute warnings before starting, as shown in Figure 2-5. If you know of any write-behind disk cache or RAM drives in use, you can choose to abort the program by hitting <Ctrl>–<Break>. Otherwise, press <Enter> to start testing. Table 2-8 presents the major chipsets detected by the program. SHOWSET will attempt to identify the system architecture, the chipset detected, any available BIOS information, and the BIOS data width.

Performance

Although SHOWSET is relatively simple and automatic, it is also several years old. This presents some limitations with i486 and Pentium-type motherboards. As shown in Figure 2-5, the program could not identify the Pentium chipset on the PC used to check the software. This means you should use SHOWSET to test only older PCs such as i286 and i386 systems.

```
ShowSet - Show motherboard chip set type
Version 1.74, Copyright 1990,1991 Erik Petrich
Micro Firmware Incorporated
Sales: 1-800-767-5465   (405) 321-8333
  BBS: (405) 321-2616

ShowSet detects an active 32-bit memory manager. This may interfere with
the chip set detection routines. For best results, run ShowSet without any
unnecessary programs or device drivers loaded.

ShowSet may need to reboot the computer after it completes to ensure system
integrity. If you are using a virtual RAM disk, you may want to abort
ShowSet and save the contents. Likewise, if you are using disk caching
software with delay-writes enabled, you may want to first flush the cache.
In any case, if you want to abort, hit Ctrl-Break, otherwise press Enter to
continue.

    >         Architecture: AT
         ShowSet detects: Unknown; large CMOS found
          BIOS indicates: No information available
               BIOS width: 32 bits
```

■ **2-5** *A typical output from SHOWS174.*

31

■ Table 2-8 Chipsets compatible with SHOWS174

Company	Chipset(s)
Acer	1207
Chips & Technologies	CS8221 (NEAT)
	CS8230
	82C235 (SCAT)
Headland Technology	HT113
	HT21
Intel	82335
	82340 (same as VLSI VL82C286)
OPTi	HiD/386 or HiB/486
	Cache Sx/AT
	386WB
Sun Electronics	Suntac
VLSI Technology	VL82CPCAT-16/20 (enhanced)
	VL82C286 (TopCat)
	VL82C386 (TopCat)

Registration

No registration is required for SHOWSET; it is freeware offered by MicroFirmware (a major commercial supplier of Phoenix BIOS). As a result, there is no technical support available for the program.

Summary

SHOWSET is one of those unique and specialized utilities that should have been updated, but was dropped. It is a simple, free tool that can help you determine the chipset used in older PCs where modern shareware or commercial utilities do not support the identification of such older chipsets.

Burn-in/stress tests

Electronic devices tend to follow one of two predictable patterns; they either fail quickly (in a matter of hours or days) or they last the life of a PC. If a new device fails quickly, it can usually be replaced while still under warranty (saving time for you and money for your customer). The idea behind a "burn-in" process is to run the new device continuously for some preset period of time; if it is weak, it should fail in a short period of time. Otherwise, you can be relatively confident that the device will work indefinitely. The products in this section help to burn-in your new (or newly repaired) system.

486TST.ZIP

Since most problems with PCs originate early in the product's life (dubbed "out-of-the-box" failures), uncovering and correcting those failures before a customer does will add tremendous reliability to the system. The 486TEST.EXE utility (Table 2-9) is intended to provide burn-in services for the major motherboard components: CPU, BIOS, math coprocessor, cache, RAM (including EMS/XMS), and video memory. The premise behind 486TEST is that, by applying a heavy computational load to the main processing components, premature failures can be triggered while the PC is still on the test bench. The author claims that 486TEST can simulate processing loads that are orders of magnitude greater than an ordinary CPU would see in a 24-hour period.

■ **Table 2-9 486TST fact sheet**

Program name:	486 System Burnin
Executable file:	486TEST.EXE
Purpose:	A utility to stress-test major processing components
Version:	6.1
Operating system:	MS-DOS 3.3 or later
Compressed file:	486TST.ZIP (archive)
Author:	Richard Levey
Address:	41 Park Row, Room 710
	New York, NY 10038
ASP member:	No
Registration:	$25 for a private license;
	$75 for a commercial license
Special notes:	Be cautious of excessive heat in motherboard components.

Installation and configuration

To achieve the best results from 486TEST, you should remove any memory managers or other TSRs by booting the system clean from a bootable floppy disk. The documentation suggests that you should copy the program to a subdirectory on your hard drive and run it from there, but if you are booting the system from a floppy disk, you can copy the program to the floppy disk instead. After the 486TST.ZIP file is copied, you can switch to the floppy drive (or the desired subdirectory on your hard drive) and run PKUNZIP to decompress the archive; this yields the 486TEST.EXE file and a documentation file. Once the archive is decompressed, you can execute the program directly; there are no configuration settings or files to deal with.

Operation

The program runs through a single DOS text screen, as shown in Figure 2-6. The window on the left side of the display presents some basic system information, while the right-hand window keeps track of the test cycles. In normal operation, the test will run automatically, but you can stop the test at any time by pressing <Esc> or the spacebar. The program worked on a Pentium 166-MHz system, but failed to detect the Pentium CPU. It did, however, detect the correct DOS version and other data.

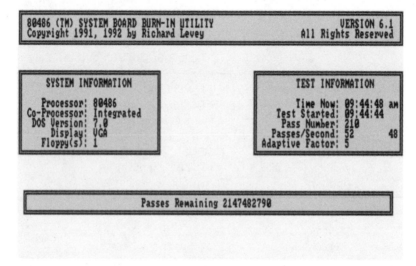

■ **2-6** *The working screen in 486TST.*

One important thing to remember is that the computational load provided by 486TEST.EXE will cause an unusual temperature rise in the main processing components of your motherboard. Depending on the design and vintage of your particular motherboard, this can have several effects. First, the key components on your motherboard will get hot—especially the CPU. If you are running the burn-in process with the PC housing removed, be extremely careful reaching inside the system. In actual practice, you should keep the outer housings in place so the computer is running under normal ventilation conditions. To be really safe, shut down the computer and allow 15 minutes for the system to cool before working inside of it. The program is supposed to be adaptive; more computational load will be applied when more powerful CPUs are detected. However, since the program did not detect the Pentium, it is unclear just how much load is being applied (or just how hot the components might become). Second, you should generally run this type of program for no more than 48 hours. If you run the program for a protracted period of time under high stress (say a week or more), you might actually shorten the working life of good components.

Performance

There is nothing fancy about 486TEST.EXE; it is a basic burn-in tool focusing on the motherboard components. If the PC hangs up or fails while the 486TEST is running, you should suspect a fault in the CPU or other processing component. If the problems appear intermittent, be sure that the CPU heat sink (if one is attached) is fitted securely with a layer of thermal grease to aid heat transfer. If no heat sink is attached, try adding one and see if the intermittent problems go away.

Registration

There are two registrations currently available for this software: personal and commercial. A personal registration ($25) licenses the use of 486TEST on only one computer at a time, by one person at a time. A commercial registration ($75) licenses the use of 486TEST on any number of computers. For busy technicians, a commercial license is often the best option. All registrations include the latest software version, free updates for one year (an update is normally issued every four to six months), and technical support via telephone or e-mail. You can purchase updates after the first year for 30 percent of the registration fee then in effect. All registered software will display registration information consisting of the owner's name and serial number.

Summary

Although version 6.1 is now several years old, 486TEST.EXE is a useful utility for stress-testing 486 motherboards, and, as a shareware version, it will provide service on even late-model Pentium systems. Newer registered versions will undoubtedly provide better support for Pentium systems.

CMOS utilities

The CMOS memory is a small amount of low-power RAM that stores the parameters used to configure the computer (i.e., date, time, drives, and so on). A CMOS setup utility allows you to change the system's configuration settings. Older PCs used a setup utility on diskette, while later 386 systems and onward incorporate the CMOS setup routine into BIOS. The CMOS memory contents are sustained by a battery while the computer power is off. Unfortunately, if the battery fails (or a circuit problem interferes with CMOS memory), the system might not boot at all. The problem with CMOS is that people rarely ever worry about its contents until something goes wrong. CMOS backup routines will help protect a system from unexpected failures.

CMOS.ZIP

Scott Hoopes' CMOS.COM is rather unique as a CMOS backup utility; it is a little over 5KB, is a small utility, and saves your CMOS data directly to the .COM file itself rather than creating a separate data file. For a technician, this makes it a simple matter to install CMOS.COM (Table 2-10) to your customer's machines without worrying about data files, installation routines, or even clean-booting the system from a bootable floppy disk.

■ Table 2-10 CMOS fact sheet

Program name:	CMOS Backup and Restore
Executable file:	CMOS.COM
Purpose:	A utility for recording and restoring CMOS data
Version:	1.0
Operating system:	MS-DOS 3.3 or later
Compressed file:	CMOS.ZIP (archive)
Author:	Scott Hoopes
Address:	62 Plaza Dr.
	New Albany, IN 47150
Phone:	812-948-8521
CompuServe:	73304,274
ASP member:	No
Registration:	Optional $5 for a collection of programs
Special notes:	None

Installation and configuration

The CMOS.ZIP archive file contains the CMOS.COM utility, along with a documentation file and some information about other shareware products. For best results, copy CMOS.ZIP to your bootable system floppy or other emergency disk, then switch to the floppy drive and decompress the archive file with PKUNZIP. Remember that, if you lose your CMOS settings, the PC will not be able to recognize the hard drive(s), so placing CMOS.COM on your hard drive is rather pointless if an emergency strikes. However, you might want to keep a copy of CMOS.COM on the hard drive in the event you create new bootable disks (and want to place CMOS.COM on those disks).

There are no special installation instructions beyond basic decompression of the archive file, and there are no special configuration issues. Once the program is decompressed, you run it simply by typing CMOS and pressing <Enter>.

Operation

The copy of CMOS.ZIP included on your DLS Diagnostic CD is blank; that is, it has not yet saved a copy of CMOS for the first time. When you first run CMOS.COM, it will ask you if you want to save CMOS to the file. After the CMOS contents have been copied to the file, subsequent runs of CMOS.COM will operate as shown in Figure 2-7. You then have the opportunity to Save (i.e., update) the CMOS data, Restore the data to CMOS RAM, Compare the data to CMOS RAM (useful to see if there are any hardware changes or battery problems), or Quit without doing anything.

```
CMOS save/restore Utility ver 1.0          by Scott Hoopes; COMPUSERVE
73304,274.
NO previously saved CMOS Data was found.

CMOS Data SAVED.
Make sure you have the file: C:\SOFTWA~1\SOFTWA~1\CMOS\CMOS.COM on your
Emergency Start-Up Disk.
```

■ **2-7** *An output generated from CMOS.*

There is one important issue to consider with CMOS.COM. Since it could be years before a battery fails or other system problems cause a loss of CMOS data, it is easy to forget about utilities like CMOS.COM. You *must* run the utility each time you make a change to the computer's hardware (which results in a change to CMOS RAM); otherwise, you could inadvertently restore an outdated copy of CMOS data and cause system problems.

Performance

As you probably have gathered from Figure 2-7, CMOS.COM is a simple and straightforward utility to operate. As such, it runs quickly and with little fanfare. The user interface is simple DOS text. Since the data in CMOS RAM is saved to the CMOS.COM file itself, you can determine the last time that CMOS data was saved by looking at the date of the CMOS.COM file. Also, CMOS.COM is a relatively recent utility, and should operate on virtually any PC (it was tested on a Pentium 166- MHz system).

Registration

There is no official registration required for the use of CMOS.COM (it is freeware), and free distribution is encouraged. However, Scott Hoopes does provide a number of utilities that he has gathered together into a "grab bag." You can get the very latest versions of all his utilities for $5. Read the GRAB-BAG file included with the CMOS.ZIP archive for a specific program listing.

Summary

CMOS.COM is the quintessential PC utility: handy, small, fast, simple, and free. Its free distribution policy makes it possible to put a copy on every PC you work on, and help all your customers preserve their valuable CMOS configurations.

CMOSRAM2.ZIP

Technicians who prefer a more conventional, menu-driven program might consider Thomas Mosteller's CMOSRAM2 program (Table 2-11) a preferable choice over similar products. Like other CMOS backup and restore utilities, CMOSRAM2 performs the typical save and restore operations quickly and efficiently. But the program's menu-based operation gives you the sensation of greater program control (though the actual operations of the program are almost identical to more automated CMOS backup/restore utilities).

■ Table 2-11 CMOSRAM2 fact sheet

Program name:	C MOS Backup and Restore
Executable file:	CMOSRAM2.EXE
Purpose:	A utility for recording and restoring CMOS data
Version:	2.0
Operating system:	MS-DOS 3.3 or later
Compressed file:	CMOSRAM2.ZIP (archive)
Author:	Thomas Mosteller
Address:	1872 Rampart Lane
	Lansdale, PA 19446-5051
CompuServe:	72637,173
ASP member:	No
Registration:	$5 voluntary registration; $10 for the latest registered copy
Special notes:	Recommend installing on your emergency disk. The program also includes CHKCMOS2.EXE, which you can use to check the validity of your CMOS IC and battery.

Installation and configuration

Since most hard drives will be inaccessible if the CMOS RAM contents are lost, you must copy CMOSRAM2.ZIP to a bootable floppy disk—preferably your emergency system disk, which should also contain other DOS utilities such as CHKDSK, FDISK, and FORMAT. Once the archive file is copied, switch to the floppy drive containing your disk, then decompress the archive file with PKUNZIP. You will find a documentation file and two programs: CMOSRAM2.EXE and CHKCMOS2.EXE. There is no indication that your PC must be clean-booted before using CMOSRAM2.EXE, but if you encounter problems a clean boot might be worth a try.

Operation

Start the program by typing CMOSRAM2. The working menu will appear with five choices, as shown in Figure 2-8. Option 1 provides some online information about CMOSRAM2 and its author, as well as some registration details. When you select option 2, the contents of your CMOS RAM will be saved to a file about 500 bytes long, called CMOS.RAM. The program will also check this file for validity. Note that this adds a new file to your disk. While the CMOS.RAM file is short, be sure there is enough space on the diskette for it. Use option 3 to restore the contents of your CMOS.RAM file to CMOS RAM itself. You will typically wait to use this option until you have replaced the CMOS backup battery, or dealt with whatever problem ruined your CMOS RAM contents in the first place. Boot the PC from your emergency disk, run CMOSRAM2, and use option 3 to restore CMOS data. Remember that the CMOS.RAM file must be in the drive and directory from which you are running CMOSRAM2. When you restore CMOS data, you will also restore the date and time copied to the CMOS.RAM file. Of course, this will not be the current date and time, so option 4 allows you to correct the real-time clock (RTC). However, correcting the CMOS date and time does not correct the DOS date and time, so you will need to reboot the PC again for DOS and CMOS clocks to match. Option 5 allows you to leave the program.

Performance and CMOSRAM2

The CMOSRAM2 program operates in a straightforward manner. The routines for setting time and date will work for any BIOS that follows the IBM guidelines (the program has been tested on machines with Phoenix, Award, and AMI BIOS), but it is possible to design a hardware/software system for which CMOSRAM2 does

```
┌─────────────────────────────────────────────────┐
│           CMOS RAM Save/Restore Program          │
│              T. Mosteller 02/25/95               │
└─────────────────────────────────────────────────┘

Desired Function:

1: About the CMOS RAM
2: Save the contents of your CMOS RAM to a disk file
3: Restore the CMOS RAM from the disk file
4: Set the CMOS clock
5: Exit
```

■ **2-8** *The main menu of CMOSRAM2.*

not work correctly. Also, versions of DOS greater than 5.0 set both the DOS system clock and date and the CMOS clock and date when you type TIME or DATE. Earlier versions set only the DOS system clock and date, not those in CMOS; that's why option 4 is included in CMOSRAM2.

Like most CMOS utilities, it is easy to forget about the utility because it could be years before you actually need the CMOS.RAM file. In that time, you could have updated the system and forgotten to update the CMOS data file. If you attempt to restore an outdated CMOS data file, you might actually compound your problems. You can run the CHKCMOS2.EXE utility from the AUTOEXEC.BAT file to test the RTC and battery, then compare the contents of your CMOS.RAM file against actual CMOS contents; if there are any differences, you will get a warning reminding you to back up your CMOS. Remember that your CMOS.RAM file must be in the same directory from which CHKCMOS2 is run. For example, if you copy the utility to your hard drive, make sure the following sequence is in your AUTOEXEC.BAT file:

```
CD\CMOSRAM2
CHKCMOS2
CD\
```

If the CMOS.RAM file is in a different directory, you will encounter an error message. Also note that the CHKCMOS2.EXE utility does not remain memory-resident, so it will not need memory once the PC boot process is complete. Finally, the program is relatively recent and has been specifically updated to version 2 for the purpose of supporting i386, i486, and Pentium-type systems.

Registration

CMOSRAM2 requires a registration if you choose to use it for more than a reasonable evaluation period (say 30 days). The registration is $10, which will get you the latest registered copy of the program; you can specify whether or not you want a 5.25 or 3.5-inch diskette. If you install CMOSRAM2 to a customer's PC (or create an emergency disk for them that contains CMOSRAM2), you should collect the registration fee and forward it to the program's author, or instruct your customer to forward the appropriate fee.

Summary

CMOSRAM2 (and CHKCMOS2) are two utilities that can easily save you and your customers hours of frustration and expensive service by creating and maintaining a copy of the CMOS RAM contents. Fast and easy to use, it should provide service on virtually any PC platform. Although a registration fee is required for continued use, it is cheap insurance against the threat of lost CMOS data.

CPU utilities

Generally speaking, there are few true CPU diagnostics; if the CPU fails, the system simply won't start. However, testing the CPU's performance and checking its upgrade potential are two useful services.

MAXSPEED.EXE

Checking the clock speed of your CPU is an important gauge of your system's performance. However, it is not always easy to determine the actual clock speed. BIOS notes appearing when the PC first boots flicker only for a moment (and don't necessarily list the speed), and CMOS setups do not always list the speed. The MAXSPEED utility (Table 2-12) tests the CPU through a series of algorithms and displays the clock speed in large numbers, as shown in Figure 2-9.

Installation and configuration

MAXSPEED.EXE requires no installation or configuration at all. It is distributed as an uncompressed .EXE file, so you can copy it directly to your general diagnostic disk, emergency boot disk, or hard drive. Once the program is copied, just type MAXSPEED to start the test.

Program name:	Clock Speed Checker
Executable file:	MAXSPEED.EXE
Purpose:	To determine the computer's effective CPU clock speed
Version:	Unknown
Operating system:	MS-DOS 3.3 or later
Compressed file:	None
Author:	Maxum Computers
Contact:	Stewart Finck
Phone:	212-505-0909
ASP member:	No
Registration:	Free ($0 shareware)
Special notes:	Run the program from DOS in a clean-booted system

■ **2-9** *The speedometer display from MAXSPEED.*

Operation and performance

MAXSPEED operation requires no user interaction; once the program starts, it will calculate and display clock speed for as long as you care to let the program run. You can terminate MAXSPEED and return to DOS by pressing any key. The program should operate properly on almost any PC platform; in spite of its overall age, MAXSPEED checked out properly on a Pentium 166-MHz computer.

Registration

MAXSPEED requires no registration, and may be distributed freely as long as no fee is charged for the program. If you have a shop with a variety of systems on the test bench, MAXSPEED is a handy program for light burn-in testing.

Summary

MAXSPEED serves as a CPU clock-speed diagnostic for just about any PC platform. It can help with commercial utilities or BIOSes that simply assume what the clock speed is.

SRXTEST.EXE

CPU upgrades are some of the most popular upgrade approaches available to PC users. By improving the processing power of the CPU, the entire system experiences a performance increase. Late-model motherboards (such as i486 motherboards) are typically designed with CPU sockets that can accommodate several different versions of microprocessor. Older systems, however, are not always so flexible—even though they are the most in need of upgrades. Upgrading an i386 CPU often requires a CPU adapter module such as the Cyrix Make-It-486, an i386-to-i486 upgrade module. Unfortunately, not all i386 CPUs are candidates for such an upgrade. Cyrix has released its SRXTEST utility (Table 2-13) to check the i386 for its upgrade potential.

■ **Table 2-13 SRXTEST fact sheet**

Program name:	Test for Cyrix Upgrade CPU
Executable file:	SRXTEST.COM
Purpose:	To test a 386SX CPU for upgrade capability
Version:	2.10
Operating system:	MS-DOS 3.3 or later
Compressed file:	SRXTEST.EXE (self-extracting)
Author:	Cyrix
Phone:	800-848-2979
ASP member:	No
Registration:	Free (freely distributed)
Special notes:	Works only with 386 CPUs

Installation and configuration

The SRXTEST program requires a "clean" DOS environment, so you should create a bootable floppy disk, then copy the SRXTEST.EXE self-extracting file to it. Switch to the floppy drive containing your bootable floppy disk and execute the self-extracting file to decompress the SRXTEST program. Once the program and its documentation file are decompressed, you can run the utility.

Operation and performance

Keep in mind that the SRXTEST utility will work only with i386 microprocessors; using the utility on a later CPU will probably hang up the PC, though there should be no damage (it hung up a Pentium system, but a simple reboot cleared the problem). After the program starts, it will provide a brief report on its assessment of the upgrade potential for your CPU.

Registration

There is no need to register the software; it is distributed freely (largely as a boost for Cyrix upgrade sales). There is little point in registration anyway, since the program will probably be used only once on any given i386 system.

Summary

Ensuring a reliable and cost-effective upgrade is a major priority for technicians and end users alike. With the cost of new motherboards continuously falling, the economic considerations of a new CPU versus a new motherboard demands careful attention. The SRXTEST utility allows you to test an i386 system in order to evaluate its upgrade potential before committing any time or money to the procedure.

44

General system tests

General system test utilities serve two basic functions. First, they can be used to test the overall operations of a defective PC; most can test such areas as memory, drives, and chipsets. Second, system test products can check the PC's configuration before (and after) you perform an upgrade. There are many different utilities that serve this type of purpose, and this section presents some of the most respected titles available.

ASQ0315.ZIP

Memory allocation and memory management are two essential considerations when optimizing any PC. Determining what memory is available, where it is located, and how it should be used are often difficult questions to answer— even for experienced technicians. Qualitas (known for their 386MAX memory management software) has developed ASQ Qualitas (Table 2-14) to serve two purposes: tutor the technician in memory management concepts, and analyze the system to aid memory management procedures. Although Qualitas no longer wields the influence it once did, ASQ0315 remains a popular system tool specially tailored for memory management.

■ **Table 2-14 ASQ0315 fact sheet**

Program name:	ASQ Qualitas
Executable file:	ASQ.EXE
Purpose:	A system configuration checker/memory management tutorial
Version:	1.3
Operating system:	MS-DOS 3.3 or later
Compressed file:	ASQ0315.ZIP (archive)
Author:	Qualitas, Inc.
Address:	7101 Wisconsin Ave.
	Bethesda, MD 20814
Phone:	301-907-6700
ASP member:	No
Registration:	$0 shareware, name and address only
Special notes:	Good online instructions

Installation and configuration

For all the information that ASQ Qualitas offers, the ASQ0315.ZIP file requires no special installation or configuration procedures. Copy the archive file to the desired subdirectory on your hard drive or to a floppy disk (which need not be bootable). Switch to the floppy drive or hard drive subdirectory containing the archive file, and decompress the archive with PKUNZIP. The actual uncompressed utility consists of an ASQ.EXE executable file and an ASQ.HLP file, which provides the text instruction used in the program. Since the system need not be booted clean, you can run the program from DOS or from a DOS window. When the program is decompressed, start the diagnostic by typing ASQ.

Operation

The program starts with the main screen illustrated in Figure 2-10. The first four options produce text information about the program, memory management, and a selection of Qualitas products. The About Memory Management option offers some good background information on the ideas and objectives of memory management. The fourth option, Tutorial Menu, provides a series of detailed memory management tutorials; this is particularly useful for PC enthusiasts and new technicians interested in broadening their knowledge.

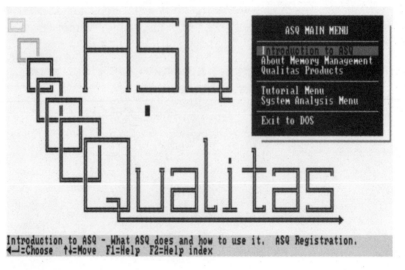

■ **2-10** *The main menu in ASQ0315.*

Of course, the program also offers a series of tests under the System Analysis Menu. The first option, Memory Analysis, brings up a submenu, as shown in Figure 2-11. From here, you can receive a general summary of the PC's memory configuration or select from a number of specific memory tests. As you scroll through each selection, a small text window on the right of the display provides additional details about the test. The Configuration Analysis menu (Figure 2-12) allows you to check a summary report or review the contents of your CONFIG.SYS

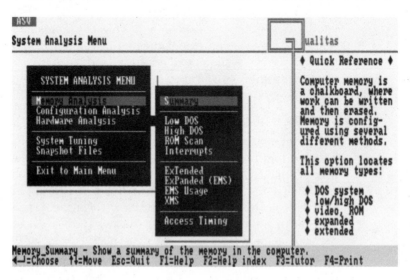

■ **2-11** *The Memory Analysis menu in ASQ0315.*

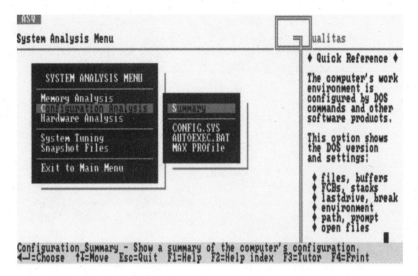

■ **2-12** *The Configuration Analysis menu in ASQ0315.*

and AUTOEXEC.BAT files. If you have 386MAX on the system, the MAX PROfile option will detail its operation. When you select the Hardware Analysis option (Figure 2-13), you can receive a summary or check the details of your video, drives, ports, BIOS, or CMOS contents.

When you select the System Tuning option, the program steps through each entry in your configuration files and makes specific recommendations about the optimum setting (if any) for each entry. This is a unique (and surprisingly thorough) feature of

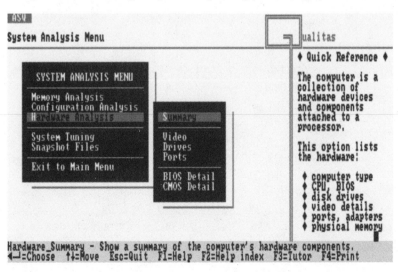

■ **2-13** *The Hardware Analysis menu in ASQ0315.*

ASQ.EXE. If you want to capture screen shots at various points (or recall previous screen shots), you can use the Snapshot Files feature. The Exit option (or <Esc> on the keyboard) will return you to the main screen.

Performance

The ASQ.EXE utility makes use of basic text symbols, so it is not very visually appealing. It does, however, provide a wealth of good system (especially memory) information, which is also well supported by clear and concise text. The keyboard navigation is consistent and intuitive, and is largely through directional arrows, <Enter>, and <Esc>. The <F4> key starts a very good printer interface, which you can use to print out system reports as well as text tutorials. Finally, the program works on a wide variety of system platforms; in spite of its age (c. 1991), the program worked well on a Pentium 166-MHz PC. Clearly, there is no CPU-specific code or testing done by the program.

Registration

ASQ.EXE is $0 shareware, but Qualitas asks that you register the product by sending in your name and mailing information. This method of generating sales leads through shareware is often referred to as *contact-ware*, and will invariably draw sales offers for 386MAX and other Qualitas products. The associated documentation promises that a registration will keep you informed of the newest releases of ASQ.

Summary

If you find yourself dealing with memory management issues, ASQ0315.ZIP is a must-have package. Not only is the system analysis information meaningful, but the companion text and tutorial information make this a uniquely valuable diagnostic and learning tool.

CHECK136.ZIP

Some technicians simply do not like the idea of menus and report screens. CHECKSYS (Table 2-15) is a basic system diagnostic that abandons the use of menu screens and windows in favor of a command line. When CHECKSYS is executed, it returns a description of the whole PC system (or an error level, if necessary). You can also use CHECKSYS to inspect specific subsystems and return one-line descriptions of system status. The command-line architecture of CHECKSYS also makes it possible to add routine diagnostic

■ Table 2-15 CHECK136 fact sheet

Program name:	Command Line Diagnostic
Executable file:	CHECKSYS.EXE
Purpose:	A command-line diagnostic for basic PC testing
Version:	1.36
Operating system:	MS-DOS 3.3 or later
Compressed file:	CHECK136.ZIP (archive)
Author:	Dan Shearer
Address:	Computer Centre
	University of South Australia
Internet:	ccdps@lux.levels.unisa.edu.au
ASP member:	No
Registration:	Public domain
Special notes:	Basic command-line interface only

functions in the system startup files (e.g., AUTOEXEC.BAT) or other batch files.

Installation and configuration

CHECK136 has no particular installation or configuration requirements, so you can copy the CHECK136.ZIP archive to any subdirectory on your hard drive or to a floppy disk. Once the archive file is copied, switch to the drive or directory containing the file, then use PKUNZIP to decompress the archive file. You will find the executable file CHECKSYS.EXE and documentation file CHECKSYS.DOC. You can start the program by typing CHECKSYS with a command-line switch; if you use CHECKSYS alone, the program will respond with a complete list of switches.

Operation

CHECKSYS should be operated through the DOS command line rather than a DOS window. When running the program, you should use one of the command-line switches listed in Table 2-16. The program will run and return a message or error level. Once the test is complete, CHECKSYS will terminate and return to the DOS prompt. The advantage of this arrangement is that you can place CHECKSYS in your AUTOEXEC.BAT file. The following line:

C:\utilities\checksys /CPU

will start CHECKSYS and perform a CPU check. The test will return an error level depending on which CPU is detected in the system. Other tests operate in a similar fashion.

■ Table 2-16 Command-line switches for CHECKSYS

Switch	Description
/ALL	Displays the messages for all tests and returns error level 0
/CPU	Returns error level 0 to 8, in order, for: 8088, 8086, V20, V30, 80188, 80186, Unknown, 80286, and 80386
/EMM	Returns error level 1 if EMM driver is installed, 0 if not
/FTP	Returns 1 if packet driver responds, else 0 if not installed
/KBD	Returns error level 1 if extended keyboard is installed, 0 if not
/MOUSE	Returns 0 for no mouse driver, else number of buttons
/NETBIOS	Returns error level 1 if NetBIOS responds, 0 otherwise
/PAR	Returns number of parallel ports recognized by BIOS
/SER	Returns number of serial ports recognized by BIOS
/VID	Returns 1 to 10, in order, for: CGA, MCGA, EGA, EGA64, EGAMon, 8514, HercMon, ATT400, VGA, and PC3270
/WIN	Returns 0 to 3, in order, for: No Windows, Win/386 2.x, Win 3.0 (/R or /S), and Win 3.x (/3)
/XMS	Returns 2 for XMS and HMA avail, 1 for XMS but no HMA, and 0 for no XMS
/87	Returns 0 to 3, in order, for: None, 8087, 80287, and 80387

Note: Each test also displays a detailed message to standard output. Switches can be abbreviated to one letter. An error level of 99 is a syntax error.

Performance

The program starts, runs, and returns its results in a matter of moments, but the program's author has identified a number of important limitations that you should keep in mind:

☐ The BIOS check for printer and COM ports is often not accurate.

☐ The FPU check gives an erroneous result when used on an NEC V20 chip with an Intel 8087 installed.

☐ The program does not check for Weitek FPUs.

☐ The program can't distinguish OS/2 DOS-boxes from Windows DOS-boxes.

☐ The program does not test for various network cards.

☐ The program does not test for a game port.

☐ The program does not provide video chipset information.

☐ The program does not detect sound cards.

Registration

CHECKSYS has been released to the public domain (c. 1992), so you are free to use the program as you see fit without cost or obligation. It may be used and distributed freely.

Summary

CHECKSYS is a basic testing/system configuration utility intended to be run from the command line. It lacks many of the testing features found in other software, but its command-line nature allows the convenience of batch file operation.

CONF810E.ZIP

Information is the technician's most vital resource whenever repairing, testing, or examining a PC prior to an upgrade. Success often lies in knowing "what's in the box." Rather than the time-consuming process of disassembling the computer and examining each item by hand, a well-written, up-to-the-minute system information utility can tell technicians everything they need to know before they even pick up a screwdriver. The long-running PC-Config (Table 2-17) series of utilities by Michael Holin is one of the most recognized and respected shareware system information utilities/benchmarking programs available. With version 8.10E now in the field, PC-Config retains its leadership as a thorough and reliable system utility.

■ **Table 2-17 CONF810E fact sheet**

Program name:	PC-Config
Executable file:	CONFIG.EXE
Purpose:	A system information and benchmarking program for PCs
Version:	8.10E
Operating system:	MS-DOS 2.0 or later (3.0 or later preferred)
Compressed file:	CONF810E.ZIP (archive)
Author:	Michael Holin
Address:	P.O. Box 1147
	65432 Florsheim
	Germany
CompuServe:	100441,1366
URL:	http://ourworld.compuserve.com/homepages/holin
ASP member:	No
Registration:	Private $20 and commercial $70; registered versions provide even more hardware data and functions
Special notes:	Can produce false information if run from a DOS window

Installation and configuration

You should begin installation by copying the CONF810E.ZIP archive file from your DLS Diagnostic CD to a subdirectory on your hard drive. You could also install the utility to a floppy disk.

Since the system does not need a clean boot to use PC-Config, your floppy disk need not be bootable (though adding it to your emergency system disk is probably a good idea). Once the archive file is copied, switch to the drive or subdirectory containing the file and use PKUNZIP to decompress the archive. This process will decompress a series of files into your directory. There are no other configuration steps needed to use PC-Config, but you do need the CONFIG.INI file in the same directory as the executable CONFIG.EXE file. Start the program simply by typing CONFIG and pressing <Enter>.

Operation

Stated simply, PC-Config provides a wealth of information. Data is presented as a series of detailed information "windows," such as the first hardware window shown in Figure 2-14. The documentation that accompanies PC-Config (the CONFIG.TXT file) provides explanations of what each entry means, and where (or how) the data was acquired. Over 12 windows of detailed data provide you with the following types of system information:

☐ Installed PC hardware

☐ Installed software (e.g., DOS and network OS details)

☐ Hard drive benchmark

☐ PCI system information

☐ CD-ROM drive benchmark

☐ Resident system software and drivers

☐ System devices (e.g., ports)

☐ Your PC compared to other PCs

☐ Detailed chipset information

☐ Memory timing specifications

☐ IRQ assignments

☐ List of logical drives installed

☐ System hints

☐ Supplemental PC hardware installed (registered version)

☐ ASPI information (registered version)

☐ Screen refresh rates (registered version)

Navigating the software is easy; the <F2> key moves you forward between individual windows, while the <F3> key moves you back. The program also supports a mouse in the DOS mode, so you can click on the appropriate place to move from window to window. If there is a specific window you need to see, you can click on

■ **2-14** *One of many comprehensive data screens in CONF810E.*

Window and select any available window immediately. PC-Config also allows you to edit your system startup files (i.e., CONFIG.SYS and AUTOEXEC.BAT).

Performance

PC-Config is an extremely detailed utility and, except for momentary delays when measuring drive benchmark performance, the program behaves quite well. As with all types of "information" utilities, however, there is always the possibility that some information will be detected incorrectly. The following issues have been identified by the program author

☐ Under Windows (and other multitasking environments), it is not possible to make short-term time measurements, so benchmark tests are impossible.

☐ Under DR-DOS 6.0's EMM386, the speed measurement test for extended memory causes privilege errors. The switch TESTEXTMEM must therefore be set to NO(NEIN).

☐ PC-Cache V5.x is recognized as Multisoft QCache.

☐ There are problems with more than one continuous area of HI-DOS.

☐ Some computers slow down their clock frequency when a floppy drive is running. PC-Config can usually recognize when it has been started from a floppy, and waits for the drive to stop. However, this recognition does not work with some Compaq computers, and the displayed value for the clock speed will be wrong.

- [ ] If all resident software is loaded in HI-DOS, this will cause problems.
- [ ] PC-Config cannot find RAM disks loaded high under QEMM.
- [ ] On some older computers (e.g., an IBM XT/286) there are problems with establishing the hard disk access times.

Registration

For users who choose to employ PC-Config regularly, there are two types of registration: private (individual), and commercial. Private registration is $20, while the commercial registration is $70. You can register through the mail (checks in U.S. currency are accepted), with a MasterCard or Visa, or through CompuServe (type GO SWREG) using the program ID number 3879. Registration will get you the latest complete version of the software with all features fully enabled.

Summary

PC-Config represents some of the best attributes of shareware; it is a thorough, highly detailed, PC information utility that is accurate, easy to use, regularly updated, well documented, and reasonably priced.

FIXCLOCK.ZIP

PCs keep time by using a real-time-clock (or RTC). Unfortunately, not all RTCs keep the correct time with total accuracy; you've probably noticed that the time you set several days ago is now off by as much as several minutes. The FIXCLOCK utility (Table 2-18) permits you to adjust the clock rate of the computer's RTC in order to speed up or slow down clocks that are not running accurately. FIXCLOCK is designed for computer systems whose RTCs can be reset with MS-DOS function calls.

Installation and configuration

To operate, FIXCLOCK.EXE must be placed on your hard drive and referenced in the AUTOEXEC.BAT file. Prepare a subdirectory on your hard drive, then copy the FIXCLOCK.ZIP file from your DLS Diagnostic CD to your hard drive subdirectory. Switch to your subdirectory with this command:

```
C:\> cd\fixclock <Enter>
```

then run PKUNZIP to decompress the archive. After you have decompressed the file, start a text editor such as DOS EDIT and load your AUTOEXEC.BAT file. Then add the following command line to the AUTOEXEC.BAT file:

■ Table 2-18 FIXCLOCK fact sheet

Program name:	Fix Clock
Executable file:	FIXCLOCK.EXE
Purpose:	To correct problems with PC time-keeping
Version:	Unknown (c. 1995)
Operating system:	MS-DOS 3.3 or later
Compressed file:	FIXCLOCK.ZIP (archive)
Author:	Irving Maron
CompuServe:	76614,2666
ASP member:	No
Registration:	$0 shareware
Special notes:	Must be installed in AUTOEXEC.BAT

c:\fixclock\fixclock

Of course, if FIXCLOCK.EXE is in a different subdirectory, make sure to use the right path. As a rule, you should place the FIX-CLOCK command line before any lines that start other drivers or TSRs. You can then save your changes to AUTOEXEC.BAT and exit your text editor. The next time you reboot the PC, FIX-CLOCK will interrupt the process and require you to enter two correction constants (in seconds per week). After you enter these values, subsequent reboots will not be interrupted. FIX-CLOCK checks the system clock at each initialization and resets the clock based on the clock-rate correction constants that you entered during installation.

The first correction constant entered (called the "real-time clock rate adjustment") accounts for clock drift on normal days when the computer is turned on and used normally. The second constant (called "additional adjustment for nonoperating days") is provided for computers that exhibit clock drift during periods of a day or more when the computer is not booted. This is a different amount of drift than that encountered when the computer is operated. The second adjustment is an incremental correction to the first correction constant. If the additional correction is not required (or if you are not sure whether or not it is required), just enter zero.

Operation

Unlike many of the other utilities covered in this chapter, FIX-CLOCK is a TSR that requires virtually no user interaction. Once the proper correction constants are entered, you need not worry about the utility any more. However, getting the correction constants correct in the first place can be tricky. To change the constants after initial installation, switch to the subdirectory containing FIXCLOCK and type:

C:\> FIXCLOCK S <Enter>

This allows you to account for any remaining clock-rate inaccuracy noted after the initial setup. When entering a new correction constant, use the previous constant, adjusted for the additional clock drift. For example, if you initially observed that, for periods when the computer is operated, the uncorrected clock gained 30 seconds per week, then the installation procedure would have guided you to enter –30 as the real-time clock rate adjustment (the negative sign indicates a slowdown). If you then note that the clock still gains five seconds every two weeks (2.5 seconds per week), you should then change the constant to –32.5. On the other hand, if the clock had begun to lose five seconds per week after the initial installation, you would change the constant to –27.5 instead. You can adjust the correction constants as many times as you like in order to find the correct values for your clock.

Whenever the correction constants are adjusted, the date and time are recorded in an ASCII file named FIXCLOCK.ADJ in the FIXCLOCK directory. This information can be useful in determining the clock drift correction. You can read the date and time recorded in FIXCLOCK.ADJ by entering:

C:\> type fixclock.adj <Enter>

Performance

The important thing to note about FIXCLOCK is that it works only on systems where the RTC can be set through DOS function calls. This is not always possible with every PC type and model, so if FIXCLOCK does not work on any one particular system, that could be the problem.

Registration

FIXCLOCK.EXE has been released as $0 shareware, so it may be freely used and distributed.

Summary

The FIXCLOCK utility is one of those unusual utilities that can prove remarkably handy in PCs that just don't seem to keep the right time; it's much more convenient than remembering to reset the time manually every few days.

OVERHEAD.ZIP

When technicians evaluate the performance of a computer, it is generally accepted that any drivers and TSRs operating in the system might slow down (or degrade) the evaluation. The more of this "overhead" software present in a system, the more performance will be affected. While the difference between such "burdened" and "unburdened" systems is often easily noticeable, there are few simple tools available to help you apply a number to this difference. OVERHEAD (Table 2-19) is a rudimentary program that can actually help determine the effects of your system overhead.

■ Table 2-19 OVERHEAD fact sheet

Program name:	System Overhead Tester
Executable file:	OVERHEAD.EXE
Purpose:	To measure the effects of overhead on your PC
Version:	Unknown
Operating system:	MS-DOS 3.3 or later
Compressed file:	none (provided uncompressed)
Author:	Ed Ross
CompuServe:	75776,151
ASP member:	No
Registration:	Public domain
Special notes:	Must be used on a normal and clean system to be effective

Installation and configuration

OVERHEAD is provided in its uncompressed form, so you should copy the OVERHEAD.EXE program and its OVERHEAD.DOC documentation file to a bootable floppy disk. Once the files are copied, you can run OVERHEAD from the DOS command prompt (as well as a DOS window). There are no setup or configuration issues involved in the use of OVERHEAD.

Operation

Simply stated, the OVERHEAD diagnostic performs several iterations of a fixed calculation, then measures the amount of time those iterations take. The more a system is burdened with drivers and TSRs, the longer those iterations will take. Start the evaluation by booting the system clean from your floppy disk, then running OVERHEAD for the first time. Note the time required to perform the iterations. Next, boot the system normally (i.e., from your C: drive with all normal drivers and TSRs loaded in your startup files). Run OVERHEAD again and note the time for the same number of iterations. The difference between the burdened and clean systems indicates the effects of system overhead on the burdened system. You can also express this difference as a percentage:

$$\frac{\text{burdened system} - \text{clean system}}{\text{burdened system}} \times 100$$

For example, suppose OVERHEAD returned the number 2.527473 for a clean system, and 3.00 for a burdened system. This means that the overhead software running on your burdened system causes a ([3.00 − 2.527473] / 3.00) × 100, or 15.75 percent slowdown in the system (if the answer were negative, it would indicate a system speed-up, which is a highly unlikely scenario).

Performance

The OVERHEAD program is simple to use. Just run the program; it will take a moment to perform several calculations, then report on the time required to perform them. After the time is reported, the program terminates. The actual amount of time needed to run the iterations depends on the speed of the PC; a Pentium 166-MHz system will blaze through the calculations in a matter of moments, while an i286-type system might take 20 to 30 seconds or more. By default, the program will run four iterations before reporting on a time. You can adjust the number of iterations by adding the number to your command line. The following command, for example:

C:\> OVERHEAD 20 <Enter>

will perform 20 iterations. As a rule, you should require faster PCs to perform more iterations.

Registration

No registration is required for the use of OVERHEAD. Based on the documentation that accompanies the program, I presume the program is in the public domain.

Summary

There's nothing fancy about OVERHEAD, but it can provide a very handy bit of performance information about a PC that few (if any) other utilities bother to address.

RESOUR11.ZIP

There is little doubt that the introduction of Windows opened up computing potential on the PC that DOS could never have matched.

But even with all the advances behind Windows, its performance is still limited by available system resources (namely memory). When problems arise on a Windows platform, the wise technician keeps an eye on system resources. Free System Resources (Table 2-20) is a Windows utility that runs in the background and reports when Windows resources are low. Not only does RESOUR11 help avoid system crashes, but it can help prevent lost data as the result of resource-related crashes.

■ Table 2-20 RESOUR11 fact sheet

Program name:	Free System Resources
Executable file:	RESOURCE.EXE
Purpose:	To track and report low Windows resources
Version:	1.1
Operating system:	Windows 3.1 or later
Compressed file:	RESOUR11.ZIP (archive)
Author:	Chet Williams
Address:	1737 Peyton Ave., K
	Burbank, CA 91504
Phone:	818-954-9128
ASP member:	Yes
Registration:	$10
Special notes:	Requires VBRUN300.DLL (not included) and installation under Windows

Installation and configuration

The RESOUR11 utility is strictly a Windows product, so you should prepare a subdirectory on your hard drive, then copy the RESOUR11.ZIP file from the DLS Diagnostic CD to your new subdirectory. Once the archive file is copied, switch to the subdirectory and use PKUNZIP to decompress the archive. As the archive decompresses into its constituent files, you will notice that virtually all the files have an underbar (_) in the extension (e.g., TOOLHELP.DL_); this indicates that the file is still in a compressed form.

Start Windows (if not already running), select File and Run, then enter the drive and path containing the SETUP.EXE file, such as the following:

c:\resour11\setup

This will start the setup program for Free System Resources. Follow the on-screen instructions to complete the program's installation.

Note that RESOUR11 requires the use of the Virtual Basic runtime module (VBRUN300.DLL), which should be installed in your main Windows\System directory. When you start the utility, you will need to configure the program by entering "trigger points" to define the resource levels at which the program will initiate its warnings.

Operation

Although the program does not normally install itself to a system's startup program group, consider installing it there so it will start automatically each time the program is run (you can apply the "run minimized" attribute). An .INI file will be created to keep track of the program's operating characteristics. In the minimized mode, memory percentages will appear on the icon's label lines, so you can check the available resources periodically without having to maximize, resize, and reminimize the window. You can also change the colors associated with backgrounds and warnings so when an error is flagged, it cannot be missed.

Performance

There are some performance points to keep in mind when using RESOUR11:

The GDI and User data space (or "heap") is limited to 64KB. If the user runs out of either of these two data spaces, an Out of Memory error message will occur. Sufficient GDI and User data space must be available to avoid problems. If your customer's work habits or applications are such that memory problems occur, RESOUR11 can be helpful in keeping the user out of trouble by setting trigger levels.

The memory (or "global heaps") managed by the virtual memory manager are less of a problem due to the way the memory manager works. Global heaps are managed as pages that can be 2048 or 4096 bytes, and the memory manager keeps track of which pages are disposable. When additional memory is required, the disposable pages are removed. Still, low disk space (virtual memory) can cause errors.

Some programs have "memory leaks," or bugs that allow programs to use memory, but do not return it to the system after the program terminates. To locate these kinds of problems, track the current percentage available during execution and after program termination to see that the resource is returned to the system. If not, you might need to change drivers or get a program patch to fix the problem.

Registration

If you plan to use RESOUR11 regularly, you must register the product with the program author. The cost for RESOUR11 is $10. Unfortunately, the registration benefits are not stated very clearly in the associated documentation. Call the program author directly to get the latest registration benefits.

Summary

One of the greatest weaknesses of Windows 3.x is its absolute dependence on limited system resources. When those resources are strained, Windows can crash (and take your current work with it). The RESOUR11 utility can help users and technicians keep track of system resources, which can warn of impending errors, and correlate resource problems with specific actions or applications.

RITM25.ZIP

Earlier in this chapter, you learned about FIXCLOCK, a utility to correct drift in a PC's real-time clock (or RTC). RighTime (Table 2-21) is the next in a line of popular clock-correction products. RighTime is a resident real-time clock-correcting program for MS-DOS, PC-DOS, and DR-DOS running on PC/AT and 100 percent compatible machines. It corrects both DOS settings and CMOS real-time clock rate errors as large as 5.5 minutes per day, and it increases the DOS clock resolution from about 0.055 seconds to 0.01 seconds. RighTime occupies only about 7KB of system RAM, and can normally be loaded into the upper memory area (UMA).

RighTime brings exceptional system time-of-day clock performance to PCs, with no additional hardware requirements. With RighTime installed, the standard real-time clock system becomes what the program author refers to as an "adaptive mathematically compensated crystal-controlled oscillator-based clock." Under stable conditions, RighTime can produce a system clock that keeps time within 0.5 second per week or better. According to RighTime's documentation, some users have reported consistent clock accuracies of 0.07 second per week.

Installation and configuration

You need to follow a procedure very similar to the one described in this section to properly install and configure RighTime. First, copy the RITM25.ZIP archive file to a subdirectory on your hard drive.

■ Table 2-21 RITM25 fact sheet

Program name:	RighTime
Executable file:	RIGHTIME.COM
Purpose:	To correct for time drift in PC clocks
Version:	2.58
Operating system:	MS-DOS 3.3 or later
Compressed file:	RITM25.ZIP (archive)
Author:	G. T. Becker
Address:	Air System Technologies, Inc.
	4232 Marsh Lane, Suite 339
	Dallas, TX 75234-3899
Phone:	214-402-9660
BBS:	214-869-2780
CompuServe:	76436,3210
ASP member:	No
Registration:	$40
Special notes:	Includes a set of other utilities, and has very complete and thorough documentation.

Switch to that subdirectory, then use PKUNZIP to decompress the archive file. You will see the main program, RIGHTIME.COM, along with the documentation file and a number of other related utilities.

Make sure you are running DOS (not a DOS window), and start the RighTime setup procedure, SETUPRT2.COM. SETUPRT2 allows you to select from among many options, but you can initially accept the defaults by simply selecting Install; you can then change them later. When asked to do so, set the time accurately, then type EXIT to continue the installation process. The program will then modify your AUTOEXEC.BAT and (if required) CONFIG.SYS files by adding a line or two to them. The existing files will be renamed with an .RT2 extension. You will normally be directed to reboot by pressing <Ctrl>–<Alt>–<Del>. This should get RighTime running each time the PC starts.

Set the time accurately for a few days, ideally immediately before you shut down your system for the night and immediately after booting in the morning. If you never shut down your system, set the time accurately a few times each day over well-spaced periods of time. You should find that your system clocks will rapidly become more accurate. If they do not, check the log file for invisible, unexpected time sets (which will confuse RighTime's learning). The name of the program that sets the time is identified in the log.

You might be surprised to find that some programs you never expect set the clock (usually incorrectly), which will always disturb RighTime.

Operation

Part of the RighTime process requires storage of some correction data. The amount of data is small and it must be stored in a place that will survive rebooting and power failures. To use RighTime, first decide where to store the corrections. There are two options: a disk file or unused CMOS RAM. It is recommended for you to try the disk option first if you can. A diskless machine cannot use the disk option, unless it is equipped with a nonvolatile RAM disk, which will appear to the system as any other disk.

Although only the first 52 bytes of a 64-byte CMOS RAM are defined by the original IBM PC standard (presumably leaving the last 12 bytes available), most modern BIOS will use these 12 bytes for other functions. For example, if you have adopted a user-specified hard disk type, your specification might be stored there. Sometimes the area is used for the power-on password in machines where passwords are enabled. Many modern machines contain 128-byte CMOS RAM areas, and others (some PS/2 models and SL-based machines) contain 256 bytes of CMOS RAM. SETUPRT2 will allow selection only of CMOS RAM addresses that allow for the proper storage of RighTime's correction data, but there is no guarantee that the address you select is unused in your machine configuration. You can run the VIEWCMOS.COM utility to look at the CMOS RAM contents, but your machine might not have a large block of zeros free and safe to use. Before attempting to use the CMOS RAM option, understand that CMOS RAM contains system setup data that RighTime might inadvertently disturb. So be prepared to reset the setup data if the CMOS RAM option is unsuccessful on your system.

If you choose the disk file option, RighTime will attempt to write to a disk file from time to time, so write access must be allowed. If the "disk" is actually a nonvolatile RAM disk card, the card must remain in the machine if this option is to work properly. If you use the disk file option on a battery-powered laptop, you can decrease the update frequency and allow your hard disk to spin down after periods of inactivity to increase the battery life. The disk file option causes RighTime to maintain an open handle to a file, which will present a problem when running a file defragmenting utility on the same disk drive that RighTime is updating. But RighTime can be killed during defragmentation and restarted afterward.

63

RighTime can also be configured with no correction storage, with consequential loss of some of its utility.

If you know how fast or slow your clock appears to run per day, you can speed up the learning process of RighTime by suggesting a correction to the program: a signed number in hundredths of seconds, positive for a slow clock and negative for a fast clock. For example, if your clock runs about two minutes fast per day, the suggested correction should be –120.00 (120 seconds). There are actually two corrections that RighTime normally applies, one while the system is running (warm) and another when the system is off (cool). If you know the cool correction, you can suggest it also. If you don't know one or either correction, RighTime will determine them anyway; it'll just take a little longer for the corrections to reach peak accuracy.

If you need to restart RighTime while it is currently resident and running, you must first kill the resident program. If appropriate, the corrections that RighTime has already learned can be suggested to the new program copy. Note: If you have been using another resident driver or TSR to correct the weaknesses of your clock, remove all references to it from your CONFIG.SYS and AUTOEXEC.BAT files, and remove the other driver or TSR from your system.

RighTime will monitor each time correction event and learn from your adjustments. Whenever you notice that the indicated DOS system time is off, reset it accurately. You will find that the clocks will become more and more accurate and the need for adjustment will decrease, becoming infrequent. However, you must set the time accurately at least once per month. Also allow sufficient time to elapse between time adjustments so that enough error exists for RighTime to use in its correction calculations. The more time you allow, the better the correction factors that are determined. Careless time sets will result in poor correction or even wild clock behavior.

When you run RighTime, the program will normally be silent. If RighTime beeps, pay close attention to its report; it is reminding or warning you of an unusual mode, condition, or failure. If ANSI.SYS is present and data highlighting is not disabled, the warning lines will be highlighted.

Performance

Now that you have seen some of the things RighTime can do, there are some things it cannot do that you should be aware of:

RighTime cannot correct clock boards or computer mother-board clocks that do not emulate the PC/AT CMOS RTC hard-ware clock and its BIOS support precisely. The large majority of current 80286, 80386, and 80486-based machines are generally compatible.

RighTime cannot properly correct an unstable clock; most clocks are slow or fast, but they are essentially unvarying. If your clock wanders aimlessly or has sudden changes in behavior, your hard-ware might need repair (perhaps simple battery or CMOS RTC module replacement).

RighTime will not run under OS/2. An OS/2 version is in devel-opment.

Registration

If you continue to use RighTime after a period of 30 days, you must register it with the program author for $40. Registered Righ-Time users receive a diskette containing the current version of the registered program, additional utilities, a printed user man-ual, and automatic notification of new releases. The registered version of RighTime is functionally identical to the shareware-distributed evaluation version, except that it lacks registration re-minders, it is smaller in size, it can operate in a nonverbose and silent mode, and it is serial-numbered to the individual or busi-ness registrant.

Summary

RighTime is one of the most popular time-correcting utilities avail-able because of its excellent (and automatic) adaptability; you just have to keep the time set accurately for a while. This eliminates the guesswork involved in correction factors, and configures most PCs for outstanding long-term time-keeping.

SNOOP330.ZIP

Knowing the hardware and software configuration of a PC can make the difference between a quick and easy upgrade or a long, perplexing nightmare. Looking inside the PC will help, but you certainly cannot identify specific components, assemblies, or setup information from a visual inspection. System information utilities fill this important information gap by analyzing a sys-tem's components, configuration, and attributes, and providing the details in a convenient screen format. Snooper by John Vias (Table 2-22) fills this need with a series of compact, data-filled displays.

■ Table 2-22 SNOOP330 fact sheet

Program name:	Snooper
Executable file:	SNOOPER.EXE
Purpose:	A detailed system information utility
Version:	3.30
Operating system:	MS-DOS 3.1 or later
Compressed file:	SNOOP330.ZIP (archive)
Author:	John Vias
Address:	Vias & Associates
	P.O. Box 470805
	San Francisco, CA 94147
Phone:	415-921-6262
ASP member:	Yes
Registration:	$39
Special notes:	Outstanding documentation

Installation and configuration

Snooper can be installed under either DOS or Windows. Copy the SNOOP330.ZIP archive from the CD to a subdirectory on your hard drive. You might also want to copy the archive to a floppy disk if you plan to keep Snooper in your toolbox. Once the archive is copied, switch to your subdirectory (or floppy drive) and use PKUNZIP to decompress the archive. Once the archive has been decompressed, you can run SNOOPER.EXE directly from the sub-directory or diskette.

If you then want to install the program under Windows, start Windows, choose an acceptable program group for Snooper, select File and New, and click on New Program Item. Where it asks for the description, enter Snooper. In the Command Line entry, type the full path to the program. For example:

c:\snoop330\snooper.exe

Note: If you want to use a .PIF file, edit it with PIFEDIT to point to SNOOPER.EXE. Then follow these instructions but make Command Line point to the .PIF file instead.

Click on Change Icon and enter the path to SNOOPER.ICO. Finally, click the OK buttons until you return to the Program Manager's main screen. Snooper's icon should appear in the selected program group. Just double-click on the icon to run Snooper.

Operation

When started, Snooper displays its Equipment screen (Figure 2-15). This one screen provides detailed CPU, memory, and drive data that identifies most of the computer's vital assemblies. The main menu is listed along the bottom of the Equipment screen. From here, you can access information about the system busses, system diagnostics, system benchmarks, your CMOS setup, network data, setup data, and configuration files (CONFIG.SYS and AUTOEXEC.BAT). You can also print reports or exit the program. The documentation accompanying Snooper outlines each parameter in detail. There is no mouse support in Snooper, so navigation is accomplished solely with the keyboard.

```
Snooper, the system checker, version 3.30 Copyright 1989-94 John Vias
┌─────────────────────────────────────────────┬────────────────────────────┐
│ Equipment                                    │ Disk [aCd]                 │
│                                              │                     Label  │
│ Computer Pentium compatible (with APM 1.01)  │ +FTWA1\SNOOP330  Directory │
│ CPU Pentium->100, V86Video VESA 2.0 SVGA 2M  │       ST32140A  IDE model  │
│ NDP internal        Ports Game S-Blaster     │    fixed disk  Drive type  │
│ Bus PCI             Serial 3F8 2F8           │            1   CMOS type   │
│ Memory              Parallel 378             │        local   Status      │
│   655,360 b Convl   BIOS  11/29/95 PnP       │           64   Heads       │
│   323,376 b Free     Exts C000 ED00          │           63   Sectrs/cyl  │
│   131,984 b Used    Mouse Microsoft 9.01     │        1,023   Cylinders   │
│    15,360 K Extended Port PS/2               │          512 b Sectors     │
│           K Ext free Keyboard 101 Support 101│       32,768 b Clusters    │
│    14,768 K XMS 3.0  Environment             │  2,109,472,768 b Total     │
│    in use HMA (A20)   Free 1,211 Total 1,424 │     919,470,080 b Free     │
│        23 K UMB     DOS MS-DOS 7.0a (HMA)    │   1,190,002,688 b Used 56% │
│    15,664 K EMS 4.0  Shell VCPI 1.0          │ ▬▬▬▬▬▬▬▬▬▬▬▬▬▬▬▬▬▬▬▬▬▬▬▬▬▬ │
│    15,008 K EMS free Files 60   Buffers 40   │ Empty        Half     Full │
│ Drives              Break off Verify  off    │                            │
│ 1 Floppy 2 Physical Cache                    ├────────────────────────────┤
│ 1 Hard   3 Logical  Network                  │ Message:                   │
└─────────────────────────────────────────────┴────────────────────────────┘
Snooper running Wednesday, August 28, 1996, at 10:02:17am
F1-help Alt->Bus Diags bEnch cmOs Network Setup Auto Config Log Print< Esc-quit
```

■ **2-15** *The main screen of SNOOP330.*

Along with the general Equipment screen, you can check the interrupt and DMA assignments, COM ports, and LPT ports using the Diagnostic screen (Figure 2-16). This Diagnostic screen also checks for the presence of a sound card. Another interesting feature of Snooper is its CMOS editing capability, shown in Figure 2-17. Major system CMOS parameters are displayed in this screen, and you can edit them without using the system setup routine. However, you must restart the PC for changes to work.

As a final note, Snooper can be executed from the command line to perform a specific check, report the necessary data, then terminate to DOS. This makes Snooper particularly useful for startup system checks.

```
Snooper, the system checker, version 3.30 Copyright 1989-94 John Vias
┌──────────────────────────────────────┬──────────────────────────────────────┐
│ Serial ports                         │  IRQ lines        DMA channels        │
│           COM1    COM2               │                                       │
│ Address   03F8    02F8               │        Timer ** 0 ** In use          │
│ UART    16550A  16550A               │     Keyboard ** 1 ** In use          │
│ Speed   19,200   1,200               │  Second 8259 ** 2 ** Floppy disk     │
│ Format    8N1     ?N1                │     COM2/COM4 ** 3 ** In use         │
│ IRQ       (4)     (3)                │     COM1/COM3    4    Available       │
│ Device                               │          LPT2    5 ** In use         │
│ Fax class                            │  Floppy disk ** 6 ** In use          │
│                                      │          LPT1    7 ** In use         │
│ Parallel ports                       │         Clock    8  (DMA report may   │
│           LPT1                       │  (from IRQ2) ** 9   be inaccurate    │
│ Address   0378                       │     Available   10  on this PC.)      │
│ IRQ                                  │     Available   11                    │
│ Selected   **                        │   MOUSE.COM ** 12  (** This          │
│ I/O error                            │  Coprocessor ** 13   IRQ line or     │
│ No paper    **                       │    Hard disk ** 14   DMA channel     │
│ Busy        **                       │       In use ** 15   is in use.)     │
├──────────────────────────────────────┼──────────────────────────────────────┤
│ Sound card Sound Blaster at port 220h│  Message:                            │
└──────────────────────────────────────┴──────────────────────────────────────┘
Snooper running Wednesday, August 28, 1996, at 10:02:54am
Alt-Log screen to file   Alt-Print screen to PRN   Esc-main screen
```

■ **2-16** *The Diags report from SNOOP330.*

```
Snooper, the system checker, version 3.30 Copyright 1989-94 John Vias
┌──────────────────────────────────────────────────────────────────────────┐
│ CMOS                                                                       │
│                                                                            │
│         DatE 08-28-96 Wednesday        CMOS status OK                      │
│         Time 11:51:42                                                      │
│                                                                            │
│ Convl Memory    640K                                                       │
│ EXt. memory 15,360K                                                        │
│                                                                            │
│ Floppy A: 3.5" 1.44M                                                       │
│ Floppy B: none                                                             │
│                                                                            │
│             Type  Heads  Secs/Cyl  Cylinders  Pre-comp  L-zone  Capacity   │
│ Hard drive 1:  1 (user-defined or invalid type)                            │
│ Hard drive 2: none, or a SCSI hard drive                                   │
│                                                                            │
│    DIsplay VGA or EGA                                                       │
│                                                                            │
│ CoProcessor installed                                                      │
│                                              ┌──────────────────────────┐  │
│                                              │ Message:                 │  │
└──────────────────────────────────────────────┴──────────────────────────┴──┘
Snooper running Wednesday, August 28, 1996, at 11:51:42am
Tab/Shift-Tab select field   +/- modify field   Alt-Log   Alt-Print   Esc-quit
```

■ **2-17** *The CMOS editor in SNOOP330.*

Performance

Snooper is an efficient and up-to-date system information utility capable of identifying an astounding amount of hardware, but there are some operational factors to keep in mind:

A few machines lock up when running Snooper. The culprit is sometimes the CPU, NDP, IDE, sound card, or IRQ detection routines. Simply specify the C, N, S, T, or O command-line switches (see the documentation to learn the operation of each switch.

Because of the way NDOS and 4DOS allocate memory in their non-swapping modes, Snooper can't find the environment and will give an incorrect environment report, such as: Free 65,536 Total 0.

Registration

If you continue to use Snooper after 30 days, you should register the program for $39. Registration provides a series of benefits for the user: a printed manual, the latest version of Snooper, upgrade and discount notices, and lifetime technical support for Snooper. Volume discounts and special sales are available from Vias & Associates.

Summary

Snooper does not provide quite as much detailed information as some other major system information utilities, but it is capable of identifying more diverse hardware. It is also simple to use (the lack of mouse support might actually be a blessing for some technicians), and is frequently updated to reflect the latest changes in PC technology.

SPC.ZIP

There are times when too much information can be a problem for technicians, especially when you need just a few crucial bits of information. Searching through pages of detailed reports can be a cumbersome (and unnecessary) exercise. In some cases, a single screen of important data can tell technicians all they need to know. The Integrated System Utility from Bob Eyer (Table 2-23) focuses on achieving the highest possible ratio of information-to-examination time in the smallest possible space. The philosophy behind SPC is that the user should not have to flip through dozens of pages of output to get a fairly complete overview. Eyer feels an overview should be quick, not require any keystrokes other than those needed to run the program, and certainly not use any nonredirectable display modes such as graphics or direct screen writing. SPC has also attempted to position itself as an "e-mail friendly" utility; the output is 71 characters wide, which is compatible with many e-mail processing screens.

Installation and configuration

SPC can be run from either a hard drive or a floppy disk, so copy the SPC.ZIP archive from the CD to a selected subdirectory (or your floppy disk). Switch to the subdirectory (or floppy drive), and run PKUNZIP to decompress the archive. Once the archive has been decompressed into its constituent files, you can run the

■ Table 2-23 SPC fact sheet

Program name:	Integrated System Utility
Executable file:	SPC.EXE
Purpose:	A PC system information utility
Version:	6.1
Operating system:	MS-DOS 3.3 or later
Compressed file:	SPC.ZIP (archive)
Author:	Bob Eyer
Address:	1100 Bloor Street West, Suite 16
	Toronto, Ontario M6H 1M8
	Canada
CompuServe:	73230,2620
Phone:	905-455-4843
ASP member:	No
Registration:	$20, money orders preferred
Special notes:	Good, single-screen summary reports

utility directly without any other setup or configuration steps. The syntax and command-line options for SPC are:

SPC [? H A P F E D S] [=*identification*] [>*file*/PRN/COMx]

? or H or HELP Brief help screen.

A Use standard ASCII character set to accommodate Epson-compatible printers. The default is to use the extended ASCII character set for display.

P Pause printer. Intended to be used *only* as an enhancement of DOS PRINT when loaded as a TSR. To resume printing, enter PRINT.

F Include drives A: and B: in drive report. The default is to include no drives. When running in a network environment, include this parameter since the A: and B: drives are likely reassigned network drives, not floppy drives.

E Exclude UNDEF drives from totals. The default is to include drives flagged as UNDEF in totals. UNDEF drives are most likely CD-ROM or WORM drives.

D Force DUPlicate detection instead of SUBSTed detection in the drive report, and net duplicates out of the totals. The default is SUBSTed detection, unless a supported network is detected, in which case SPC defaults to DUPlicate detection to avoid confusion between SUBSTed detection and drive reassignment under network configuration. The D or S options are used for overriding these defaults.

S Force SUBSTed detection instead of DUPlicate detection in the drive report, and net SUBSTed drives out of the totals.

= Identification string. SPC puts your identification string on the right half of line 1 of the display, overriding the author credit, if you use = followed by your selected identification information. SPC looks for the occurrence of the equals sign on the command line and interprets everything following it (up to but not including redirection and piping symbols) as an identification string rather than an option. The maximum length is 14 characters.

Operation

When SPC runs, it produces a single-page information display, as shown in Figure 2-18. As you can see, the display screen is not large, but it does contain an assortment of useful information. Line 1 of the display informs you that the machine is run under DOS 7, has a VGA color monitor with a two-button Microsoft-type (M) mouse. LPT1: is connected to a selected printer (labeled S; other values are 1 or 2, which might have different meanings to different printers). Line 2 provides the model number (FC, typical of AT-class machines), the BIOS revision date, and the type of motherboard bus architecture (ISA or MCA). This is immediately followed by technical motherboard information, specifically: E (wait for external event installed), K (keyboard intercept used), R (real-time clock installed), 8259 (slave 8259 installed), and 3 (HD BIOS uses DMA channel 3). This is followed by the keyboard status group: E (enhanced keyboard), I (insert mode on), C (caps lock set), N (num lock set), and S (scroll lock set). Finally, line 2 provides the identity and speeds of the processor and coprocessor (if any). The graph markers (X, 1, 2, and so on) on the next line correspond to the lower speed boundary for each type of machine. Table 2-24 outlines each drive boundary.

Line 3 presents the speed graph for both the processor (marked *) and the coprocessor (marked !). The maximum of the scale is 18,000 and the scale is logarithmic. At the end of this line is total environment usage in bytes (marked 240 in Figure 2-18). The next group of lines, labeled Resident, presents a listing of any TSRs currently in memory with the size of each appended (without environment and data segments). This list is presented only where the DOS version is 4 or later. The Memory line then presents—in sequence—the verify status (VER), a reserved area for future

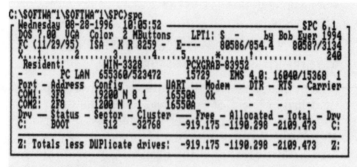

```
C:\SOFTWA~1\SOFTWA~1\SPC)spc
  Wednesday 08-28-1996  10:05:52 ────────────────── SPC 6.1
  DOS 7.00  VGA   Color  2 MButtons      LPT1: S -      by Bob Eyer 1994
  FC (11/29/95)  ISA - X R 8259 -    E----   80586/854.4   80587/3134
  X...1.......2.......3.......4....5....*....!........... 240
   Resident!       WIN-3328        PCXGRAB-83952
  -        PC LAN  655360/523472      15729    EMS 4.0: 16040/15368  1
  Port - Address  Config  ───── UART — Modem — DTR - RTS - Carrier
  COM1! 3F8      19200 N 8 1      16550A  Ok      -     -      -
  COM2! 2F8      1200 N ? 1       16550A  -       -     -      -
  Drv — Status - Sector - Cluster — Free - Allocated - Total - Drv
  C:    BOOT      512    -32768   -919.175 -1190.298 -2109.473  C:

  Z: Totals less DUPlicate drives!  -919.175 -1190.298 -2109.473  Z:
```

C:\SOFTWA~1\SOFTWA~1\SPC)

■ **2-18** *A typical system screen shot generated with SPC.*

■ **Table 2-24 SPC drive speed boundaries**

Machine	Rating	Clock range
8086 (X)	1	4.77 to 10 MHz
80186 (1)	2	4.77 to 10 MHz
80286 (2)	7	6 to 20 MHz
80386 (3)	26	16 to 33 MHz
80486 (4)	100	16 to 33 MHz
80586/Pentium (5)	300	60 to 200 MHz

development, the type of network or multitasking environment detected (Windows, PC LAN, Novell, MS NET, or DV or DDOS), total/free conventional memory, available extended memory in KB, and information about expanded memory (where detected), including the number of EMS handles in use.

Port information follows on the next line. First, the UART indicator is designed to work in DOS environments. Windows reconstructs DOS to a large extent, but errs in certain areas. For this reason, the UART indicator might not read correctly under Windows. Second, the modem function detector is based on the assumption that the modem's DSR line is high when the modem is powered on. Most modems and NVRAM factory defaults satisfy this condition, but others might not. The drive status indicators also need some explaining:

BOOT The drive used for booting the computer (DOS 4 or later).

CSPEC Drive where the CONFIG.SYS variable COMSPEC says COMMAND.COM is located.

SUBST A drive defined by redirection, usually through use of a DOS SUBST command.

DUP A drive that has the same free space as some other drive. Except in extremely rare circumstances, such a drive will be the same as if it had been a SUBSTed drive on a stand-alone machine. In a network, many drives might be defined as redirected to begin with—in which case, each ought to appear in SPC's display as an original drive.

UNDEF A drive that has more than 65,534 clusters (such as a CD-ROM drive). The default mode of SPC is to count such drives in space totals.

Performance

The program is complete in just a few moments. After the report is generated, SPC terminates to DOS. This makes SPC ideal for batch-file operation or startup checking in a system's AUTOEXEC.BAT file. Perhaps the most important issue surrounding SPC is the need to learn a myriad of (sometimes cryptic) symbols and flags in order to interpret the data screen correctly; this can hinder the use of SPC with novice users.

Registration

You can register SPC directly with the program author for $20. In return, you will receive the latest version of SPC and an enhanced program documentation file. When ordering SPC, the program author prefers money orders over personal or business checks. If you intend to install SPC on every PC you work on, you should contact the program author to discuss a license.

Summary

In some circumstances, a "snapshot" of a system's configuration can prove more effective than pages of detailed technical information. The SPC utility offers a surprising amount of system information condensed into a single, convenient text display.

SYSCHK40.ZIP

System Checker by Paul Griffith (Table 2-25) is the next in a long line of powerful system information utilities designed to provide enthusiasts and technicians alike with a detailed view into the workings of a PC. This is accomplished with 13 different information screens you can select from the main menu (Figure 2-19). SYSCHK40 can provide information on the CPU, BIOS, I/O devices, disks, networks, video, memory, device drivers, CMOS, interrupt assignments, and Windows. In addition, SYSCHK40 also supports a speed-checking feature to help gauge system performance. Online help is available through the <F1> key.

■ **Table 2-25 SYSCHK40 fact sheet**

Program name:	System Checker
Executable file:	SYSCHK.EXE
Purpose:	A system information utility
Version:	4.0
Operating system:	MS-DOS 3.3 or later
Compressed file:	SYSCHK40.ZIP (archive)
Author:	Paul Griffith
Address:	Advanced Personal Systems
	105 Serra Way, Suite 418
	Milpitas, CA 95035
CompuServe:	70323,136
ASP member:	Yes
Registration:	$29
Special notes:	None

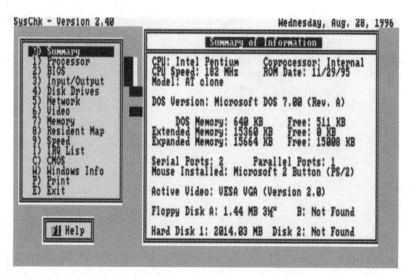

■ **2-19** *The summary page in SYSCHK40.*

Installation and configuration

As a system information utility, SYSCHK.EXE can (and often should) run from a normally configured system, so it should not be necessary to perform a clean boot. Still, you might want to install SYSCHK40 to a floppy disk to keep in your toolbox. Copy the SYSCHK40.ZIP archive file to a subdirectory on your hard drive or to a floppy disk. Switch to the subdirectory (or floppy drive) and run the PKUNZIP utility to decompress the archive. Once the files are copied, you can run the SYSCHK.EXE file directly. Although you might be able to install SYSCHK40 under Windows, you should really use the program from the DOS mode only in order to ensure the most accurate results.

Operation

SYSCHK40 supports a mouse, so you can use any Microsoft-compatible mouse to navigate between screens on the main menu. If a mouse is not installed, use the corresponding keys to select each screen.

One of the most interesting attributes of SYSCHK is its printer support. Many programs allow you to print the current screen, but when you select the Print option in SYSCHK you get a printout of *all* system data. This makes it very convenient to get comprehensive printed information without having to view and print each screen of information. You can also store the complete system report to a disk file for later viewing. If you want to configure your report by determining which information you would like to have included, press S and a series of questions will guide you through which information you want included or excluded from the system report. This will create a configuration file named SYSCHK.INI. If no SYSCHK.INI file is found, the program will simply print out its default system report. Most information is enabled by default except for the CONFIG.SYS, AUTOEXEC.BAT, and CMOS values.

You can also use standard output redirection in batch files by simply adding /F as a SYSCHK command-line parameter. For example, the following:

SYSCHK /F > MYINFO.TXT

will create a file called MYINFO.TXT, or SYSCHK /F will display a text file to the console screen. You can print a configuration file from within SYSCHK, or enter SYSCHK /F > LPT1 to redirect the file to your LPT1 printer port.

To automatically include the video speed and hard disk speed with your configuration file, include the /T switch to test those devices without any user intervention. If you want to automatically add any text to the printout (e.g., a company price list or sales notice), create a file called COMMENTS.TXT and place it in the same directory as SYSCHK. When you print out a configuration sheet, SYSCHK will automatically add that text to the top of the printout. If you use the /F parameter and do not want anything displayed on the screen, use the /B option to bypass the on-screen message.

Performance

To get the best performance from SYSCHK, you have to master its array of command-line switches:

/F Redirects all output to standard output. This allows you to run SYSCHK in a batch file and create a configuration report, or output directly to a printer or the console. For example, to redirect to a file, you would enter SYSCHK /F > MYINFO.TXT.

/N If you are connected to a Novell network, this switch creates a report file with the same physical ID as the filename. For example, entering SYSCHK /N will create a file named 12345678.dat (if your physical ID is 1234:5678).

/B If you also entered /F or /N for redirection and you need to bypass any on-screen copyright messages, enter /F /B or /N /B to redirect without sending any copyright messages to the screen.

/T Executes the video and disk speed tests if you also entered /F for redirection. This allows you to include the speed ratings in your redirected file.

/S Disables detection of hard disk controllers. On some SCSI host adapters, controller detection can cause the SCSI bus to hang.

/V Disables detection of video card's chipset, which can occasionally cause the system to hang.

/I Disables I/O IRQ detection.

/U Disables UMB detection.

/M Uses a monochrome display.

/R Creates a record file called SYSCHK.REC, which includes execution trace for debugging purposes.

/? Help screen.

Registration

If you plan to keep SYSCHK in your toolbox after 30 days, you should register the software with the program author. For the registration fee of $29, you get the registered version of SYSCHK, along with a free copy of the Advanced Personal System's Deluxe Utility Disk (assorted other PC productivity utilities). There is also an offer for the Windows version of SYSCHK (when it becomes available). You can register through CompuServe by entering GO SWREG and billing your CompuServe account. The registration ID for SYSCHK is 497.

Summary

SYSCHK ranks among the best system information utilities that are now available. It is comprehensive, easy to navigate, accurate, and frequently updated. The batch file and reporting features of SYSCHK allow convenient batch file (or AUTOEXEC.BAT) operation.

SYSINF.ZIP

Having the proper system information plays an important role in any upgrade or configuration planning. Tobin Fricke's SysInfo program (Table 2-26) provides a general selection of basic information that defines key areas of a PC. Results generated from SysInfo can be directed to the screen, printer, or a file. SysInfo is not as comprehensive as other system information utilities, but it might be handy for general-purpose testing.

■ **Table 2-26 SYSINF fact sheet**

Program name:	SysInfo
Executable file:	SYS-INF.EXE
Purpose:	A general-purpose system information utility
Version:	2.5 (c. 1993)
Operating system:	MS-DOS 5.0 or later
Compressed file:	SYSINF.ZIP (archive)
Author:	Tobin Fricke
Address:	25271 Arion Way
	Mission Viejo, CA 92691-3702
CompuServe:	76660,3110
ASP member:	No
Registration:	$5
Special notes:	Might not work on newest systems

Installation and configuration

Like most of the system information utilities covered in this chapter, SysInfo can be executed from either the hard drive or a floppy disk. Copy the SYSINF.ZIP archive file to a subdirectory on the hard drive (or a floppy disk). Switch to the subdirectory (or floppy drive) and use the PKUNZIP utility to decompress the archive. When the archive is decompressed, you can run the SYS-INFO.EXE file directly. No other configuration steps are required to use the software.

Operation

The first step in running SysInfo is to select an output device; you can choose from the display, a file, or the printer. If you choose the printer as an output device, SYS-INFO will ask about the printer type, print quality, and whether or not you want color. Once an output device is selected, SysInfo will analyze the computer and produce its report.

Performance

SysInfo was designed to work on older computers, such as i386 and i486 systems; the CPU speed check (and the entire program) crashed when tested on a Pentium 166-MHz system. No later shareware versions are available, but the issues are believed to be corrected in the registered version.

Registration

If you plan to use SysInfo regularly, you should register the program. The $5 registration buys you the latest version of the utility and regular upgrades (for S & H costs only). When registering, submit your payment with the completed BETATEST.TXT form.

Summary

SysInfo is a relatively simple system information utility, but it is rather dated in its current shareware version—so it might not recognize the equipment in late-model i486 and Pentium systems.

I/O, IRQ, and DMA tests

Interrupt (IRQ) lines, direct memory access (DMA) channels, and input/output (I/O) ports are the resources that controllers and other expansion devices need in order to operate properly. As a technician, you will need to check these resources to both configure new devices properly and track down possible resource conflicts with other devices in a computer.

CHKIO.ZIP

It is often difficult to know how some cards use I/O space. This can present a problem when you are faced with locating unusual hardware or troubleshooting an unusually configured system. The CHKIO utility (Table 2-27) aids a technician by locating ports used by various installed devices. CHKIO can use four different "spying" methods to perform this search. Even better, it can be run as a TSR in order to monitor some devices that keep a low profile in the system and do not reveal their presence unless their I/O ports are activated.

■ **Table 2-27 CHKIO fact sheet**

Program name:	Check I/O Ports
Executable file:	CHKIO.EXE
Purpose:	To check the assignments of system I/O ports
Version:	1.2a
Operating system:	MS-DOS 3.1 or later
Compressed file:	CHKIO.ZIP (archive)
Author:	PhG
ASP member:	No
Registration:	$0 shareware
Special notes:	No author support and no future versions planned

Installation and configuration

The CHKIO utility can be run from a hard drive or floppy disk. Copy the CHKIO.ZIP archive from the CD to a floppy disk or subdirectory on your hard drive. After the archive is copied, switch to the subdirectory (or floppy drive) and use PKUNZIP to decompress the archive. You can then run CHKIO.EXE directly without any further configuration. Keep in mind that CHKIO is designed to run as a DOS-only program, so do not run the program through DOS windows. To run CHKIO as a TSR, you will need to install the program on your hard drive and add a command line to a batch file, such as:

CHKIO SAMPLE 18 $300 32

The command-line switches listed later in this section present all the options available for the program.

Operation

The CHKIO utility will affect the performance of your PC (especially when running it as a TSR). As a consequence, some programs might not get the data they expect for normal operation. You should use the program to examine only specific activity, then re-boot the PC to clear the effects of CHKIO. Fortunately, CHKIO does not write anything to your system, so there is no chance of data corruption, but the timing might interfere with other devices.

Performance

As a stand-alone utility, you can check used and unused I/O ports. As a TSR, you can monitor port activity and record it to the CHKIO.RPT file. CHKIO requires one or more command-line switches to define its operation:

<port> [count] Checks a number of I/O ports starting from the defined port address (usually in the $0000 – $03FF range). The count default value is 16. Values are given in decimal form, unless they begin with a $, for hexadecimal. For example:

```
CHKIO $220
CHKIO $330 8
```

FREE Shows the most probable unused I/O ports in the $0200 – $03FF range. For example:

```
CHKIO FREE
```

USED Shows the most probable used I/O ports in the $0200 – $03FF range. For example:

```
CHKIO USED
```

<method> SAMPLE <ticks> <port> [count] Installs the program as a TSR. The ticks value is the sampling frequency (one tick is 1/18.2s). The method value is the type of test used to check the ports (M0 is the default). Method 0 (M0) reads a byte from a port address, then a byte from address + 1, and checks if the word value just read equals $FFFF. Method 1 (M1) reads a byte from a port address, then a byte from address + 1, and checks if the two bytes differ from one another. Method 2 (M2) reads two bytes in succession from a port address, and checks if they are both equal to $FF. Method 3 (M3) reads two bytes in succession from a port address and checks if the two bytes differ from one another. The default is M0. For example:

```
CHKIO M2 SAMPLE 32 $220
```

RESET Reinitializes results obtained from the TSR. For example:

```
CHKIO RESET
```

REPORT Dumps current results to the CHKIO.RPT file. A previous file of the same name is kept as CHKIO.BAK. For example:

CHKIO REPORT

STATUS Shows the current TSR status.

UNLOAD Tries to unload the CHKIO program from memory. If this fails (or erratic behavior continues), you will have to reboot the PC. For example:

CHKIO UNLOAD

Registration

CHKIO is $0 shareware, so no registration is required. Although the program author retains all rights to the program, you can use and distribute it freely as long as no modifications are made to the files.

Summary

Whether you are a programmer or a technician, CHKIO can assist you in finding active and inactive ports in the PC. The utility is quite basic, but it can help to identify free I/O addresses or locate devices that make only occasional use of certain ports (with potentially disastrous hardware conflicts if you install new hardware at those locations).

IRQINFO.ZIP

Virtually all expansion devices (sound boards, drive controllers, and so on) rely on the use of resources in order to interact with the system. Resources include I/O addresses, DMA channels, and interrupt (IRQ) lines. Of these three resources, interrupts are arguably the most important. One of the main reasons for this importance is that there are only 16 interrupts available in today's PCs — and out of that 16, only 4 or 5 are usually available. This presents some unique problems when upgrading a system, because you must accurately detect which IRQ lines are already in use. Now many of the system information programs listed earlier in this chapter will display a readout of interrupt assignments, but IRQInfo from CTS, Inc. (Table 2-28) specializes in identifying the detailed status of each system interrupt by performing a series of eight separate tests. IRQInfo makes no assumptions about the status of any interrupt line.

Installation and configuration

IRQInfo can be run from your hard drive, but this is the type of tool that you should probably keep on a diskette in your toolbox. If you plan to use the program on your hard drive, copy the IRQINFO.ZIP file from the CD to a subdirectory on your hard drive. For floppy

Program name:	IRQInfo
Executable file:	IRQINFO.EXE
Purpose:	To test and identify IRQ line assignments
Version:	1.60A (c. 1996)
Operating system:	MS-DOS 3.3 or later
Compressed file:	IRQINFO.ZIP (archive)
Author:	Computer Telecommunication Systems, Inc.
Address:	3847 Foxwood Road, Suite 1000
	Duluth, GA 30136-6100
Phone:	770-263-8623
Internet:	support@comminfo.com
CompuServe:	76662,2315
URL:	http://www.comminfo.com/
ASP member:	Yes
Registration:	$24 for IRQInfo; $35 for IRQInfo Pro
Special notes:	None

installations, copy the archive to your floppy disk. The PC need not be clean booted to run IRQInfo, so the floppy does not have to be bootable. Once the archive file is copied, switch to the subdirectory (or your floppy drive) and run PKUNZIP to decompress the archive. No other configuration steps are required. You can start the program by typing IRQINFO. Keep in mind that IRQInfo must be run from the DOS mode; it is incompatible with Windows or any DOS window.

Operation

When started, IRQInfo begins a series of tests to determine the usage of each interrupt. A series of questions helps the program make more accurate assessments. When the tests are complete, a summary screen appears, as shown in Figure 2-20. The summary consists of four columns: the IRQ number, the common use, its use in this system, and its availability. As you can see from the figure, there are four interrupts that are never available, nine interrupts that are in use, one interrupt that is uncertain, and only two interrupts that are free to use. This is vital information to have before upgrading a system.

Performance

IRQInfo is usually quite automatic in its testing and it requires a minimum of user interaction, but there are some command-line switches that can streamline the program's operation:

IRQ	Standard/Common Use	Used in This System	Available
0	System Timer	Yes - System Timer	Never
1	Keyboard	Yes - Keyboard	Never
2	2nd IRQ Controller	Yes - 2nd IRQ Controller	Never
3	Com2 (Serial Port)	Yes - Com2	No-In Use
4	Com1 (Serial Port)	Yes - Com1	No-In Use
5	LPT2/Sound Card/Modem	Yes - Sound Blaster (E)	No-In Use
6	Floppy Disk Drive	Yes - Floppy Disk Controller	No-In Use
7	LPT1/Sound Card	Possibly - (?) LPT1	???
8	System Clock	Yes - RealTime System Clock	Never
9	Video/Add-in Card	Possibly - Enabled but not active	???
10	Add-in Card	* Nothing Detected	Yes
11	Add-in Card	* Nothing Detected	Yes
12	PS2 Mouse/Add-in Card	Yes - PS/2 Mouse	No-In Use
13	Numeric Coprocessor	Yes - Coprocessor Detected	No-In Use
14	Hard Drive Controller	Yes - Hard Drive Controller	No-In Use
15	Add-in Card	Yes - CD-ROM	No-In Use

Press a key to continue   (this is NOT required in registered versions)

■ **2-20** *One of the report pages produced with IRQINFO.*

/? Enter the following command to display a short help screen:

IRQInfo /?

/L Use this switch to create a log file that contains a copy of all screen displays. To create the log file IRQINFO.LOG, enter the command line:

IRQInfo /L

/LA Use the following command to add to an existing log file:

IRQInfo /LA

/P Use this command to print a copy of the log file on the system printer:

IRQInfo /P

Registration

If you plan to keep IRQInfo in your toolbox, you should register the product with CTS, Inc. for $24. When you order the IRQInfo software, you will receive the most current version of IRQInfo and an option to upgrade to IRQInfo Pro, which includes a printed user guide. (This is optional; please indicate if you would like the user guide.) You will also get special discounts on SwapIRQ and PortFix utilities, and announcements about updates and other new products.

Users interested in a more full-featured tool might prefer IRQ-Info Pro, which includes additional device tests, more detailed summary information, and an IRQ-monitoring TSR. IRQInfo Pro is available to registered users for $35.

Summary

IRQInfo provides technicians with a powerful and reliable diagnostic tool for evaluating the performance of a system's IRQs and preventing a major cause of system upgrade problems. Good documentation makes this an ideal learning tool.

PORT11.ZIP

Like interrupts, I/O ports are vitally important resources for devices that must interact with a PC. While most system information utilities reveal most I/O devices currently on the systen, you might need to interact with I/O ports manually. This allows you to check the actual operation of some devices, especially unusual devices that don't respond well to standard tests or diagnostics. PORT (Table 2-29) is written to facilitate working with I/O ports on the PC or Intel processor-based hardware. Generally speaking, it allows you to debug new hardware, reverse-engineering old hardware, find out where an adapter card decodes its ports, and otherwise manipulate I/O ports.

■ **Table 2-29 PORT11 fact sheet**

Program name:	Port
Executable file:	PORT.EXE
Purpose:	To alter the assignments of I/O ports
Version:	Unknown (c. 1991)
Operating system:	MS-DOS 3.3 or later
Compressed file:	PORT11.ZIP (archive)
Author:	John De Armond
Address:	C/O Rapid Deployment Systems, Inc.
	P.O. Box 670386
	Marietta, GA 30066
Phone:	404-578-9547
ASP member:	No
Registration:	$0 shareware
Special notes:	No telephone support

Installation and configuration

PORT can be installed to either a hard drive or a floppy disk. Copy the PORT.ZIP archive to a subdirectory on your hard drive or to a floppy disk. Switch to the subdirectory (or the floppy drive) and run PKUNZIP to decompress the archive file. Once the constituent files are decompressed, you can start PORT.EXE with its proper command-line attributes. Remember that PORT is designed to operate in the DOS mode only; it will not function properly through Windows or a DOS window.

Operation

In order to run PORT properly, you must correctly specify two optional arguments, if needed. The first argument is interpreted as the port address, and the second is interpreted as the data (or bit pattern). These must be specified in hexadecimal with no leading modifiers. For example, use a sequence like:

port 3b4 0111

You can also redirect a configuration file into PORT, such as the following:

port < config

This file should contain PORT commands just as if you had typed them from the command line (rather like a batch file). PORT will execute the commands and then wait for keyboard input.

Performance

When using a program like PORT, remember that it is possible to crash the system by placing the wrong data at the wrong port. This is one of the advantages of working in DOS; a system crash won't ruin swap files or system registries. To get the most from PORT, you should also master some of the command-line arguments that are used with it:

r Read the port

w Write the port

e<xd> Enter a byte (word in designated mode, hex or decimal)

m<xdbw> Mode (x = hex, d = dec, b = byte, w = word)

tn Toggle bit <n>

c Clear all bits

s Set all bits

p Set port address

g<io> Go in or go out, perform action continuously

i Increment port address one count

d Decrement port address one count

q Quit

< Redirect commands from a file

? Help

Registration

PORT is $0 shareware; it is freely distributed, and the C source code is included for custom modifications. If you do make any changes or additions to the program, however, the program's author would like to know.

Summary

PORT is a truly unique tool for testing and verifying I/O port activity. Though its usefulness might seem limited when compared to some of the full-featured system utilities that are available, PORT can be invaluable in tracking down exotic, old, or unusual devices.

SPYDOS.ZIP

Few diagnostics are truly capable of tracking the behavior of a CPU, but SPYDOS (Table 2-30) can provide a wealth of information about the interrelationship between software interrupts and CPU registers. The SPYDOS program is a high-performance int86x software interrupt analyzer program that hooks into up to three user-selected software interrupts, and tracks all (real-mode) CPU registers used with the int86x function call. This program is useful for debugging the behavior of different versions of DOS, Windows, and Windows-NT. For programmers, it also has proved useful for debugging incorrect compiler switches and settings used for the application program.

Installation and configuration

SPYDOS requires a clean system for proper operation, so any memory managers, drivers, TSRs, and even disk compression utilities should be shut down for this. As a result, you should install SPYDOS to a bootable floppy disk. Copy the SPYDOS.ZIP archive from the CD to your bootable floppy disk, then use PKUNZIP to decompress the archive into its constituent files.

Next, you need to create an AUTOEXEC.BAT file on your floppy disk to configure and load SPYDOS. Basically, the batch file consists of three parts: creating environment variables that define IRQ hooks, starting SPYDOS, and starting READSPY to initialize and

■ Table 2-30 SPYDOS fact sheet

Program name:	Software Interrupt Analyzer
Executable file:	SPYDOS.EXE
Purpose:	A utility to check system-software-driven interrupts
Version:	1.30.00
Operating system:	MS-DOS 5.0 or later
Compressed file:	SPYDOS.ZIP (archive)
Author:	Wolfgang Heck
CompuServe:	71730,2657
ASP member:	No
Registration:	$9.95 (private), $99.95 (commercial), and $199.95 (site)
Special notes:	Contact author via CIS or Internet for latest registration information

read the data generated by SPYDOS. The documentation for SPYDOS covers the actual configuration steps in more detail, but here is a typical AUTOEXEC.BAT file:

```
mode con: lines=50
rem CONFIGURE THE SPYDOS INTERRUPT ROUTINE
SET DOSINTA=80
SET DOSINTB=21
SET DOSINTI=7D
rem Load SPYDOS
SPYDOS.EXE
rem Initialize SPYDOS
READSPY.EXE
```

Operation

Once SPYDOS is operating, it will store the contents of your CPU's registers in arrays for later analysis (minimizing the time overhead used during the interrupt call). A second program (READSPY) is used to read out the contents of these arrays and print them on your standard I/O device, such as a printer or display. A typical output is shown in Figure 2-21. One thing to remember about SPYDOS is that it cannot be unloaded once it has been started; you must reboot the PC.

Performance

The unregistered shareware version supports the analysis of nine interrupt calls, and the internal buffer is not reset after printout. By comparison, the registered version supports the analysis of 1,600 interrupt calls, and the internal buffer is reset after printout.

However, SPYDOS does have a known problem if DOS interrupt 2Fh is monitored; if a disk command failed (DIR, FORMAT, and so

```
G:\INTER>READSPY

READSPY U T I L I T Y  V1.30.00: Activate/Read SPYDOS Data
(C)1995, 1996 W. Heck ALL RIGHTS RESERVED

Activating Data collection function of SPYDOS now...

—-- Number of internal calls saved: 3 —--

C#:   1 Int: 0x80
Call al:  4C ah:   4 bl:  4D bh:   4 cl:  4E ch:   4 dl:  4F dh:   4 cf:3A16
      cs:3D77 ip:1D14 ss:   0 sp:   0 bp:1D1E ds: 453 es: 452 si: 450 di: 451
C#:   2 Int: 0x80
Call al:  4C ah:   4 bl:  4D bh:   4 cl:  4E ch:   4 dl:  4F dh:   4 cf:3A16
      cs:3D77 ip:1D14 ss:   0 sp:   0 bp:1D1E ds: 453 es: 452 si: 450 di: 451
C#:   3 Int: 0x80
Call al:  4C ah:   4 bl:  4D bh:   4 cl:  4E ch:   4 dl:  4F dh:   4 cf:3A16
      cs:3D77 ip:1D14 ss:   0 sp:   0 bp:1D1E ds: 453 es: 452 si: 450 di: 451
READSPY: Program Stop.
```

■ **2-21** *A typical SPYDOS printout.*

on), the system will not accept keyboard data for the Retry, Abort, Fail command. You have to either correct the error or reboot the system. The current versions of SPYDOS V1.1$x.xx$ do not run under DR-DOS and are not tested under OS/2. The environment variable DRDOSCOMP should allow the program to run under DR-DOS, but this configuration is not yet tested with versions V1.20.0x and V1.3$x.xx$.

Registration

One of the problems with the shareware version of SPYDOS is that it works only the first time it is run after being loaded. Even though it supports the same functions found in the full version, you might need to reload SPYDOS several times in order to evaluate it properly. There are three types of registrations available for SPYDOS: a private user license for $9.95, a single-user business license for $99.95, and a company site license for $199.95. For specific registration instructions, contact the program's author at 71730.2657<\@>COMPUSERVE.COM. Upon receiving payment, the author will e-mail you the latest full release of SPYDOS and its associated utilities.

Summary

SPYDOS is a powerful and aggressive utility for debugging software-driven interrupts. While it might be of more use to programmers, it can help technicians debug difficult problems between the CPU and software.

SWAPIRQ.ZIP

One of the most perplexing problems with modern PC communications is the limitation of IRQ ports for modems. The limitation of

IRQ 3 and IRQ 4 in supporting COM 1 through COM 4 has caused countless hours of configuration headaches for new users and experienced technicians alike. The SwapIRQ program (Table 2-31) is a powerful but tiny DOS utility that allows your existing communications software to use any interrupt supported by your serial port or modem. You can also use SwapIRQ in a DOS session under Windows to provide access to an IRQ not supported by a DOS application. SwapIRQ works under DOS versions 2.0 and higher, and uses less than 1KB (actually, less than 800 bytes) of memory.

■ **Table 2-31 SWAPIRQ fact sheet**

Program name:	SWAPIrq
Executable file:	SWAPIRQ.EXE
Purpose:	Allows comm software to use nonstandard IRQs
Version:	1.1 (c. 1996)
Operating system:	MS-DOS 2.0 or later
Compressed file:	SWAPIRQ.ZIP (archive)
Author:	Computer Telecommunication Systems, Inc.
Address:	3847 Foxwood Road, Suite 1000
	Duluth, GA 30136-6100
Phone:	770-263-8623
Internet:	info@comminfo.com
CompuServe:	76662,2315
ASP member:	Yes
Registration:	$20
Special notes:	Works under DOS and Windows

Installation

Since SwapIRQ is intended to augment a PC, it must be resident on the individual system's hard drive. Create a subdirectory on your hard drive, then copy the SWAPIRQ.ZIP archive from the CD to your subdirectory. Switch to the subdirectory and use the PKUNZIP utility to decompress the archive into its constituent files.

You do not have to add SwapIRQ to AUTOEXEC.BAT, but if you make changes to your IRQ lines frequently, this is a great way to automate the process. Rather than modifying AUTOEXEC.BAT, you can create multiple batch files to run SwapIRQ—each for different configurations. You can also run SwapIRQ directly from the DOS command line. For example, create a batch file in the directory of the program that requires SwapIRQ. The batch file will start SwapIRQ, run the communication application you need, and then unload SwapIRQ when you have finished:

```
rem swap IRQ 5 to IRQ 4
c:\swapirq\swapirq /i5 /i4
rem put the program startup string here
c:\utility\commprog
rem unload SwapIRQ
c:\swapirq\swapirq /d
```

Configuration and operation

SwapIRQ must be started before the communication application that requires the special handling. You can then unload SwapIRQ when it is no longer needed. For a listing of help information, simply type SWAPIRQ from the command line. There are several possible ways of using SwapIRQ (each example can be run from a batch file). See the documentation with SwapIRQ for specific Windows instructions.

Method 1: SwapIRQ /ih /is to install the SwapIRQ program and swap hardware IRQ /ih to software IRQ /is. That is, the serial port is using IRQ /ih to signal the software, which is looking for IRQ /is. So /ih is the IRQ generated by the hardware and /is is the IRQ expected by the software. The valid /ih and /is values are decimal 2 to 7 for an IBM PC/XT computer, and 3 to 7, 9 to 12, 14, and 15 for an IBM AT or compatible machine. The following command line:

```
swapirq /i5 /i4
```

will translate IRQ 5 generated by the serial port to IRQ 4 for the software. Note that the software interrupt cannot be used by a hardware device at the same time that SwapIRQ is in use. In the previous example, the IRQ 4 line must be dedicated to SwapIRQ. The COM1 serial port (which normally uses IRQ 4) must be inactive while SwapIRQ is loaded.

Note: if your board has a setting for IRQ 2, it is actually using IRQ 9 in an IBM AT or compatible computer. You should use IRQ 9 as the hardware IRQ. You can use IRQ 2 as the software IRQ.

Method 2: SwapIRQ /ih /is /n /M The /n switch (where /n is a valid serial port number from 1 to 8) instructs SwapIRQ to disable interrupts from serial port /n. Use this switch if you are switching a hardware interrupt over to an interrupt line used by another serial port. This will prevent a stray interrupt from the serial port from contesting with the swapped interrupt. If you add an /M switch to the command line, this will completely disable a serial mouse on port /n. Applications that use a mouse might require this command format to run correctly with SwapIRQ.

Method 3: SwapIRQ /ih /is /Aaaa /M You can use this option to disable interrupts from a serial port at address aaa (where aaa is a valid serial port address in hexadecimal). Use this command if you are swapping a hardware IRQ over to an IRQ line used by a nonstandard serial port.

Performance

In most circumstances, SwapIRQ should be very effective at redirecting IRQs. However, there are some known problems with America Online and Prodigy for DOS programs. The program author is also in the process of compiling a list of games and other programs that might have problems when SwapIRQ is in use.

Registration

Once you start using SwapIRQ, be sure to forward the $20 registration fee directly to the program author. This licenses SwapIRQ and gets you the very latest version of the program. If you install SwapIRQ on a customer's PC, be sure to collect the registration fee from the customer and forward it to the program's author, or direct your customer to remit the registration fee directly.

Summary

This is one of those out-of-the-way utilities that won't really prove its worth until you actually have an IRQ crunch to resolve. With so few IRQs available on today's PCs, swapping IRQs to streamline the use of communication products is an option worth considering with SwapIRQ.

Memory/cache tests

Next to the CPU, a system's memory is probably the most crucial processing element in the PC. Given the sheer volume of memory that is now typical in today's computers, even one bad RAM address can disable the system. Testing RAM, cache, and memory performance has become a major challenge for technicians. Fortunately, there are a number of good shareware utilities for memory testing.

486TEST.ZIP

Measuring the amount of time required to write a word to memory can often serve as an important benchmark of a system's performance. The 486TEST utility (Table 2-32) is an extremely basic tool for measuring the memory write performance on 386 and 486 systems. It has also been tested on a Pentium system.

■ **Table 2-32 486TEST fact sheet**

Program name:	Memory Write Test
Executable file:	486TEST.EXE
Purpose:	To test the speed of memory writes
Version:	Unknown (c. 1992)
Operating system:	MS-DOS 3.3 or later
Compressed file:	486TEST.ZIP (archive)
Author:	Michael Abrash
ASP member:	No
Registration:	None ($0 shareware)
Special notes:	A very basic and limited test

Installation and configuration

The 486TEST utility can be run from a hard drive or floppy drive, but for best results the system should be booted clean to remove any TSRs or drivers that might interrupt the write-timing loop. Copy the 486TEST.ZIP archive from the CD to a subdirectory on your hard drive or to a floppy disk. Switch to the subdirectory (or floppy drive) and use PKUNZIP to decompress the archive files into constituent files. Once the files are decompressed, you can run the utility by typing 486TEST. If you are not sure just how much resident drivers or TSRs will affect the timing measurement, try running 486TEST from a normal boot, then from a clean boot—and see how the two numbers compare.

Operation

486TEST runs an elementary counter/timer to test how fast the system can perform 1,000 memory-write operations. When the operations are complete, a single line of information is produced, such as:

Timed count: 17017 microseconds

According to the scant documentation, the timing figure divided by 1,000 is the time required to move one word—in nanoseconds. For the previous example, it would presumably take (17,017 ÷ 1,000) or 17 nanoseconds to write a single word. Given an extremely fast PC with L1 cache, that timing figure is probably reasonable.

Performance

The 486TEST utility performs only one memory-write loop, then terminates to DOS without any user interaction. As a result, the actual test process is quite fast. There are no known problems with the test, but you should not regard these timing results as foolproof.

Registration

486TEST is technically classified as $0 shareware simply because the term *public domain* isn't contained in the program or documentation. Since there is no author contact or copyright information included with the product, however, it can be used and distributed freely.

Summary

This tool can serve as a starting point in an investigation of memory performance, but it is an extremely simple tool and its accuracy is difficult to prove. Fortunately it's free, so it might be worth a try for curious technicians or enthusiasts.

CACHECHK.ZIP

A surprising part of today's PC performance improvements have come through the use of cache memory; by placing a small amount of extremely fast RAM between the CPU and main memory, the CPU can run with few (if any) wait states. Most system utilities can detect the amount of cache in a computer, but CACHECHK (Table 2-33) is one of the few utilities that can actually test cache access speed. CACHECHK will run access tests using all the memory in your machine, so you can verify that all the memory is cached.

■ **Table 2-33 CACHECHK fact sheet**

Program name:	Cache Check
Executable file:	CACHECHK.EXE
Purpose:	To test the cache performance of PCs
Version:	4.0 (c. 1996)
Operating system:	MS-DOS 3.3 or later
Compressed file:	CACHECHK.ZIP (archive)
Author:	Ray Van Tassle
Address:	1020 Fox Run Lane
	Alqonuin, IL 60102
Phone:	708-658-4941
ASP member:	No
Registration:	Voluntary contribution
Special notes:	Excellent cache and memory performance data

Installation and configuration

CACHECHK will run from your hard drive or a floppy disk. Copy the CACHECHK.ZIP file from your CD to a subdirectory on the hard drive or to a floppy disk. Switch to the subdirectory (or your floppy drive) and run PKUNZIP to decompress the archive file into its constituent files. Once the archive has been decompressed, you can run CACHECHK.EXE. While CACHECHK will run under Windows, the results can be wildly inaccurate. Run CACHECHK from DOS; if there are bizarre results, try clean-booting the system. No other steps are needed to configure the program.

Operation

Once CACHECHK is executed, it will begin to test the system cache. As the test progresses, the program will produce test results similar to the display in Figure 2-22. There is no user interaction required and, once the test is complete, the program terminates to DOS. The first five report lines identify the installed memory, CPU type, and clock speed.

```
CACHECHK v4 2/7/96  Copyright (c) 1995 by Ray Van Tassle. (-h for help)
****** WARNING *******
            CPU is in V86 mode!      Timings may not be accurate!
CMOS reports: conv_mem= 640K, ext_mem= 15,360K, Total RAM= 16,000K
"GenuineIntel"  Pentium Clocked at 166.5 MHz
Reading from memory.
MegaByte#:       -------- Memory Access Block sizes (KB) -----
         1     2    4    8   16   32   64  128  256  512 1024 2048 4096 <-- KB
0:       5     5    5    5    8    8    8    8    8    8   --   --   --  µs/KB
2:       5     5    5    5    8    8    8    8    8    8   13   13   13  µs/KB
3  4  5  6  7  8  9 10 11 12 13 14 15  <--- same as above.

Extra tests----
Wrt  12   12   12   12   12   12   12   12   12   12   12   12   12<-Write
mem
This machine seems to have both L1 and L2 cache. [read]
    L1 cache is   8KB -- 225.3 MB/s   4.7 ns/byte  (265%) (166%)   3.0 clks
    L2 cache is 512KB -- 135.2 MB/s   7.8 ns/byte  (159%) (100%)   4.9 clks
    Main memory speed --  84.8 MB/s  12.4 ns/byte  (100%) [read]  7.9 clks
    Effective RAM access time (read ) is   99ns (a RAM bank is 8 bytes wide).
    Effective RAM access time (write) is   92ns (a RAM bank is 8 bytes wide).
    "GenuineIntel"  Pentium Clocked at 166.5 MHz.  Cache ENABLED.
Options:  -t0
```

■ **2-22** *A typical output from CACHECHK.*

The test table indicates the speed of memory versus cache block sizes. Figure 2-22 illustrates that 1 through 8KB can be cached at 5 µs/KB. For 16 through 512KB, the cache runs at 8 µs/KB. Any entry marked with an underscore (_) could not be tested. The tests are repeated several times to ensure optimum accuracy. You might notice that tests 3 through 15 are marked "Same as above" because the results were exactly the same as previous test runs. Below the test results, you will see several summary lines about the cache size and speed. If you look at these performance numbers closely, this is a surprisingly comprehensive evaluation of cache and main memory. Good documentation outlines the meaning of every entry in more detail.

Performance

The CACHECHK utility takes up to several minutes to run, so you might want to get a coffee while each test line generates. For more control over the program, use the following command-line switches:

-4 Override CPU check, treat this as a 486.

-h? Print this help text.

-f Perform tests with cache disabled.

-q Quick (faster but not as accurate).

-qq Each q is two times quicker, but less accurate.

-tn Top of memory to test (n = nth MB).

-v Verbose. (-vv is positively chatty!)

-xN Extra tests. N is bit-mapped number: 1 = write 2 = read with cache off 4 = read with byte offsets The switch -x7 will do all three.

-w Do memory write (otherwise memory read).

-z Slower (like q, but the other direction).

When running CACHECHK, keep in mind that it will not touch extended memory that is already allocated or in use. If you have a memory manager installed, it usually occupies the first portion of the second megabyte, so CACHECHK will not be able to check that.

CACHECHK directly accesses the timer chip to get a high-precision timer (0.838 ms resolution). In some motherboards (notably reported to be "UMC with fake cache chips"), there is a problem with this timer. Version 2 addressed this problem, but the work-around might not function on some boards.

Registration

CACHECHK has a rather unique registration requirement: sending the program author a postcard (this is sometimes referred to as *postcard-ware*). If you find the program to be truly valuable, the program author welcomes a monetary contribution at your discretion.

Summary

This is one memory/cache program that you should add to your toolbox. The documentation is good, and it contains a lot of information about PC cache technology. The program itself provides a selection of system data that is difficult to find in other diagnostics.

MEMSCAN.ZIP

Technicians might often find it helpful to investigate the detailed contents of the first megabyte of memory. The MEMSCAN utility is designed to display raw memory contents contained from 0MB to 1MB in a PC. MEMSCAN allows full- screen viewing in printable ASCII, or a combination of ASCII and hexadecimal display for all memory. It also allows you to display or change any random-access memory byte within the entire system. You can view the BIOS contents, but you cannot change them. (See Table 2-34.)

■ **Table 2-34 MEMSCAN fact sheet**

Program name:	Memory Scan
Executable file:	MEMSCAN.COM
Purpose:	A utility to inspect the first one megabyte of RAM
Version:	Unknown (c. 1990)
Operating system:	MS-DOS 3.3 or later
Compressed file:	MEMSCAN.ZIP (archive)
Author:	James B. Penny
Address:	Coastal Computer Consulting
	415 East Beach Dr., Suite 506
	Galveston, TX 77550
ASP member:	No
Registration:	$15
Special notes:	Limited to the first one MB

Installation and configuration

Since the MEMSCAN utility is designed to read memory, you can use it with any TSRs or drivers loaded; changing the value at an address might cause the system to hang, but you should be able to read any address regardless of how the PC is booted. As a result, you can install the utility to your hard drive or a floppy disk. Copy the MEMSCAN.ZIP archive from the CD to your subdirectory or floppy disk. Switch to the subdirectory (or floppy drive) and run PKUNZIP to decompress the archive.

Operation

You can see a typical MEMSCAN display in Figure 2-23. The memory address (in page:offset format) is shown on the left, the actual memory data is displayed in hexadecimal notation in the middle, and the ASCII interpretation of the data is shown in the right column. The advantage of an ACSII interpretation is that you can read words (text) embedded in program code. You can navigate through memory using up and down arrows or the <Page Up> and <Page Down> keys. Press <Esc> to terminate the program.

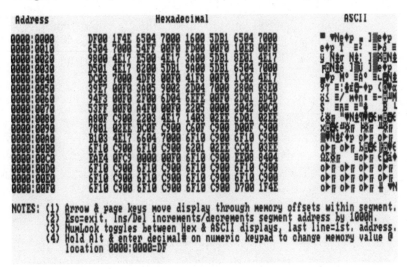

■ **2-23** *An interactive memory display produced by MEMSCAN.*

At startup, the screen displays the 0:0 area. *Do not change the data in this area*; this is where the interrupt vectors are located. Byte changes here will invariably cause the system to hang. These vectors dispatch the program counter to all parts of the operating system, so a change could send the computer off into an unexpected program area when the interrupt is activated by the operating system or BIOS code.

You change bytes simply by holding the <Alt> key while typing the decimal value of the new byte on the numeric keypad. The byte change happens when you release the <Alt> key. The byte that is changed is the first byte displayed on the screen. The address and hexadecimal value of the byte to be changed is given on the last line of the screen. If you don't press <Alt>, you can use the arrow keys to move around in order to place any memory byte in the first screen position.

Performance

Generally speaking, you can use MEMSCAN to explore any location within your first megabyte of RAM; there should be no adverse system effects. However, changing bytes can easily cause software performance problems and can result in system hang-ups. If the system should hang while in the DOS mode, you need only reboot the PC to clear the problem. To prevent damage to your Windows swap file or registry, do not attempt to change bytes using MEMSCAN under Windows.

Registration

The registered version of MEMSCAN comes complete with program source code, and will run as a TSR. It also provides information on the memory stack used for interrupt operations. The registration fee is $15 to the program author.

Summary

MEMSCAN is a versatile tool for reviewing the first one megabyte of RAM in your system, and observing how that memory is used. While you can alter RAM contents with MEMSCAN, it isn't wise to do so unless you know exactly what effect that change will have.

RAMMAP.ZIP

More so than reviewing the specific byte-by-byte contents of RAM, a technician might find it more helpful to identify the drivers and TSRs that are active in memory. The RAMMAP utility by Marc Perkel (Table 2-35) is designed to serve two functions: display the software that is active in memory, and free up wasted memory blocks (if possible). The program can also return an error level to a batch file in order to indicate which TSRs are in memory.

■ **Table 2-35 RAMMAP fact sheet**

Program name:	RAMmap
Executable file:	RAMMAP.EXE
Purpose:	Displays the software active in memory
Version:	1.3 (c. 1990)
Operating system:	MS-DOS 3.3 or later
Compressed file:	RAMMAP.ZIP (archive)
Author:	Marc Perkel
Address:	Computer Tyme
	411 North Sherman, Suite 300
	Springfield, MO 65802
Phone:	417-866-1222
ASP member:	Yes
Registration:	$10 to $250
Special notes:	Might not display all active software

98

Installation and configuration

Since RAMMAP is designed to show you the active drivers, TSRs, and OS software running on a system, you can use it from the hard drive or a floppy disk, though the floppy would be most convenient if you take RAMMAP on the road. Copy the RAMMAP.ZIP archive from the CD to a subdirectory on your hard drive or a floppy disk. Switch to the subdirectory (or floppy drive) and run PKUNZIP to decompress the archive file. Once the archive is decompressed, you can execute RAMMAP.EXE directly without any further configuration or setup.

Operation

You can run RAMMAP without any command-line switches, in which case the utility will return a screen report similar to the one shown in Figure 2-24. But there are two other command options available. One is the FREE option. When loading TSRs, each program has its own environment space. Generally, this is wasted memory. Running RAMMAP FREE after each TSR load can recover this "lost" memory. It won't gain a lot, but there are some situations where every byte counts.

```
Computer Tyme * 411 North Sherman, Suite 300 * Springfield Mo. 65802
(800) 548-5353 Sales * (417) 866-1222 Voice * (417) 866-1665 Data

Shareware Version. This program is not registered. Usage requires purchase.
These programs are part of the DOS To
Blk  Own    Size Program Name Type Parent Program     Command Line Parameters
—— ——   ——— — ————————— ——— —————————
0205 0008   9840
046D 0008     64
0472 0A83     16
0474       24544 ??           Prog 9D3A
0A73 0A83    240 - Master -   MEnv
0A83        3328 ÿÿÿÿÿÿÿÿÿÿÿÿÿ Bat  9D39
0B54 0B66    272 PCXGRAB.EXE  Env
0B66       83952 PCXGRAB.EXE  Prog EE02 command.com  /i
1FE6 0B66   1024 PCXGRAB.EXE  data
2027 2038    256 RAMMAP.EXE   Env
2038      523376 RAMMAP.EXE   Prog EE02 command.com
```

■ **2-24** *A typical report from RAMMAP.*

The second command option is InMem, which tests to see what TSRs are loaded in memory. If the specified program is found, RAMMAP will return an error level of 1. Otherwise, it will return an error level of 0. Besides finding TSRs, InMem will also find batch files that are running. This can be handy if you are using a menu-driven batch file to configure the PC differently depending on what software is running.

Performance

As you can see in Figure 2-24, RAMMAP should be able to identify several important pieces of information about the software running on a system. However, not everything was detected in the tests I performed, and some of the items that were detected were not identified completely. This is attributed to the overall age of the program (c. 1990), so it might not interact properly with the latest PC hardware.

Registration

RAMMAP carries a registration fee of $10 for single users, $25 for 10 users, $100 for 100 users, and an unlimited license for $250. Make it a point to evaluate this utility very carefully before registering.

Summary

This is definitely a utility that you need to check out for yourself, and try on several different PCs to evaluate its performance. It is handy (similar to DOS MEM) in its ability to identify software, but it is clearly a dated product and does not detect everything successfully.

SHADTEST.ZIP

One of the problems with BIOS ICs is their slow access speed. While RAM is surging below 60 ns, BIOS ROMs are still in the range of 100 to 150 ns. Since most PCs regularly use BIOS calls, the delays presented by BIOS really add up. PC designers have responded to this by copying (or shadowing) BIOS to free areas of RAM. This effectively increases the speed of BIOS (at the expense of RAM space). Technicians can use SHADTEST to check if shadow RAM is working. (See Table 2-36.)

■ **Table 2-36 SHADTEST fact sheet**

Program name:	Shadow RAM Test
Executable file:	SHADTEST.EXE
Purpose:	Test the operation of shadow RAM
Version:	1.0 (c. 1991)
Operating system:	MS-DOS 3.3 or later
Compressed file:	SHADTEST.ZIP (archive)
Author:	Unknown
ASP member:	No
Registration:	$0 shareware (believed to be in the public domain)
Special notes:	None

Installation and configuration

The SHADTEST utility can be run from the hard drive or a floppy disk, but you might get better results by booting the system clean, in which case you should probably install the software to a floppy disk. Copy the SHADTEST.ZIP archive from your CD to a hard drive subdirectory or a bootable floppy disk. Switch to the subdirectory (or floppy drive) and use PKUNZIP to decompress the archive. Once the archive is decompressed, you can run the SHADTEST.EXE program directly. If the program returns unusual results, try booting the system clean and run the utility again.

Operation

SHADTEST calculates access times for main RAM and BIOS memory. The actual test cycle can take up to 30 seconds or more. By comparing these two measurements, the program can make a reasonable assumption as to whether a shadow RAM feature is enabled. If shadow RAM is working, then access time for the BIOS area will be less than or equal to the access time for main RAM memory. If shadow RAM is disabled, access time for BIOS memory will be much longer because wait states are inserted in the memory cycle to accommodate the slower BIOS ROM. SHADTEST does not test the actual quality of the RAM because shadow RAM is normally write-protected. SHADTEST simply reports the ratio of the access times, as shown in Figure 2-25. The program bases its decision on whether the ratio of BIOS to main RAM access time is less than 106 percent.

```
SHADOW TEST ver 1.0   determines the presence of shadow ram control circuitry.

TESTING  . . . about 30 seconds,

It appears that shadow ram is disabled and that wait states
are being inserted during access to the BIOS.

The ratio of access time of BIOS MEMORY to MAIN RAM is 10963 percent.
```

■ **2-25** *A typical output from SHADTEST.*

Performance

Try running SHADTEST twice, once with shadow RAM enabled (usually accomplished through CMOS) and once with it disabled. This will give you a benchmark for reference. Save the numbers for comparison if you ever suspect problems with your motherboard's shadow RAM circuitry.

Registration

Technically, SHADTEST is not in the public domain since there is no note to that effect in the program or its associated documentation. However, there is no author listed, no copyright date claimed, and no contact information provided. As a result, the program should be regarded as freely distributed $0 shareware.

Summary

Though the program is dated, SHADTEST can be handy when you're trying to evaluate the differences between normal RAM and BIOS ROM access through the use of shadow RAM.

Video tools

Of all the advances being made in modern PCs, few are as fast or as exciting as those in video technology. Once considered a major bottleneck of PC performance, new bus architectures and chipsets are bringing video adapters to a new level of prominence. However, technicians need a suite of reliable tools to make the most of today's video systems and diagnose the myriad of operating problems that can occur. This chapter focuses on shareware and public-domain products dedicated to optimizing and testing PC video systems (Table 3-1). Refer to Chapter 8 for details about the commercial MONITORS utility included on the DLS Diagnostic CD.

■ **Table 3-1 Video diagnostics and utilities**

Filename	Description
Video ID/BIOS tools	
ATMEM10.ZIP	VGA BIOS identifier
IS_VID.EXE	Video detection utility
PSV10.ZIP	VGA/SVGA utilities
Screen/palette tools	
HISCAN.ZIP	Screen refresh rate enhancer
PALU15.ZIP	Palette adjusting utility
PSPS30.ZIP	PostScript screen print utility
VGAHUE.ZIP	VGA palette utility
Alignment tools and diagnostics	
CHKPXLS.ZIP	Checks LCD pixels
CNVRGE.ZIP	Monitors convergence utility
CRTAT2.ZIP	Windows CRT alignment utility
VIDEO.EXE	Video diagnostics
VIDEOT.ZIP	Video test utilities
VIDSPD40.ZIP	Video speed diagnostic

Important It is impossible to test these programs on every possible configuration of PC hardware. If you cannot get the program to run (or encounter unexpected results), contact the program's author for more information.

System backup I highly recommend that you perform a complete system backup before attempting to use system diagnostics and utilities. In the event that system errors or unexpected program results accidentally damage your programs or data, a backup will allow you to restore your information quickly and easily.

Virus warning As a general operating procedure, you should never attempt to run a new program without first checking it for viruses. Decompress the program and then run your virus checker. If a virus is detected, take all necessary steps to neutralize it.

Video ID/BIOS tools

Evaluating a video system requires a great deal of information about the capabilities of a particular video board and the video BIOS it's using. Once this information is known, a technician can decide whether a video board is incompatible with certain video modes or if it has trouble working with operating systems such as Windows or Windows 95. The following programs are designed to either identify the video system in use or provide important details about the video BIOS.

ATMEM10.ZIP

The problem with video board ID programs is their overall inability to learn; with new video boards being introduced to the market at an astounding rate, video ID routines can be obsolete in a matter of months. Charles Vachon's ATMEM10 program (Table 3-2) takes an unusual approach to video board detection by allowing you to actually create and update a text data file to use as the testing database. As a result, you can keep ATMEM10 current.

Installation and configuration

As a detection utility, ATMEM10 can be installed to your hard drive, but if you want to keep ATMEM10 in your toolbox, you would probably be better off installing the program to a floppy disk. Copy the ATMEM10.ZIP archive to a subdirectory on your hard drive or to a floppy disk. Switch to the subdirectory (or floppy drive) and use PKUNZIP to decompress the archive file. Once the archive is decompressed, you can run the ATMEM.EXE program. No other configuration is required. If you encounter problems getting ATMEM to identify hardware properly, try clean-booting the PC from a floppy disk.

■ Table 3-2 ATMEM10 fact sheet

Program name:	Video Board Detector
Executable file:	ATMEM.EXE
Purpose:	Utility to detect video board installed in system
Version:	1.0 (c. 1992)
Operating system:	MS-DOS 3.3 or later
Compressed file:	ATMEM10.ZIP (archive)
Author:	Charles Vachon
Address:	170 De Bray
	BerniSres, Quebec G7A 1T3
	Canada
Internet:	CVACHON@VM1.ULAVAL.CA
ASP member:	No
Registration:	$0 shareware
Special notes:	Contains a companion utility, C000

Operation

ATMEM uses a text file that contains all data and instructions for board identification. You can name the data file whatever you like, since the information that identifies the data file is passed as the first parameter on the command line. An example file named ATMEM.DAT shows you the general format:

```
ATMEM VERSION 1.0 DATA FILE
VBOARD=UNKNOWN
$C000 $0035 VBOARD=PAR256 003056-007COPYRIGHT PARADISE
$C000 $002D VBOARD=PAR1024 PARADISE003145-110
<EOF>
```

The first line identifies the data file to ATMEM; this line *must* be present! The second line tells ATMEM what it should report in case no subsequent data lines match the PC's memory. This line will be written as a SET command in a batch file, whose complete name is specified as the second parameter on the command line (optional). Next come the data lines. There has to be at least one if you want ATMEM to do something useful, and you can add as many lines as you like. The format of a data line is:

```
$C000 $002D VBOARD=PAR1024 PARADISE003145-110
```

The first string (blank delimited) represents the segment of memory to search. It has to be a positive integer either in decimal or hexadecimal notation. If hexadecimal, a $ sign must precede the number. The second string is the offset of memory to search. The third string (blank delimited, so no embedded blanks are allowed in this string) contains the string to write as the SET command in the batch file if the ID string matches the memory at the address given by segment and offset. Please note that part of the string is case-sensitive (being a SET value). The rest of the line, from the fourth string onward, is the ID string; this is the data that ATMEM will try to match against memory. Please note that this string is case-sensitive, and that embedded blanks are significant (that is, they will be used in comparisons as any regular characters). Then comes the end of the file. Don't place the <EOF> in your file.

Performance

You can run ATMEM using a command line such as the following:

ATMEM *data_file batch_filespec*

where *data_file* is the name of the ATMEM data file (e.g., AT-MEM.DAT) and *batch_filespec* is the batch file that receives the results of ATMEM. If no parameter is passed, ATMEM will display a help screen. If no *batch_filespec* is passed to ATMEM, it will simply write to the standard output, such as the display. ATMEM reports on an abnormal termination with self-explanatory error messages and an error level of 1 (0 for normal completion). The data lines are all read into memory before being compared against memory, and the lines are processed sequentially. Processing stops at the first data line that matches the memory contents.

Finally, a small utility called C000.EXE is included with the AT-MEM10.ZIP archive. It simply dumps the first 256 characters at BIOS address C000:000 into a file named C000.DAT. This can be a handy utility in actually finding meaningful strings to compare against.

Registration

ATMEM10 is available as $0 shareware, so you may use and distribute it freely (barring any specific restrictions in the program's documentation. No later release of ATMEM is known to be available at this time.

Summary

ATMEM is a uniquely flexible tool for technicians who deal extensively with video systems. By maintaining your own data file of video board "signatures," you can identify virtually any video board (and many other types of boards).

IS_VID.EXE

The IS_VID utility (Table 3-3) is designed to display the specific type of video system installed in a PC by searching for video

Program name:	Video Detector Utility
Executable file:	ISVIDEO.EXE
Purpose:	Detects the video system characteristics in a system
Version:	1.0 (c. 1994)
Operating system:	MS-DOS 3.3 or later
Compressed file:	IS_VID.EXE (self-extracting)
Author:	Barry St. John
CompuServe:	76247,264
ASP member:	No
Registration:	$0 shareware
Special notes:	Can return results to a batch file

identification information between C000h and C7FFh. The program explores the range of addresses typically occupied by video boards, and reports the text strings that it finds. These text strings can almost always provide you with enough information to determine the video type and maker. A typical printout, shown in Figure 3-1, lists the video board as a Matrox/Millennium VGA/VBE board.

```
Video could be identified by the following signature:

ÿ IBM COMPATIBLE MATROX/MILLENNIUM  VGA/VBE BIOS (V1.5 )PCIR+@838-4ÿ@efet"=t.33ÿ
.F.3U3:h]eS@[e]3e
@
```

■ **3-1** *A typical report from IS_VID.*

Installation and configuration

Since this is a detection utility, ISVIDEO.EXE can be installed to your hard drive, but if you want to keep ISVIDEO in your toolbox, you should install the program to a floppy disk. Copy the IS_VID.ZIP archive from your CD to a subdirectory on your hard drive or to a floppy disk. Switch to the subdirectory (or floppy drive) and use PKUNZIP to decompress the archive file. Once the archive is decompressed into its constituent files, you can run the ISVIDEO.EXE program. No other configuration is required. If you encounter problems getting ISVIDEO to report its findings properly, try clean-booting the PC from a floppy disk.

Operation

To get help using ISVIDEO, run ISVIDEO with no command-line parameters (or with /?). Use the /A (auto detect) switch to see the text contained in video BIOS. This is not true detection, but the text will usually contain the video type and maker. The output from a video board with a Quadtel S3 chipset could appear in the following way, with video identified by the following signature:

```
Quadtel S3 86C801/805 Enhanced VGA BIOS. Version 2.13.06
Copyright 1987-1992 Phoenix Technologies Ltd.
Copyright 1992-1993 S3 Inc.
All Rights Reserved
```

Instead of using the auto detect feature, you can tell ISVIDEO to look for a specific text string, such as the following:

```
ISVIDEO Quadtel
ISVIDEO S3
ISVIDEO 86C801/805
```

If the chipset search string matches, a DOS error level of 1 will be returned to the batch file that called ISVIDEO. If there is no match (or you display syntax help), an error level of 0 will be returned. When running the program in auto detect mode, /V (verbose output) is set automatically. DOS error levels are returned regardless of the /V switch status.

Performance

The ISVIDEO program works quickly and with little fanfare, but keep in mind that, in order for the video detection to function correctly, your video system must be installed in the typical video address range between C000h and C7FFh.

Registration

ISVIDEO is $0 shareware, which means it can be used and distributed freely (barring any specific limitations in the program's documentation).

Summary

ISVIDEO is a particularly handy utility for identifying video systems because it can quickly display meaningful text from the video BIOS without requiring you to maintain your own database (as with ATMEM10.ZIP).

PSV10.ZIP

Whether you're a technician or an end user, you have probably searched for ways to check and streamline your video system. Patrick Swayne's VGA/SVGA Utilities (Table 3-4) is a collection of programs designed to help you get more out of your VGA or Super VGA (SVGA) video system. The collection includes utilities to help you adjust your color monitor, test your video system performance, set up custom color palettes, and explore the various video modes supported by your system configuration.

Program name:	VGA/SVGA Utilities
Executable file:	n/a (various files)
Purpose:	Utilities to support VGA/SVGA functions
Version:	n/a (c. 1991–1994)
Operating system:	MS-DOS 3.3 or later
Compressed file:	PSV10.ZIP (self-extracting)
Author:	Patrick Swayne
Address:	428 Cauthen Ct.
	Ellenwood, GA 30049-2919
ASP member:	No
Registration:	$15 (U.S.) and $20 (international)
Special notes:	Contains a large assortment of utilities

Installation and configuration

Installation can be a bit tricky with PSV10.ZIP. Because there are several different programs to contend with (both diagnostics and utilities), you might actually find yourself taking a few programs along with you on a floppy disk and installing some of the utilities on a hard drive. As a rule, you will probably benefit most by installing the whole suite of utilities to a hard drive, then transferring any useful files to a floppy later on.

Copy the PSV10.ZIP archive from the DLS Diagnostic CD to a subdirectory on your hard drive (preferably a subdirectory pointed to in a PATH statement in AUTOEXEC.BAT). Switch to the subdirectory containing the archive file and use PKUNZIP to decompress the archive. Once the constituent files are decompressed, you can set up or run each program as required. Most of the programs have a help feature that you can access by typing the name of the desired file followed by a question mark, such as:

VM ? <Enter>

Operation and performance

CM (Color Master) The Color Master utility lets you change the 16 colors that are available in text modes on a VGA/SVGA card. You can assign any color from a palette of 64 colors to each of the 16 visible colors and to the screen border (which is normally black). You can make colors more vibrant or softer, or change color schemes entirely. To run Color Master, just type:

C:\> CM <Enter>

CP (Color Protector) This is a utility that can protect the custom colors you set up with Color Master. It is a TSR (terminate and stay resident) program that watches for video mode changes and reloads the color registers with your custom colors each time the system changes to a text mode. To load Color Protector, first make sure your custom colors are loaded, then type:

C:\> CP <Enter>

TCOLORS In the color text modes, a VGA or SVGA card can display up to 16 colors (plus a border) on the screen at any one time. These colors are taken from a palette of 64 colors. TCOLORS can display all of these colors at once. The colors are in numbered rectangles, which represent the color register values used to create the colors. You can jot down the numbers of the colors you want to include in your custom color set, then run Color Master to set up those colors. To run TCOLORS, type:

C:\> TCOLORS <Enter>

SAVCOLOR If you have programs that run in the text mode and produce unusual colors while they're running, they might be manipulating the color registers. The SAVCOLOR utility allows you to save modified color registers in a file that can be used by Color Master. SAVCOLOR is a TSR program that you can activate while running other programs. To load SAVCOLOR into memory, type:

C:\> SAVCOLOR <Enter>

VL (VESA list) This utility lists the video modes that your video card supports. It requires an SVGA video card with the VESA extensions. If the board does not come with VESA extensions in BIOS, you might need to run a VESA driver before using VL. To use the utility, just type:

C:\> VL <Enter>

If your video card does not support VESA, VL will display "No VESA support detected." If your card does support VESA, VL will display information about your video card and/or VESA extensions, and list the video modes supported by your card in the format shown in Figure 3-2 on the next page.

VM (video mode selector) You can use this utility to set any of the VGA or VESA video modes that your video card supports. Type:

C:\> VM *n* <Enter>

replacing *n* with a number representing the actual video mode (such as the mode numbers in Figure 3-2 on the next page). You can use

```
PS's VESA BIOS information lister, v 1.0
Copyright (C) 1994 by Patrick Swayne.  All Rights Reserved.
Type VL ? for help.

VESA version:    1.1
OEM name:        Acumos AVGA2
Estimated memory: 256k

Video modes supported by this adapter:

Mode      Type  T/G   Resolution Colors Memory model
18/012h   VGA   Graph 640x480       16  16-color(EGA)graphics
19/013h   VGA   Graph 320x200      256  packed pixel graphics
87/057h   OEM   Text  132x25         2  text
258/102h  VESA  Graph 800x600       16  16-color(EGA)graphics
265/109h  VESA  Text  132x25        16  text
266/10Ah  VESA  Text  132x43        16  text
```

■ **3-2** *A typical display from the VL utility.*

either a decimal or hexadecimal mode number. If you use a hexadecimal number, put an h at the end (e.g., 102h). If you wanted to set the VESA 132 × 43 character text mode, for example, you would type:

C:\> VM 109H <Enter>

or:

C:\> VM 265 <Enter>

You can also use VM to determine which mode is active. Just type:

C:\> VM <Enter>

VMD (Video mode disabler) If your video adapter supports VESA video modes that your video monitor does not support, you can use VMD to disable those modes and prevent programs from setting them. To use VMD, type:

C:\> VMD *nn*[,*nn*...] <Enter>

where *nn* is a decimal video mode. If you use hexadecimal notation, add an h after the mode number. For example, if your card supports the 16- and 256-color 1024 × 768 graphics modes but your monitor does not, you can type:

C:\> VMD 104H,105H,... <Enter>

or:

C:\> VMD 260,261,... <Enter>

Lines If you run your video card in a mode you are not familiar with, and you want to see how many lines and columns of text that mode supports, you can use LINES or LINES0. To use either program, just type the name of the program at the DOS prompt, and press <Enter>. Numbers will appear at the top of the screen indicating the number of columns, and along the left side numbering the lines. LINES.COM begins numbering with 1, and LINES0.COM numbers starting with 0. Press any key when you are through checking the numbers.

VTEST_T, VTEST_G (video speed test utilities) These utilities can test the speed of your video system, and you can use them to compare the speed of different systems. To use either one, just type its name at the DOS prompt and press <Enter>. VTEST_T.COM tests your system in the text mode, while VTEST_G.COM tests it in the graphics mode. VTEST_T uses a page fill test and a scrolling test, and reports the time of each test. A shorter time means a faster system. VTEST_G performs a BIOS test, a pixel video memory test (data is written to the screen one pixel at a time), and a byte video memory test (data is written one byte at a time). If your system turns in fast times for the memory tests, but a slow time for the BIOS test, it probably means that your video BIOS is not shadowed. Consult the owner's manual or the SETUP help screens for your computer to see if you can shadow your video BIOS to optimize performance.

VCOLORS (VGA color display) VCOLORS.COM displays all the colors available in the default palette of the VGA 256-color mode. The colors are displayed in numbered squares on the screen. To run VCOLORS, just type:

C:\> VCOLORS <Enter>

You can use VCOLORS to adjust the brightness and contrast (or picture) controls on your VGA monitor. You should adjust these so the brightest colors are not hazy and the dimmest colors can be just barely seen (the dimmest color in the default 256-color palette is color number 17, a very dark gray). Colors 0 and 16 are both black, so you should not see anything at those squares. Colors 248 through 255 are usually black, but if you have run a graphics program just before using VCOLORS, they might not be black. These colors are individually programmable, and will retain the colors entered by any program until they are changed by another program.

HATCH (crosshatch utility) The HATCH.COM program can display a crosshatch or a dot pattern on your screen. You can use these patterns to make several adjustments to the monitor display. You might need a technical manual for your monitor in order to locate the controls for some of these adjustments. To run HATCH, type:

C:\> HATCH <Enter>

CLF (fade to clear utility) CLF.COM is a replacement for the DOS CLS command. It clears the screen to black by fading, and then fades back in with just the DOS prompt on the screen. When CLF fades back in, it uses the foreground and background colors that were active at the cursor at the time it began to clear the screen. To use CLF, just type the following whenever you want to clear the screen:

C:\> CLF <Enter>

You can also modify the way CLF works using command-line parameters. If you type:

C:\> CLF F <Enter>

CLF will fade out and back in twice as fast as it normally does. If you type:

C:\> CLF C <Enter>

CLF will fade out, but come back instantly, with the colors set to the standard light gray on black like CLS does. You can also combine the F and C parameters (CLF F, C or CLF C, F).

COLOR (screen color utility) The COLOR utility lets you set the foreground and background colors on your screen while you are at the DOS prompt. To use it, type:

C:\> COLOR f,b <Enter>

where f is the number of the foreground color and b is the number of the background color.

Registration

If you continue to use any portion of the PSV10 package after 30 days, you must register it with the program author. For your $15 registration ($20 for international orders), you will receive a VGA Screen Banner utility, which produces scrolling messages on the screen, as well as the latest versions of each utility. Print out the file REGISTER.DOC, fill in the blanks, and mail it with a $15 check or money order. If you install and set up PSV10 on someone else's PC, you should collect the registration fee and forward it to the author, or instruct your client to remit the proper registration fee.

Summary

Though Windows users would probably be most interested in the DOS-based utilities, the PSV10.ZIP package is a uniquely versatile set of programs for your DOS-based video system. Good documentation explains each feature thoroughly.

113

Screen and palette tools

There is little doubt that the video display plays a vital role in an individual's comfort when using a PC. Displays with starkly contrasting or awkward color schemes (especially under DOS) can quickly cause eye fatigue and headaches. By establishing screen, text, and border colors that are more pleasing to the eye, user comfort improves. While Windows does a good job at controlling a display's characteristics, DOS is simply not that sophisticated; DOS colors and resolutions depend on the actions of the individual applications and specialized DOS drivers. To achieve colors and contrasts that are most pleasing to an individual user, you need to optimize the video palette by using DOS utilities such as those in the following section.

HISCAN.ZIP

A great many mobile PC users choose to use their notebook or laptop system with an external monitor in a "docking station" configuration when working in a desktop environment. At high resolutions, however, users often complain of excessive screen flicker (especially at resolutions of 800×600 and higher) and having to adjust the display position each time they switch from DOS to high-resolution video modes.

If your notebook PC has a video controller using a Chips and Technologies F655xx Series chipset, the HiScan utility (Table 3-5) allows you to set a refresh rate of 80 Hz or more for almost all extended video modes using the special capabilities of that particular chip family (the maximum refresh rate is limited only by the monitor itself). The current refresh rate is measured and displayed in real time. HiScan provides an easy way to adjust and save the horizontal screen position for each video mode individually. In some cases, HiScan will even make new modes available that you could not use before because the default refresh rate was not compatible with your monitor. For instance, the $640 \times 480 \times 16.7$ million color mode of the F65540 chipset does not work on most multisync monitors because the factory-set default refresh rate is too low. HiScan lets you adjust the refresh rate for your monitor so you can enjoy your favorite JPEGs in 16 million colors. All Windows accelerator modes and VESA modes are supported. HiScan can also increase the number of visible text lines for most DOS-based applications to 28 or even 50 lines instead of the usual 25.

Installation and configuration

In order for HiScan to work, it must be installed on your hard drive. Copy the HISCAN.ZIP archive to a subdirectory on your

■ Table 3-5 HISCAN fact sheet

Program name:	HiScan
Executable file:	HISCAN.EXE
Purpose:	Optimize scan rates of external monitors
Version:	1.2 (c. 1996)
Operating system:	MS-DOS 3.3 or later
Compressed file:	HISCAN.ZIP (archive)
Author:	Joerg H. Arnu
CompuServe:	100326,564
URL:	http://ourworld.compuserve.com/homepages/joerg
ASP member:	No
Registration:	$18
Special notes:	Designed for laptop PCs using external monitors

hard drive, switch to that subdirectory, and use PKUNZIP to decompress the archive. Once the constituent files are decompressed, you can start HiScan directly; no further setup is required. If you get an error message saying that VESA support is not installed, you will need to install the VESA extension driver (usually included with your video board's utilities diskette) when the system starts.

HS-TSR.COM is a memory-resident driver that will set up the modified refresh rate parameters each time a new video mode is selected. To operate, HS-TSR should be loaded into memory at system start-up in your AUTOEXEC.BAT system startup file. Edit the AUTOEXEC.BAT file with the DOS EDIT utility and add a line such as the following:

C:\HISCAN\HS-TSR

where C:\HISCAN is an example path where you might have decompressed HiScan; if you have chosen a different path, use that instead. You can also load the TSR into the upper memory area using the LH command:

LH C:\HISCAN\HS-TSR

Operation

When you start HISCAN.EXE, it will check for the presence of a C&T F655xx chipset. If the chipset is found, HISCAN will respond with a list of modes that can be enhanced. Some modes might be grayed-out, which means they cannot be selected because your hardware does not support them. In addition to the mode list, there are some more options:

Set all modes to their defaults Cancels all changes for all modes and uses the factory settings instead.

Save changes Saves settings for all video modes to HISCAN.DAT after you are done. Note: this option is disabled in the unregistered shareware version.

Enable/disable TSR if installed Toggles the active state of the TSR module (if it is installed). The current state is displayed in the status line above the main menu.

Exit to DOS Quit HISCAN. If you have made any changes, you are reminded to save them before you quit.

When you select a video mode to enhance, you will see the Enhance Mode menu. You can enhance the refresh rate only if the external display system is enabled on the laptop. If both displays (or only the internal LCD display) are enabled, you cannot enter the Enhance Mode menu. To switch to the external monitor, you usually have to press a certain key combination on the laptop. These vary from system to system, so refer to the documentation for your particular system.

In the upper part of the main menu, you will find the current status of HS-TSR.COM (enabled or disabled). To change the status, press the <Tab> key. Below the status display, there are options for the number of text lines (25/28/50). The current number of lines is highlighted. To change the number of visible lines, press the left or right cursor key. Note that this feature has no effect if the TSR is globally disabled; if the TSR module is not loaded, the number of displayed lines cannot be changed.

Performance

HiScan is specially designed to operate with the Chips & Technologies F655xx Series video controller chipset. To see if it works for your hardware, just execute the main module HISCAN.EXE; it will detect if your mobile PC has a compatible video controller, and exit with an error message if the appropriate chipset is not found (without affecting your video system).

Registration

If you plan to use HiScan beyond the 30-day evaluation period, you should register the software with the program author. For the $18 registration fee, you will receive a registration code that enables the Save Changes option; this allows you to save the settings for all video modes, and load them automatically when the system boots if you install the TSR module. For online registration via CompuServe, use the CompuServe shareware registration service (GO SWREG) and select the shareware registration ID #8518. The registration is honored for all future versions of HiScan, with no additional registration fee. Technical support is also provided for registered users.

Summary

HiScan is a one-of-a-kind video utility that can really improve the display of an external monitor, and there is good documentation to back it up. But you must be using a PC with a C&T F655xx video chipset in order for the utility to work.

PALU15.ZIP

Although Windows allows you to alter screen attributes with a few clicks of the mouse, DOS provides no such flexibility. For DOS users who are tired of the stark, colorless DOS display, palette adjusters such as the PALU15 package (Table 3-6) often prove to be the only means of altering screen, text, and border colors at will. The program can be loaded as a driver in AUTOEXEC.BAT so it loads the preset color scheme automatically.

■ Table 3-6 PALU15 fact sheet

Program name:	Palette Adjuster
Executable file:	PAL.EXE
Purpose:	Alter the palette of DOS video colors
Version:	1.5 (c. 1994)
Operating system:	MS-DOS 3.3 or later
Compressed file:	PALU15.ZIP (archive)
Author:	Lincoln Beach Software
Address:	P.O. Box 1554
	Ballwin, MO 63022
Phone:	314-861-1500
ASP member:	Yes
Registration:	$10
Special notes:	Intended for operation under DOS

Installation and configuration

Palette Adjuster is designed to work from your hard drive. Copy the PALU15.ZIP archive to a subdirectory on your hard drive, switch to that subdirectory, and use PKUNZIP to decompress the archive. Once the constituent files have been decompressed to the hard drive, you can start PAL.EXE directly; no further setup is required.

If you want to load PAL.EXE as a utility in your AUTOEXEC.BAT file, you need to copy the PAL.EXE and CUSTOM.PAL files to your root directory (or add the subdirectory containing the PALU15 files to the system's PATH command line) and insert the following line in the AUTOEXEC.BAT file:

PAL /L

To reset the original 16 colors at any time, type:

PAL /R

Operation

When you start PAL.EXE, you are given a screen with all the default colors preset, as shown in Figure 3-3. The pick-list box on the left will put a border around the screen with the color that matches a selected color. Keep in mind that anything issuing a CLS (clear screen) will erase the border. On the right side of the screen are the 15 colors that can be adjusted (you cannot adjust black, so it is left out). To the left of each color is a Reset button, which will reset the individual color back to its original state. There are three columns: red, green, and blue. You can enter a value ranging from 0 to 63, 0 being the least of a color and 63 being the highest saturation allowed for the color. Thus, an entry of 63,0,0 would result in a *very* bright shade of red. Adjust these three numbers for each color to get the look you want.

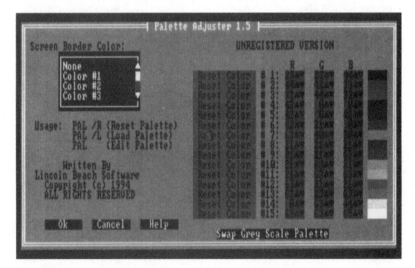

■ **3-3** *The interactive palette display in PALU15.*

If you have a monochrome monitor, select the Swap Gray Scale Palette button to change the colors to their respective shades of gray. Press it again to return the color palette. Once you have the colors you need, simply press or click on the OK button, and the palette will be saved to a file named CUSTOM.PAL. If you hit

Cancel, the palette will not be saved and your screen colors will return to what they were before PAL.EXE was run. If you delete the CUSTOM.PAL file, you will need to start your color selection over again.

Performance

The PAL.EXE utility works only under DOS; there is simply no need for it under Windows 3.1x or Windows 95. As a result, you will find a need for Palette Adjuster only when working with DOS applications or in the DOS mode.

Registration

If you choose to use Palette Adjuster beyond a 30-day evaluation period, register the software with the program author for $10. For the registration fee, you will receive the latest version of the utility. If you install Palette Adjuster on another PC, you should also remit the registration fee to the author, or instruct your customer to remit the fee directly.

Summary

Programs such as Palette Adjuster were quite popular in the days when DOS ruled the PC world. Now that Windows is largely the OS of choice, palette programs are usually regarded as esoteric. Still, the PALU15 package can be a good complement to systems still running DOS or those that work frequently in the DOS mode.

PSPS30.ZIP

Screen captures and printer dumps have always been a handy feature of PCs, but the basic ASCII dumps under DOS often did not capture the desired image properly or cleanly. The PSPS30 package (Table 3-7) provides a versatile screen-dump tool for Postscript printers. PSPS.EXE allows you to use the conventional <Print Screen> key (or <Shift>–<Print Screen>) to capture screens into Postscript file format. MDA, CGA, Hercules, EGA, MCGA, VGA, and VESA SVGA video modes are all supported, and the printing can take place in monochrome, reverse monochrome, grayscale, reverse grayscale, color, and reverse color. In addition, PSPS.EXE can output the capture to an LPT port using encapsulated or normal Postscript.

Installation and configuration

Since PSPS.EXE must be running as a TSR (and saves files that can be quite large), you will typically get your best performance by installing the program to your hard drive. Start by copying the

119

■ **Table 3-7 PSPS30 fact sheet**

Program name:	PostScript Print Screen
Executable file:	PSPS.EXE
Purpose:	Capture video displays to PostScript printers
Version:	3.0 (c. 1994)
Operating system:	MS-DOS 3.3 or later
Compressed file:	PSPS30.ZIP (archive)
Author:	A.N.D. Technologies
Address:	P.O. Box 64811
	Los Angeles, CA 90064
Phone:	213-467-8688
Internet:	andtech@netcom.com
CompuServe:	71011,3570
ASP member:	No
Registration:	$25 (single user)
Special notes:	Requires a PostScript printer

PSPS30.ZIP archive from the DLS Diagnostic CD to a subdirectory on your hard drive. Switch to the subdirectory and run PKUNZIP to decompress the PSPS30 archive file. Once the archive is decompressed, you can run PSPS.EXE directly without further configuration, or add the PSPS command line to AUTOEXEC.BAT, like this:

C:\PSPS\PSPS [*command-line options*]

PSPS requires 12KB of RAM in normal operation, and can be unloaded when you're not using it. Also keep in mind that you can load PSPS into the UMA, but you'll need a 21K block of free memory to do it.

Operation

PSPS.EXE is normally started with several command-line options. The specific options you choose depend on the type of screen mode you will be capturing in, the orientation and contrast of the images, and the Postscript characteristics you want to use. You can also run PSPS with the U command to unload the program. Simply typing PSPS will show the program's current settings. The command-line options are as follows:

E Eject page, flush unprinted text screens

F=E,P Output to new EPS or PS file: PSPS*xxxx*.(E)PS; *xxxx* = 1–9999

FS=fsname File server for queue (must come before queue)

L=N[B,H] Output to LPT port where N = 1, 2, or 3 [B = BIOS, H = HW Port]

M=M,RM,G,RG,C,RC Mode: mono, reverse mono, gray, reverse gray, color, or reverse color

ND No graphics status display

O=P,L Orientation: portrait or landscape

PSL=N PostScript level to use for graphics; N = 1 or 2

Q=qname Output to Novell print queue "qname"

S=N Screens per page; N = 1, 2, or 3

U Uninstall

X=N,Y=N Dimensions of graphics screen that PSPS can't detect

Performance

Although PSPS.EXE should work with many different video modes (and most video systems that support BIOS interrupt 10 calls), the program will not work with the extended graphics modes of 8514/A or XGA video systems. Of course, PSPS requires connection to a PostScript-compatible printer.

Registration

If you find PSPS30 to be a useful package, you should register the product with the program author. If you install the program on someone else's system, either remit the registration fee or instruct your customer to remit the fee directly. The shareware version has all the same features as the registered version, but the "unregistered version" notice does not appear in the registered version. The registration is $25 for a single-user license and $125 for a site license. There are other available registration options detailed in the documentation, or you can contact the program author. Purchase orders are accepted. After you register, you will be sent the newest version of PSPS.EXE by e-mail. If you require a diskette mailed to you, add an extra $5 for shipping and handling.

Summary

If you or your customer are looking for a good PostScript screen capture and printing utility, PSPS is certainly a tool to consider—if you have an extra 12KB or so of memory available in your system.

VGAHUE.ZIP

The VGAHues program (Table 3-8) is another utility you can use to alter the text, screen, and border colors of a DOS video system. By selecting colors to best suit your tastes and needs, you can reduce eye fatigue, strain, and headaches. Unlike other utilities that use text-rich screens to mark each color, VGAHues employs a graphic interface such as the one shown in Figure 3-4 on the next page. The interface allows you to adjust several different screen attribute colors with "slider" controls. As the corresponding color changes, you can see the new color in the graphic at the upper part of the display.

■ **Table 3-8 VGAHUE fact sheet**

Program name:	VGAHues
Executable file:	VGAHUES.EXE
Purpose:	Adjust RGB components of VGA color in the DOS mode
Version:	Unknown (c. 1994)
Operating system:	MS-DOS 3.3 or later
Compressed file:	VGAHUE.ZIP (self-extracting)
Author:	GMH Code
Address:	P.O. Box 2117
	Lowell, MA 01851
ASP member:	No
Registration:	$5
Special notes:	Can be used in DOS mode only

Installation and configuration

Ideally, VGAHues should be run from the hard drive because, in order to reset the DOS colors each time the PC is initialized, the program has to be run from AUTOEXEC.BAT (although it is not a TSR). Copy the VGAHUE.ZIP archive into a subdirectory on your hard drive, switch to the subdirectory, and run PKUNZIP to decompress the archive. Once the archive has been decompressed, you can run VGAHUES.EXE directly without any further installation or configuration.

Operation

You can select and adjust colors using either the keyboard or the mouse. Mouse control is really quite intuitive, and you can alter various colors by "dragging" and "dropping" each R, G, or B color bar as desired. A selection of buttons on the left side of the control panel allows you to control the program and save changes made to

■ **3-4** *The interactive graphic display in VGAHUE.*

the color scheme. Keyboard operations are a bit more complicated, so you should refer to the program's detailed documentation (or online help) for specific information.

Performance

In normal operation, the program runs quite well and is relatively
easy to master once you realize which color bars control which attributes of the screen. The mouse support also adds a great deal of
intuitiveness to VGAHues. Unfortunately, the program does not run
as a TSR or load its data file, VGAHUES.SAV, automatically. This
means that user interaction is required each time the program runs,
which makes VGAHues unsuitable for use in AUTOEXEC.BAT. You
have to run the program specifically each time the computer starts.

Registration

If you decide to use VGAHues after a 30-day evaluation period,
you need to register it with the program author. Your $5 registra-
tion provides a more complete set of instructions outlining the
program's command-line functions, as well as some additional features, such as a shortcut back to the default VGA text mode, data
on the current VGA display mode, the ability to set your card to
any VGA display mode, the ability to view or reset the first 16 colors of a VGA color map, and the ability to set your video card to
run in VGA monochrome (grayscale) emulation.

Summary

VGAHues is an interesting (and surprisingly visual) tool for investigating the VGA color palette and exploring how red, green, and blue levels contribute to the creation of various colors. As a working tool, however, the need to run it discretely each time the PC powers up makes its regular use a bit inconvenient.

Alignment tools and diagnostics

When a monitor needs repair, it often needs to be checked for proper alignment and then realigned if necessary. Alignment tools provide a technician with a selection of "standard" reference images that can be used to optimize such attributes as linearity and centering. Most alignment utilities depend on DOS, but there are a few that will operate under Windows.

CNVRGE.ZIP

Color monitors produce their colors by directing three electron beams around a CRT face coated with color phosphors. In order for the colors to be pure and true, each beam must be precisely synchronized so all three beams converge at the proper locations. If any of the beams are off by even a small degree, the resulting colors produced in the display will be incorrect. When monitors are repaired (especially important repairs such as the CRT or deflection yokes), you must realign the beam convergence. The CNVRGE package from Brent Turner (Table 3-9) produces a display VGA pattern that a technician can use during convergence tests.

■ Table 3-9 CNVRGE fact sheet

Program name:	Convergence Test
Executable file:	CONVERGE.EXE
Purpose:	Test the color convergence of monitors
Version:	Unknown (c. 1993)
Operating system:	MS-DOS 3.3 or later
Compressed file:	CNVRGE.ZIP (archive)
Author:	Brent Turner
Address:	P.O. Box 3612
	Fullerton, CA 92634-3612
ASP member:	No
Registration:	$5
Special notes:	Dedicated to color convergence tests

Installation and configuration

Since CONVERGE.EXE is a diagnostic, it can be run from the hard drive, but you might have better results putting the program on a floppy disk and keeping it in your toolbox. Copy the CNVRGE.ZIP archive from the DLS Diagnostic CD to a subdirectory on your hard drive or a floppy disk. Switch to the subdirectory containing the archive (or your floppy drive), then run PKUNZIP to decompress the archive file. Once the archive has been decompressed into its constituent files, you can run CONVERGE.EXE with no further installation or configuration. You should not have to clean-boot the PC to use CONVERGE.EXE.

Operation

When CONVERGE.EXE is executed, it checks for the presence of a VGA (or higher) video system. If VGA is present, a convergence grid is displayed. The grid used in CONVERGE.EXE employs yellow vertical lines and magenta horizontal lines surrounded by a white border. There are also a number of color purity screens; blue, green, red, and white. You can cycle through each screen in turn by pressing the spacebar. To exit the program, press the <Esc> key. Note that if you specify a particular screen in the CONVERGE.EXE command line, the spacebar will have no effect.

Performance

The CONVERGE.EXE program is straightforward, and runs well under DOS. It has been tested under Windows 95 in the full-screen mode. Instead of using the spacebar to cycle between different displays, you can select a specific display by using the following command-line switches:

? Echoes a brief help text on the screen; no action is taken

/b Displays the blue color purity screen

/c Displays the convergence grid where each square is on exactly a 1:1 pixel aspect ratio (each side is exactly the same number of pixels in length)

/g Displays the green color purity screen

/r Displays the red color purity screen

/w Displays the white color purity screen

Registration

If you choose to continue using this program after a reasonable evaluation period, forward a registration fee of $5 to the program author. For registering the software, you will get the latest version of CONVERGE.EXE. Be sure to specify which disk size and density you need (e.g., 3.5-inch high density).

Summary

Color convergence is an important attribute of monitors, and the CONVERGE.EXE program is a handy and inexpensive tool for checking convergence as well as color purity.

CRTAT2.ZIP

There are very few Windows-based diagnostics, but the CRTAT2 package (Table 3-10) is an important exception. This Windows diagnostic is designed to test monitors for such attributes as convergence, linearity, and color purity while working in the current Windows resolution and color depth. Another interesting part of CRTAT2 is that the documentation is provided as a Windows help file. While the program predates Windows 95, it does appear to work properly in a Windows 95 environment.

■ **Table 3-10 CRTAT2 fact sheet**

Program name:	CRT Alignment Tools
Executable file:	CRTAT.EXE
Purpose:	Test and align color CRTs
Version:	2.0 (c. 1994)
Operating system:	Windows 3.1x or later
Compressed file:	CRTAT2.ZIP (archive)
Author:	Stephen Jenkins
Address:	1310 S. Taylor St. #22
	Arlington, VA 22204-3718
Internet:	stephenj@ix.netcom.com
CompuServe:	76666,1066
ASP member:	No
Registration:	$0 shareware
Special notes:	Requires VBRUN300.DLL and Windows

Installation and configuration

Like most diagnostics, CRTAT2 will provide the best service if it is installed to a floppy disk that you can carry in your toolbox, but it will also work directly from a system's hard drive. Copy the CRTAT2.ZIP archive from the DLS Diagnostic CD to a subdirectory on your hard drive or to a floppy disk. Switch to the subdirectory (or floppy drive) and run PKUNZIP to decompress the archive file. Once the archive is decompressed into its constituent files, you should add a copy of VBRUN300.DLL to the subdirectory or disk. Most copies of Windows and Windows 95 already have VBRUN300.DLL somewhere on the system, so you might try a directory search from the hard drive root directory, such as:

```
C:\> dir vbrun300.dll /s <Enter>
```

This will search the entire hard drive for the file. If you find it, copy it to the disk or directory containing the files for CRTAT2.

Most Windows programs are installed as an icon under a program group or as a member of a Start menu, but since CRTAT.EXE is a diagnostic, you can typically avoid the extra installation hassle by simply launching CRTAT.EXE from a Windows command line. For Windows 3.1x, select File and Run, enter the disk, directory, and filename:

```
a:\crtat.exe
```

then press OK (this example assumes the diagnostic is in the root directory of a floppy disk). For Windows 95, you can launch CRTAT.EXE from Windows Explorer.

Operation

When you launch CRTAT.EXE, you will see a set of default color bars, along with the program control panel (Figure 3-5 on the next page). The program supports five different CRT tests: color purity, static convergence, dynamic convergence, white purity, and aspect ratio (linearity). You also have three (somewhat more subjective) checks to choose from: resolution, readability, and color bars. You can switch back and forth between tests at will and hide the control panel for full-screen operation (any key will bring the control panel back).

Performance

Program operation is simple and straightforward, and uses familiar Windows mouse support. Program documentation is available as a hypertext-linked Windows help file, so you can navigate the detailed documentation with ease. Unfortunately, the documentation is not very clear on how to interpret each test or what steps to take in order to correct problems; it assumes a great deal of knowledge on the part of the individual technician. Also, the program requires VBRUN300.DLL to operate. If you do not already have a copy of VBRUN300.DLL somewhere on your Windows system, you need to obtain a copy before using CRTAT.EXE.

■ **3-5** *The Windows display of CRTAT2.*

Registration

The CRTAT2 package is offered as $0 shareware, so you may use the program freely.

Summary

CRTAT.EXE is a free and handy tool that might be ideal for Windows pundits, but the need for VBRUN300.DLL could present problems if you do not already have a copy on your system.

VIDEO.EXE

Technicians and end users alike need to know what video mode an adapter is in, as well as the modes a particular video board is capable of. This is not only important for choosing compatible monitors, but also for choosing software. The Video package (Table 3-11) provides you with a simple tool for checking and setting video modes, and other features such as foreground and background color setting, monochrome operation, and inverted display attributes.

Installation and configuration

Choosing whether to install VMODE.EXE to a floppy disk or hard drive depends on just how you intend to use it (defined by a series

Program name:	Video Mode Controller
Executable file:	VMODE.EXE
Purpose:	Video mode checker/setting utility
Version:	1.6 (c. 1992)
Operating system:	MS-DOS 2.0 or later
Compressed file:	VIDEO.EXE (self-extracting)
Author:	Paul Lee
Address:	Abri Technologies, Inc.
	HCR62, Box 100K
	Great Cacapon, WV 25422
ASP member:	Yes
Registration:	$6
Special notes:	Can be used in DOS mode only

of command-line switches). If you plan to use VMODE.EXE as a diagnostic to investigate video modes, you might have better results installing the program to a floppy disk for your toolkit. If you plan to use the program to adjust colors or preset video modes, you will have better performance if you install it to a subdirectory on your hard drive (then add the VMODE.EXE command line to AUTOEXEC.BAT).

Copy the VIDEO.EXE self-extracting archive to a subdirectory on your hard drive or the root directory of a floppy disk. Switch to the subdirectory (or floppy drive) and run VIDEO.EXE. The archive will extract its constituent files automatically. If you plan to use VMODE as a diagnostic, you can run the program directly with no further installation. If you plan to use VMODE as a configuration tool, however, make sure the subdirectory holding the program is included in the DOS PATH line in AUTOEXEC.BAT and also add the VMODE command line to AUTOEXEC.BAT. For example:

C:\VIDTOOLS\VMODE /C1e

will set the screen attributes to 1 (blue) foreground and e (yellow) background. Each time the system starts, VMODE will execute through AUTOEXEC.BAT and set the colors accordingly. If the program directory is in the PATH, you can omit the directory path in the VMODE command line.

Operation

VMODE is a command-line program. To test the available video modes, use the /A switch:

129

VMODE /A

The program will return the compatible video modes, as shown in Figure 3-6. Use the <Page Down> key to display each successive page of available modes. The following list illustrates other command-line switches for VMODE:

VMODE Displays the current video mode

VMODE /A Displays all available video mode numbers

VMODE /C Lists background/foreground attributes

VMODE /Cbf[mm] Sets video background/foreground color (or monochrome screen attributes)

VMODE /I Inverts screen attributes

VMODE -X Sets the video mode to x (and large cursor)

```
Unregistered Shareware - Please Register
        BIOS Video Modes:

0   CGA 40x25 B/W text, (8x8 character dots)
1   CGA 40x25 Colour text, (8x8)
2   CGA 80x25 B/W text,   (8x8)
3   CGA 80x25 col. text, (8x8)
4   CGA 320x200 4-col. graphics,
5   CGA 320x200 4-col. graphics (col. off),
6   CGA 640x200 Black & White Graphics,
7   Mono 80x25 text or 720x348 Hercules
8   PC Jr. 160x200 16-col. graphics,
9   PC Jr. 320x200 16-col. graphics,
10  PC Jr. 640x200 4-col. graphics,
13  EGA 320x200 16-col. graphics,
14  EGA 640x200 16-col. graphics,
15  EGA 640x350 B/W graphics,
16  EGA 640x350 4/16-col. graphics,
17  VGA 640x480 2-col. graphics,
18  VGA 640x480 16-col. graphics,
19  VGA 320x200 256-col. graphics,
20  VGA 132x25 16-col. text (8x16) *
84  VGA 132x43 16-col. text (8x8)

        PgDn - Any other key exits
```

■ **3-6** *A screen mode summary from VIDEO.*

Performance

While the VMODE program is relatively versatile, there are some issues you should be aware of. First, the background/foreground screen color functions are not available if the DOS ANSI.SYS driver is running. Second, when it finds the current video mode, VMODE.EXE returns the DOS error level number corresponding to the video mode. When it sets the video mode, VMODE returns DOS error level 1 with an error message, or an error level 0 otherwise. This feature might be useful to batch file programmers.

Registration

If you plan to use VMODE.EXE after a reasonable evaluation period, you must register the software with the program author. Registration is $6 ($5 + $1 shipping and handling). Registered users receive the latest version of VMODE and software support for at least three months. If you install VMODE on someone else's system, you should forward the registration fee to the program author or direct your client to forward the appropriate fee.

Summary

VMODE is a rare "all in one" program that can provide information like a diagnostic, but also serve as a video configuration utility under DOS. The low registration fee makes this an economical addition to your toolbox.

VIDEOT.ZIP

Virtually all modern video adapters are capable of operating over a wide range of resolutions and color depths. Unfortunately, determining the exact resolution and color depth of a system at any given time is hardly an intuitive exercise. You need a diagnostic that can interrogate the hardware of a video board and report on the corresponding video mode. The VIDEOT.ZIP package from Aaron Johnson (Table 3-12) is one such diagnostic to consider.

131

■ Table 3-12 VIDEOT fact sheet

Program name:	Video Adapter Test Program
Executable file:	VIDEOTST.EXE
Purpose:	Test the various modes of a video board
Version:	Unknown (c. 1991)
Operating system:	MS-DOS 3.3 or later
Compressed file:	VIDEOT.ZIP (archive)
Author:	Aaron Johnson
ASP member:	No
Registration:	$0 shareware
Special notes:	None

Installation and configuration

You can install the VIDEOT package successfully to either your hard drive or a floppy disk. Since this is a diagnostic, however, you will probably get the best results by installing the program to a floppy disk to keep in your toolkit. Copy the VIDEOT.ZIP archive from the CD to a subdirectory on the hard drive or to a floppy disk. Switch to the subdirectory (or your floppy drive) and use PKUNZIP to decompress the archive file. Once the archive is decompressed into its constituent files, you can run the VIDEOTST.EXE program directly without any further configuration.

Operation

VIDEOTST.EXE attempts to test the various modes of a video adapter by setting a mode, then drawing moving lines across the display (until you press the <Esc> key). Pressing the spacebar during the line-drawing process will reset the lines. The program can be run in three basic modes:

VIDEOTST A This mode attempts to identify your adapter, tell you the kind of VGA card detected, list the amount of video memory detected, and list the video modes that are most likely to be available (Figure 3-7). It will then attempt to call the highest 256-color mode and the highest 16-color mode available (and use the drawing routine). If no VGA card is installed, VIDEOTST will only identify the adapter.

```
Attempting Video card identification

Adapter type = VGA

VESA          : 256k      Cirrus      : No
Video7        : No        Tseng       : No
Tseng4000     : No        Paradise    : No
Chips & Tech  : No        Trident     : No
ATI           : No        Everex      : No
Ahead A       : No        Ahead B     : No
Oak Tech      : No

Valid Modes in table:
X-res  Y-res  Colors  Mode #
-----  -----  ------  ------
 640    400    256      4f02
 640    480    256    (Non-Standard) mem needed = 300k (Insufficient Video Memory)
 800    600    16     (Non-Standard)
 800    600    256    (Non-Standard) mem needed = 468k (Insufficient Video Memory)
1024    768    16     (Non-Standard) mem needed = 384k (Insufficient Video Memory)
1024    768    256    (Non-Standard) mem needed = 768k (Insufficient Video Memory)
1280   1024    16     (Non-Standard) mem needed = 640k (Insufficient Video Memory)
1280   1024    256    (Non-Standard) mem needed = 1280k (Insufficient Video Memory)


Press any key to continue:

This program has determined that the maximum resolutions you can use are:
640 by 400 by 256 colors, and 800 by 600 by 16 colors.

This program will now attempt to test the maximum available
video modes for your card.  During the drawing routine, press
the SPACE BAR to re-genenerate the drawing, and ESC to exit

Press any key to attempt auto max 256 color video mode set:
 Resolution 640x400 with 256 colors
Sorry - Mode Set was unsuccessful.
Press any key to attempt auto max 16 color video mode set:
 Resolution 800x600 with 16 colors
Sorry - Mode Set was unsuccessful.
```

■ **3-7** *A typical report generated by VIDEOT.EXE.*

VIDEOTST M# This mode will tell you what resolution the # mode results in, where # is the mode, in decimal, to pass to register AX.

VIDEOTST # This mode attempts to set a mode based on an internal mode list, where # is a number taken from the video mode list in Table 3-13.

■ **Table 3-13 Video mode numbers available for VIDEOTST.EXE**

#	Mode	#	Mode
0	CGA 320×200×4	1	CGA 640×200×2
2	EGA 320×200×16	3	EGA 640×350×2
4	EGA 640×350×16	5	MCGA 320×200×256
6	VGA 640×480×2	7	VGA 640×480×16
8	SVGA 800×600×16	9	SVGA 1024×768×16
10	SVGA 640×400×256	11	SVGA 640×480×256
12	SVGA 800×600×256	13	SVGA 1024×768×256
14	VGA 320×400×256	15	VGA 320×480×256
16	VGA 360×480×256	17	VGA 376×564×256
18	VGA 400×564×256	19	VGA 400×600×256
20	VGA 704×528×16	21	VGA 720×540×16
22	VGA 736×552×16	23	VGA 752×564×16
24	VGA 768×576×16	25	VGA 784×588×16
26	VGA 800×600×16		

Performance

While the VIDEOTST.EXE program runs quickly and seems to have no adverse system effects, there are some points to keep in mind. First, most video boards in the DOS mode require a VESA driver in order to reach resolutions and color depths higher than 640 × 480 × 16. If you cannot get those modes to work, check the video driver disk that accompanied the video board for any DOS VESA drivers. If there are no native drivers available, you can often use a generic VESA driver such as UNIVBE, which is available from online sources such as CompuServe in the PC Hardware Forum (GO PCHW). Second, there is some question as to how well the program works with new video adapters; it failed to identify the correct amount of video memory on the Matrox/Millennium VESA board.

Registration

VIDEOTST.EXE is available freely as $0 shareware, so you may use it without cost. However, there is no technical support from the author and there is no known revision for this diagnostic.

Summary

Ultimately, VIDEOTST.EXE is a somewhat dated utility, but it is free and could prove useful for basic tests on older PCs and late-model 486 systems.

VIDSPD40.ZIP

Video performance has long been a bottleneck for PC operations. As a result, technicians often search for ways to measure video speed in comparative terms. The VIDSPD40 package (Table 3-14) is one of the few software tools to provide hard measurement of video reading and writing operations for any given video mode.

■ **Table 3-14 VIDSPD40 fact sheet**

Program name:	Video Speed Analyzer
Executable file:	VIDSPEED.EXE
Purpose:	To check video reading and writing speed
Version:	4.0 (c. 1992)
Operating system:	MS-DOS 3.3 or later
Compressed file:	VIDSPD40.ZIP (self-extracting)
Author:	John Bridges
ASP member:	No
Registration:	$0 shareware
Special notes:	None

Installation and configuration

You can install The VIDSPD40 package successfully to either your hard drive or a floppy disk. But since this is a diagnostic, you will probably get the best results by installing the program to a bootable floppy disk to keep in your toolkit. Copy the VIDSPD40.ZIP archive from the DLS Diagnostic CD to a subdirectory on the hard drive or to a floppy disk. Switch to the subdirectory (or your floppy drive) and use PKUNZIP to decompress the archive file. Once the archive is decompressed into its constituent files, you can boot the system clean and run the VIDSPEED.EXE program directly without any further configuration.

Operation

VIDSPEED.EXE must be run from the DOS command line. You can test the video performance at different screen modes by using the correct mode switch, as shown in Table 3-15 (you can get this table by simply running VIDSPEED.EXE without any command-line argument. When you decide on what mode to test, run VIDSPEED with the corresponding mode letter, such as:

C:\> VIDSPEED M

which runs the program in VGA ($640 \times 480 \times 16$) mode. It will take several moments for the program to operate, and you might see some graphic fragments displayed as the timing is calculated. For a Pentium 166-MHz system with a Matrox/Millennium video board, the results are shown in the following typical report:

80486 with VGA Oak Tech 4meg Vesa VBE support

8212W 1773R Bytes per millisecond 28.65KHz 59.67Hz 640x480x16 (VGA)
21557W 3205R 16 bit writes/reads
33550W 5633R 32 bit writes/reads

While the program failed to recognize the CPU and video board properly, the timing details and results are essentially correct. You can also force VIDSPEED to check every available video mode by using the + switch.

■ Table 3-15 Test video modes available under VIDSPEED.EXE

*	Normal RAM (for comparison)	+	All valid video modes
0	40×25 color text	1	80×25 color text
3	EGA 80×43, VGA 80×50 color text	4	VESA 80×60 color text
5	VESA 132×25 color text	6	VESA 132×43 color text
7	VESA 132×50 color text	8	VESA 132×60 color text
A	CGA 4 color	C	CGA 640×200 2 color
D	EGA 640×200 16 color	E	EGA 640×350 2 color
F	EGA 640×350 4 color	G	EGA 640×350 16 color
I	VGA 640×350 16 color	J	EGA 320×200 16 color
L	VGA/MCGA 320×200 256 color	M	VGA 640×480 16 color
O	VGA/MCGA 640×480 2 color	P	EGA/VGA 800×600 2 color
Q	EGA/VGA 800×600 16 color	R	S-VGA 640×400 256 color
S	S-VGA 640×480 256 color	T	S-VGA 800×600 256 color
U	S-VGA 1024×768 2 color	V	S-VGA 1024×768 16 color
W	VGA 360×480 256 color	X	S-VGA 1024×768 256 color
Y	S-VGA 1280×1024 16 color	Z	S-VGA 1280×1024 256 color
L2	S-VGA 320×200 Hicolor 16	S2	S-VGA 640×480 Hicolor 16
T2	S-VGA 800×600 Hicolor 16	X2	S-VGA 1024×768 Hicolor 16
Z2	S-VGA 1280×1024 Hicolor 16	L3	S-VGA 320×200 Hicolor 24
S3	S-VGA 640×480 Hicolor 24	T3	S-VGA 800×600 Hicolor 24
X3	S-VGA 1024×768 Hicolor 24	Z3	S-VGA 1280×1024 Hicolor 24

You read the report starting at the top line, which indicates that the access speed of the video card for writing is 8212 bytes/ms and for reading is 1773 bytes/ms, while the monitor is using a horizontal scan frequency of 28.65 KHz and a vertical scan frequency of 59.67 Hz (~60Hz). The board operated in the $640 \times 480 \times 16$ mode for the test. The subsequent two lines show the resulting bytes/ms when working with 16- and 32-bit data.

Performance

Since the program was last updated in 1992, it will not identify a lot of CPU and video board hardware, but the timing tests should be quite accurate under DOS (operation under Windows or with DOS TSRs might affect the system timing). Do not type or use any other hardware while the test is running; interrupts such as keyboard handlers will also upset system timing.

Registration

The VIDSPEED.EXE program is $0 shareware, so you may use and distribute it freely. However, there is no support from the author and there is no known update for the program.

Summary

VIDSPEED.EXE is a unique and reasonably accurate tool for determining the reading and writing performance of video systems at different resolutions and color depths.

Printer and parallel port tools

4

The parallel port is perhaps the single most used port on the PC; printers, dongles (parallel port hardware encryption keys), external tape drives, and all manner of other peripherals compete for space on the LPT port. When there is trouble with the parallel port, it has a profound impact on your ability to use the computer; just imagine not being able to print a document. Printers also have their share of ills, which can often be addressed by a set of good diagnostics. This chapter outlines parallel port diagnostics (Table 4-1), as well as a suite of utilities to check and optimize a printer.

■ Table 4-1 Printer and parallel port tools

Filename	Description
Parallel port utilities	
PARAMO.ZIP	Parallel data capture utility
EZSET.ZIP	Printer configuration utility
Printing utilities	
LASMAN.ZIP	Laser print manager
PRINTGF.ZIP	Image printing utility
PRNTGL.ZIP	Pen plotter emulator
ZC33.ZIP	Printer control utility
Printer maintenance utilities	
LASERTST.ZIP	HP self-test utility
LZC26.ZIP	Laser cleaning utility
PRN-TEST.ZIP	Printer test utilities

Important It is impossible to test these programs on every possible configuration of PC hardware. If you cannot get the program to run (or encounter unexpected results), contact the program's author for more information.

System backup I highly recommend that you perform a complete system backup before attempting to use system diagnostics and utilities. In the event that system errors or unexpected program results accidentally damage your programs or data, a backup will allow you to restore your information quickly and easily.

Virus warning As a general operating procedure, you should never attempt to run a new program without first checking it for viruses. Decompress the program and then run your virus checker. If a virus is detected, take all necessary steps to neutralize it.

Parallel port utilities

Printers rely on the uninterrupted flow of proper data from a computer. When trouble occurs in the printing process, verifying the parallel port's operation is a major priority for a technician; a working parallel port means the problem is either in the printer cable or the printer itself. Once you know the parallel port is working, the remaining troubleshooting is simplified. The two diagnostic programs in this section are designed to track data and handshaking signals at the PC parallel port.

PARAMO.ZIP

The PARAMO package (Table 4-2) is a data capture program that works on any standard LPT1 port. It will capture a file of any size from any type of host computer sending data along a standard Centronics port. Version 1.2 can capture data at a rate of 20,000 characters/second, which means it can keep up with a throughput of 135 pages a minute. You can also capture data in the background within a DOS window in Windows 3.1 (or Windows 95). PARAMO can create a single file of any size, or it can maintain a wraparound file from 3 to 10MB in size. You can view, edit, and retransmit the captured file to the printer using standard DOS commands. The capture process is very simple; users simply connect the PARAMO cable, start the PARAMO program, wait for the data from a sending computer, and press F10 when the data is finished.

Installation and configuration

In order to provide the best results, PARAMO should be run with a minimum of "overhead" software, such as drivers and TSRs, so you should probably clean-boot the PC from a bootable floppy. Copy the PARAMO.ZIP archive from your CD to a bootable floppy disk. Switch to the floppy drive and run PKUNZIP to decompress the

■ Table 4-2 PARAMO fact sheet

Program name:	Printer Capture Utility
Executable file:	PARAMO.EXE
Purpose:	To capture data generated by the LPT1 port
Version:	1.2-04b (c. 1993)
Operating system:	MS-DOS 3.1 or later
Compressed file:	PARAMO.ZIP (archive)
Author:	Jean-Georges Marcotte
Address:	45 Grenier Ste-Anne de Bellevue, Quebec H9X 3L2 Canada
Internet:	JGM.Dorval@XCI.Xerox.Com
CompuServe:	70065,1220
ASP member:	No
Registration:	$75
Special notes:	Needs a specialized cable

archive. Once the archive has been decompressed, you can start PARAMO.EXE with no further configuration.

Operation

There are three things you need in order to operate PARAMO: the cable, the configuration, and the host computer. The cable is the physical wire that goes from the LPT1 port of the PC monitoring the data to the parallel port of the monitored printer, including the connector that receives the "host" parallel plug. The only way to capture data is to connect to it. You can construct the cable using the information included in PARAMO.DRW. The configuration is the set of parameters needed to run the program correctly. Those parameters have to set using a menu in PARAMO. They are saved in PARAMO.CFG. The configuration also includes the characteristics of the monitoring PC. A host is the device sending data to the printer.

Performance

When you start PARAMO.EXE, a main menu will appear, as shown in Figure 4-1 on the next page. There are five options to choose from. The first three options define the way PARAMO captures data. The fourth option allows you to set up the program's configuration. The final option lets you exit the program. If you choose options 1 or 3, the program will ask you for a filename (by default, the name will be CAPTURE.DAT). If the file already exists, PARAMO will ask you if you want to overwrite the file. Type another filename or press <Enter> to overwrite it. There is no filename choice for menu 2 because the filename in that case is always CAPTUREx.DAT (x being the buffer number).

PARAMO, the simple parallel data monitor
By Jean-Georges Marcotte, version 1.2-04b

1 Capture and save using a 64Kbytes rolling buffer

2 Capture a rolling 3 meg. with 3 files of 1 meg. each.

3 Capture and save the complete job

4 PARAMO setting and utility

5 Quit

■ **4-1** *The main menu in PARAMO.*

Once the capture program is actively collecting data, only the <F10> key is active; you can use F10 to exit from the capture session (you might have to press the key more than once). You can also break from the program using <Ctrl>–<Alt>–<Del>, but you will lose the capture file. During the capture process, you can see the amount of data captured and the status of several different port signals. Once the capture terminates, PARAMO will ask if you want to see the captured data. If you press Y, the file will print out. You can continue to trap other data, or exit to take a look at the file using your favorite text editor.

Perhaps the most notable disadvantage of PARAMO is that it needs a cable that you will probably need to build. However, the plans for building the cable are outlined in the PARAMO.DRW file.

Registration

If you continue to use PARAMO beyond a reasonable evaluation period, you must register the software with the program author. The registration fee for a single-user license is $75.

Summary

PARAMO is a powerful data tracking tool that technicians can use to help track down the presence (or absence) of data between a PC and printer. You need a cable and a free computer to monitor the flow of data. For many users, the demands of PARAMO will outweigh the benefits, but serious technicians will find the program to be a real asset.

EZSET.ZIP

In order to provide their myriad of advanced features, virtually all modern printers use a series of sophisticated *escape codes* (the <Esc> character followed by a sequence of several other characters). This makes it possible for printers to be designed with almost limitless functionality. However, the program that drives the printer must understand and use those codes. If the program that operates the printer does not use particular codes, the printer will not provide the corresponding features. The EZSET program (Table 4-3) is designed to supplement other printer software, or allow you to test specific printer functions by entering desired control sequences.

■ Table 4-3 EZSET fact sheet

Program name:	EZSET
Executable file:	EZSET.EXE
Purpose:	Printer control utility
Version:	2.1 (c. 1993)
Operating system:	MS-DOS 2.1 or later
Compressed file:	EZSET.ZIP (archive)
Author:	T. C. McAdams
Address:	McAdams Associates
	P.O. Box 835505
	Richardson, TX 75083-5505
ASP member:	No
Registration:	$20
Special notes:	You must know the printer control codes.

Unlike other programs that come with a predefined library of printer codes or require you to write BASIC programs or batch files, all you need to use EZSET effectively is your printer's user manual. EZSET allows you to send your printer's control codes from the DOS command line or from batch files. In addition, EZSET printer strings can be customized to go automatically to any printer port, using any printer online return value.

Installation and configuration

Deciding where to install EZSET depends on how you plan to use it. If you need EZSET as a supplemental printer configuration tool, you should install it to your hard drive so it can be referenced in AUTOEXEC.BAT. If you plan to use EZSET as a diagnostic or testing tool, you might get better performance by installing the program to a floppy disk you can keep in your toolbox. Copy the EZSET.ZIP archive file from the DLS Diagnostic CD to a subdirectory on your hard drive or to a floppy disk. Switch to the subdirectory (or floppy drive) and run PKUNZIP to decompress the archive file. Once the archive has been decompressed into its constituent files, you can run EZSET.EXE directly with no further configuration.

Operation

EZSET.EXE has two modes of operation: an editor mode and a command-line mode. You use the editor mode to input and edit printer strings, and the command-line mode to send strings to a printer. To start EZSET in the editor mode, type:

C:\> EZSET <Enter>

Once the program starts, you have three options: exit the program, edit an existing printer control string, or enter a new printer control string. If there are already some printer control strings defined (in a file called EZSET.LIB), choosing the Edit option lets you modify them or send them to the printer immediately (Figure 4-2). Note that EZSET.LIB can be located in any directory defined in your PATH environment variable. The New command option allows you to enter a new string (and determine which printer port the string will go to) and define what the online return code should be.

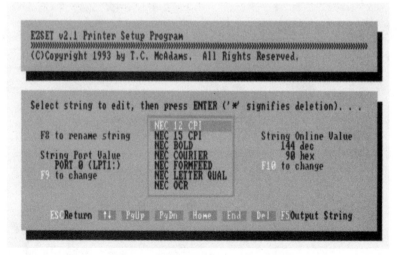

■ **4-2** *The working display in EZSET.*

142

After you have entered at least one printer control string (using EZSET in the editor mode), you can send the string to your printer by typing:

C:\> EZSET *stringname* <Enter>

where stringname is the name of the desired printer control string saved in EZSET.LIB. If the printer is online, the string is sent to it. If the printer is offline (not available), you are told so and EZSET will exit with a return code of 255. EZSET's ability to return an exit code allows you to perform conditional branching in a batch file. You can also place the EZSET command line within your AUTOEXEC.BAT file to automatically adjust the printer's configuration during system startup. When a printer is offline, a message to that effect is printed to the screen. Also, if you type a nonexistent string name (one that isn't in the library file), EZSET will say so and produce a return code of 255.

Performance

EZSET will manage a printer string library containing a maximum of 255 printer strings, with each printer string a maximum of 255 characters in length. EZSET will output strings only through parallel ports 1 through 3 (LPT1, LPT2, and LPT3). EZSET supports parallel ports only and will not output through serial ports.

143

Registration

EZSET is shareware; if you continue to use the program beyond a reasonable evaluation period, you should register the software with the program author for $20. A check or money order is preferred. Your registration provides you with one year of free telephone and e-mail support, free bug fixes or patches, the latest version of EZSET, and some extra utility programs. If you install EZSET on a customer's PC, you should remit the registration fee to the program author or instruct your customer to remit the proper registration fee.

Summary

EZSET.EXE provides technicians with a versatile tool for configuring a printer to suit a unique system or testing the printer's individual functions. However, you need to have access to a user manual or other printer documentation that lists the printer's control codes.

Printing utilities

No matter how many functions a modern printer is capable of performing, there never seem to be enough functions to perform every task. Users are always trying to squeeze that extra ounce of performance and capability from their printer investment. Users often need tools that allow you to manipulate fonts and page sizes, and print multiple pages on the same sheet, as well as sophisticated image and plot file printing utilities. The programs in this section are designed to help users achieve that extra element of customized operation.

LASMAN.ZIP

Users often print text files with a word processor, but straight ASCII text (without formatting or format control characters) can be a real disappointment. The Laser Manager package (Table 4-4) will print ASCII text on a laser (or ink jet) printer in any of several hundred styles. Such styles and enhancements include portrait or landscape orientation, five font sizes, multiple text pages per sheet, pamphlet format, and book format. Extensive documentation outlines the myriad of features that are available.

■ **Table 4-4 LASMAN fact sheet**

Program name:	Laser Manager
Executable file:	LASR_MAN.EXE
Purpose:	Print files to laser printers in a variety of formats
Version:	6.05 (c. 1994)
Operating system:	MS-DOS 3.0 or later
Compressed file:	LASMAN.ZIP (archive)
Author:	MicroMetric
Address:	98 Dade Ave.
	Sarasota, FL 34232-1609
Phone:	813-377-2515
Fax:	813-377-2091
BBS:	813-371-2490
ASP member:	Yes
Registration:	$40 (single user) and $200 (site license)
Special notes:	Extensive documentation

Installation and configuration

For best results, install LASMAN.ZIP to the hard drive of your PC. Create a subdirectory for LASMAN.ZIP on your hard drive, then copy the archive file from the CD to a *temporary* subdirectory. Switch to the temporary subdirectory and run PKUNZIP to decompress the archive file. Once the archive is decompressed, you still need to install the program. Type INSTALL and follow the instructions on the screen. When asked for the destination directory, enter the path to the directory you just created. If you have not created a subdirectory yet (or prefer the default subdirectory offered by the installation routine), you can install the program there and remove your newly created subdirectory later. Once installed properly, you can run the LASR_MAN.EXE program either directly from DOS or through a DOS window.

Operation

You can navigate through LASR_MAN.EXE by using its full-screen menu, as shown in Figure 4-3. The top line of the display indicates the menu level (Expert) and display type (Normal), as well as the current date and time. A shareware notice is provided on the third line from the bottom, and the second line from the bottom shows the program's copyright notice. The bottom of the display lists the various function key features, such as <F1> for help, <F8> to adjust the background information, and <F9> to alter the display type.

■ **4-3** *The LASR_MAN working window.*

The real features of LASR_MAN.EXE are in the main menu selections listed on the second display line: Setup, Options, Files, Print, and Exit. When the Setup option is selected, a drop-down menu allows you to define the drive and directory where the files to be printed are located. You can select the options for printing, such as printing style, font, cover file, lines/page, and so on. Then you can select the Files menu, which lists the files available in the drive and directory specified under Setup and allows you to tag the desired files for printing. Finally, choose the Print option to begin the printing process. Once printing is complete, you can select Exit to leave the program. By default, there are a minimum of choices listed under each menu option. You can increase (or decrease) the number of items listed by pressing <F8> (menu detail).

Performance

Laser Manager is compatible with a wide range of laser and ink-jet printer models. In addition to a readily accessible menu system, LASR_MAN.EXE also has a selection of command-line and environment options (Table 4-5). The documentation provides highly detailed descriptions and examples for each option, along with some examples that help you learn how to use LASR_MAN.EXE.

Registration

If you continue to use LASR_MAN.EXE beyond a 30-day evaluation period, you must register the software with the program author. Once you register, you will receive a 7×8.5-inch printed and bound manual, phone or mail support for one year, notification of the next major program release, and a diskette containing the latest version of the program, along with supplemental files that include additional soft font typefaces.

A single-user license is $40, which entitles a user to unlimited use of the program on a single computer. A site license is $200, which entitles the user to unlimited use of the program on all computers (including networks) at a single location. Add $5 for shipping and handling within the U.S. and $12 outside of the U.S. Don't forget to specify your disk size.

Summary

The LASMAN package is one of the more comprehensive DOS printer enhancements available. Recent and very well documented, LASR_MAN.EXE will provide excellent service on a wide selection of laser and ink-jet printers.

PRINTGF.ZIP

While printers are adept at printing text, images are often another matter, especially under DOS. PrintGF (Print Graphics Files) is a shareware image printing utility for DOS and Windows systems (Table 4-6). It includes a DOS program (PRINTGFD.EXE) that can be run from the command line or menu, along with an equivalent Windows program (PRINTGFW.EXE). It prints .BMP, .DCX, .GIF, .PCX, and .PNG files. PrintGF is also compatible with a wide range of printers, such as Epson and IBM 9-pin printers; Epson, Fujitsu, IBM, NEC, and Toshiba 24-pin printers; Canon BJ, BJC, and LBP ink-jet printers, Epson Stylus, Fargo Primera, HP Laser-

■ Table 4-5 Command-line options for LASR_MAN.EXE

Options	Description
A (Archive Bit Status)	Define which files will be displayed for selection
C (Change Configuration File)	Modify the printer command parameters for this execution only
V (Cover File)	Specify a cover file to print before other selected files
D (Drive/Directory Path)	Define the drive and directory from which files will be selected and printed
F (File/File Mask)	Specifies the file to be printed or the file mask to use for selection
G (Graphics)	Specify how fast the logo animation will be displayed
I (Line/Page Limit)	Define the maximum lines per page for the selected files
M (Monitor)	Force a different display mode
M (Mouse)	Adjust the mouse parameters of sensitivity and button assignment
O (Option File)	Specify the option file of saved setting to load
W (Option Switches)	Select individual option switch settings
T (Output To_)	Define the port or file to which output is to be directed
B (Paper Source Bin)	Specify the paper source bin of paper on which to print
U (Printer Type)	Specify the type of printer to be supported
N (Print Font Usage)	Specify which pitch should be loaded for soft fonts
R (Reverse Second Pass Printing)	Reverses the order in which the second printing pass will be done
E (STAMP-IT!)	Include a halftone "rubber" stamp
S (Style of Output File)	Outline the selected style of output options
H (Title)	Specify the text page header/footer
P (Typeface)	Specify the selected typeface to use
Y (User Display Level)	Control the background information display
U (User Menu Level)	Select the function menu options that will be available

147

Jet, DeskJet, PaintJet, and HP-RTL printers, IBM ExecJet and LaserPrinter printers; and PostScript printers. It will also display images on CGA, EGA, HGC, VGA, and VESA SVGA, and generate DCX and PCX bitmaps.

PrintGF outputs color or black-and-white images with pattern and/or error diffusion dithering, brightness, contrast, and gamma for each plane, gray balance, blur and sharpen, edge smoothing,

■ Table 4-6 PRINTGF fact sheet

Program name:	Print Graphics Files (PrintGF)
Executable files:	PRINTGFD.EXE (DOS) and PRINTGFW.EXE (Windows)
Purpose:	Print graphics files to a printer
Version:	1.24b (c. 1995)
Operating systems:	MS-DOS 3.3 or later and Windows 3.1x or later
Compressed file:	PRINTGF.ZIP (archive)
Author:	Cary Ravitz
Address:	Ravitz Software Inc. P.O. Box 25068 Lexington, KY 40524-5068
BBS/Fax:	606-268-0577
CompuServe:	70431,32
Internet:	70431.32@compuserve.com
ASP member:	Yes
Registration:	$34
Special notes:	DOS and Windows versions are both included in the package

user-selected clipping area, print area, and portrait or landscape orientation.

Installation and configuration

You could run PrintGF from a floppy disk, but you will get the best results by installing PrintGF to the hard drive. Create a subdirectory for the program and copy the PRINTGF.ZIP archive from the CD to the subdirectory. Switch to the subdirectory and use PKUNZIP to decompress the archive. If you want to use PrintGF from any application, be sure to include the PrintGF subdirectory in your PATH statement.

To install PRINTGFW.EXE as an icon in the Windows 3.1x Program Manager, select File, New, then Program Item to bring up the Program Item menu. Enter the item name PrintGF/W with a command line similar to C:\PRINTGF\PRINTGFW, and the working directory (wherever you keep your image files). You can choose from three icons designed for 2, 16, and 32K color setups. Under Windows 95, you can create a shortcut on the desktop or launch the program from Windows Explorer.

Operation and performance

When you start PrintGF, you will see a menu such as the one in Figure 4-4 on the next page. The first column of main menu options is dedicated to menu functions. These include running PrintGF, alternate configurations, exiting the program, saving the configurations, and menu setup options. The Alt Config item rotates between five configurations (the current configuration name is on line 2). The Save Configs item saves the current configurations by writing them to the .EXE file. Only the first nine lines of the image file list are saved. You can create multiple .EXE files with different names and each can have its own configurations. The Menu Config item lets you set the configuration name and screen colors. For PrintGF/W, you can also use the − and * keys as color modifiers. These keys are effective only with 15, 16, or 24-bit color setups. To use the default Windows colors, blank out the desired line of colors. For PrintGF/W, you can choose the screen font height and selected from current "fixedsys" fonts.

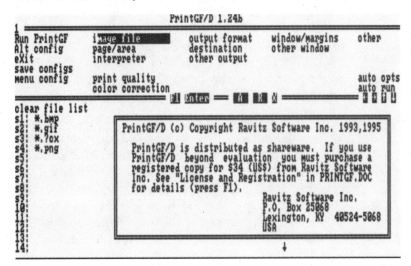

■ **4-4** *The main menu for PRINTGF.*

Column two of the main menu lets you choose which image files to print, as well as features like the image page number (/N), picture area/mode (/A), image interpreter (/E), print quality (/F), brightness (/B), contrast (/C), image gamma correction (/U), output gamma correction (/Z), and gray balance (/Y). You can enter up to 99 image files in the Image File main menu option. Each file can be preceded by a repetition count from 2 to 5. To choose from a list of files, enter a mask name and press <Enter> (the cursor must be on the mask). The menu will then display a list of corresponding files. Select any number of the files by moving the cursor to the desired file and pressing the spacebar or the right mouse button. Consecutive presses will increment the repetition count. If no files are selected, then pressing <Enter> will select the file under the cursor. The selected files are added to the file list below the cursor. Files

149

that would overflow the 99th position on the image file list are dropped.

Directories are shown at the top of the file list and are designated by a trailing slash (\). If you select a directory, then you can use that to display a new file list. This is handy for navigating a disk to search for image files. The first nine plot files are saved when you select Save Configs. When you select Run PrintGF, the program is run for each file in the image file list (masks are ignored). For any files that PrintGF does not successfully process, an arrow is inserted in front of the filename. You can view the results from the Image File main menu item.

The third column of options specifies the destination (/D), output format (/F), and other output options (/LF = form feed, /XP = pause to load paper, /J = prefix codes, and /K = suffix codes). In the Output Format menu, printers that support color have a color option. This lets you specify a black-and-white output. Output formats that do not support color do not have this option and always convert to black and white.

The fourth column of main menu options includes Window/Margins and Other Window, which lets you specify the print area and its position on the paper (/L = page layout). Other options are in column five. The Other option lets you turn off use of the upper memory block and enter command-line options to override anything on the menu. At the bottom of column five are the Auto Run options. The lower right corner of the menu includes Auto Opts and Auto Run. In Auto Run mode, the disk is continually searched for new files that match the mask or file specified in Auto Opts. Whenever one is found, PrintGF is run on that file. This is useful with multitasking systems such as DESQview and Windows. Run in PrintGF's Auto Run mode and switch it to the background. Then you can output files and they will be printed automatically.

The Auto Run mask might include the # character (the same as ?), but when a file matches the mask, the character that matches the # selects the PrintGL configuration. The first character of the configuration title must match the selected configuration. Auto Run mode uses one of two ways of choosing new files (specified under Auto Opts). The first is by the time/date stamp. In this mode, it will catch only files that have a time/date stamp later than when Auto Run mode was started and later than the last file processed in Auto Run mode. The file with the earliest time/date stamp is processed first. Copying a file does not change its time/date stamp, so copying a file to the Auto Run mask will not cause it to be seen as a new file. The second mode uses an archive bit. When Auto Run mode is started, any file that matches the mask and has its archive bit set will be processed, regardless of when it was created. The file with the earliest time/date stamp is processed first. After it is chosen, its archive bit is reset so it will not be chosen again. This lets you copy files to the Auto Run mask to print them.

Registration

If you continue to use PrintGF after a reasonable evaluation period, you must register the software with the program author. The registration for a single-user license is $34.

Summary

PrintGF is a particularly handy utility for printing graphics through DOS or Windows. Extensive documentation details each function and feature.

PRNTGL.ZIP

With the growth of CAD programs and other design packages, users frequently save files in a plotter format. Unfortunately, plotters are a rare and expensive PC peripheral. PrintGL (Table 4-7) is a DOS and Windows shareware package that emulates pen plotters; it allows you to print plot files on impact, ink-jet, or laser printers. It includes a DOS program that can be run from the command line or through its menu. The PRINTGL package contains the DOS utility (PRINTGLD.EXE), an equivalent Windows program (PRINTGLW.EXE), and a resident DOS program that intercepts plotter data as it is being written to file (PRINTCAD.EXE).

Even if your graphics program supports your printer, you will probably find that PrintGL is faster, gives better print quality, and provides more formatting flexibility. PrintGL uses the best graphics modes available for each printer it supports and uses data compression to improve print speed on many printers. And it provides options such as paper size, orientation, magnification, and pen width, color, and shading.

Installation and configuration

You could run PrintGL from a floppy disk, but you will get the best results when installing PrintGL to your hard drive. Create a subdirectory for the program and copy the PRINTGL.ZIP archive from the CD to the subdirectory. Switch to the subdirectory and use PKUNZIP to decompress the archive. If you want to use PrintGL from any application, be sure to include the PrintGL subdirectory in your PATH statement.

151

■ Table 4-7 PRNTGL fact sheet

Program name:	Pen Plotter/Emulator (PrintGL)
Executable files:	PRINTGLD.EXE (DOS), PRINTGLW.EXE (Windows), and PRINTCAD.EXE (DOS CAD)
Purpose:	Print pen plots on a conventional printer
Version:	1.56c (c. 1995)
Operating systems:	MS-DOS 3.3 or later and Windows 3.1x or later
Compressed file:	PRINTGL.ZIP (archive)
Author:	Cary Ravitz
Address:	Ravitz Software, Inc.
	P.O. Box 25068
	Lexington, KY 40524-5068
BBS/Fax:	606-268-0577
CompuServe:	70431,32
Internet:	70431.32@compuserve.com
ASP member:	Yes
Registration:	$50
Special notes:	Contains both DOS and Windows versions

To install PRINTGLW.EXE as an icon in the Windows 3.1x Program Manager, select File, New, then Program Item to bring up the Program Item menu. Enter the item name PrintGL/W with a command line similar to C:\PRINTGL\PRINTGLW, and the working directory, wherever you keep your image files. You can choose from three icons designed for 2, 16, and 32K color setups. Under Windows 95, you can create a shortcut on the desktop or launch the program from Windows Explorer.

Operation and configuration

When you start PrintGL, you will see a menu like the one in Figure 4-5 on the next page. The first column of menu items is dedicated to menu-related functions such as running PrintGL, using an alternate configuration, exiting the program, saving the configurations, setting menu options, and creating a batch file corresponding to the current configuration. The Alt Config item rotates between five available menu configurations. The current configuration name is in the upper left corner. The Save Configs item saves all the current menu configurations by writing them into the .EXE file. Only the first nine lines in the plot file list are saved. You can copy the .EXE file to a different name, and it will have its own configurations. The Menu Config item lets you set the configuration name, screen colors, and the name of the batch file created with the Create BAT option.

Column two of the main menu lets you choose which files to plot, the plot page number, the output destination, output format, and

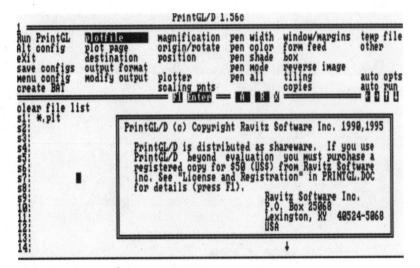

■ **4-5** *The main menu for PRINTGL.*

modifications to the output such as compression mode (/F), horizontal and vertical size multiplier (/F), and prefix and suffix printer codes (/J and /K). You can enter up to 99 plot files in the Plot File submenu, and precede each file with a repetition count from 2 to 5. To choose from a list of files, enter a mask name and press <Enter> (the cursor must be on the mask). The menu will then display a list of corresponding files. Select any number of the files by moving the cursor to the desired file and pressing either the spacebar or the right mouse button. Consecutive presses will increment the repetition count. If no files are selected, then pressing <Enter> will select the file under the cursor.

The selected files are added to the file list below the cursor. Files that would overflow the 99th position on the plot file list are dropped. Directories are shown at the top of file lists and are designated by a trailing slash (\). If you select a directory (repetition counts are not allowed), then you can use that to display a new file list. This is handy for navigating a disk to search for image files. The first nine plot files are saved when you select Save Configs.

When you select Run PrintGL, the program is run for each file on the plot file list, and masks are ignored. For any plot files not successfully processed, an arrow is inserted in front of the plot filename. You can view the results from the Plot File main menu item. Printers that support color have a color option that lets you specify a black-and-white printer even if you have set up colors with the Pen Color menu. Output formats that do not support color do not have this option and always convert the selected colors to black and white.

The third column of menu items in Figure 4-5 define how the plot is processed. The options include magnification, origin, position, plotter configuration, and initial scaling points. The fourth column of main menu items covers the pen characteristics: width, color and opaque/transparent mode, and shade. With each of these submenus you use the up and down cursor keys to select a pen, and the left and right cursor keys to choose an attribute. The Pen All submenu combines the four other submenus to let you choose all of a pen's attributes at once. The fifth column of main menu items covers the page layout. The first three items are suboptions of the /L option: print window and margins, form feed, and box. Tiling options and multiple copies are also controlled here. Other options are available in column six. These include the temporary file name and, under Other, pausing to load paper, suppressing unsupported command messages, and so on.

The lower right corner of the menu includes Auto Opts and Auto Run. In Auto Run mode, the disk is continually searched for new files that match the mask or file specified in Auto Opts. Whenever one is found, PrintGL is run on that file. This is useful with multi-tasking systems such as DESQview and Windows. Run in PrintGL's Auto Run mode and switch it to the background. Then you can output files and they will be printed automatically.

Auto Run mode lets you choose files in one of two ways (specified under Auto Opts). The first is by using a time/date stamp. In this mode, the program will catch only files with a time/date stamp later than when Auto Run mode was started and later than the last file processed in Auto Run mode. The file with the earliest time/date stamp is processed first. Copying a file does not change its time/date stamp, so copying a file to the Auto Run mask will not cause it to be seen as a new file. The second way of choosing files is by using an archive bit. When Auto Run mode is started, any file that matches the mask and has its archive bit set will be processed, regardless of when it was created. The file with the earliest time/date stamp is processed first. After it is chosen, its archive bit is reset so it will not be chosen again. This lets you copy files to the Auto Run mask to print them.

Registration

If you continue to use PrintGL after a reasonable evaluation period, you must register the software with the program author. The registration for a single-user license is $50.

Summary

PrintGL is a remarkably convenient utility for printing plotter files through any impact, ink-jet, or laser printer. Excellent documentation explains all command-line and menu functions in the program.

ZC33.ZIP

Many DOS applications simply do not support all of a printer's features (especially given the proliferation of features in today's laser printers). ZAPCODE (Table 4-8) allows you to directly enter control codes in order to configure your printer. For example, with ZAPCODE you can reset your printer, turn on condensed print, or eject the page. You can also use ZAPCODE to automatically enter printer codes into your word processor, spreadsheet, or any other program. This is ideal for applications that don't support all your printer's features, but allow you to embed printer control codes inside your documents. Pop up ZAPCODE, select the desired printer option(s), and then let ZAPCODE enter the printer codes for you. ZAPCODE is ideal for all types of printers, including dot-matrix and laser printers, even plotters.

■ **Table 4-8 ZC33 fact sheet**

Program name:	ZapCode
Executable file:	ZAPCODE.COM
Purpose:	Control the operations of a printer
Version:	3.3 (c. 1990)
Operating system:	MS-DOS 2.0 or later
Compressed file:	ZC33.ZIP (archive)
Author:	Robert L. Morton
Address:	Morton Utilities International
	81-887 Tournament Way
	Indio, CA 92201
Phone:	619-347-7563
CompuServe:	70132,3707
Internet:	70132.3707@compuserve.com
ASP member:	Yes
Registration:	$19.95 (single user) and $499.95 (site license)
Special notes:	You can use shareware version for a 14-day trial period only.

Installation and configuration

ZAPCODE can be run from either the hard drive or a floppy disk. Your best results will depend on how you plan to use the program. If you use ZAPCODE as a printer enhancement, you should probably make it resident on the hard drive (and place ZAPCODE's directory in the PATH statement). If you plan to use ZAPCODE as a diagnostic tool—allowing you to check the various functions of a printer—you should probably install the program to a floppy disk.

Copy the ZC33.ZIP archive from your CD to a subdirectory on your hard drive or to a floppy disk. Switch to the subdirectory (or floppy drive) and run PKUNZIP to decompress the archive. Once the archive has been decompressed into its constituent files, you can run ZAPCODE.COM directly. You can choose to run ZAPCODE in a stand-alone mode, or install it in memory. Start the program by typing:

C:\> ZAPCODE <Enter>

Operation

Once the program starts, you will see a window listing all the printer drivers in the current directory, as shown in Figure 4-6. Ideally, you should find the printer driver that matches (or emulates) your printer. Use the up and down arrows and <Page Up> and <Page Down> keys to select the desired driver. The <Enter> specifies the selected file in stand-alone mode, installs the selected driver in memory (the hot key is <Ctrl>–<Alt>–<Z>), removes the last driver installed in memory, <E> allows you to edit the selected driver, and <A> lets you add a new driver file. To exit the program, press <Esc>.

You can install as many copies of ZAPCODE as available memory allows in your particular system. If you have installed more than one copy and each copy shares the same hot key, press the hot key

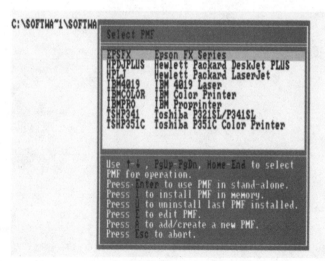

■ **4-6** *The printer selection menu for ZC33.*

once to activate the copy installed last. Press the hot key again to activate the copy installed prior to that, and so on. If you have installed more than one copy, the last copy installed will be removed first. Uninstalling again will cause the copy installed prior to that one to be removed. If you have loaded other memory-resident utilities after ZAPCODE, ZAPCODE might not be able to remove itself. If this happens, the message "Cannot uninstall" will be displayed.

The program can also perform all these functions through command-line switches. The complete syntax for ZAPCODE is:

ZAPCODE [*filename*] [/I] [/U] [/E]

where *filename* is the name of the printer file (it is not necessary to type the .PMF extension). The /I switch installs ZAPCODE (and the specified printer file) in memory. The /U switch removes the last installed copy of ZAPCODE. The /E switch invokes the printer file editor. You must also specify the name of the driver file you want to edit; if the file does not exist, it will be created.

You can specify ZAPCODE to be loaded automatically each time the computer is started by adding the ZAPCODE command line to your AUTOEXEC.BAT file. If other memory-resident utilities are loaded in AUTOEXEC.BAT and conflicts result when loading ZAPCODE, try changing the order in which the drivers are loaded.

Performance

ZAPCODE runs efficiently as long as there is memory to hold the program, but it offers a remarkable suite of features, outlined in the program's documentation. For example, ZAPCODE supports any parallel printer attached to LPT1, LPT2, or LPT3 and any serial printer attached to COM1 through COM4. The printer drivers are completely customizable; you can easily modify the included printer drivers to suit any printer configuration, or even create your own. Stand-alone or memory-resident operation gives you maximum flexibility in using the program. Menu colors and hot keys can all be specified. Multiple installation capability allows you to support systems with more than one printer, but the copies can be uninstalled to save RAM.

Registration

If you plan to use ZAPCODE beyond a 14-day evaluation period, you must register the software with the program author for $19.95. A site license can be purchased for $499.95. In exchange for your registration, you receive the latest registered version of ZAPCODE, a professionally printed and bound 33-page manual, the latest library of printer driver files, and six months of technical support.

Summary

ZAPCODE is a tool that is ideal for making your printer(s) work in conjunction with your DOS applications by taking the fullest advantage of your printer's particular features. You can also use the program to help diagnose problems by testing certain printer features.

Printer maintenance utilities

Even if a printer is connected and running properly, it should still be tested periodically, as well as during routine maintenance. This gives you a standard benchmark with which to judge the printer's operation and keep the printer running longer. The following programs provide technicians with an assortment of tools for printer maintenance.

LASERTST.ZIP

The LASERTST.COM program (Table 4-9) causes any HP Laser-Jet printer to run a self-test and eject the printed results. The actual test process should take only a minute or two. Depending on the particular model of printer, the results might include an example of the default font, ROM dates, installed memory, and number of pages printed since it was manufactured. The program might also work on some LaserJet clones.

Installation and configuration

Since LASERTST.COM is intended to serve as a diagnostic, you should get the best results by installing the program to a floppy disk and keeping it in your toolbox (though hard drive installations

■ **Table 4-9 LASERTST fact sheet**

Program name:	HP Self-Test Utility
Executable file:	LASERTST.COM
Purpose:	Causes HP laser printers to run a self-test
Version:	Unknown (c. 1993)
Operating system:	MS-DOS 3.3 or later
Compressed file:	LASERTST.ZIP (archive)
Author:	Michael Bruss
Address:	569 Villanova Drive
	Davis, CA 95616
ASP member:	No
Registration:	Public domain
Special notes:	Limited to HP laser printers and some clones

will operate just as well). Copy the LASERTST.ZIP archive to your floppy disk or a subdirectory on your hard drive. Switch to the subdirectory (or floppy drive) and use PKUNZIP to decompress the archive. Once the archive file is decompressed, you can run LASERTST.COM directly.

Operation

The program operates automatically; once LASERTST starts, no user interaction is required. It might then take several minutes for the printer to produce its self-test printout.

Performance

LASERTST.COM is designed specifically for Hewlett-Packard laser printers, so will not operate on all laser printers. Some HP clone printers might respond properly to LASERTST, but there is no clear way to tell which ones are compatible.

Registration

LASERTST.COM has been released to the public domain, so you may use and distribute the program freely.

Summary

This is a unique and useful program that allows you to test HP laser printers without having to decode the control-panel keystrokes required to produce a self test. However, non-HP laser printers might not work with this utility.

LZC26.ZIP

Laser printers operate by using light to discharge areas of a charged drum. The *EP drum* is basically an aluminum cylinder coated with light-sensitive material. If some areas of the drum remain charged for long periods, the drum could encounter a bit of difficulty in discharging those areas of the drum. This can lead to unusually light areas when printing dark images or complex graphics. The LaserClean program (Table 4-10) is designed to print an all-black image that discharges the drum evenly and improves the overall image quality.

Installation and configuration

Since LaserClean is intended to be used as a diagnostic, you should install it to a floppy disk and keep it in your toolkit (but the program will operate from a hard drive just as well). Copy the LZC26.ZIP archive file from the DLS Diagnostic CD to your hard drive subdirectory or a floppy disk. Switch to the subdirectory (or

■ Table 4-10 LZC26 fact sheet

Program name:	LaserClean
Executable file:	LZC.EXE
Purpose:	To clean a laser printer
Version:	2.6 (c. 1992)
Operating system:	MS-DOS 3.3 or higher
Compressed file:	LZC26.ZIP (archive)
Author:	David Witt
Address:	Spacebook Consulting
	17 Skylark Drive #32
	Larkspur, CA 94939
ASP member:	No
Registration:	$10
Special notes:	Needs a laser printer to work

floppy drive) and use PKUNZIP to decompress the archive. Once the archive file is decompressed, you can run LZC.EXE directly.

Operation

Once you start LZC.EXE, you will see a main menu with three choices: learning about the program, running the drum cleaning cycle, and exiting the program. There is very little explanation required here; run a cleaning cycle for the prescribed period, then quit the program.

Performance

The LZC.EXE program should be run exclusively from DOS (rather than a DOS window). While the program requires a laser printer to be attached in order to run properly, it will not damage ink-jet printers. Consider running LZC.EXE every thousand pages or if you notice unusually light areas in an image (that are not toner-related). Finally, keep in mind that you might need to run the program through more than one cycle in order to achieve the desired results.

Registration

LaserClean is a shareware product. If you plan to use it beyond a 30-day evaluation period, you should register the software with the program author. The registration fee is $10.

Summary

LaserClean is not a program you will use frequently, but when used properly, it can reveal (and sometimes correct) charge problems in the EP drum, possibly preventing unnecessary replacement of the printer drum and engine and resulting in a major cost savings for your customer.

PRN-TEST.ZIP

There is little doubt that impact printers have lost their appeal in the business community; their incredibly low cost can no longer outweigh the superior image quality and speed of a laser (or even an ink-jet) printer. Still, impact printers do have a place in homes and offices, and they need to be tested during maintenance and repairs. The PRN-TEST.ZIP package from Harry Calevas (Table 4-11) provides some simple tools for testing impact printers.

■ **Table 4-11 PRN-TEST fact sheet**

Program name:	Printer Test Utilities
Executable file:	Several different applications
Purpose:	To test the operation of various printer types
Version:	Unknown (c. 1989)
Operating system:	MS-DOS 3.3 or later
Compressed file:	PRN-TEST.ZIP (self-extracting)
Author:	Harry P Calevas
Address:	P.O. Box 830 Trenton, GA 30752
Phone:	404-657-5484
ASP member:	No
Registration:	$15
Special notes:	Designed for impact-type printers using the Centronics instruction set

Installation and configuration

Since the programs with PRN-TEST.ZIP are intended to be used as diagnostics, you should install them to a floppy disk and keep the disk in your toolkit (but the programs will operate from a hard drive just as well). Copy the PRN- TEST.ZIP archive file from the CD to your hard drive subdirectory or a floppy disk. Switch to the subdirectory (or floppy drive) and use PKUNZIP to decompress the archive. Once the archive file is decompressed, you can run the required program directly. If you have trouble using any of these programs, try booting the system from a clean floppy disk.

Operation

The PRN-TEST.ZIP package is not one program, but several different programs designed to test several different printers: the

Centronics 102A and Okidata (both text and graphics mode). In actual practice, however, the program will work on just about any compatible impact printer.

The C102TEST.EXE program will test a Centronics 102A printer or any printer (in the draft mode) that responds to the older Centronics instruction set. Since the Centronics printer supports only limited functions, keep in mind that the expanded-print test might fail on some draft-type printers. To run C102TEST.EXE, just type:

C:\> C102TEST <Enter>

The next two programs are designed for Okidata printers. The OKI-TEST.EXE program tests the printer in the standard mode using a Centronics instruction set. The GRPH-TST.EXE program was written to test Okidata printers with the PC_Writer (graphics) module installed. This program will work with any printer that emulates the IBM Graphics printer. To run either program, type:

C:\> OKI-TEST <Enter>

or:

C:\> GRPH-TST <Enter>

Performance

Perhaps the most important factor to consider when using the PRN-TEST programs is that they were designed for relatively old and simple printers. The tests might not work on newer impact printers or other contemporary moving-carriage printers like ink-jet systems.

Registration

If you continue to use the PRN-TEST.ZIP programs after a reasonable evaluation period, you must register the software with the program author. Your $15 single-user registration fee entitles you to future versions of the utilities for two years for a disk fee of $5 each.

Summary

With impact printers in their waning days, the need for an impact printer diagnostic is questionable. Still, though the programs included with PRN-TEST.ZIP are dated, they provide a possible diagnostic resource when working with impact printers.

Modem and
communication tools

5

One of the fastest growth areas in the last couple of years for personal computers has been in PC communication. The use of commercial online services and the Internet for research, technical support, and entertainment has resulted in a proliferation of modem use. The use of modems and other serial devices (e.g., serial printers and mice) demands that the computer's COM ports be configured properly. The software utilities presented in this chapter (Table 5-1) are intended to help you analyze serial data and control signals to verify the operation of each COM port.

■ **Table 5-1 Modem and communication tools**

Filename	Description
Port/data analyzers	
BBX201.ZIP	Breakout box utility
COMPRT25.ZIP	COM port testing/management
COMRESET.ZIP	Resets the COM port
COMTAP21.ZIP	Serial line monitor software
COMTEST.ZIP	Serial port test utility
CTSSPU22.ZIP	Serial port utilities
SIMTRM.ZIP	Serial port diagnostic
UARTTS.ZIP	UART tester utility
Modem utility	
LISTEN10.ZIP	Modem ring utility

Important It is impossible to test these programs on every possible configuration of PC hardware. If you cannot get the program to run (or encounter unexpected results), contact the program's author for more information.

System backup I highly recommend that you perform a complete system backup before attempting to use system diagnostics and utilities. In the event that system errors or unexpected program results accidentally damage your programs or data, a backup will allow you to restore your information quickly and easily.

Virus warning As a general operating procedure, you should never attempt to run a new program without first checking it for viruses. Decompress the program and then run your virus checker. If a virus is detected, take all necessary steps to neutralize it.

Port/data analyzers

When trouble occurs with serial data, you need to know whether the problem is with the COM port data lines, the handshaking signals, or the device at either end. By tracking the operation of data lines and handshaking signals, you can isolate the cause of the problem. The port/data analyzer software presented in this section will reveal the data being passed between the COM port and device, along with control signals like CTS and RTS.

BBX201.ZIP

When testing serial ports, one of the most popular tools is known as a *breakout box*, a hardware tool that displays data and handshaking signals as a series of LEDs. The BBX201.ZIP package from David Foley (Table 5-2) is a software version of the classic breakout box. It displays the status of any COM port in the PC. The status of the various port flags are also displayed on the screen and are updated in real time as port activity happens. As an added bonus, BBX201.ZIP also displays the data lines and control signals for LPT (parallel) ports.

Installation and configuration

The BRKBOX.COM program will run equally well from a hard drive or a floppy disk, but you might get better performance by installing the program to a floppy disk that you can keep in your toolbox. Copy the BBX201.ZIP archive to a subdirectory on the hard drive or a floppy disk. Switch to the subdirectory (or floppy drive) and use PKUNZIP to decompress the archive file. Once the archive has been decompressed into its constituent files, you can run the program directly with no further configuration. If you choose to install BRKBOX.COM to a floppy disk, consider using a bootable floppy disk so you can boot the test system clean.

■ Table 5-2 BBX201 fact sheet

Program name:	Breakout Box
Executable file:	BRKBOX.COM
Purpose:	Serial port debugging tool
Version:	2.01 (c. 1991)
Operating system:	MS-DOS 3.3 or later
Compressed file:	BBX201.ZIP (self-extracting)
Author:	David R. Foley
Address:	Foley Hi-Tech Systems
	172 Amber Drive
	San Francisco, CA 94131-1642
Phone:	415-826-6084
Fax:	415-826-1706
BBS:	415-826-1707
CompuServe:	70262,1463
Internet:	70262.1463@compuserve.com
ASP member:	No
Registration:	$19
Special notes:	Will report on serial or parallel ports

Operation

When you run BRKBOX.COM, you need to specify the port to be monitored and any options (see *Performance*). The program will display port register contents such as handshake status. For serial ports, BRKBOX will display the status of DTR, DSR, CTS, DRS, RI, and DCD. You will also see values for the current data rate (300 to 115200 bps), parity (none, even, or odd), data bits (7 or 8), and stop bits (0, 1, or 2). You can also specify the monitoring of a parallel port, which will display registers such as BUSY, ACK, PAPER, ONLINE, ERROR, and TIMEOUT. By default, each condition is displayed along the top of a DOS text screen (though you can change the screen location where data is displayed). You can use the <Alt>–<C> key combination to toggle the display on and off, or remove the program from memory when no longer needed.

Performance

At a little over 5KB in size, BRKBOX is a simple TSR; like most TSRs, there are no bells and whistles. The program needs only two command-line switches: which port to monitor and which option(s) to use. A typical syntax for BRKBOX is:

C:\> BRKBOX [*port*] [*options*] <Enter>

where port can be COM1 through COM4, or LPT1 through LPT3. The following options are supported:

+ Enable display

− Disable display

/nn Multiplexer I.D. number

/nnnn Define a new hot key for toggling the display.

/Lxx Display location, with xx being any combination of r for right side, l for the left side, t for the top of the screen, and b for the bottom of the screen. EGA and VGA 43- and 50-line modes are supported by the bottom display.

/NOH Suppress header

/U Remove program from memory. BRKBOX must be the last TSR installed for this to work.

Registration

If you continue to use BRKBOX.COM beyond a reasonable evaluation period, you should register the product with the program author. The registration fee is $19, which will get you the latest registered version of BRKBOX.

Summary

BRKBOX is a small and simple port monitoring tool. Easy to run and removable, it can prove very handy when you are troubleshooting communication problems with a serial or parallel port device.

COMPRT25.ZIP

In order for a technician to work with the communication ports of a computer, it is necessary to know just what ports are actually installed in the computer in the first place; this is especially important when working with an unknown machine. The COMPort package from OSR (Table 5-3) addresses this issue by analyzing the system's configuration to find the installed ports, their I/O address, the UART installed (for each COM port), and other pieces of information that you can select. The program also allows you to add or remove COM or LPT ports from DOS at any address through the use of command-line switches.

Installation and configuration

The program operates equally well from a hard drive or floppy disk, but the method you use to install COMPort will depend on how you plan to use it. If you plan to use COMPort as a simple diagnostic, you will probably get the best results by installing it to a

Program name:	COMPort
Executable file:	COMPORT.EXE
Purpose:	Display COM and LPT port information
Version:	2.5 (c. 1993)
Operating system:	MS-DOS 3.3 or later
Compressed file:	COMPRT25.ZIP (archive)
Author:	OSR Open Systems Resources, Inc.
Address:	105 Route 101A, #19
	Amherst, NH 03031-2244
E-mail:	osr@world.std.com
CompuServe:	71477,2703
ASP member:	No
Registration:	$14.75
Special notes:	Simple program to use

bootable floppy to keep in your toolbox. If you plan to use the program to help configure port activity on a particular system, you should install COMPort to your hard drive (preferably a subdirectory that is added to your PATH statement).

Copy the COMPRT25.ZIP archive from the CD to a bootable floppy disk or subdirectory on your hard drive. Switch to the floppy drive (or subdirectory) and use PKUNZIP to decompress the archive. Once the archive has been decompressed into its constituent files, you can run the COMPORT.EXE program directly or add a command line to your AUTOEXEC.BAT file. If you intend to use COMPORT.EXE from anywhere in the directory tree, be sure to add the program's subdirectory to the PATH statement in AUTOEXEC.BAT.

Operation

The basic use of COMPORT.EXE is to display the number and addresses of the serial and parallel ports in a system. Serial ports will also carry a specification for the UART in use). To run the program, simply type:

```
C:\> COMPORT <Enter>
```

The program will generate a report similar to the one shown in Figure 5-1. You can also use COMPort to display the IRQ of each serial port in your system by adding the /I switch to the command line:

```
C:\> COMPORT /I <Enter>
```

Note: you should run this command with your network software
unloaded, and nothing running in the background. This means you
should boot the system clean before proceeding.

```
COMPORT V2.5
Copyright (c) 1993 - OSR Open Systems Resources, Inc.
This is the UNREGISTERED version of COMPORT.
COMPORT is Shareware...
If you find COMPORT useful, PLEASE register it!

Type <CR> to continue:DOS Equipment List Initially Indicates:
       2 serial ports
       1 parallel ports

Current Port Addresses and Types:
       COM1: 03F8h, Type=16550AFN
       COM2: 02F8h, Type=16550AFN

       LPT1: 0378h
```

■ **5-1** *A typical report produced by COMPRT25.*

Performance

While you can use COMPORT.EXE as a simple diagnostic, the program offers a large number of options for reporting. Many other
options, outlined in this section, allow you to use COMPort to configure the system's ports. You can get more detailed information
from the program's manual.

/A[-] Displays addresses of parallel and serial ports known to
DOS, as well as types of serial port UARTS. The default is /A
(enabled).

/E[-] Displays the number of COM and LPT ports known to DOS
according to the BIOS data area equipment list word, as COMPort
starts to run. Therefore, any ports found by COMPort configuration options are not included in these counts. The default is /E
(enabled).

/I[-] Displays the IRQ line associated with each COM port. The default is /I- (disabled).

/? or /H Displays a short screen of help information.

/S[-] Requests COMPort to scan for additional COM and LPT ports
at their typical default addresses; if any are found, they are added
to DOS. The default is /S- (disabled).

/Cn=x Requests COMPort to configure COM (serial) port n ($n = 1$
$- 4$) in DOS at port address x (the hex address without a trailing h
or leading $0x$). The default is none.

/Ln=x Requests COMPort to configure LPT (parallel) port n ($n = 1$ – 3) in DOS at port address x (the hex address without a trailing h or leading $0x$). The default is none.

/R=k Allows you to register your version of COMPort, using the registration key (k) provided to you by the author. Registering your copy of COMPort removes the gentle but annoying registration reminder that requires you to type an <Enter> to continue COMPort's execution. This option supersedes any others on the command line.

Registration

If you plan to use COMPort beyond a 30-day evaluation period, you must register the product with the program author. Registration is $14.75, which gets you the latest version of COMPort, free updates and support for 90 days, and a printed manual. If you install COMPort on a customer's system, you should collect and remit the registration fee to the program author, or instruct your customer to remit the registration fee directly.

Summary

COMPort is a uniquely versatile piece of software. It can report on existing ports in the computer and also help you to reconfigure those ports under DOS, which might be an ideal fix for crowded or strangely configured systems.

COMRESET.ZIP

Older versions of Windows do not fully reset the COM port circuitry after Windows communication programs finish. This can often cause problems when attempting to rerun communication programs under DOS used after Windows exits. The COMRESET.EXE program from FBN Productions (Table 5-4) is specifically designed to reinitialize your PC's COM port(s) after exiting Windows. While the program was intended to correct an issue with Windows 3.0 running in 386 enhanced mode, you can employ this utility after using Windows 3.1 or 3.11.

Installation and configuration

COMRESET.EXE is intended to serve as a system utility; as a result, it should be installed to your system hard drive. Create a subdirectory for the program and copy the COMRESET.ZIP archive from your CD to the subdirectory. Switch to the subdirectory and use PKUNZIP to decompress the archive into its constituent files. Once the archive is decompressed, you should add the subdirectory to your PATH statement, and include the COMRESET command line

169

Program name:	COM Port Reset
Executable file:	COMRESET.EXE
Purpose:	Utility to reset stuck COM ports after Windows exits
Version:	1.0 (c. 1990)
Operating system:	Windows 3.0 or later
Compressed file:	COMRESET.ZIP (archive)
Author:	FBN Productions
Address:	917 W. Columbia Ave. Champaign, IL 61821
BBS:	217-359-2874
ASP member:	No
Registration:	$0 shareware
Special notes:	Intended to correct a deficiency in Windows 3.0

in a batch file that can be executed when Windows exits. You could also use COMRESET as needed without adding it to a batch file.

Operation

The command line for COMRESET is very straightforward; simply list the numbers of each COM port you want to reset on the COMRESET command line, and execute the command line (or batch file) after Windows exits. Generally, you should reset all the ports that are installed in your system. Include only the number, and separate each number with a space. COMRESET recognizes ports COM1 through COM4 and will exit with an error message if you specify a port that is out of range. If a COM port is specified but does not actually exist in your system, COMRESET will note that with an error message, but other existing ports you might have specified will still be reset. For example, to manually reset ports COM1, COM2, and COM4, enter the command:

C:\> COMRESET 1 2 4 <Enter>

COMRESET assumes that the serial ports are at the "standard" addresses and interrupts for COM1 through COM4: COM1 at 03F8h using IRQ4, COM2 at 02F8h using IRQ3, COM3 at 03E8h using IRQ4, and COM4 at 02E8h using IRQ3. If you have rearranged these specifications using any other utilities (such as COMPORT.EXE), COMRESET might fail.

Performance

In actual operation, COMRESET shows no headers, reports, or other outward behavior. As a result, you might not even know the program has executed. COMRESET was designed to correct a deficiency in Windows 3.0, but you should be able to use the utility (if necessary) after running Windows 3.1 and Windows 3.11.

Registration

The COMRESET program is $0 shareware, so you can use and distribute it freely.

Summary

Chances are that you will never need COMRESET, but it might be just the tool to get you out of trouble when using a modem under DOS after exiting Windows.

COMTAP21.ZIP

When serial communication problems occur, it is often necessary to analyze the flow of data and control signals between the computer and serial device. The ComTAP program (Table 5-5) allows your PC to function as a passive or active RS-232 data and signal line monitor/ protocol analyzer that can eliminate guesswork when dealing with serial transmissions. ComTAP can resolve individual character arrival times to the microsecond, collect up to 8MB of time-stamped data, control all collection parameters, operate at up to 115,200 bps, and provide context-sensitive hypertext help for all program modes.

Installation and configuration

ComTAP will run equally well from a hard drive or floppy disk. Since the program is intended to be used as a diagnostic, however,

■ Table 5-5 COMTAP21 fact sheet

Program name:	ComTAP
Executable file:	PALS.EXE
Purpose:	Serial protocol analyzer
Version:	2.1 (c. 1993)
Operating system:	MS-DOS 2.1 or later
Compressed file:	COMTAP21.ZIP (archive)
Author:	Paladin Software, Inc.
Address:	3945 Kenosha Avenue San Diego, CA 92117
Phone:	619-490-0368
Fax:	619-490-0177
ASP member:	Yes
Registration:	$169
Special notes:	Extensive online help files

you might get better performance by installing ComTAP to a bootable floppy disk. Your first step should be to copy the COM-TAP21.ZIP archive to your floppy disk or a temporary subdirectory on the hard drive. Switch to the subdirectory (or floppy disk) and run PKUNZIP to decompress the archive file. Once the archive is decompressed, you will need to execute the INSTALL.EXE routine to complete the program installation. Note that you can exit the utility at any time by pressing <Ctrl>–<Break>, but the comTAP installation will not be complete. Do not attempt to run the program if you have aborted the installation process! You will be prompted for the type of monitor you are using, the letter of the source drive containing your copy of the comTAP program, the destination drive letter, and the name of the destination directory you want to contain the program files. Installation then concludes quickly.

Operation

You can launch ComTAP by typing PALS from the DOS command line. When the program starts, you will see a main screen similar to the one in Figure 5-2. The main menu is presented along the top of the display: File, Display, Configure, and Log. You can select each feature by pressing and holding down <Alt> and then typing the corresponding menu letter. The File menu allows you to create a new file, open an existing file, learn more about ComTAP, or exit to DOS. The Display menu lets you configure the way data is presented and control the buffers that hold sampled data. The Configure menu supports logging activity, hardware configurations, and defining other system options. Finally, the Log menu controls system logging activity.

You can define which windows are shown in the display (up to four), but by default you will see only three: Buffer, Log, and Characters. Buffer activity is shown in the upper left window, and the display indicates how the buffer fills (up to 128KB). The Log window shows the state of the system log, and keeps track of its activity. The Character window actually tracks the data being monitored by ComTAP.

Performance

ComTAP is a fairly sophisticated monitoring program capable of very fast operation. In addition, there are some other features that affect performance, such as macro display settings; you can record up to six display combinations for one-touch recall. Com-TAP provides resolution that can pick out individual data events to the microsecond. Context-sensitive hypertext provides extensive help. A hypersetup feature links directly to program setup

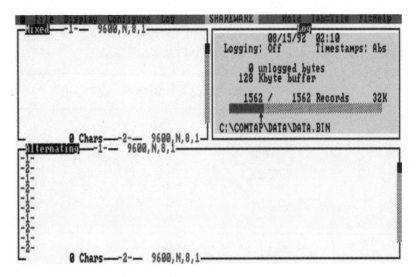

■ **5-2** *The Data Analysis menu/display in COMTAP.*

fields to allow interactive hypertext-prompted setup. Four user color sets (color, monochrome, grayscale, or LCD) support all display types, even laptops. The program has an 8MB archive capacity with auto-halt (when full) and continuous (wraparound) modes. You will need ample disk space for such a large archive. A snapshot disk logging feature allows you to log the RAM buffer data to disk at any time. Finally, all COM ports, data rates, and UART types are supported.

Registration

If you plan to use ComTAP beyond a reasonable evaluation period, you must register the program with the program author. The registration for ComTAP is $169, which includes the latest program version, unlimited program support, and a 60-day money-back guarantee.

Summary

Though expensive, ComTAP provides serious technicians with a powerful and versatile tool for tracking serial data and port operation.

COMTEST.ZIP

Testing the serial connection between a computer and a serial device is an important task for technicians. There are tools to check the computer's hardware and tools to monitor the flow of serial signals, but COMTEST (Table 5-6) is one of the few tools for testing a serial connection by sending a command string to the device and reporting the response. You can use any command string you want by modifying the strings in COMTEST.TXT.

■ **Table 5-6 COMTEST fact sheet**

Program name:	ComTest
Executable file:	COMTEST.EXE
Purpose:	To test a PC's serial port and device
Version:	2.0 (c. 1993)
Operating system:	MS-DOS 3.3 or later
Compressed file:	COMTEST.ZIP (archive)
Author:	Bert Whetstone
ASP member:	No
Registration:	$0 shareware
Special notes:	None

Installation and configuration

COMTEST.EXE will work equally well from the hard drive or floppy disk, but since the program is intended to be a diagnostic, you might have better results installing the program to a bootable floppy disk. Copy the COMTEST.ZIP archive from the CD to a floppy disk or a subdirectory on your hard drive. Switch to the floppy drive (or subdirectory on the hard drive) and run PKUNZIP to decompress the archive file into its constituent components. Once the archive is decompressed, you can run COMTEST.EXE directly with no further installation requirements.

Operation

After COMTEST starts, the display will appear as shown in Figure 5-3. The main menu runs along the top of the display with six options: File, Baud, COM Port, Receiver, Transmitter, and Window. The File menu allows you to learn more about the program or exit to DOS. You can use the Baud menu to select working baud (bps) rates between 1,200 and 9,600. The COM Port menu lets you select COM1, COM2, COM3, and COM4. The Receiver and Transmitter menus optimize the way data is exchanged through the program. Finally, the Window menu allows you to adjust the display.

The lower part of the display lists the command strings available for use. For a one-time test, select the command of interest and

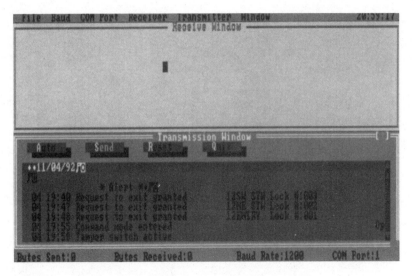

■ 5-3 *The Transmit/Receive windows of COMTEST.*

click on Send; this transmits the command, and any response is shown in the Receive window. You can automatically transmit a range of control strings for any given count, entering new commands in COMTEST.TXT. To use this feature, click on Auto in the Transmit window. A dialog box will appear with three fields: Count, From, and To. COMTEST will transmit a number of strings (specified by Count) that are selected randomly from the list box in the range From-To. When you have filled in these fields, click OK and the program will begin sending. To stop (or see how many iterations remain), just click on Auto again and enter 0 into the Count field.

Performance

The COMTEST program is relatively straightforward to operate, and its mouse support makes navigating between the menus very quick and easy. The program supports 1,200 to 9,600 bps, but it supports a data frame of only 8 data bits, no parity bit, and 1 stop bit (8, N, 1). COMTEST does have another known limitation; although serial receive interrupts are used, some data can be lost at higher baud rates when the data is transferred from the receive buffer to the display buffer.

Registration

COMTEST is $0 shareware, so you may use and distribute the program freely.

Summary

The COMTEST program sends predefined command strings to a serial peripheral and reports any result data, so it is particularly useful for testing devices like modems, which develop known responses to various commands.

CTSSPU22.EXE

Serious technicians need to know every facet of the serial port's operation, and take control over a PC's serial ports. The Serial Port Utilities from CTS (Table 5-7) provide you with a collection of DOS-based serial port tools that perform such advanced tasks as detecting multiple serial ports installed at the same address, informing you which trigger level is used in the 16550A UART, reporting the presence of "enhanced" serial ports (e.g., Telcor T/Port, Hayes ESP, and Practical Peripherals HSSP), and reporting the presence of emulated UARTS. Each of the CTS utilities support all standard and user-defined serial ports (defined in the command line or in the system environment variables).

Installation and configuration

The programs contained in your CTSSPU22 package will run equally well from the hard drive or floppy drive, but your choice

■ **Table 5-7 CTSSPU22 fact sheet**

Program name:	Serial Port Utilities
Executable file:	PORTINFO.EXE (and several other utilities)
Purpose:	To test serial port operation and performance
Version:	2.20a (c. 1994)
Operating system:	MS-DOS 3.3 or later
Compressed file:	CTSSPU22.EXE (self-extracting)
Author:	John Jerrim
Address:	Computer Telecommunication Systems, Inc. 3847 Foxwood Road, Suite 1000 Duluth, GA 30136-6100
Phone:	404-263-8623
Fax:	404-263-0124
CompuServe:	76662,2315
Internet:	76662.2315@compuserve.com
ASP member:	Yes
Registration:	$20 to $79, depending on the license
Special notes:	Perhaps the most comprehensive set of tools available for serial ports

of installation will depend on which programs you intend to use. Diagnostic programs such as PORTINFO are usually best installed to a bootable floppy disk kept in your toolbox. On the other hand, utilities such as COM_FMT that are used to control the serial port are often best installed to the system's hard drive. If you do install the programs to a hard drive, it is often advisable to include the subdirectory in the system's PATH statement.

If you plan to install CTSSPU22 to a hard drive, create a subdirectory for it. Copy the self-extracting CTSSPU22.EXE file to the subdirectory or floppy disk. Switch to the subdirectory (or floppy drive) and run CTSSPU to extract the archive into its constituent files. Once the archive is decompressed, you can run each of the utilities directly without any further installation.

Operation

There are a number of important programs provided with your CTSSPU22 package. The following sections outline the purpose and general operation of each program.

PORTINFO.EXE

PORTINFO is a comprehensive diagnostic tool that tests a computer system to determine everything possible about your serial ports (including interrupt and address conflicts). If a problem is detected, PORTINFO will provide you with appropriate failure and warning messages about actual and possible conflicts. You can launch the program by typing PORTINFO. When you launch PORTINFO, you will see a data report, as shown in Figure 5-4.

```
PortInfo Summary Screen

                          Serial 1     Serial 2    Serial 3    Serial 4

    Port Address (Hex)       3F8          2F8         3E8         N/A
    Interrupt (IRQ)           4            3          10
    IRQ (Out2) Enabled       No           Yes         No

    DOS uses port as        Com1         Com2        Com3         N/A
    Device Detected      ExtFAXModem     Mouse      FAXModem     Display
    FAX Service Class      0,1,2.0                    0,1

    Type of Port           T/Port        16450       16550A
    Buffer - Trigger        None         None        On-8
    Speed                  19200         1200        2400
    Bits / Character          8            7           8
    Parity                  None         None        None
    Stop Bits                 1            1           1

    Clear to Send            On           Off         Off
    Data Set Ready           On           Off         Off
    Ring Indicator          Off           Off         Off
    Data Carrier Detect      On           Off         Off
    Data Terminal Ready     Off           On          Off
    Request to Send         Off           On          Off
```

■ **5-4** *A typical PORTINFO summary report.*

The detailed report provides a complete breakdown of serial port operation and conditions, such as:

☐ The actual IRQ used by each port and the current IRQ status

☐ The DOS port assignments (e.g., COM1 through COM4 and mouse)

☐ The UART identification (e.g., 8250, 8250A/16450, 16550, 16550A, T/Port, both types of Hayes ESPs, Practical Peripherals' HSSP, and some emulated UARTs)

☐ The FIFO status (if FIFO is ON, the current FIFO receiver trigger level is displayed)

☐ All programmable port parameters, such as speed, format, parity, and current RTS or DTR settings

☐ The current status of modem lines, such as Ring Indicator, Carrier Detect, Clear to Send, Data Set Ready, and an indication of when the lines are tied together (looped back)

As you might expect, the PORTINFO program uses a fair number of basic and advanced command-line switches. The most common are as follows:

/n The port number (1 through 8 and 0 for all ports)

/Q Performs a quick test and skips conflict testing

/L Generates a log file called PORTINFO.LOG

/Axxx Tests the port at the specified address (in hex)

/? Displays help information

/B Installs all detected ports to the BIOS data area

/ESP Enables Hayes ESP port detection

/LA Appends the existing log file

/LP Prints the log file to LPT1

/Plug Detects the presence of a loop-back plug on the port

/S Generates a short report

Xaxxx Excludes the port at the specified address from testing

Xixx Excludes the specified IRQ line from testing

For example, to perform a quick test of the port at address 2E8 and create a log file, use the PORTINFO command with the following syntax:

C:\> PORTINFO /A2E8 /Q /L <Enter>

PORTINFO provides warnings under a variety of important conditions:

☐ When multiple serial ports are used at the same address (e.g., two COM1 ports)

☐ When interrupt conflicts occur between a bus mouse and a serial port

☐ When interrupts are shared (two serial ports or a serial port and a serial mouse sharing an IRQ)

☐ When the local loop-back test accurately identifies failed serial ports

☐ When conflicts occur between COM4- and 8514/A-compatible monitors

☐ When unusual serial port setups (BIOS and DOS port assignments) are detected

☐ When serial ports cannot generate interrupts

PORTINFO also serves as an information tool by:

☐ Helping to determine when interrupts can be shared

☐ Identifying which ports have active modems (and possibly determining if the modem is internal or external)

☐ Identifying fax-modem installation (with supported fax classes included in the summary report)

BUFFER.EXE

The BUFFER utility allows you to control the FIFO buffers in a current 16550A or compatible UART. You can turn the buffers on and off and set the receiver trigger level. The syntax for BUFFER is:

C:\> BUFFER [/port] [/On /Off] [/T trigger]

where the port number is 1 to 8 (0 for all ports), /On and /Off rurn the FIFO on or off respectively, and the trigger term can be 1, 4, 8, or 14 (the default). For example, to set the COM1 buffer trigger on for eight characters, use:

C:\> BUFFER /1 /On /T8 <Enter>

COM_BPS.EXE

COM_BPS allows you to set a port's data rate (in bits per second, or *bps*) to any standard value supported by the serial port. This utility is normally used as a replacement for the DOS MODE command. The syntax for COM_BPS.EXE is:

C:\> COM_BPS.EXE [/*port*] [/S *data rate*]

where *port* is the port number 1 to 8 (0 for all ports). You can replace this by using a specific port address with the /A*xxx* switch (e.g., /A3F8). The *data rate* is any standard entry from 110 to 115,200 bps. To set port 1 for 9,600 bps, for example, use the following command:

C:\> COM_BPS /1 /S9600 <Enter>

COM_FMT.EXE

COM_FMT allows you to set a port character format to any standard value supported by the serial port. This utility is normally used with COM_BPS as a replacement for the DOS MODE command. The syntax used with COM_FMT.EXE is:

C:\> COM_FMT.EXE [/*port*] [/F *format*]

where *port* is the port number from 1 to 8 (0 for all ports). This can be replaced with a specific port address with the /A*xxx* switch (e.g., /A3F8). The *format* can be any standard combination of data bits, parity, and stop bits (in that order). For example, a format of 8 data bits, no parity, and 1 stop bit would be denoted 8*n*1. To set the data format at port 1 for 7 data bits, even parity, and one stop bit, you would use the following command:

C:\> COM_FMT /1 /F7e1 <Enter>

DOS_COM.EXE

You use DOS_COM to insert a serial port in the BIOS data area used by DOS. Only two command-line switches are available: /# (1 to 4), which assigns a "standard" port address for the corresponding port, and /A*xxx*, which adds the base address of a port if the address is nonstandard. For example, to set COM4 to address 2E8, you would use the following command:

C:\> DOS_COM /4 /A2E8 <Enter>

DOS_SWAP.EXE

DOS_SWAP allows you to exchange two serial ports in the port list used by DOS. In the command line, you simply need to specify which two standard ports (1 to 4) you want to exchange. For example, you could exchange COM ports 1 and 3 with this command:

C:\> DOS_SWAP /1 /3 <Enter>

DTR.EXE

DTR gives you command-line control of the Data Terminal Ready (DTR) line of any serial port. You can turn the DTR line on or off for any standard port (1 to 8, or 0 for all ports), or any port address with the /A*xxx* switch. For example, to turn off the DTR line for port 1, use the following command:

C:\> DTR /1 /Off <Enter>

IRQ.EXE

IRQ allows you to enable and disable the interrupts from any serial port (1 to 8, or 0 for all ports). Instead of using standard port numbers, you can control specific port addresses using the /A*xxx* switch. For example, to disable the IRQ for COM1, use this command:

C:\> IRQ /1 /Off <Enter>

RESETCOM.EXE

The RESETCOM utility resets a serial port to its "power-up" configuration: port interrupts are disabled, the data rate is set to 2,400 bps, and the character format is set to eight data bits, no parity, and one stop bit. If the port is a 16550A-type device, then the FIFO buffers are disabled. This utility will often restore a port that doesn't work after you've run an ill-behaved application. To use the utility, you simply need to specify the port number (1 to 8, or 0 for all ports). For example, to reset COM2, use this command:

C:\> RESETCOM /2 <Enter>

RTS.EXE

RTS gives you command-line control of the Request To Send (RTS) line of any serial port. You can turn the RTS line on or off for any standard port (1 to 8, or 0 for all ports) or any port address with the /A*xxx* switch. For example, to turn off the RTS line for port 1, use the following command:

C:\> RTS /1 /Off <Enter>

Performance

Generally, each program runs quickly and cleanly with a minimum of user interaction (if any); this makes the programs ideal for use in AUTOEXEC.BAT or other specialized batch files. The extensive documentation and help files explain each program's operation in detail.

Perhaps the only issue relates to modems and PORTINFO. Some internal modems require the computer to have a "hard reset" before running PORTINFO to obtain correct results. If you observe a problem where PORTINFO does not detect an internal modem or the IRQ used by the modem, then either turn the computer off and back on to perform a hard reset or use the Reset button. Then try running PORTINFO again.

Registration

If you plan to use the CTSSPU programs beyond a 30-day evaluation period, you should register the package with CTS. There are four different types of registration depending on your particular needs: a single-user license is $20, an enhanced single-user license is $35, a professional single-user license is $59, and an enhanced professional single-user license is $79. Your registration buys the latest registered version of all utilities, printed documentation, bonus utilities, free updates for 12 months, and free support. If you install any portion of CTSSPU on a customer's PC, you should collect and forward the registration fee to the program author, or direct your customer to forward the registration fee directly.

Summary

The CTSSPU package is a first-rate, reasonably priced set of tools that every serious technician should consider acquiring. Each utility is small, easy to use, and specific in its task.

SIMTRM.ZIP

The SIMTRM package (Table 5-8) is a shareware terminal emulator that can assist users in isolating and resolving serial communication problems. With SIMTRM, you can open up to four serial ports at a time using any hardware-supported baud rate. Comprehensive handshaking control, loop-back tests, and configurable triggers make SIMTRM a flexible troubleshooting tool. There is also a monitor mode, which monitors communications between a DTE and DCE.

Installation and configuration

The SIMTRM package will run equally well from a hard drive or floppy disk. Since the program is intended to be used as a diagnostic, however, you will probably get the best results by installing the program to a bootable floppy disk. Create a subdirectory on your hard drive, then copy the SIMTRM.ZIP archive to the subdirectory or a floppy disk. Switch to the subdirectory (or floppy drive) and use PKUNZIP to decompress the archive file. Once the archive is decompressed, you can run the SIMPTERM.EXE program directly with no further configuration.

Operation and performance

Once you launch SIMPTERM.EXE, the program display will appear as shown in Figure 5-5. The main menu is along the top of

■ Table 5-8 SIMTRM fact sheet

Program name:	Simple Terminal Emulator (SimpTerm)
Executable file:	SIMPTERM.EXE
Purpose:	Utility to aid in the troubleshooting of serial problems
Version:	1.0
Operating system:	MS-DOS 3.3 or later
Compressed file:	SIMTRM.ZIP (archive)
Author:	Rick Hardy
Address:	B&B Electronics Mfg. Co. P.O. Box 1040 Ottawa, IL 61350
Phone:	815-434-0846
ASP member:	No
Registration:	$50
Special notes:	A good serial troubleshooting tool

the display, with the following options: Port, Control, Options, Display, and Config. The Port menu opens the desired serial port(s) for testing. Control options handle tasks like RTS, DTR, and FIFO management. The Options menu allows you to define operating attributes like triggers and test modes. Entries in the Display menu let you define how data is presented in the display. Finally, the Config menu supports the loading and saving of current test conditions. You can access all the menus in SIMPTERM by pressing and holding down <Alt>, then typing the appropriate menu key. Use the right and left arrow keys to move to the next or previous menu, and the up and down arrow keys to move to the next or previous layer of menu items. Some of the menu items have a key or key sequence to the right of the option; this is a "hot key" that you can use at any time to access that menu function.

The large open area just beneath the main menu is the terminal screen. This is the area where all the characters that are transmitted and received are displayed. On color monitors, the transmitted characters are displayed in yellow and the received characters are represented in cyan. On a monochrome monitor, the transmitted characters are displayed in white and the received characters are shown in gray. If an overrun error, parity error, framing error, or break interrupt is detected, the character will blink. When a port is in split mode, a horizontal line divides the terminal screen, displaying the transmitted characters (DTE) in the upper half and the received characters (DCE) in the lower half. A 45-line circular buffer is maintained for each of the opened ports.

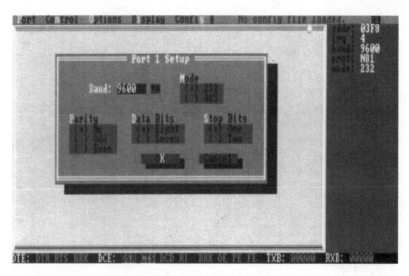

The Setup dialog in SIMTRM.

The Setup window is located on the right side of the terminal screen when the Settings option is selected. This is a constant reminder of the port settings, such as address, IRQ, baud rate, and data format. As the port settings change, the data in this windows will change to reflect it.

The handshake line is located at the bottom of the display screen. This line of information keeps track of each handshaking state of the monitored port. The line is split up into four sections. The DTE section displays the state of DTR (data terminal ready), RTS (request to send), and BRK (break). The DCE section displays the state of DSR (data set ready), CTS (clear to send), DCD (data carrier detect), and RI (ring indicator). The third section outlines the error flags: BRK (break), OE (overrun error), PE (parity error), and FE (framing error). If one or more of these errors occur on a receive character, the state will be set until the next receive or transmit character is displayed. The fourth section tracks the current size of the TXB (transmit) and RXB (receive) buffers.

Registration

If you plan to use SIMPTERM beyond a reasonable evaluation period, you should register the product with the software author. For $50, you will get the latest version of SIMPTERM, a printed manual, and technical support. You can also register SIMPTERM via CompuServe by typing GO SWREG and entering registration number 5281.

Summary

SIMPTERM can be an important tool for any technician testing the connection between a PC serial port and peripheral. Its low cost and flexible configuration options make the program ideal for a wide variety of hardware configurations.

UARTTS.ZIP

When working with serial ports, it is often necessary to obtain accurate identification of the corresponding UART; older UARTs can provide immediate clues to limited data rates and other serial port problems. The UARTTS.ZIP package (Table 5-9) provides technicians with a simple and straightforward port analysis tool that can identify the UART in use. Other programs reviewed in this chapter also report on the type of UART, but UARTTS.ZIP offers a simpler, more direct, and less expensive tool.

■ Table 5-9 UARTTS fact sheet

Program name:	UART Port Identifier
Executable file:	UART.COM
Purpose:	To identify COM port hardware characteristics
Version:	1.2 (c. 1993)
Operating system:	MS-DOS 3.3 or later
Compressed file:	UARTTS.ZIP (archive)
Author:	Rodey Green
ASP member:	No
Registration:	$0 shareware
Special notes:	Tests UARTs only

185

Installation and configuration

The UARTTS package will run equally well from a hard drive or floppy disk, but the program is intended to be used as a diagnostic so you will probably get the best results by installing the program to a bootable floppy disk. Create a subdirectory on your hard drive and copy the UARTTS.ZIP archive to the subdirectory or floppy disk. Switch to the subdirectory (or floppy drive) and use PKUNZIP to decompress the archive file. Once the archive is decompressed, you can run the UART.COM program directly with no further configuration.

Operation

UART.COM is designed to operate on the four standard COM ports (COM1 through COM4) and it can detect 8250, 16450, 16550AF, and Type 3 DMA-style UART operation. Running UART.COM is relatively simple; you need only specify the port to test, such as:

C:\> UART COM4 <Enter>

Once the program executes, you will see a report similar to this one:

COM4: is at hex port address: 02E8.
AT style 16450 unbuffered UART.
Port correctly configured to IRQ 3.

Performance

The UART.COM program can be fooled by OS/2, which falsely images all UART chips to look like the old 8250. DESQview can prevent UART.COM from accessing COM ports if you don't give permission in the DESQview PIF. Don't use UART on COM ports that are being actively used by a mouse or modem (UART works by temporarily reprogramming the port and sending it an NUL character).

Registration

UART.COM is $0 shareware, so you may use and distribute it freely.

Summary

UART.COM is one of those free tools you don't think about until you need it, but for quick checks of a serial port's UART, the program can be indispensable.

Modem utilities

The serial port software discussed in the previous section is very effective at checking a port's operation or serial port connections, but it is not always effective when it comes to actually checking peripherals such as modems. A few shareware tools specialize in testing modems, and this part of the chapter outlines the available products.

LISTEN10.ZIP

The LISTEN10.ZIP package (Table 5-10) is a batch file utility that allows you to test remote access situations (where a PC is powered on remotely). The computer has no way of knowing whether it was powered on by hand or by telephone. Most configurations use a special pause command in batch files that waits a specific amount of time for a key press. If no key is pressed, the batch file will load the remote communication software. The LISTEN utility monitors the modem for a ringing status. If there is no ringing, LISTEN tells the batch file (usually AUTOEXEC.BAT) that there is no ringing, so the batch file can branch off accordingly. If there *is* ringing, it also notifies the batch file of the situation. This method means that an operator doesn't need to watch the computer boot up and wait.

■ **Table 5-10 LISTEN10 fact sheet**

Program name:	Modem Listen Utility
Executable file:	LISTEN.EXE
Purpose:	To listen for incoming ring signals
Version:	1.0 (c. 1994)
Operating system:	MS-DOS 3.3 or later
Compressed file:	LISTEN10.ZIP (archive)
Author:	No Preservatives Software
Address:	5135 E. Evergreen St. #1272 Mesa, AZ 85205
Phone:	602-924-4878
ASP member:	No
Registration:	$10
Special notes:	Used mainly with remote access systems

Installation and configuration

LISTEN is designed as a batch file utility for returning conditions that a batch file (usually AUTOEXEC.BAT) can use to select different system configurations. As a result, you should install the program to your hard drive and run it from your AUTOEXEC.BAT file. Create a subdirectory on the hard drive and copy LISTEN10.ZIP from the CD to the subdirectory. Switch to the subdirectory and use PKUNZIP to decompress the archive.

To use LISTEN, you must activate it in the AUTOEXEC.BAT file. When using the program, you must also include two command-line arguments: the serial port number (1 to 4) and the ring delay (in seconds, using the -s switch). The following example AUTOEXEC.BAT file will run LISTEN with a ring delay of 6.5 seconds and a modem at COM2:

```
@ echo off
prompt $p$g
c:\dos\smartdrv.exe
c:\dos\doskey
listen 2 -s6.5
if not exist ring goto end
c:
cd \host
host
:end
```

Operation and performance

The full syntax for LISTEN is as follows:

LISTEN [*port*] [-s*delay*] [-m]

where port is the serial port where the modem is attached (1 to 4). Note that LISTEN automatically determines the port address for your computer's COM ports. For a list of them, type LISTEN with no parameters. The -s parameter specifies the maximum number of seconds to wait for ring status (optional). The default (if no delay specified) is 7 seconds. The -m parameter uses the modem status register (optional). Use this if the standard mode doesn't recognize rings or if you don't have a Hayes-compatible modem. This method detects rings faster, but is less compatible with all modems.

Registration

If you continue to use the program after 30 days, you must register LISTEN with the program author for $10. If you install LISTEN on a customer's PC, collect and forward the registration fee to the program author or direct your customer to remit the proper fee directly.

Summary

The LISTEN.EXE program is a handy tool for remote system operation when the system configuration depends on whether the system is activated locally or remotely. It is not a program you will use regularly, but it might be just the tool for remote use.

188

Drive tools

6

Now, more than ever before, PC drives are defining computer performance and capabilities. Quick access times, fast data transfer rates, and truly massive storage capacities are literally changing the way we use computers. The floppy drive still remains a standard medium for easy file exchanges, backups, and basic program distribution. Virtually all PCs are fitted with one 3.5-inch 1.44MB floppy drive. Hard drives now offer more than 2GB of storage space (with access times under 10 ms). Such huge amounts of on-line storage open possibilities for large operating systems (e.g., Windows 95) and their applications. Hard drives also commonly supplement RAM by serving as virtual memory, so drive performance now has a profound effect on overall system performance. CD-ROM drives offer large blocks of permanent storage, and their discs are now the medium of choice for distributing major software packages and databases. Plus, the traditionally slow access and data transfer times of CD-ROM drives are continually improving. This chapter presents you with a suite of tools (Table 6-1) for testing, cleaning, and optimizing these different types of drives.

Important It is impossible to test these programs on every possible configuration of PC hardware. If you cannot get the program to run (or encounter unexpected results), contact the program's author for more information.

System backup I highly recommend that you perform a complete system backup before attempting to use system diagnostics and utilities. In the event that system errors or unexpected program results accidentally damage your programs or data, a backup will allow you restore your information quickly and easily.

Virus warning As a general operating procedure, you should never attempt to run a new program without first checking it for viruses. Decompress the program and then run your virus checker. If a virus is detected, take all necessary steps to neutralize it.

■ Table 6-1: Drive tools and diagnostics

Filename	Description
General drive tools	
DAAG310.ZIP	Disk-at-a-glance utility
DATA_REC.ZIP	Data recovery utility
DDARP_13.ZIP	Device driver information utility
DISKUTIL.ZIP	Disk drive utility
DKI191.ZIP	Disk analyzer 1.91
SREP.ZIP	SmartDrive report utility
Floppy drive tools	
AUTOTEST.ZIP	Floppy/hard drive speed test
CHKDRV.ZIP	Floppy changeline diagnostic
CLEAN4.ZIP	Floppy cleaning utility
DFR.ZIP	Diskette recovery software
Hard drive tools	
BOOTRX.ZIP	Boot sector reporter
CSCTEST2.ZIP	HDD evaluation utility
DUGIDE.ZIP	IDE identifier utility
FIPS10.ZIP	Partition splitting utility
HDCP.ZIP	Hard disk backup utility
HDINFO.ZIP	Hard drive information utility
IDATA.ZIP	Identifies ATA drives
PARTITV1.ZIP	Partition analyzer
CD-ROM drive tools	
CDCP10.ZIP	CD audio player utility
CDQCK120.ZIP	CD cache utility
CDSPEED.ZIP	CD-ROM drive tester
CDTA.ZIP	CD-ROM speed tester
DA7.ZIP	CD audio player utility

General drive tools

While PC drives have grown in importance, they can also be a weakness; drive failures have been known to corrupt files and lose data, resulting in the loss of weeks (if not months) of work. The general drive tools in this section provide technicians with several important capabilities, such as determining drive capacities, recovering lost data, and checking the performance of disk cache tools. While many of these tools will work on floppy drives or hard drives, the most common subject for these tools is the hard drive itself.

DAAG310.ZIP

When working on a customer's system, a technician must often be able to determine the existence and location of important files and subdirectories. Windows allows you to do this with programs such as the File Manager or Explorer; under DOS, however, the traditional DIR and CD commands prove to be slow and cumbersome. The Disk at a Glance utility (Table 6-2) provides you with a tree-structured directory map of your selected disk. With DAAG310, you can move quickly and easily between directories and subdirectories. In addition to a directory tree, DAAG310 provides graphic statistics of file and directory sizes, you can locate files by typing in partial names, and you can produce printed reports to help customers track the software installed on their respective machines.

■ Table 6-2: DAAG310 fact sheet

Program name:	Disk at a Glance
Executable file:	DAAG.EXE
Purpose:	Utility designed to display disk contents in a tree structure
Version:	3.10 (c. 1992)
Operating system:	MS-DOS 3.3 or later
Compressed file:	DAAG310.ZIP (archive)
Author:	Steve Leonard
Address:	212 Green Springs Ln. Madison, AL 35758
CompuServe:	73557,203
Internet:	73557.203@compuserve.com
ASP member:	No
Registration:	$15 (single user) and $149 (site license)
Special notes:	Ten-day evaluation period only for shareware

Installation and configuration

You can install DAAG310 to a hard drive or floppy disk, but since the program will be most useful in your toolbox, you will probably get the best results by installing it on a floppy disk, where you can take it from machine to machine. If you choose to use DAAG310 only on your own PC, go ahead and install it to the hard drive. If you choose a hard drive installation, add the subdirectory to your PATH statement. Create a subdirectory for DAAG310, then copy the DAAG310.ZIP archive file to the subdirectory or floppy disk.

Switch to the subdirectory (or floppy drive) and run PKUNZIP to decompress the archive. Once the constituent files are decompressed, you can run DAAG.EXE directly.

Operation

When you start DAAG310, the tree menu will appear, as shown in Figure 6-1. The menu lists each directory, the directory size, cumulative size, the number of files in the directory, and the percentage of total disk space used by the files in that directory. At the bottom of the tree, a summary line details the total amount of space on the drive, the space used, and the space remaining. You navigate around the menu and scroll through the tree by using the up and down arrow keys, <Page Up> and <Page Down> keys, and the <Home> and <End> keys. As an alternative, begin typing the name of the desired directory, and the highlight will jump to that directory as you type. DAAG310 is also mouse-aware, so you can scroll around the menu tree by using the scroll bars, then click on the directory of interest.

After you highlight a directory, pressing <Enter> will provide a summary of the highlighted directory and display a scrolling window of files and sizes, grouped by extension. Hitting any key will cause the highlight to jump to the first entry beginning with that letter. Pressing <Enter> (or clicking the left mouse button with the cursor on the OK box) will open up a third scrolling window of filenames containing the highlighted extension. This window can also be sorted by filename or size. You can delete individual files in this

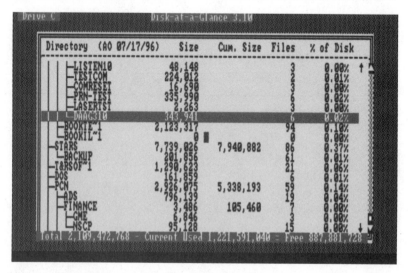

■ **6-1** *The disk tree structure shown in DAAG310.*

scrolling window by hitting the <Del> key or clicking on the Del button.

When working with the menu tree, there are some hints to help you understand the information better. First, the AO Date is the date that the menu tree file was last generated. You should periodically regenerate this tree with the <F7> key. Second, hidden directories appear with an H following the directory name. Next, the Cumulative Size column for any directory refers to the number of bytes in all the child directories of that directory, plus the number of bytes in the directory itself. If the directory has no subdirectories, the cumulative value is left blank.

Hitting <F2> from the main window will present you with a list of other available logical disk drives (A: and B: are not included). Use the arrow keys to select a drive and hit <Enter>. You can also type the drive letter or click on the desired letter to change to a particular drive.

DAAG310 can produce three different types of graphs (note that this requires EGA and higher graphics): a pie chart (Figure 6-2) showing the top 16 directories <F3>, a pie chart showing the top 16 first-level subdirectories <F4>, and a pie chart showing the top directories in the current branch <F5>. Once you press <Esc> or <Enter>, a bar graph will be displayed. Bar graphs shows all directories, but only about 50 can be displayed at a time (or the directory names start to collide). The density of the bar graphs is controlled by <F3> (increase by 5) and <F4> (decrease by 5). Hit or click the left and right arrow keys to shift the bar graph left or right one bar at a time. Hit <Ctrl>–<left arrow> or <Ctrl>–<right arrow> to shift left and right five bars at a time. Press <Enter> or <Esc>, or click the Exit button to return to the menu tree.

Hit the <F8> key or click on the asterisk (*) on the bottom line to print the menu tree report. A dialog box will prompt you to enter an optional machine ID, which is useful if you manage several different machines. If using a mouse, you can click within the dialog box to get the on-screen keyboard and type in the machine ID entirely with the mouse.

Performance

Once you master a few basic keys, DAAG310 is a fairly simple and straightforward program to operate. Just keep in mind that it needs about 370KB of RAM to run, so run the program from DOS and remove any unnecessary TSRs.

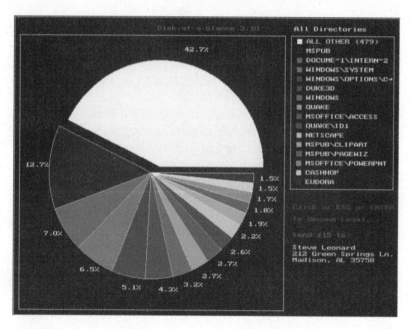

Disk at a Glance 3.10   All Directories

- ALL OTHER (479)
  MSPUB
- DOCUME~1\INTERN~2
- WINDOWS\SYSTEM
- WINDOWS\OPTIONS\C+
- DUKE3D
- WINDOWS
- QUAKE
- MSOFFICE\ACCESS
  QUAKE\ID1
- NETSCAPE
- MSPUB\CLIPART
- MSPUB\PAGEWIZ
- MSOFFICE\POWERPNT
- CASHHOP
  EUDORA

42.7%

12.7%

7.0%

6.5%

5.1%   4.3%   3.2%   2.7%   2.7%   2.6%   2.2%   1.9%   1.8%   1.7%   1.5%   1.5%

Send $15 to:

Steve Leonard
212 Green Springs Ln.
Madison, AL 35758

■ **6-2** *A pie chart breakdown of drive contents in DAAG310.*

Registration

If you continue to use DAAG310 after a 10-day evaluation period, you must register with the program author. A single-user registration is $15, and a site license is $149. You will receive the latest registered version of DAAG, as well as six handy bonus programs.

Summary

Disk at a Glance provides a quick and convenient means of navigating the contents of a hard drive without having to load Windows. This can be an invaluable asset if Windows is corrupted or malfunctioning, or other DOS-based troubleshooting is underway.

DATA_REC.ZIP

There is little that is more frustrating and frightening than a hard drive crash. Even with your work fully backed up, the time and expense of troubleshooting and drive replacement can be an expensive proposition. If you're caught unprepared, a drive crash can destroy weeks (or months) of invaluable hard work. Recovering data from a crashed hard drive is more of an art than a science and few tools are actually up to the task, but Tiramisu (Table 6-3) is one of the only shareware tools available that can reconstruct data from failed drives. Tiramisu is designed to help drives that have been hit by a virus, scratched by a head crash, accidentally formatted or partitioned, corrupted by a power failure, or damaged by buggy applications. Tiramisu scans the drive even when there is physical damage, then analyzes and reconstructs the found data. The program works on drives without a readable boot sector, FAT, or directory entries—even drives that are no longer recognized by DOS.

Tiramisu automatically creates a virtual drive in memory. This virtual drive looks like a file manager, allowing you to see the lost directories and files of your crashed drive, then copy them to a safe medium. Tiramisu is nondestructive and read-only. It does not record any data onto your crashed drive. Recovered data is restored to another destination (e.g., another hard disk, diskette, or network).

■ **Table 6-3: DATA_REC fact sheet**

Program name:	Tiramisu Data Recovery
Executable file:	TIRAMISU.EXE
Purpose:	To recover data from a failed hard drive
Version:	Unknown (c. 1996)
Operating system:	MS-DOS 3.3 or later
Compressed file:	DATA_REC.ZIP (archive)
Author:	Uwe Gissemann
Address:	Plug 'n Play
	Crellestr. 6
	D-10827 Berlin
	Germany
E-mail:	101457.1447@compuserve.com
WWW:	http://ourworld.compuserve.com/homepages/data_recovery
ASP member:	No
Registration:	$99
Special notes:	Works best with plenty of available RAM

Installation and configuration

Assuming the hard drive has failed, you should install Tiramisu on a bootable floppy disk. Copy the DATA_REC.ZIP archive from the DLS Diagnostic CD to your floppy disk, switch to the floppy drive, and run PKUNZIP to decompress the archive file. Once the archive is decompressed, you can boot the faulty PC and use TIRAMISU.EXE directly. The boot disk should be as "clean" as possible, but it should have a minimum CONFIG.SYS file available to load basic memory-management functions. A typical CONFIG.SYS file is as follows:

```
files=25
device=himem.sys
device=emm386.exe
```

If the CMOS contents have been lost or changed, make sure the correct drive geometry is entered in CMOS.

Operation

When you launch Tiramisu, the main display appears as shown in Figure 6-3. The program identifies your system's first hard drive and its geometry in the left window. If you have a second hard drive, its information will be shown in the right window. When recovery is in operation, the progress is displayed in the bottom window. The main menu along the top of the display lets you configure and control program operation through File, Info, Options, and Help.

To start recovery, select File and Start Recovery. You can specify where the recovered files should go. By default, Tiramisu uses EMS as the active swap area. If for some reason there is no (or not enough) EMS, you can specify a swap area on disk. Select Options and Data Recovery, tag Disk Allowed, and specify the path. (Caution: do not swap to the drive you intend to recover.) Tiramisu will start processing. Depending on your system's speed and drive size, this can take anywhere from five minutes up to an hour.

Performance

There are some things to keep in mind when running Tiramisu. First, the program can handle only drives with 16-bit FATs (which applies to most systems); fortunately, only old (e.g., 10MB) drives have 12-bit FATs. If you have more than one partition, you can re-

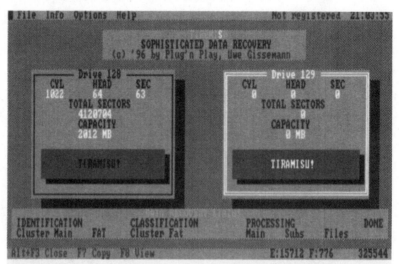

■ **6-3** *The main data recovery screen in DATA_REC.*

196

cover only the first one. There is a work-around, however; physically copy the partition you want to recover to another drive. Finally, Tiramisu is very memory-hungry and your PC might run out of memory. If you encounter this problem, install a memory manager with as much RAM and EMS as possible. Watch the available memory displayed at the bottom line. The value displayed at the far right shows the free RAM. The E:xxx figure shows the free EMS, and the F:xxx figure shows the fragmentation. Note that the RAM should not go below 50KB.

Registration

You are welcome to try Tiramisu for a reasonable evaluation period, but if you continue to use the program, you should register it with the program author. The registration is $99, which allows you to copy recovered files from a specified set of drives. The unregistered version has all functions for recovering your crashed hard drive, but only the registered version of Tiramisu allows you to actually copy files from your recovered drive. You can find more about the specific registration procedure in the accompanying documentation.

Summary

Tiramisu is one of the few shareware programs that allows you to recover damaged or corrupted files. The registration price is extremely reasonable considering how indispensable the program can be if your hard drive crashes and you lose crucial data.

DDARP_13.ZIP

One of the problems with TSRs and device drivers is that there are no rules for how they should work together. As a result, they often conflict. Since driver conflicts usually affect drive systems, technicians troubleshooting a drive problem should be sensitive to the drivers running on that particular system. Booting a system clean can clear driver-related problems, but knowing which drivers are the culprits requires a tool to show you which drivers are running. DDARP (Table 6-4) can display the installed device drivers in memory and rename a driver in memory.

Installation and configuration

The DDARP package can be run from the hard drive or a floppy disk. If you simply plan to use DDARP as a diagnostic tool, either installation would suffice. If you plan to use DDARP to rename drivers that might be conflicting, you should install the program

■ Table 6-4: DDARP_13 fact sheet

Program name:	Driver Display and Rename Program
Executable file:	DDARP.EXE
Purpose:	To identify and rename device drivers
Version:	1.3 (c. 1993)
Operating system:	MS-DOS 5.0 or later
Compressed file:	DDARP_13.ZIP (archive)
Author:	Robert Stuntz
Address:	2120 Aspen Dr. Woodstock, IL 60098
CompuServe:	71043,117
ASP member:	No
Registration:	$0 shareware
Special notes:	A handy tool to use when drivers conflict

to a hard drive. Copy the DDARP_13.ZIP archive file to a subdirectory on the hard drive or a floppy disk. Switch to the subdirectory (or floppy drive) and use PKUNZIP to decompress the archive. Once the archive is decompressed, you can run DDARP.EXE directly.

Operation

With no command-line arguments, DDARP reports the device drivers currently installed, producing a report such as the one shown in Figure 6-4. There are five columns of information; Address, Name, Type, Driver Attribute, and Driver File. The Address column lists the address of the driver's header in memory. Name specifies the name of the driver; if the driver is a block device, this field will be the number of block units associated with the driver. Character drivers have an eight-character name (which can include trailing spaces). The Type specifier is either blk or chr, depending on the driver type (block or character). The Driver Attribute is a 16-bit value describing the driver's capabilities. Finally, if the driver has its own memory control block (or MCB), then the name of the file it came from is shown in the Driver File column.

The drivers are displayed in ascending order, though you can use command-line switches to adjust the display. You can also use DDARP to rename a driver, using the following syntax:

C:> DDARP [*drvname1*] [*drvname2*] <Enter>

The first argument, *drvname1*, should be the name of the driver you want to rename. The second argument, *drvname2*, is what

```
DDARP  v1.3   Robert Stuntz

(Use /? for help)

Address      Name        Type   Driver Attribute      Driver File
---------    ---------   -----  --------------------  -----------
E003:0000    IFS$HLP$    (chr)  1101 0000 0000 0000   IFSHLP
0070:0016    CON         (chr)  1000 0000 0001 0011
0070:0028    AUX         (chr)  1000 0000 0000 0000
0070:003A    PRN         (chr)  1010 0000 1100 0000
0070:004C    CLOCK$      (chr)  1000 0000 0000 1000
0070:005E     3 unit(s)  (blk)  0000 1000 1100 0010
0070:006A    COM1        (chr)  1000 0000 0000 0000
0070:007C    LPT1        (chr)  1010 0000 1100 0000
0070:008E    LPT2        (chr)  1010 0000 1100 0000
0070:00A0    LPT3        (chr)  1010 0000 1100 0000
0070:00B8    COM2        (chr)  1000 0000 0000 0000
0070:00CA    COM3        (chr)  1000 0000 0000 0000
0070:00DC    COM4        (chr)  1000 0000 0000 0000
0070:012D    CONFIG$     (chr)  1100 0000 0000 0000
E0B6:0000    SETVERXX    (chr)  1000 0000 0000 0000   SETVER
00C9:0048    NUL         (chr)  1000 0000 0000 0100
0247:0000    XMSXXXX0    (chr)  1010 0000 0000 0000   HIMEM
0290:0000    EMMXXXX0    (chr)  1100 0000 0000 0000   EMM386
039E:0000    CMxRF121    (chr)  1000 0000 0000 0000   DWCFGMG
C803:0000    WP_CDROM    (chr)  1100 1000 0000 0000   WCD
```

■ **6-4** *A typical report from DDARP.*

you want to rename the driver. For example, to rename LPT1 to PRINTER1, you could use the following command:

C:> DDARP LPT1 PRINTER1 <Enter>

DDARP will generate a message reporting whether the rename was successful or not. When renaming a driver, DDARP starts at the beginning of the driver chain and searches for *drvname1*. All driver names are in uppercase, but you don't have to type the arguments in uppercase. Only chr-type drivers can be renamed. If you want to rename a driver to all spaces, specify =BLANK= as *drvname2*. Since you can't specify a name of eight spaces on the command line, =BLANK= will change the driver's name to all spaces (20h, 20h, 20h, 20h, 20h, 20h, 20h, 20h). You can also specify =BLANK= as *drvname1* when naming the driver back to what it was.

Performance

DDARP uses a number of command-line switches in order to optimize the program's operation:

/l Displays in ascending order, the default order. This is included in case you're used to using command-line arguments.

/d Displays in descending order.

/c Displays in the order the drivers are arranged on the driver chain.

/A Displays a brief explanation of the driver attribute word. A good programming book would probably describe these bits in greater detail.

/?, ?, z or /H Displays a small help screen on the program's syntax.

Registration

DDARP is $0 shareware, so you may use and distribute it freely.

Summary

DDARP can be a handy tool to use when device driver conflicts (or buggy drivers) cause problems with drive operation.

DISKUTIL.ZIP

The DISKUTIL package from Rich Belgard (Table 6-5) provides a technician with three different DOS tools for IDE drives. DISKTYPE. EXE lets you identify the hard disk manufacturer and/or model, and other geometry factors such as cylinders, heads, sectors per track, serial number, and firmware revision. IDLE.EXE serves as an "idle timer" to allow a drive motor to spin but shut off other functions. The STANDBY.EXE utility acts as a "standby timer" to shut down all drive power. The timer utilities are particularly useful with power-conscious systems such as notebook or laptop computers.

Installation and configuration

The choice of hard drive or floppy drive installation depends on your particular needs. You can use the DISKTYPE.EXE diagnostic from the hard drive, but you might prefer to install the program to a floppy disk and keep it in your toolbox. The IDLE.EXE and

■ **Table 6-5: DISKUTIL fact sheet**

Program name:	Disk Utilities
Executable file:	Several different utilities
Purpose:	To provide specialized services for IDE hard drives
Version:	1.0 (c. 1994)
Operating system:	MS-DOS 3.3 or later
Compressed file:	DISKUTIL.ZIP (archive)
Author:	Rich Belgard
America Online:	RICHB89600@aol.com
ASP member:	No
Registration:	$0 shareware
Special notes:	Will not work under Windows

STANDBY.EXE utilities are usually loaded each time the PC starts, so you will need to install them on a hard drive. Copy the DISKUTIL. ZIP archive to a subdirectory on the hard drive or a floppy disk. Switch to the subdirectory (or floppy drive) and use PKUNZIP to decompress the archive file. Once the archive is decompressed, you can run DISKTYPE.EXE directly. To run IDLE.EXE or STANDBY.EXE, you need to add their respective command lines to AUTOEXEC.BAT (or other batch file).

Operation

The three utilities included in DISKUTIL.ZIP are relatively straightforward to use, but each has their own subtle command-line differences. The following sections review each program.

DISKTYPE.EXE

When installing a new hard drive, you must enter the correct drive geometry (cylinders, heads, and so on) in CMOS. This allows BIOS to interact with the drive properly. While some drive manufacturers are getting better about listing the drive geometry on the drive itself, most unknown drives more than a few years old require you to contact the manufacturer to obtain the correct geometry numbers. This can also be a perplexing problem when CMOS contents are lost due to a failed battery. DISKTYPE.EXE reports the drive geometry, which you can then use to set CMOS contents. To run DISKTYPE, just start the program and use the drive number (0 for the first hard drive and 1 for the second hard drive), such as:

C:\> DISKTYPE [*drive* #] <Enter>

A report will be generated, as shown in Figure 6-5. IDE/AT disk controllers support two drives, a "master" and a "slave." The master is always drive 0. If there is only one disk present, it is the master. If two drives are present, drive 0 is the master and drive 1 is the slave. In the simplest case, drive 0 corresponds to the C: drive and drive 1 corresponds to the D: drive. Jumpers on the drive and/or CSEL line on the cable to the IDE controller determine which drive is which. DISKTYPE.EXE might even work correctly when the jumpers on a drive are improperly configured.

IDLE.EXE

The IDLE.EXE utility sets an idle timer, present on compatible IDE disk drives. This is a power management timer by which the drive can automatically lower its power consumption after a specified

```
Model Number: ST32140A

    Number of Cylinders: 4095
    Number of Heads:       16
    Sectors/Track:         63
    Serial Number:              JB181459
    Firmware Rev: 07.07.01
```

■ **6-5** *A typical report from DISKTYPE.*

amount of time (if it has not been accessed). In this idle mode, the
spindle motor is supposed to be running (the platters are spinning),
but other power is disabled. This allows fast access to the drive because the drive doesn't have to spin up, but it still saves some power.
Some drives do not conform to the IDE specification and will not
work with IDLE.EXE. The IDLE program requires two command-
line arguments: a drive number (0 or 1), and the timeout period (0
or 5 to 1200 seconds). Using 0 as a timeout period will disable the
timeout feature. Note that IDLE.EXE is not a TSR and requires no
memory after initial execution. A typical line to set drive 0 to a timeout of one minute might appear in AUTOEXEC.BAT such as this:

IDLE 0 60

STANDBY.EXE

The STANDBY.EXE utility runs much like IDLE, but STANDBY.EXE
powers down a compliant hard drive almost entirely (including the
spindle motor). This results in a much better power savings for the
computer, but once the platters spin down, it could take several moments for the drive to spin up again when an access is attempted.
The STANDBY program requires two command-line arguments: a
drive number (0 or 1) and the timeout period (0 or 60 to 1000 seconds). Using 0 as a timeout period will disable the timeout feature.
Note that STANDBY.EXE is not a TSR and requires no memory after its initial execution. A typical command line to set drive 0 to a
timeout of one minute might appear in AUTOEXEC.BAT like this:

STANDBY 0 60

Performance

IDLE and STANDBY are most useful in mobile computers, but you can
also use them to save power and drive life in desktop systems that are
left on overnight. Note that all three programs *must* run under DOS;
they will not work under Windows or in a DOS window. Also note that
the utilities might not run properly with a disk-caching controller.

Registration

The utilities in DISKUTIL.ZIP are provided as $0 shareware, so you may use and distribute them freely.

Summary

The DISKUTIL.ZIP package offers technicians a handy investigative tool, as well as some power-saving options for both mobile and desktop computers.

DKI191.ZIP

When working on an unknown system, it is often helpful to have a complete set of information about available drives and their characteristics. The DKI191.ZIP package from Philippe Duby (Table 6-6) provides complete information (as well as file management features) for IDE, SCSI, CD-ROM, network, and compressed drives. This ability to work with different popular drive types has made DKI popular as an administration tool, and a suite of command-line switches allows you to tailor the program's operation depending on your needs.

Installation and configuration

The DKI191.ZIP package can be installed to either a floppy disk or your hard drive. If you plan to use DKI as a diagnostic, you will probably get better results installing the program to a floppy disk

■ **Table 6-6: DKI191 fact sheet**

Program name:	Disk Information Utility
Executable file:	DKI.EXE
Purpose:	Determine information about all available drives
Version:	1.91 (c. 1994)
Operating system:	MS-DOS 3.3 or later
Compressed file:	DKI191.ZIP (archive)
Author:	Philippe Duby
Address:	7 rue Jules Vallss
	69100 Villeurbanne
	France
CompuServe:	73551,1561
E-mail:	duby@lanpc1.univ-lyon1.fr
ASP member:	No
Registration:	$10
Special notes:	Provides a very complete report

so you can carry it in your toolkit. Since DKI also reports on network and compressed drives, it should not be necessary to boot the PC clean before using the program. Copy the DKI191.ZIP archive to your floppy disk or a subdirectory on the hard drive. Switch to the floppy drive (or a subdirectory) and run PKUNZIP to decompress the archive file. Once the archive has been decompressed into its constituent components, you can run DKI.EXE directly.

Operation and performance

DKI is basically a command-line-driven program. The DKI command and switches allow you to tailor the report output you see (a complete listing of the DKI switches is shown in Table 6-7). The easiest way to use DKI is simply to run the program with no switches, such as this:

```
C:\> DKI <Enter>
```

This will produce a complete report of all drives detected in the computer. You can also limit the report to specific drives by adding the desired drive letter(s), such as:

```
C:\> DKI C: D: <Enter>
```

If you are interested only in the physical information related to your drive(s), use the /p switch:

```
C:\> DKI /p <Enter>
```

When there are too many lines of information to fit on a single DOS screen, you can display up to 50 lines in the maxscreen mode with the /m switch:

```
C:\> DKI /m <Enter>
```

DKI also supports verbose reports (/v), which count all files and directories:

```
C:\> DKI /v <Enter>
```

When you need information about particular directories only, you can specify the disk and path:

```
C:\> DKI c:\ <Enter>
C:\> DKI \windows <Enter>
```

Note that you can also mix several commands on the same command line, such as:

```
C:\> DKI c: d: <Enter>
C:\> DKI c:\dos c:\windows d: <Enter>
```

If you just want to study your PATH directories, use the /e switch:

C:\> DKI /e <Enter>

You can use DKI to obtain a summary of disk contents by subdirectory using the /0, /1, or /2 switches. The /1 switch will list all the first-level directories and /2 will list all second-level directories. The following command will provide a report of all the subdirectories from \windows, detailing the number of files inside and the size occupied by the directory on the disk:

C:\> DKI \windows /0 <Enter>

DKI can also be quite specific in the way it lists particular files. If you needed to find all the .GIF files in the first-level subdirectories of drive D:, you could use the following command:

C:\> DKI d:*.gif /1 <Enter>

If you needed to list all the programs in the DOS directory of your C: drive, you could use this command:

C:\> DKI c:\dos*.exe <Enter>

To delete unwanted files or directories, you can use the /d switch. However, there is no "safety catch" with the /d switch; once a file or directory is deleted, it's gone. Note: if DKI encounters a read-only file, it will ask you for confirmation before deleting it. Suppose you wanted to delete the \windows directory. You could use the following command:

C:\> DKI c:\windows /d <Enter>

DKI will also help you analyze your drive's contents. The /s switch lists the 10 biggest files from the current directory (sorted by decreasing size):

C:\> DKI /s <Enter>

You can put a number after /s to override the default of 10 files. For example, you could list the 30 biggest files under Windows using the 50-line display mode, with a command such as:

C:\> DKI d:\windows /ms30 <Enter>

The /t switch allows you to list files in the current directory that have been modified on the current date. Files are listed chronologically. For example:

C:\> DKI /t <Enter>

205

You can put a date after the /t switch to override the current date. For example, to list all the files on your computer that were updated or modified on 1/1/94, use a command such as:

C:\> DKI $: /t1/1/94 <Enter>

DKI can provide you with drive benchmark figures if you use the /b switch. Note that a disk cache will affect the test results, so you might have to disable the disk cache. This test will also work on CD-ROM drives, but you have to disable CD-ROM caching.

C:\> DKI c: /b <Enter>

Registration

If you continue to use DKI after a reasonable evaluation period, you must register it with the program author. A single-user registration is $10 and volume discounts are available. Registration will get you the latest version of DKI.

Summary

DKI is a remarkably versatile DOS-based disk reporting tool that can be invaluable to technicians preparing to upgrade a PC, or system administrators trying to keep an eye on their networks.

■ **Table 6-7: Summary of command-line switches for DKI191**

Switch	Description
/?	Command summary
/0	Lists all the directories scanned during a file search
/1,2	Same as above, but for directories before level 1 or 2
/a	Displays with ASCII 7 bit filter and no color, to allow for storing the result into a BBS message
/b	Unit drive benchmark
/d	Delete mode, to delete recursively directories and specified files
/g	Debugging information
/e	Scans the directories of the DOS PATH variable
/i	Facilitates DKI's installation by looking for an appropriate location to copy DKI and updating your AUTOEXEC.BAT file to add DKI and an XDEL macro
/m	Switches to Maxline mode (50 lines)
/p	Physical information
/s	Displays the n biggest files (sorted by size)
/t	Displays files modified by day (default is today, sorted by time)
/v	Verbose mode
/*	Full-information mode
/-	Bypass ASPI-SCSI detection

SREP.ZIP

Caching has become one of the most effective means of increasing disk performance. By storing often-used pieces of information in memory, disk accesses are reduced and apparent speed improves. Windows provides its own caching monitor, but there is no DOS-based tool to measure cache performance. The SmartReporter utility (Table 6-8) is a DOS-based solution for tracking the performance of SmartDrive. The "hit ratio" is of special importance; a low ratio means few cache hits, which means more memory must be allocated to SmartDrive.

Installation and configuration

SREP can be installed to a hard drive or floppy disk. Since the program is really intended for occasional or diagnostic use, you might get better results by installing SREP to a floppy disk and keeping it in your toolbox. Copy the SREP.ZIP archive to a floppy disk or subdirectory on the hard drive. Switch to the floppy drive or subdirectory, then run PKUNZIP to decompress the archive. Once the archive file is decompressed, you can run SMARTREP.COM directly.

Operation

When launched, SMARTREP.COM will load into memory and show the hit ratio for SmartDrive in the upper corner of your screen while you go about your normal computing activities. The hit percentage will print in green if your ratio is over 50 percent

■ Table 6-8: SREP fact sheet

Program name:	SmartDrive Monitor
Executable file:	SMARTREP.COM
Purpose:	Monitor SmartDrive performance under DOS
Version:	Unknown (c. 1994)
Operating system:	MS-DOS 3.3 or later
Compressed file:	SREP.ZIP (archive)
Author:	Scott Alan Hoopes
Address:	62 Plaza Drive
	New Albany, IN 47150
Phone:	812-948-8521
CompuServe:	73304,274
Internet:	73304.274@compuserve.com
ASP member:	No
Registration:	$5
Special notes:	Designed for DOS use

and red if it falls below 50 percent. You can upload SMARTREP.COM from memory by typing SMARTREP /U.

Performance

SMARTREP.COM is a simple utility that displays its data in basic text mode. As a result, it might not work properly (if at all) with some graphic programs, including Windows. Make it a point to use SMARTREP.COM with standard 80 × 25 DOS text programs. The program also might not work with caching programs other than SmartDrive.

Registration

If you continue to use SMARTREP.COM beyond a reasonable evaluation period, you must register it with the program author. The registration is $5 and includes the latest version of SMARTREP.COM, as well as a suite of additional utilities.

Summary

SMARTREP.COM is a basic tool for checking the performance of SmartDrive while running under DOS, and is particularly useful if Windows is corrupted or otherwise inoperative.

Floppy drive tools

Traditionally, the floppy drive has been the "lowest common denominator" among PCs, allowing you to exchange programs and data through very inexpensive floppy diskettes. Today, the explosive growth of networking, PC-to-PC data exchange, and online file transfers has reduced the need for floppy drives, but you can still find at least one in every desktop and tower PC. The following programs provide you with the means to test and clean typical floppy drives.

AUTOTEST.ZIP

Part of drive testing often involves measuring performance. While performance is not a crucial factor with floppy drives, poor performance (usually in conjunction with other DOS errors) might suggest a failing drive or the presence of a hardware conflict. The AUTOTEST.EXE diagnostic (Table 6-9) is designed to measure floppy drive performance by putting the drive through a series of random and sequential reads. Unusually long read times might suggest problems with the R/W heads, track-stepping motor, or spindle motor.

■ Table 6-9: AUTOTEST fact sheet

Program name:	Access Time Test Utility
Executable file:	AUTOTEST.EXE
Purpose:	Test the access times for floppy and hard disks
Version:	Unknown (c. 1987)
Operating system:	MS-DOS 3.3 or later
Compressed file:	AUTOTEST.ZIP (archive)
Author:	Unknown
ASP member:	No
Registration:	$0 shareware
Special notes:	No author or contact information

Installation and configuration

AUTOTEST can be installed to a hard drive or floppy disk. Since the program is really intended for occasional or diagnostic use, you might get better results by installing AUTOTEST to a floppy disk and keeping it in your toolbox. Copy the AUTOTEST.ZIP archive to a floppy disk or subdirectory on the hard drive. Switch to the floppy drive (or subdirectory), then run PKUNZIP to decompress the archive. Once the archive file is decompressed, you can run AUTOTEST.EXE directly.

Operation

The operation of AUTOTEST.EXE is automatic; simply type AUTOTEST and press <Enter>. The program will ask for the drive number to be tested (e.g., 0 for A: and 1 for B:). As the program runs over the course of several minutes, it will generate a performance report, such as the one shown in Figure 6-6. The report indicates the total number of sectors on the disk, then details the read times for both sequential and random tests. Note that there must be a diskette in the drive before AUTOTEST.EXE will run.

Performance

After you specify which drive to test, the AUTOTEST.EXE program runs automatically without the need for user input. You need to place a diskette in the drive before proceeding, and the diskette must be formatted. For best results, the diskette should contain a reasonable number of files (about 50 percent of the disk's capacity). The data should be safe because there are no write operations performed, but you might want to prepare a simple data disk with general files on it (things you don't need or have backed up

```
drive number (0=a , 1=b ...):
total number of sectors = 2847
Sequential Reads
   1 sectors            -    0.019 Sec/read
   8 sectors            -    0.137 Sec/read
  16 sectors            -    0.269 Sec/read
  24 sectors            -    0.404 Sec/read
Random Reads  -  1 sector
  0.10 width seeks      -    0.110 Sec/read
  0.33 width seeks      -    0.205 Sec/read
  0.50 width seeks      -    0.205 Sec/read
  0.90 width seeks      -    0.305 Sec/read
Random Reads  -  8 sector
  0.10 width seeks      -    0.179 Sec/read
  0.33 width seeks      -    0.280 Sec/read
  0.50 width seeks      -    0.379 Sec/read
  0.90 width seeks      -    0.470 Sec/read
```

■ **6-6** *A typical report from AUTOTEST.*

elsewhere). You should also consider write-protecting the disk to provide an extra measure of data safety.

Registration

The AUTOTEST.EXE program is provided as $0 shareware, so you may use and distribute it freely.

Summary

This is one of the only tools that can affix a quantitative number to your floppy drive's performance. It is a basic diagnostic, but it is free.

CHKDRV.ZIP

One of the most perplexing problems with floppy drives is the notorious "phantom directory," where the directory listing of a new diskette remains the same as the diskette just removed. The problem is innocuous unless you try writing to the new disk, which can overwrite and corrupt files on the new disk. The CHKDRV.ZIP package (Table 6-10) is designed to test the floppy drive for a working CHANGELINE signal. The absence of the CHANGELINE signal might indicate a floppy failure or a problem in the floppy signal cable.

Installation and configuration

CHKDRV can be installed to a hard drive or floppy disk, but since the program is generally intended for occasional or diagnostic use, you will probably get better results by installing CHKDRV to a floppy disk and keeping it in your toolbox. Copy the CHKDRV.ZIP archive to a floppy disk or subdirectory on the hard drive. Switch to the floppy drive (or subdirectory), then run PKUNZIP to decompress the archive. Once the archive file is decompressed, you can run CHKDRV.EXE directly without any further installation.

Operation

The CHKDRV.EXE program requires a command-line switch to specify which drive must be tested (A or B, with no colon), so a test of the A: drive would require the following command:

C:\> CHKDRV A <Enter>

During normal operation, CHKDRV.EXE first verifies that a valid floppy drive letter (A or B) was entered on the command line. The computer hardware is checked to ensure it will properly execute the program before attempting any disk access. You are then prompted to put a disk in the floppy drive. Note that any formatted floppy disk will work; CHKDRV.EXE never writes anything to the disk. If you want, you can set the write-protect tab for additional safety. Once the program verifies a disk in the drive, it will start the drive and prompt you to remove the disk. If the disk removal is detected, the CHANGELINE signal is working properly. Otherwise, try a new floppy drive.

Performance

There are several notes for using CHKDRV.EXE. First, wait for at least three seconds before removing a disk from the floppy drive; if

■ Table 6-10: CHKDRV fact sheet

Program name:	Changeline Check Utility
Executable file:	CHKDRV.EXE
Purpose:	Checks the activity of floppy-drive change-line signals
Version:	1.0 (c. 1991)
Operating system:	MS-DOS 3.3 or later
Compressed file:	CHKDRV.ZIP (archive)
Author:	Douglas S. Parman
Address:	Software Specialists 300D Versailles Drive Melbourne Beach, FL 32951
Phone:	407-984-0219
ASP member:	No
Registration:	$0 shareware
Special notes:	Used for all standard floppy drives

the program senses the disk's removal before that time, it will assume an error has occurred. Second, you can press the <Esc> key at any time during program execution and return to DOS. Finally, some drives are installed and configured with utilities such as DRIVER.SYS or the DOS DRIVPARM command. If a drive so configured does not respond properly, verify that the /C option is present in the DRIVER.SYS (or DRIVPARM command) entry for that drive, such as:

```
device=c:\dos\driver.sys /d:2 /t:80 /s:9 /c
```

Registration

The CHKDRV.EXE program is provided as $0 shareware, so you may use and distribute it freely.

Summary

The CHKDRV.EXE program can help technicians isolate a CHANGELINE problem quickly and effectively rather than having to swap drives or drive cables indiscriminately.

CLEAN4.ZIP

While the floppy drive is running, the R/W heads are always in contact with the diskette media. This scrapes off minute quantities of magnetic material. Eventually, magnetic material (as well as dust and debris from the surrounding air) accumulates and causes the heads to malfunction. Floppy drive R/W heads should be cleaned periodically to remove foreign matter. The CLEAN4.ZIP package (Table 6-11) is designed to help you clean your floppy drives. The program uses random tracks to accomplish the cleaning cycle, so you use more of the cleaning disk.

Installation and configuration

CLEAN4.ZIP can be installed to a hard drive or floppy disk, but since the program is generally intended for occasional or periodic use, you will probably get better results installing CLEAN4 to a floppy disk and keeping it in your toolbox. Copy the CLEAN4.ZIP archive to a floppy disk or subdirectory on the hard drive. Switch to the floppy drive (or subdirectory), then run PKUNZIP to decompress the archive. Once the archive file is decompressed, you can run CLEAN.EXE directly without any further installation.

Note: you need to insert a cleaning diskette in the desired drive before using CLEAN.EXE. You can obtain cleaning diskettes from almost any computer store or department store that sells computers.

Program name:	Floppy Drive Cleaning Utility
Executable file:	CLEAN.EXE
Purpose:	To clean the floppy drive
Version:	Unknown (c. 1990)
Operating system:	MS-DOS 3.3 or later
Compressed file:	CLEAN4.ZIP (archive)
Author:	Randy Stack
Address:	6222 Brookhill Circle
	Orlando, FL 32810
ASP member:	No
Registration:	$4
Special notes:	Works from a hard drive or floppy drive

Operation

The CLEAN.EXE program requires two command-line arguments: the number of seconds to run and the drive number to be used (A: is 0 and B: is 1). To run a cleaning cycle on drive A: for 60 seconds, you would use the following command:

```
C:\> CLEAN 60 0 <Enter>
```

Once the program starts, you will be prompted to insert a cleaning disk. After the cleaning cycle has started, you can terminate the cycle at any time by pressing any key. CLEAN works with 5.25 and 3.5-inch floppy drives in both high-density and double-density formats. As a measure of user protection, CLEAN will not permit access to fixed disk drives, nor will it affect any existing data on noncleaning disks, so files will be safe if you forget to insert a cleaning disk.

Performance

In actual operation, the program determines whether there is a disk in the drive to be cleaned (it will abort if a disk is not detected). CLEAN.EXE steps through all tracks and sectors of the disk, which allows complete use of your cleaning disk. The 5.25-inch cleaning disk must have an index hole for CLEAN.EXE to recognize that a disk is in the drive. The index hole is the small hole located $\frac{1}{2}$ inch from the center hub hole. Cleaning disks are sometimes supplied without this index hole, but you can cut one. The 3.5-inch disk does not use an index hole.

In the event that you are executing CLEAN.EXE from the same floppy drive you'll be cleaning, you will be prompted to insert the cleaning disk and press any key. Upon completion of the cleaning process, the "remove cleaning disk" message will be displayed. Take out your cleaning disk and replace it with the original disk from which CLEAN was executed, then press any key.

Registration

If you continue to use CLEAN.EXE after a reasonable evaluation period, you should register it with the program author. Registration is $4.

Summary

Floppy drives require regular cleaning. CLEAN.EXE is an inexpensive tool that will run the drive and maximize the use of your cleaning disk. This utility should have a place in your toolkit.

DFR.ZIP

Sometimes the data on a floppy disk is just as valuable as the data on a hard drive. When the floppy diskette fails, the loss of data or programs on it could be catastrophic. The DFR package from Mark Vitt (Table 6-12) is a highly automated recovery tool that specializes in recovering files from floppy disks. DFR can recover files to a hard drive or another floppy disk.

Installation and configuration

The DFR program can be run from either the hard drive or the floppy drive. Since you are trying to recover data from a floppy disk, however, you will probably get better results by installing the program to your hard drive (unless you have a second floppy drive

■ **Table 6-12: DFR fact sheet**

Program name:	Disk Recovery Utility
Executable file:	DFR.EXE
Purpose:	To recover data from a diskette
Version:	1.01 (c. 1991)
Operating system:	MS-DOS 3.3 or later
Compressed file:	DFR.ZIP (archive)
Author:	Mark Vitt
CompuServe:	70053,2236
Internet:	70053.2236@compuserve.com
ASP member:	No
Registration:	$0 shareware
Special notes:	Designed for floppy disks

available). Copy the DFR.ZIP archive to a subdirectory on the hard drive or a floppy disk. Switch to the subdirectory (or floppy drive) and run PKUNZIP to decompress the archive. Once the archive has been decompressed into its constituent files, you can run DFR.EXE directly.

Operation

There is little real documentation for DFR.EXE, but the program's operation is fairly automatic. The DFR command line requires three arguments: the source drive, the filename to be recovered, and the destination drive. You can use a fourth switch (T) to make text readable (this is optional). The generic command-line syntax is as follows:

C:\> DFR [*drive:filename*] [*destination drive*] [T]

For example, suppose you need to recover the file LIST.TXT from a failed floppy in drive A:, and you want to save the file to drive C:. You would issue the following command:

C:\> DFR A:LIST.TXT C: <Enter>

Performance

Ideally, recovery should take place between two identical floppy drives, but few PCs provide two identical floppy drives. In actual practice, files are recovered to a hard drive (often to the root directory), and those files can be copied to a fresh floppy disk later on.

Registration

The DFR.EXE program is provided as $0 shareware, so you may use and distribute it freely.

Summary

Although there is no real documentation for the program, DFR is quite straightforward to run. It might be just the tool for saving data on a failing floppy disk.

Hard drive tools

The hard drive is probably the single most important drive type. Its huge capacities and fast operation have made possible many of the powerful applications we now take for granted. As a technician, you need to be able to identify the hard drive(s) in a system quickly and accurately. Another important aspect of hard drive operation are performing backups, protecting your data from drive failures and computer viruses. Finally, hard drives can be separated into logical partitions. This is normally performed with the DOS FDISK utility, but there are third-party utilities that allow you to adjust partition sizes "on the fly." The software reviewed in this section provides you with tools to identify drive types, back up drive contents, and alter partition arrangements.

BOOTRX.ZIP

The boot record of a hard drive contains a great deal of information that is absolutely vital for the system's proper initialization. The BOOTRX.ZIP package (Table 6-13) is designed to read the data contained in a boot sector, then display the results in a report-type format. If you encounter problems with a drive's boot behavior, the BOOTRX program is an ideal tool for detecting missing or inconsistent data.

■ **Table 6-13: BOOTRX fact sheet**

Program name:	Boot Record Reporter
Executable file:	BOOTREX.COM
Purpose:	Displays the boot record parameters of a drive
Version:	1.2 (c. 1989)
Operating system:	MS-DOS 3.3 or later
Compressed file:	BOOTRX.ZIP (archive)
Author:	Jack A. Orman
Address:	P.O. Box 858
	Southaven, MS 38671
CompuServe:	72261,677
Internet:	72261.677@compuserve.com
ASP member:	No
Registration:	$20
Special notes:	Does not alter boot record information

Installation and configuration

The BOOTREX.COM program will run equally well from either a hard drive or a floppy disk, but since the program is intended to serve as a diagnostic, you might get better results by installing it to a floppy disk to keep in your toolbox. Copy the BOOTRX.ZIP archive to your floppy disk or a subdirectory on the hard drive. Switch to the floppy drive (or subdirectory) and use PKUNZIP to extract the archive. Once the archive has been decompressed, you can run BOOTREX.COM directly.

Operation

BOOTREX.COM uses only one command-line argument, the hard drive to be checked (such as C: or D:). Keep in mind that BOOTREX.COM will work on drives only up to D:. Once started, the program runs automatically and generates a report that is displayed on the monitor.

Performance

The BOOTREX.COM program runs quickly and accurately, but it does not write any information to your boot record. As a result, your boot record is safe.

Registration

If you use BOOTREX.COM for more than 30 days, you must register it with the program author. Registration is $20, which will get you the latest version of BOOTREX.COM, along with a supplemental utility disk from Jack Orman.

Summary

Fast and safe to use, BOOTREX.COM might be just the tool to help you track down problems with a drive's boot record.

CSCTEST2.ZIP

Drive performance is becoming an ever more important aspect of system performance, and technicians need to have some means of measuring drive performance. The CSCTEST2 package from Corporate Systems Center (Table 6-14) measures drive performance in both data access times (sequential and random) and data transfer rates (sequential and random). The results are displayed graphically.

Installation and configuration

CSCTEST2.ZIP can be used from a hard drive or floppy disk. Since the program is generally intended for occasional or diagnostic use, you will probably get better results by installing CSCTEST to a floppy disk and keeping it in your toolbox. Copy the CSCTEST2.ZIP archive to a floppy disk or subdirectory on the hard drive. Switch to the floppy drive (or subdirectory), then run PKUNZIP to decompress the archive. Once the archive file is decompressed, you can run the CSCTEST.BAT batch file directly without any further installation.

■ Table 6-14: CSCTEST2 fact sheet

Program name:	Hard Drive Benchmark
Executable file:	CSCTEST.BAT
Purpose:	To measure the performance of a hard drive
Version:	2.0 (c. 1991)
Operating system:	MS-DOS 3.3 or later
Compressed file:	CSCTEST2.ZIP (archive)
Author:	Corporate Systems Center
Address:	730 North Pastoria Ave. Sunnyvale, CA 94086
Phone:	408-737-7312
ASP member:	No
Registration:	$0 shareware
Special notes:	Might not work on all current drives

Operation

CSCTEST's operation is entirely automatic, and no user input is required. Once the batch file is started, the program evaluates drive performance; you will see a fancy hard drive graphic displayed while the test is in progress. After the test is complete, you will see the results displayed as a series of graphs, as shown in Figure 6-7. The graph on the left illustrates the data access time (in accesses per second) for both sequential and random reads. The graph on the right shows the data transfer rate (in sectors per second) for both sequential and random reads.

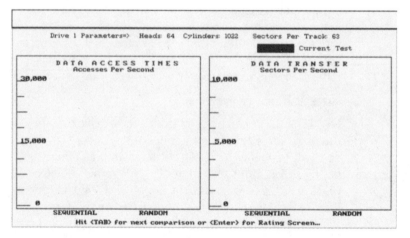

■ 6-7 *The graphic performance summary in CSCTEST2.*

Performance

The CSCTEST program is one of the more visually appealing diagnostics, but it is not quite as robust as many other reporting/benchmarking tools; the program failed to work with a 2GB hard drive on a Pentium 166-MHz system, though smaller drives on other systems appeared to check correctly.

Registration

CSCTEST is provided as $0 shareware, so you may use and distribute it freely.

Summary

CSCTEST clearly has its limitations, but, as a free tool, it's probably worthwhile for testing the performance of smaller hard drives.

DUGIDE.ZIP

Every hard drive ever manufactured has its own "geometry," the number of cylinders, heads, sectors, and so on that define the way the drive retains data. When a new drive is installed, an old drive is replaced, or the contents of CMOS are lost, a technician is faced with the prospect of tracking down and restoring the geometry figures for each hard drive. While most hard drive manufacturers make their data readily available through online and fax-back services, it still takes time and effort to perform that research. On the other hand, programs like DUG_IDE.EXE (Table 6-15) interrogate a hard drive and display the resulting details for quick reference.

219

Installation and configuration

The advantage of a program like DUG_IDE.EXE is that it can report disk and BIOS figures for a wide array of drives. As a result, the program is most handy on a diskette where it can be taken from machine to machine (though it will run equally well from the hard drive itself). Copy the DUGIDE.ZIP archive file from the DLS Diagnostic CD to your floppy disk or a subdirectory on your hard drive. Switch to the floppy drive (or subdirectory) and run PKUNZIP to decompress the archive. Once the archive is decompressed, you can run DUG_IDE.EXE directly.

Operation and performance

The DUG_IDE.EXE program runs automatically from the command line; there are no command-line switches. When the program runs, it generates a report such as the one shown in Figure 6-8.

Program name:	IDE Drive Information Utility
Executable file:	DUG_IDE.EXE
Purpose:	To provide information about IDE drives in a system
Version:	1.0 (c. 1993)
Operating system:	MS-DOS 3.3 or later
Compressed file:	DUGIDE.ZIP (archive)
Author:	Doug Merrett
Address:	P.O. Box 432 Stones Corner Q 4120 Australia
E-mail:	dcm@mincom.oz.au
ASP member:	No
Registration:	$0 shareware
Special notes:	A simple utility that might not work on all new EIDE drives

There are basically three parts to the report: the summary, the hard disk response, and the BIOS response. The summary provides details of the drive, controller type, and data transfer. The hard disk response details the physical drive parameters returned from the drive itself. The BIOS response indicated the drive "translation" geometry used in the CMOS setup.

The DUG_IDE.EXE program does have some limitations; it assumes that the drive controller uses basic hardware addresses. This is not always the case with new drive controllers. As a result, the program might not work with all advanced or EIDE drives and controllers.

Registration

DUG_IDE.EXE is provided as $0 shareware, so you may use and distribute it freely.

Summary

This might be just the tool for identifying an unknown drive and getting a customer's system configured quickly, but it might not work on all drive systems.

FIPS10.ZIP

One of the problems with partitions is their inefficient use of space (especially in large drives). Some users choose to manage space better by creating several smaller logical partitions on the same

```
DRIVE 0:

Model Number_____: WDC AC2700F
Serial Number_____: WD-WT3140250216
Controller Revision Number_____: 27.25C38


Able to do Double Word Transfer___:      No
Controller type_____:    0003
Controller buffer size (bytes)____:       0
Number of ECC bytes transferred___:       4
Number of sectors per interrupt___:   32784


Hard Disk Reports
Number of Cylinders (Fixed)_____:    1416
Number of Heads_____:      16
Number of Sectors per Track_____:      63


BIOS Reports
Number of Cylinders_____:     708
Number of Heads_____:      32
Number of Sectors per Track_____:      63


Press a key_
```

■ **6-8** *A typical report from DUGIDE.*

physical drive. Unfortunately, dividing an existing partition usually means repartitioning the entire drive (requiring you to back up and restore all data now on the drive). The FIPS10.ZIP package (Table 6-16) is designed to split an existing DOS partition without deleting the data on it. So you can split a partition without losing any data, provided there is enough free space for the new partition at the end of the old one.

Installation and configuration

Since you will be using the program to affect a hard drive, it is usually advisable to run FIPS.EXE from a floppy drive using a bootable floppy disk. If you have a second hard disk, you could just as easily run the program from there. Copy the FIPS10.ZIP archive to your bootable floppy disk or a subdirectory on the hard drive. Switch to the floppy drive (or subdirectory) and run PKUNZIP to decompress the archive. Once the archive has been decompressed, you can run FIPS.EXE directly. Make sure that the files RESTORRB.EXE, FIPS.EXE, and ERRORS.TXT are available on

■ Table 6-16: FIPS10 Fact Sheet

Program Name:	First Interactive Partition Splitting Program
Executable File:	FIPS.EXE
Purpose:	To split partitions on a physical hard drive
Version:	1.0 (c. 1994)
Operating system:	MS-DOS 5.0 or later
Compressed file:	FIPS10.ZIP (archive)
Author:	Arno Schaefer
E-mail:	schaefer@rbg.informatik.th-darmstadt.de
ASP member:	No
Registration:	$0 shareware
Special notes:	Lots of limitations; be sure to back up first

the disk. It is also advisable to try booting the PC from that floppy, making sure you can switch to the hard drive.

Operation

The FIPS program was designed with data safety in mind. On startup, it checks the partition table, boot sector, and FAT for any inconsistencies. If the program finds anything suspicious, it will tell you so. If there are errors, FIPS will not proceed. You can also write backup copies of your root directory and boot sector to a floppy disk before proceeding; if something goes wrong, you can then restore these with the RESTORRB.EXE utility. After you have entered the start cylinder for the new partition, FIPS checks if the new partition is completely empty by examining the FAT of the old partition. FIPS will stop if the new partition is not empty.

Note: There are some special procedures to use when using FIPS on systems with disk compression (e.g., Stacker or DoubleSpace) or systems with OS/2. Refer to the documentation provided with FIPS for detailed information.

It is important to prepare your hard drive before using FIPS. First, you must defragment the hard drive. Under DOS and Windows 3.1*x*, use the DOS DEFRAG utility. Windows 95 provides its own Windows-based defragmentation program. This is necessary because *all* the drive space used for the new partition must be completely free. You should also run a program like CHKDSK or SCANDISK to resolve any problems with the file structure before proceeding. Second, since the Windows swap file is usually not moved during defragmentation, you should remove it (in the 386 Enhanced part of the Windows control panel) and reinstall it after using FIPS. Third, if you use IMAGE or MIRROR, the last sector of the hard disk contains a hidden system file with a pointer to your mirror files. You must delete this file before using FIPS (don't worry; it will be recreated the next time you run mirror). Use either of the following commands:

attrib -r -s -h image.idx

or:

attrib -r -s -h mirorsav.fil

in the root directory, then delete the file.

Note: If you use a DOS version lower than DOS 5.0, do not try to move DOS hidden system files (e.g., IO.SYS and MSDOS.SYS). You will end up with a hard disk that won't boot any more. Since these files are already in the first sectors of the partition, it is not necessary to move them.

Once you have prepared your hard drive for the new partition, reboot the computer using your bootable diskette that contains the FIPS package and then start FIPS.EXE. You can exit from the program any time by pressing <Ctrl>–<C>. FIPS checks the OS in use, which should be DOS. The program can run under Windows, Desqview, or a Linux DOS emulator, but you do so at your own risk. Then FIPS checks your hard disks; if you have more than one, the program will ask you which one you want to work on (you can also use the /d command-line switch to specify the desired drive).

Note: FIPS.EXE changes your partition table, which can profoundly affect your data. Even though FIPS is designed to be as safe as possible, you should still perform a complete system backup before using the FIPS.EXE program.

FIPS checks the boot sector and displays the partition table, which is useful information when identifying partitions. It then checks the boot sector for errors. If you have more than one partition on the disk, you will be asked which one you want to split. The program then reads and displays boot sector information. FIPS checks if this information is consistent with the partition table, and tries to detect other errors. It verifies that the two copies of the FAT are identical. If they are not, FIPS will exit with an error message. If everything checks out, FIPS will look for free space at the end of the current partition. The new partition must have at least one cylinder, so if the last cylinder is not free, you have no chance of splitting the partition and FIPS will exit with an error message (you probably forgot to remove a mirror or image file).

Then you must enter the cylinder number on which the new partition should start. Use the left and right cursor keys to increase or decrease the cylinder count. The size of the remaining partition and the new partition are displayed in the process, so you should have no trouble choosing the right cylinder. You can change the count in steps of 10. When ready, press <Enter> to continue. FIPS checks again to see that the space for the new partition is empty. FIPS then calculates the changes to the boot sector, checks the changes, and displays the new partition table. You can then choose to re-edit the partition table or to continue. If you continue, FIPS will write the changes to the disk and exit. This should complete your new partition.

Your new partition will be recognized by DOS after your first reboot. Make sure to disable all programs that write to your disk in CONFIG.SYS and AUTOEXEC.BAT before rebooting (or boot the system from a clean floppy disk). After rebooting, use CHKDSK or Norton Disk Doctor to make sure your old (now smaller) partition is working properly. If you don't find any errors, reboot with your normal CONFIG.SYS and AUTOEXEC.BAT. Start some programs and make sure you can still read your data. If you want to use your new partition under DOS, you must first format it. If you have multiple partitions on the drive already, make sure to format the right one; the drive names might have changed!

Note: If FIPS does not offer as much disk space for creating the new partition as you would expect, you might still have too much data in the remaining partition (consider making the new partition smaller or deleting some of the data, or there might be some hidden files in the space of the new partition that were not moved by the defragmentation program.

Performance

FIPS supports a number of command-line switches that can streamline the program's operation:

/t or /test A test mode that prohibits writes to the disk.

/d or /debug A debug mode, not normally used. In this mode, a complete transcript of your session, along with some additional information, is written to the file FIPSINFO.DBG in the current directory. You can send this file to the program author to assist with technical support.

/h or /help or /? Displays the help page.

/d [*num*] Selects drive [*num*] and preselects the drive number with this switch. You can also use this switch to override the automatic drive detection; if for any reason your drive is not found by FIPS, try this switch.

/p [*num*] Selects partition [*num*] to be split and preselects the partition number (1 to 4). Only valid partitions are accepted.

/c [*num*] Preselects a new start cylinder, [*num*], for your new partition. Only valid cylinder numbers are accepted.

/omb Overrides the "more than one bootable partition" error message. Some boot programs do not complain about more than one bootable partition; they just use the first one. If you have such a program in your boot sector and the PC boots normally, you can use this switch to skip the error message.

/obf Overrides the "invalid bootable flag" error message. By modifying the bootable flag and the boot program, you can theoretically boot from the second hard drive. If you happen to have such a configuration, use this switch to skip the error message.

/ore Overrides the "number of rootdir entries must be multiple of 16" error message. An invalid number of root directory entries is accepted by DOS. If you have no other means to correct the entry, you can use this switch to skip the error message.

/olf Overrides the "FAT too large" error message. Since the number of sectors per FAT is a two-byte number, it is theoretically possible to have up to 65,535 sectors per FAT. This is acceptable by DOS, but a number greater than 256 is not useful since the largest possible FAT has 256 sectors.

/osf Overrides the "FAT too small" error message. If the number of clusters in the partition is larger than there are entries in the FAT, DOS will use only part of the partition. Something has gone very wrong with the partition, but all is not lost; use this switch and reduce the new partition to a size that can be properly managed.

/omd Overrides the "wrong media descriptor byte in FAT/bootsector" error message. The media descriptor byte should be F8h for a hard disk, but other values like FCh are accepted by DOS, so you can override the error message with this switch.

There are some other limitations to using FIPS. FIPS will work only with hard drive BIOS versions that use interrupt 13h for low-level hard disk access. I think this is true for practically all PCs. Also, FIPS will work only on disks with a sector size of 512 bytes. Third, FIPS will not split partitions with 12-bit FATs. Next, FIPS will split only DOS partitions of MS-DOS 3.0 and later. This

225

shareware version of FIPS does not work on extended DOS partitions. FIPS will not work if you already have four partitions, since it needs one free partition entry to work in. Finally, FIPS will not reduce the original partition to a size with less than 4,085 clusters.

Registration

FIPS.EXE is available as $0 shareware, so you may use and distribute it freely.

Summary

FIPS is a very specialized tool with lots of restrictions, but it might be just the thing to create new logical drives without the hassle of backing up, repartitioning, and restoring the hard drive.

HDCP.ZIP

The Hard Disk Copy Program (HDCP) shown in Table 6-17 performs a "mirroring" feature by copying files from one hard disk or image file to another hard disk or image file. This makes HDCP ideal for backing up or setting up multiple systems. HDCP copies hard disks sector by sector. The process is fast and smooth, and the number of hard drive seeks is reduced to a minimum. Moreover, HDCP has a fast mode that allows users to copy only the portion of hard disk that contains useful data. For system administrators or PC shop owners, the nightmare of having to spend hours or even days setting multiple computers to the same configuration is over; with HDCP, it can be done in minutes. You can even save the configuration in an image file for later use. Another application is that one can use HDCP to save an entire hard disk to an image file, and remote transfer it to another computer.

Installation and configuration

The HDCP utility can run equally well from a hard drive or a floppy drive. However, there is little reason to transfer HDCP along with the rest of a drive's contents, so you will probably get better results (and save a little drive space) by installing the utility to a floppy disk. Copy the HDCP.ZIP archive to your floppy disk or subdirectory on the hard drive. Switch to the floppy drive (or subdirectory) and run PKUNZIP to decompress the archive. Once the archive has been decompressed, you can run HDCP.EXE directly with no further configuration.

■ **Table 6-17: HDCP fact sheet**

Program name:	Hard Disk Copy
Executable file:	HDCP.EXE
Purpose:	To copy disk contents sector by sector
Version:	1.0 (c. 1996)
Operating system:	MS-DOS 2.0 or later
Compressed file:	HDCP.ZIP (archive)
Author:	Chang Ping Lee
Address:	DCF Software
	P.O. Box 60064
	Palo Alto, CA 94306
ASP member:	No
Registration:	$25
Special notes:	Source and destination drives must be the same capacity

Operation

Note: HDCP requires that the source disk and destination disk be the same capacity, and the disks must use the DOS file structure.

After launching HDCP.EXE, you will see a display such as the one in Figure 6-9. The main menu is listed along the top of the display: Source, Target, Action, Go, Bench, Option, and Quit. Use the left and right arrow keys to switch between main menu choices, and the up and down arrows to select the desired option within a menu. Press <Enter> to choose a highlighted selection. You can use the <Esc> key to back out of a menu or interrupt a read/write operation. The program is also mouse-aware, so a left click equates to <Enter> and a right click corresponds to an <Esc>.

The Source menu specifies the source disk (either a hard drive or an image file previously created by HDCP). The Target menu determines whether the copy is made to a hard drive or image file. The Action menu selects a particular action to be performed (only Copy is available in the shareware version). Once you have set up the operation, select Go to initiate the procedure. HDCP also provides a benchmark of the drive's sequential read speed through the Bench menu. The Option menu supports two main options: a Fast On option, which does not read or write empty areas, and a Boot On option, which includes the drive's boot sector in the operation. Finally, Quit returns you to DOS.

Performance

HDCP supports a number of command-line arguments to enhance the program's performance. The HDCP arguments are followed by

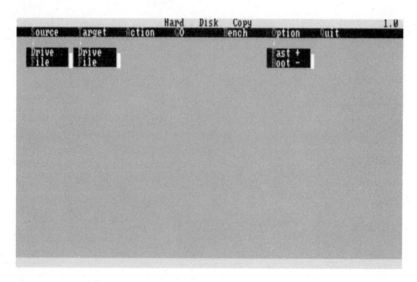

Source   Target   Action   CO   Bench   Option   Quit

Drive   Drive   Fast +
File   File   Boot –

■ **6-9** *The disk copy work area in HDCP.*

either a + or – sign to turn the corresponding function on or off. If you omit the + sign, the feature is assumed to be turned on.

/b [+/–] Sets the boot sector on/off. When on, the program also copies the boot sector (sector 0). Otherwise, the copy process starts at sector 1. Note that this option does not apply when the target is an image file, which always includes the boot sector of the source disk). By default, this option is off.

/f [+/-] Sets Fast On/Off. When on, the program reads/writes only the portion with active data, and skips empty portions of the hard disk. The default for this option is on.

/i [+/-] Sets the interface on/off. When on, the program goes to the interactive menu after the initialization stage. Otherwise, it performs the copying process in the command-line mode. When set to off, the source and target also need to be specified on the command line. The default for this option is off.

/o [+/-] Sets the monochrome in color mode. In a color system, you can use /o+ to force HDCP to run in black and white. The default is off.

/s [+/-] Sets sound on/off. The default is on.

To run HDCP with the boot sector on and fast mode off, the command line would appear something like this:

C:\> HDCP /b + f – <Enter>

Or you could copy the C: drive to the I: drive without using the interactive interface, using the following command:

C:\> HDCP /i- C: I: <Enter>

Registration

If you continue to use HDCP.EXE beyond a 30-day evaluation period, you must register it with the program author. The registration fee is $25, and you will receive the latest registered version of the program with more commands that allow you to compare and copy with on-the-fly comparison. Batch file users can enjoy no-keystroke operation. You will also get free telephone support.

Summary

HDCP provides technicians with a unique tool for mirroring drive contents to an image file or another drive. Though the drives must be the same size, HDCP can be an efficient alternative to manual system reconfiguration.

HDINFO.ZIP

One of the most difficult areas to configure in CMOS is the hard drive area; parameters such as cylinders, heads, and sectors are certainly not obvious (even to experienced technicians). Unless the drive's geometry is printed on the drive itself or contained in associated documentation, you need to contact the drive maker for the information. If your CMOS setup routine is not capable of auto-detecting the hard drive(s), you can use the HDINFO utility (Table 6-18), which is designed to eliminate the guesswork of unknown drives by reading the boot sector and displaying the partition information, including head, cylinder, and sector data. You can then use this data to restore crucial CMOS settings and get the system running again.

Installation and configuration

HDINFO will run equally well from a floppy disk or hard drive, but since the program is intended to be used only when the CMOS contents are lost, the hard drive will likely be inaccessible anyway, so you should strongly consider installing the diagnostic to a floppy disk. Copy the HDINFO.ZIP archive to your floppy disk or a subdirectory on the hard drive. Switch to the floppy drive (or subdirectory) and run PKUNZIP to decompress the archive. Once the archive is decompressed, you can start HDINFO.EXE directly.

Operation

HDINFO.EXE operates automatically with no user interaction. When the program executes, it generates a report such as the one

■ Table 6-18: HDINFO fact sheet

Program name:	Hard Drive Information Utility
Executable file:	HDINFO.EXE
Purpose:	To provide drive geometry information
Version:	1.0 (c. 1994)
Operating system:	MS-DOS 3.3 or later
Compressed file:	HDINFO.ZIP (archive)
Author:	Shane Gilbert
America Online:	ShaneG7108
ASP member:	No
Registration:	$0 shareware
Special notes:	Might not work on all newer drives

shown in Figure 6-10. A typical report lists the number of heads, cylinders, and sectors per track. This data can be used directly in CMOS. The report also lists other information, such as the active byte, partition type, and the signature byte. These last three pieces of hexadecimal data are not useful in the CMOS setup, but might be handy for other drive troubleshooting and configuration endeavors.

Performance

The program's operation is quick and direct, but it assumes standard IDE register locations and commands. As a result, HDINFO might not work on all drives, especially large (EIDE) drives. If you have trouble using HDINFO, try booting the PC clean if you are not already using a bootable floppy disk for the program.

Registration

HDINFO.EXE is provided as $0 shareware, so you may use and distribute the program freely.

```
Partition Info by Shane Gilbert ver 1.0
Read Sector OK_
First Partition is:
Number of Heads      -> 64
Number of Cylinders -> 1023
Number of Sectors    -> 63
Active Byte     <HEX>-> 80
Partition Type <HEX>-> 6
Signature       <HEX>-> aa55
```

■ 6-10 *A typical report from HDINFO.*

Summary

The HDINFO.EXE program is a simple and free tool that might just save you hours searching for obscure hard drive parameters. Still, the program might not work with all current EIDE drives.

IDATA.ZIP

The Identify ATA (or IDATA) program (Table 6-19) is another type of hard drive information reporter that displays the information returned by the IDE Identify Device command. When issued to an ATA device, the command reads and returns information regarding the drive's operating parameters. You can then use this drive geometry information to quickly correct lost CMOS settings and restore operation to a PC.

■ **Table 6-19: IDATA fact sheet**

Program name:	Identify ATA
Executable file:	IDATA.EXE
Purpose:	To identify ATA drive geometry parameters
Version:	1.0 (c. 1996)
Operating system:	MS-DOS 3.3 or later
Compressed file:	IDATA.ZIP (archive)
Author:	Brian Ryan
CompuServe:	103043,357
ASP member:	No
Registration:	Public domain
Special notes:	Might not identify all current drive types

Installation and configuration

IDATA.EXE will run equally well from a floppy disk or hard drive, but since the program is intended to be used only when the CMOS contents are lost, the hard drive will likely be inaccessible, so you should strongly consider installing the diagnostic to a clean bootable floppy disk. Copy the IDATA.ZIP archive to your floppy disk or a subdirectory on the hard drive. Switch to the floppy drive (or subdirectory) and run PKUNZIP to decompress the archive. Once the archive is decompressed, you can boot the PC clean and start IDATA.EXE directly.

Operation

The IDATA program runs automatically with no user interaction. Once the program starts, it generates a report such as the one shown in Figure 6-11. The first three entries list the number of cylinders, heads, and sectors per track. The right side of the report displays additional information detailing the data transfer modes the drive is capable of supporting. The lower part of the report lists drive controller information such as model number, serial number, and firmware revision.

```
IDentify ATA, v1.0
A public domain Freeware program.

***************************** PORT 0 *** DRIVE 0 ********************
2111 Cylinders                   PIO Mode(s): 0 1 2 3 4 (ATA-2)
 16  Heads                       LBA & DMA modes supported
  63 Sectors/Track               DMA Mode(s): s0 s1 s2 d0 d1 d2
 256 KB Buffer Size,     32 Sectors/Interrupt,   2,127,888 User sectors
1,089,478,656 User bytes

Model Number: M1606TA
Serial Number: 06057538
Firmware: 7D-13-23

No ATA DRIVE 1 available at PORT 0
```

■ **6-11** *A typical report from IDATA.*

Performance

IDATA should be run from the native DOS mode rather than from a DOS window. You should also be sure to boot the system clean to ensure that no disk drivers, caching software, or other drivers interfere with the interpretation of your drive's specifications. Also, the drive being checked must respond to the Identify Device command. Otherwise, no drives will be detected in the system and the program will terminate. Finally, use a /2 switch to display drive information for the secondary IDE port (170h to 177h), and use the /A switch to display drive information for both the primary and secondary port.

Registration

The IDATA program is in the public domain, so you may use, distribute, and modify the program freely.

Summary

IDATA is a free tool that provides a surprising amount of drive data transfer information, but it might not recognize all current EIDE drives.

PARTITV1.ZIP

One of the problems with DOS is that it stores files on disk in terms of clusters instead of sectors (where a cluster can be two, four, eight, or more sectors). The actual number of sectors in a cluster depends on the overall partition size; larger logical drives use more sectors per cluster, because there can only be 65,536 clusters in any one partition. Large clusters waste space because every file commands at least one cluster, so a small file (say 2KB) in a large cluster (maybe 16KB) leaves some substantial space (16KB – 2KB = 14KB) unused. For a large number of small files, this kind of waste can be enormous. The Partition Cluster Analyzer program (Table 6-20) analyzes wasted space, which could help technicians make educated judgments on how to repartition drives to achieve optimum partition sizes.

Installation and configuration

PARTIV1.ZIP is a Windows-based program that requires a separate installation routine. As a result, you will get the best results installing PARTIV1.ZIP to your hard drive. Create a subdirectory for the actual program, but copy the PARTIV1.ZIP archive to a temporary subdirectory. Switch to the temporary subdirectory and use PKUNZIP to extract the archive into the temporary subdirectory. Once the archive has been decompressed, you can select File and Run from within the Windows 3.x File Manager, then enter the directory and name of the setup file (SETUP.EXE). The SETUP.EXE program allows you to install the program to its final directory, and create a program group and icon. If you are running Windows 95, use the Start and Run selections, then enter the directory and name of the setup file. After the Windows installation is complete, you can launch PARTIT.EXE from its icon or Start menu entry.

233

■ Table 6-20: PARTITV1 fact sheet

Program name:	Partition Cluster Analyzer
Executable file:	PARTIT.EXE
Purpose:	To evaluate hard disk cluster size and approximate space wasted
Version:	1.0 (c. 1996)
Operating system:	Windows 3.1x or later
Compressed file:	PARTIV1.ZIP (archive)
Author:	Bill Holt
Address:	KayakR Software 430 Morningside Road Ridgewood, NJ 07450
America Online:	KayakRBill
ASP member:	No
Registration:	$3 (voluntary)
Special notes:	Provides analysis only; does not alter partition information

Operation

When you launch PARTIT.EXE, you will see a main information display, as shown in Figure 6-12. The work screen is divided into six major areas: the drive/directory dialog, analysis control panel, drive information display, directory and file status display, system status display, and partition analysis data. The drive and directory window located in the upper left portion of the display allows you to select the drive and directory to be analyzed. When a specific directory is selected, only it and its subdirectories are analyzed. The analysis control window in the upper right part of the display lets you select how much data is displayed while the files are being analyzed. Display File Data displays data as each file size is analyzed, Fast~R Scan~R displays data only as each directory is analyzed, and Fastest Scan~R updates the display only periodically. The drive information display runs along the bottom of the analysis control window. This area displays the partition size and used/available cluster space. The green part of the bar graph depicts the percent of available space, and the yellow part shows the used space on the drive. The directory and file status window runs along the middle of the display. This shows the current directory being scanned, with a bar graph of the cumulative percentage of space wasted in the directory. If the Display Files Scanned option is selected, each filename (along with a bar graph of the percentage of space wasted by the file), the number of files in the directory, and the average file size for the directory being scanned are displayed. The system status display runs just below the directory and file status window, and displays totals for the number of directories and files scanned, the total bytes used by the files, and the average file size. The yellow bar graph in the Bytes box depicts the percentage of used clusters analyzed.

The bottom portion of the display is used by the partition and cluster analysis window. The five columns you see in the display represent potential cluster sizes, with the highlighted column indicating your disk's current partition and cluster size. The title bar tracks the analysis in progress. A series of entries provide detailed data:

Clusters Alloc. This row indicates how many clusters would be allocated to store your scanned files.

Alloc'd Bytes This row shows how much disk space would be used by the allocated clusters.

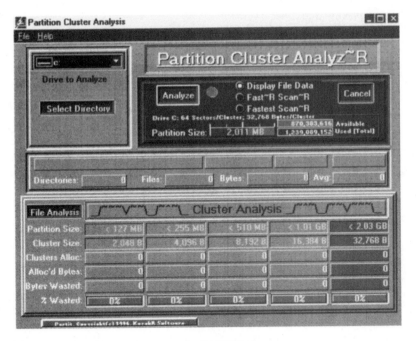

■ 6-12 *The main work screen in PARTITV1.*

Bytes Wasted This row shows the difference between how many cluster bytes would be allocated and the actual size of the files stored in the allocated clusters. Use this data to evaluate what your recovery of wasted space would be if you moved the files to a different sized partition.

% Wasted This row graphically displays the percentage of space that would be wasted for each potential cluster size.

Performance

Keep in mind that PARTIT.EXE performs a suggestive analysis only; it does not alter partition information. If you do need to make changes to your drive's partition structure, try the FIPS10.ZIP utility presented earlier in this chapter.

Registration

PARTIT.EXE is provided as 0$ shareware, but the program author welcomes a $3 voluntary contribution if you continue to use the program after a reasonable evaluation period.

Summary

PARTIT.EXE is a safe, easy-to-use utility that can provide a technician with valuable insight into the state of a hard drive's partition.

CD-ROM drive tools

The compact disc, read-only memory (CD-ROM) has proven to be an indispensable asset to PCs. The fact that each replaceable disc can hold over 600MB of data opens limitless possibilities for all kinds of software applications, especially computerized reference books and databases and other data-intensive applications like multimedia. The software in this section provides a technician with three types of tools: cache software to improve a CD-ROM drive's performance, testing software to verify the drive's operation, and CD music player software to check the drive and sound board together.

CDCP10.ZIP

Since CD-ROM drives grew out of CD audio players, it is only natural that CD-ROM drives can read and play back CD audio (red-book audio). In order to support CD audio, however, the computer must run software to read the audio tracks and handle the constant stream of audio data properly. The CDCP10.ZIP package (Table 6-21) is one such CD audio player utility. Running as a TSR, CDCP can remain resident in the background, then "pop up" as needed. CDCP uses Microsoft's CD extensions (MSCDEX) for all of its commands, so the program is portable among different systems with multiple CD interface cards (as long as MSCDEX and the correct low-level driver are loaded properly).

Installation and configuration

Since CDCP10.ZIP is intended to be a resident utility rather than a diagnostic, you will probably get your best results by installing

■ Table 6-21: CDCP10 fact sheet

Program name:	CD Control Panel
Executable file:	CDCP.EXE
Purpose:	Utility to play red book CD audio through a CD-ROM drive
Version:	1.01 (c. 1994)
Operating system:	MS-DOS 5.0 or later
Compressed file:	CDCP10.ZIP (archive)
Author:	Ray Polczynski
Address:	133 Hickory Road Lake in the Hills, IL 60102
ASP member:	No
Registration:	$10
Special notes:	Runs as a TSR; be careful of conflicts with other system TSRs

the software to your hard drive. Create a subdirectory on the hard drive and copy the CDCP10.ZIP archive file to the subdirectory from your DLS Diagnostic CD. Switch to the subdirectory and run PKUNZIP to decompress the archive. Once the archive has been decompressed, you can run CDCP.EXE directly.

Operation

CDCP is designed to make use of MSCDEX, so you need to load and run the CD-ROM drive's low-level driver and MSCDEX before starting CDCP.EXE. If the drivers are all in place, you can launch CDCP.EXE. The program will display the following message when loading:

CD-Rom Control Panel, Version 1.01
(c) Copyright 1994, by Raymond Polczynski
Press Shift+NUMLOCK to activate.
Re-run from the command line to uninstall.

This message indicates that CDCP has loaded into memory. You can now insert an audio CD and press <Shift>–<NumLock> to activate the pop-up control panel (Figure 6-13). Note that the control panel provides six buttons. From left to right and top to bottom, they are: Play, Pause, Stop, Eject, Previous Track, and Next Track. Use your arrow keys on the keyboard to move between the buttons. When the desired button is highlighted, press <Enter> to make the selection. Also note a thin line and "slider" at the bottom of the control panel. This is a volume control, which you can adjust with the + and – keys. Moving the slider to the left decreases volume, and vice versa.

The length of the inserted disc is displayed on the Total: line. As the disc is playing, the running times for the current track and the

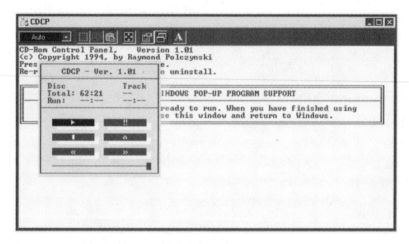

■ **6-13** *The CD control panel in CDCP10.*

disc, as well as the current track number being played, are continuously updated. To remove CDCP from memory, run the CDCP.EXE program again.

Performance

CDCP.EXE needs a proper low-level driver designed for your specific CD-ROM drive and MSCDEX (Microsoft CD extensions), version 2.21 or later. You can take audio directly from the audio jack on your CD-ROM drive, but if you plan on using speakers, there must also be a properly configured sound board and speakers in the system. Keep in mind that CDCP.EXE is designed for DOS, though it will work through a DOS window.

Registration

If you continue to use CDCP.EXE after a reasonable evaluation period, you should register it with the program author. The registration fee is $10, which entitles you to unlimited use of the program on all your PCs. If you install CDCP.EXE on someone else's computer, however, you must collect and remit the registration fee to the program author or direct your customer to remit the registration fee directly.

Summary

CDCP.EXE is a handy entertainment utility and test tool that is capable of checking a CD-ROM drive, sound board, and speakers in the same process.

CDQCK120.ZIP

CD-ROM drives are notoriously slow devices, and their data transfer rates are relatively low. As a result, cache software can dramatically affect the apparent performance of your CD-ROM drive. By storing frequently read sectors in fast XMS memory, disc reads are almost instantaneous. The CD-Quick program (Table 6-22) uses an intelligent caching algorithm and dynamic read-ahead buffering to ensure top performance. CDQ.EXE is compatible with virtually all types of CD-ROM hardware and software. It works with CD-ROM applications that require a DOS drive letter, as well as software that bypasses Microsoft CD extensions (MSCDEX.EXE) to access the CD-ROM device driver directly. The software also works seamlessly with Microsoft Windows, and will not conflict with hard disk caching software.

Installation and configuration

CD-Quick must be installed to your hard drive, and can be added to your AUTOEXEC.BAT file for use at system startup. Create a

Program name:	CD Quick Cache
Executable file:	CDQ.EXE
Purpose:	To improve CD-ROM performance through caching
Version:	1.20 (c. 1995)
Operating system:	MS-DOS 3.1 or later
Compressed file:	CDQCK120.ZIP (archive)
Author:	Peter Volpa
Address:	Circuit Systems
	48 Church Rd.
	Sicklerville, NJ 08081-1727
Phone:	609-875-5433
CompuServe:	72202,3403
ASP member:	Yes
Registration:	$29
Special notes:	Requires XMS for caching

239

temporary subdirectory on your hard drive and copy the CDQCK120.ZIP archive to your subdirectory. Switch to the temporary subdirectory and run PKUNZIP to decompress the archive. After the archive file has been successfully decompressed, you must run the INSTALL.EXE utility to complete the installation and setup for CD-Quick.

When you start INSTALL.EXE, you will first be asked for the source (where the CD-Quick files are) and destination (where you want CD-Quick copied) drive and path. When you provide this information, the installation program creates a subdirectory on your hard drive called \CDQUICK. The default source drive is the drive where INSTALL.EXE is located, and the default destination drive is drive C:. You can change these to any other drives or directories as needed. INSTALL.EXE will copy all the necessary CD-Quick files to the new directory. Then you will be asked if you want CD-Quick to determine the amount of memory to use for data caching, or if you would rather assign this figure yourself.

INSTALL.EXE scans your AUTOEXEC.BAT file, looking for at least one line containing MSCDEX.EXE. If found, the command to load CD-Quick will be added to your AUTOEXEC.BAT file, a backup of your unmodified AUTOEXEC.BAT file will be saved in the file AUTOEXEC.CDQ, and the number of buffers MSCDEX uses will be lowered to 6. If your memory manager includes software to optimize upper memory use (e.g., QEMM), you might want to rerun it after CD-Quick is installed.

Operation

Before actually installing CD-Quick, you should use the CDTEST.EXE utility to evaluate your CD-ROM drive's performance without a cache installed. To run CDTEST, switch to the subdirectory containing the program and type CDTEST and <Enter>. You must have MSCDEX.EXE loaded to run CDTEST. If you are running any version of Microsoft Windows, exit Windows and return to DOS for this test. If you have more than one CD-ROM drive, you can select which drive to test. When comparing the performance of one drive to another, be sure to test with the same CD in each drive.

With a CD in your drive, select the Walk Directories test. This test will scan the entire CD, searching for the largest file. When it finishes the scan, it reports the time taken. Next, select Do Read Test. This test will read the largest file found (which must be at least 2MB), first sequentially and then randomly. The test is repeated three times. and individual and total times are reported. After you complete the testing, note the results so you can compare the performance figures for your cached drive.

Performance

CD-Quick allows you to set several command-line parameters when it loads. The only argument required in order to load is the name of your CD-ROM hardware device driver. Other arguments are optional. Command-line parameters can be specified in any order. The generic syntax for CDQ.EXE is:

CDQ [/D:*drivername*] [*cachesize*] [/C] [/F] [/NAME=*username*]
  [/KEY=*code*] [/NOHMA] [/ON] [/OFF] [/HELP] [/?]

/D:*drivername* This parameter tells CD-Quick the name of your CD-ROM's hardware device driver, and is required for CD-Quick to work. The device driver is loaded by a line in your CONFIG.SYS file, which usually looks something like this:

DEVICE=CDROMDRV.SYS /D:MSCD001

cachesize This parameter sets the amount of memory allocated to CD-Quick's cache. It is expressed in KB. If you set cachesize to zero or omit the parameter altogether, CD-Quick will determine its cache size itself based on the amount of free XMS memory in your system.

/C If CD-Quick doesn't always recognize disc changes, you should try using the /C switch. When this switch is specified, CDQ.EXE will flush its cache whenever your CD-ROM device driver says the disc has changed or if it isn't sure. Older drives are more likely to need this option than newer drives. Don't use this option unless you need it.

/F After CD-Quick is installed, you can use the /F switch to flush the cache for all CD-ROM drives. Normally, CD-Quick will do this automatically as needed. This option has been added for old CD-ROM drives that might not report disc changes properly.

/NAME=_username_ This parameter is for people who have registered CD-Quick. When you register, you receive a key code that is derived from your name. This parameter is necessary so CD-Quick can compare your key code to your name. If they match, the opening shareware screen will not be displayed. Replace any spaces in your name with underscores.

/KEY=_keycode_ This is the companion parameter for /NAME=. Registered users receive a four-digit hexadecimal number as their key code. If your name is John Smith and your key code is 5A27, you should have the following command line:

CDQ /NAME=JOHN_SMITH /KEY=5A27

/NOHMA If you are using DOS 5.0 or later and have DOS loaded in the high memory area (HMA), CD-Quick will attempt to use any free HMA memory to store its cache index. There are a few other programs that can also use free memory in the HMA. This switch allows you to disable CD-Quick's use of the HMA and make more of it available to other applications. The cache index will be allocated in conventional memory instead. This option should rarely be used.

/ON After CD-Quick is installed, it is possible to turn the cache on and off. The default when loaded is on. If you have previously turned it off, this option will re-enable it.

/OFF It is possible to turn CD-Quick's caching on and off. This switch will disable caching for all CD-ROM drives.

/HELP or /? Gives a brief summary of CD-Quick's command-line options.

CD-Quick is a TSR; its only requirement is that it must be loaded before MSCDEX.EXE. When loaded, CD-Quick is positioned between your CD-ROM's hardware device driver and MSCDEX. MSCDEX interacts with CD-Quick instead of your device driver. CD-Quick will run just fine with SmartDrive, but if you have SmartDrive version 5.0 or later (included with MS-DOS v6.2), you need to add the /U switch when loading SmartDrive; this turns off SmartDrive's CD-ROM caching. If you used INSTALL.EXE, this will be done for you automatically.

If you encounter problems with CD-Quick or need to remove the software for any other reason, just use the DOS COPY command to copy AUTOEXEC.CDQ to AUTOEXEC.BAT, then delete the CD-Quick files.

The CD-Quick installation program can automatically determine a cache size. The amount of XMS memory allocated for the cache depends on the amount of free XMS memory in your system when CD-Quick loads. If you let CD-Quick choose the amount of memory, the following guide will be used:

☐ If less than 512KB is free, all available XMS memory will be used.

☐ If less than 1MB is free, 512KB will be used for the cache.

☐ If less than 4MB is free, 1MB will be used for the cache.

☐ If more than 4MB is free, 2MB will be used for the cache.

Registration

If you continue to use CD-Quick beyond a reasonable evaluation period, you must register the software with the program author. The registration fee is $29, for which you will receive the latest registered version of CD-Quick and a personal key code to turn off the initial shareware screen. You are also entitled to free lifetime upgrades and technical support. You can register CDQCK120.ZIP via CompuServe by selecting GO SWREG, then selecting registration number 4214. If you install CD-Quick on a client's PC, you must collect and remit the registration fee or direct your client to remit the registration fee directly.

Summary

Caching is a proven way to enhance the performance of almost any drive, but it is most effective on slow CD-ROM drives. CD-Quick is an effective and inexpensive CD cache utility that works well in most PC configurations.

CDSPEED.ZIP

As a technician, you will eventually need to measure and evaluate the performance of a CD-ROM drive during the course of a troubleshooting or upgrade procedure. The CDSPEED.ZIP package (Table 6-23) provides you with a tool to measure the sustained data transfer rate of a CD-ROM drive, the efficiency of the CD-ROM device driver in service, and the overall usage of CPU processing power (which helps you determine just how much of a load the CD-ROM drive actually is on the system).

Installation and configuration

CDSPEED will work equally well from a hard drive or floppy disk, but since the program is designed as a diagnostic, you might get best results installing to a floppy disk to keep in your toolbox. Keep in mind that drivers and TSRs could affect the timing results, so you might need to use a bootable floppy disk with a minimum

■ **Table 6-23: CDSPEED fact sheet**

Program name:	CD Speed Test
Executable file:	CDSPEED.EXE
Purpose:	To measure the data transfer rate of a CD-ROM drive
Version:	Unknown (c. 1991)
Operating system:	MS-DOS 5.0 or later
Compressed file:	CDSPEED.ZIP (archive)
Author:	Unknown
Registration:	$0 shareware
Special notes:	No author contact information

CONFIG.SYS and AUTOEXEC.BAT file to load the low-level CD-ROM driver and MSCDEX. For a report of "real" timing, CD-ROM cache software should be disabled.

Copy the CDSPEED.ZIP archive from the DLS Diagnostic CD to your floppy disk or a subdirectory on your hard drive. Switch to the floppy drive (or subdirectory) and run PKUNZIP to decompress the archive file. After the archive has been decompressed into its constituent files, you can insert a CD into the drive and run CDSPEED.EXE directly.

Operation

The CDSPEED program has several command-line arguments: a test filename and other options. The generic syntax is:

C:\> CDSPEED *filename* [*options*]

In actual practice, the filename can be any file 1.5MB or larger for best timing results. There are also a suite of command-line options (covered in the next section) for enhancing the program's operation. You can get a complete list of command-line options from the program by simply typing CDSPEED. When the program runs, it generates a report similar to the one shown in Figure 6-14. The accompanying documentation for CDSPEED defines each element of the report in detail. The actual operating cycle takes a minute or two, but the program runs automatically.

Performance

CDSPEED is designed to be run from DOS. If you are running any version of Windows, leave Windows and go to the DOS mode before using the program. You will also need the 2.21 version (or later) of MSCDEX to ensure proper operation. Finally, CDSPEED uses a number of command-line options in order to streamline the program's operation:

filename Specifies the path and name of file to test. The filename is required for operation of CDSPEED.

/r:[*transfer_rate*] Specifies the transfer rate in bytes per second. The transfer rate can range from 1 to 4,294,967, with a default of 150 kilobytes per second. Use this value to specify the sustained data read rate that might be assumed by an application.

/b:[*block_size*] Specifies the number of bytes read in each read request. The blocksize parameter can range from 1 to 65,535, with a default of 10 kilobytes.

/p:[*primer_bytes*] Specifies the number of bytes used to prime the buffer. This parameter fills a read-ahead buffer before the transfer

```
CDSPEED Settings:
                Test File Name: speed.rtf
                   Environment: DOS V7.00, MSCDEX V2.23, 1 Unit
        Requested Transfer Rate:    153600 bytes/sec (150 kb/sec)
            Delay Between Reads:        67 milliseconds
          Allowed Percent Block:        40 % (26 ms/read)
                Read Block Size:     10240 bytes (10 kb)
                   Primer Size:     10240 bytes (5 sectors)

              Preparing for tests...Done.
    Priming 10 kb--waiting  67 ms...Done.
    Performing transfer rate tests...Done.

                 Total Data Read: 51200 bytes (50 kb, 25 sectors)
                Total Time Expired: 0.3 seconds (335 milliseconds)
        Reads Exceeding  26 ms: 1 of 5 (20.0% of reads)
        Reads Exceeding  67 ms: 0 of 5 (0.0% of reads)
    Longest Time Blocked by Read: 29 ms on read #2
   Shortest Time Blocked by Read: 0 ms on read #4
          Overall Transfer Rate: 149.3 kb/sec (152836 bytes/sec)
   Percent Time Blocked by Reads: 9.6%
             Background CPU Usage: 1.1%

            Overall CPU Utilization: 10.6%
```

■ **6-14** *A typical report from CDSPEED.*

rate timing begins. This is useful when testing transfer rates approaching the maximum rate available for CD-ROM drives. The number of bytes range from 0 to 65535, with a default of 10 kilobytes.

/a:[*percent_blocked*] Specifies the maximum percentage of a read time interval the CPU should be blocked to perform the read request of data. The default is 40 percent. This value is used for scaling performance measurements, but otherwise has no effect on actual returned values.

/t Uses terse output, which is useful for processing and analyzing with a spreadsheet program. The default is verbose output.

/? Displays the list of command-line options.

Registration

CDSPEED.EXE is $0 shareware, so you may use and distribute it freely.

Summary

CDSPEED is one of the most comprehensive CD-ROM drive timing/analysis programs available for shareware, but the large number of command-line options and assumed defaults could make the program difficult for novice technicians to use accurately.

CDTA.ZIP

Timing and performance are vital aspects of all drives, so most technicians will eventually need to measure the performance and data throughput of new or replacement CD-ROM drives. The CDTA.ZIP package (Table 6-24) is designed to test the data throughputs and access times for most CD-ROM drives using conventional low-level drivers and MSCDEX.

Installation and configuration

CDTA.EXE will work equally well from a hard drive or floppy disk, but since the program is designed as a diagnostic, you will probably get the best results installing to a floppy disk to keep in your toolbox. Also keep in mind that drivers and TSRs could affect the timing results, so you might need to use a bootable floppy disk with a minimum CONFIG.SYS and AUTOEXEC.BAT file to load the low-level CD-ROM driver and MSCDEX. For a report of "real" timing, CD-ROM cache software should be disabled.

Copy the CDTA.ZIP archive from your DLS Diagnostic CD to your floppy disk or a subdirectory on your hard drive. Switch to the

■ Table 6-24: CDTA fact sheet

Program name:	CD-ROM Timing Analyzer
Executable file:	CDTA.EXE
Purpose:	To measure data throughput of a CD-ROM drive
Version:	Unknown (c. 1992)
Operating system:	MS-DOS 3.3 or later
Compressed file:	CDTA.ZIP (archive)
Author:	Eric Balkan
Address:	14704 Seneca Castle Ct. Gaithersburg, MD 20878
ASP member:	No
Registration:	$0 shareware (voluntary contribution)
Special notes:	Needs low-level CD driver and MSCDEX

floppy drive (or subdirectory) and run PKUNZIP to decompress the archive file. After the archive has been decompressed into its constituent files, you can insert a CD into the drive and run CDTA.EXE directly.

Operation

CDTA.EXE should be run from DOS rather than a DOS window, so be sure to exit any version of Windows before using the program. There are no command-line switches, so the program will run automatically without any user input. CDTA.EXE takes up to three minutes to run, and the report (Figure 6-15) is displayed on the monitor.

Performance

CDTA runs without any user interaction, and the actual test cycle might take several minutes to complete. For the most accurate readings, make sure that any CD-ROM caching software and other unnecessary drivers or TSRs are disabled.

Registration

CDTA is provided as $0 shareware, so the program may be used and distributed freely. However, if you find the program to be useful, the program author welcomes a voluntary contribution.

Summary

CDTA does not provide as much information as other CD-ROM drive performance tools, but the absence of command-line options makes CDTA easier to use.

```
CD-ROM Timing Analyzer

   Copyright 1992 by Eric Balkan.
   Packet Press BBS: 301-294-0756
   Distribute freely.  All other rights reserved.

This program will take about 3 minutes to run.  Go get some coffee.
Now checking data throughput by reading adjacent sectors...

Data throughput rate (after 30 seconds): 586478 bytes/sec
Data throughput rate (after 60 seconds): 595387 bytes/sec


Reading time per 2K sector (adjacent sectors): 3 ms

Now checking access time by reading random sectors...
This will take 2 minutes.

Average access time (exclusive of data transfer): 109 ms
Average access time (including data transfer): 112 ms


Note: The tests were done assuming a 450 MB disc.
      To determine performance with a full 680 MB disc,
      a fudge factor can be added to the readings,
      producing a truer average access time:  164 ms
```

■ **6-15** *A typical report from CDTA.*

DA7.ZIP

The ability to play red-book CD audio through your CD-ROM drive
provides a handy source of entertainment, as well as a convenient
means of checking your CD-ROM drive, sound card, and speakers
all at the same time. The DA7 package (Table 6-25) is a DOS-
based utility designed to play audio CDs through almost any CD-
ROM drive that uses conventional low-level drivers and MSCDEX.

Installation and configuration

The DA7.ZIP package will run equally well from a hard drive or floppy
disk, but if you're interested in using DA7 for entertainment, you
should probably install the program to a hard drive. Copy the DA7.ZIP
archive from the DLS Diagnostic CD to a subdirectory on the hard
drive. Switch to the subdirectory and run PKUNZIP to extract the
archive. Once the archive is decompressed, you can run DA7.EXE directly from DOS or launch it in a DOS window through Windows Explorer (under Windows 95). If you plan to use DA7 as a diagnostic, go
ahead and install it to a floppy disk. Remember that if the floppy disk
is bootable, it should also contain CONFIG.SYS and AUTOEXEC.BAT
files to load the low-level CD-ROM driver and MSCDEX.

Operation

Once you start the program and insert an audio CD, you will see the
DA7 display, as shown in Figure 6-16. Press D to select an alternate

247

■ Table 6-25: DA7 fact sheet

Program name:	Digital Audio CD Player
Executable file:	DA7.EXE
Purpose:	To play red book CD audio
Version:	7.0
Operating system:	MSDOS 3.3 or later (Windows 3.1x or later)
Compressed file:	DA7.ZIP (archive)
Author:	T. Roscoe
Address:	AVIXIVA Reflective Systems
	11367 Wright Rd., #3
	Lynwood, CA 90262
ASP member:	No
Registration:	$10
Special notes:	Will work under a DOS window

CD-ROM drive. You can select any one of up to 10 drives for play (the first drive is 0, the second is 1, and so on). Drive icons are shown at the bottom of the display. The color of the disc lines indicates audio (green), program CD (yellow), or mixed data/audio (red). Once a disc is installed and playing, the time scales should appear (make sure you have an audio disc in the drive). If CD audio goes through the mixer in your sound card, you must activate the card volume with the DOS utility that came with the card.

DA7 starts audio play automatically, even on mixed-mode discs. If the disc has alternating audio and data tracks, it will avoid the data tracks. You will need to enter the tracks to play via track Rev/Advance, Slidecue, or the track digit keys. When a disc is installed or playing, press the H key for the help screen.

Performance

Program operation is good, but a mouse is not supported and the icon-type player buttons are not clearly coupled to their keyboard equivalents. You will probably need the online help to make full use of DA7. Also remember that you need a low-level CD-ROM driver and MSCDEX (version 2.1 or later) in order to use DA7. There are no command-line options for the program.

Registration

If you use DA7 beyond a reasonable evaluation period, you must register it with the program author. The registration fee is $10. If you install DA7 on a client's PC, you must collect and remit the registration fee to the program author or direct your client to remit the registration fee promptly.

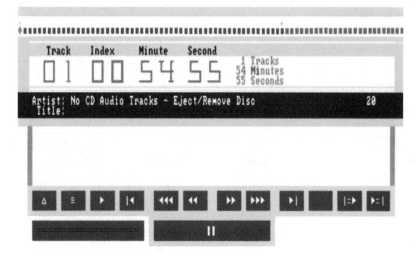

■ **6-16** *The CD control panel in DA7.*

Summary

DA7 is a good audio utility, but you need to read the documentation and online help very carefully to get the best operation.

7

General support tools

Previous chapters have covered utilities for your system, parallel ports, serial ports, video adapters, and PC drives. Still, no technician's toolbox is complete without a suite of supplemental tools to handle functions like system backup, boot management, input diagnostics, and sound diagnostics. This chapter also presents several excellent reference utilities, along with text/hex editors and some important PC security tools (Table 7-1).

Important It is impossible to test these programs on every possible configuration of PC hardware. If you cannot get the program to run (or encounter unexpected results), contact the program's author for more information.

System backup I highly recommend that you perform a complete system backup before attempting to use system diagnostics and utilities. In the event that system errors or unexpected program results accidentally damage your programs or data, a backup will allow you to restore your information quickly and easily.

Virus warning As a general operating procedure, you should never attempt to run a new program without first checking it for viruses. Decompress the program and then run your virus checker. If a virus is detected, take all necessary steps to neutralize it.

Backup utilities and organizers

One of the most important aspects of PC service is the system backup (saving the contents of a system's drives before proceeding with a repair or major upgrade). Unfortunately, this is also one of the most neglected areas of PC service. All too often, novice technicians neglect to perform a system backup until a serious problem or accidental erasure shuts down the system (and ruins the customer's hard work). The programs in this section are designed to provide hard drive backup and floppy disk copy services. Other utilities handle DOS-based disk management functions.

■ Table 7-1 General support tools

Program	Description
Backup utilities and organizers	
BACKEE28.ZIP	Drive backup utility
CF537D.ZIP	Disk/file manager utility
DCF49.ZIP	Disk copy fast 4.9
DUP59.ZIP	Disk duplicator
SUPDIR10.ZIP	Super system directories
Boot managers	
BOOTSY.ZIP	Boot configuration utility
CCS103.ZIP	Computer configuration system
Editors	
HW16V210.ZIP	Professional hex editor
RAVED.ZIP	Text editor/outliner
XEV43.ZIP	Hex editor/display utility
Input devices	
CALJOY22.ZIP	Joystick calibration utility
JOY2.EXE	Joystick calibration utility
SCODE22.ZIP	Keyboard scan code utility
STKVGA31.ZIP	Joystick calibration utility
TMTX.EXE	Mouse testing utility
Reference works	
CARDG2.ZIP	PC card guide
LOCATO.ZIP	Electronic component locator
THEREF43.ZIP	Hard drive and controller reference
Sound utilities	
SBBEEP.ZIP	Sound blaster beep utility
SNDST.ZIP	Sound board utility
Speed utilities	
SLOZIP.EXE	Slow down fast PCs
System security	
GUARD.ZIP	The Guardian hard disk security
RWARD2.ZIP	Reward notice utility

BACKEE28.ZIP

The Backer, by Bernd Cordes (Table 7-2), provides technicians and computer users with a tool to compare two different versions of a file by examining their creation dates and times. This provides the means to accomplish several important tasks. First, you can save vital system files to diskette and restore those files in the event there is ever a problem with the computer. You can also use The Backer to update data between two computers by synchronizing both file versions; newer versions replace older ones, and absent files are added. This type of synchronization can be made to work in either only one direction or both ways. Such a feature is particularly useful for synchronizing files between several computers (e.g., a desktop and mobile computer). You can also save work files to diskette. Though diskette space is pretty small, you can create work files for different projects so it's a simple matter deciding which data files can fit onto a diskette. If data loss does occur, The Backer allows you to restore work files from the diskette(s). Finally, The Backer allows you to compare directory trees, even without updating.

■ **Table 7-2 BACKEE28 fact sheet**

Program name:	The Backer (System Backup Utility)
Executable file:	BACKER.EXE
Purpose:	A utility to backup, restore, and synchronize files
Version:	2.8 (c. 1995)
Operating system:	Windows 3.1x or later
Compressed file:	BACKEE28.ZIP (archive)
Author:	Bernd Cordes
Address:	Wiesingerweg 34
	20253 Hamburg
	Germany
CompuServe:	100334,375
ASP member:	No
Registration:	$25
Special notes:	Requires Windows 3.1x or Windows 95 in order to run

Installation and configuration

Since The Backer is a Windows utility, it should ideally be installed to your hard drive. Create a subdirectory on your hard drive for The Backer. Copy the BACKEE28.ZIP archive file from the DLS Diagnostic CD to your new subdirectory. Switch to the subdirectory, then run PKUNZIP to decompress the archive file. Once the archive is decompressed into its constituent files, you can run The Backer. There is no installation routine for The Backer, so you can create a new program group and icon for it, or launch it from your File Manager (or Windows Explorer). When the program begins, you will see a small shareware reminder dialog.

Operation

After you acknowledge the shareware terms in the initial shareware reminder dialog box, the main work window appears (Figure 7-1). A main menu along the top gives you control over File, Configuration, Update, and Help features. Just below the main menu is a set of control buttons: Exit, File Select, Destination, Options, and Start Update. The large window and list below the control buttons lists the setup characteristics of The Backer. Once the program is running, you can back up system files, synchronize files, back up and restore files, and compare directory trees.

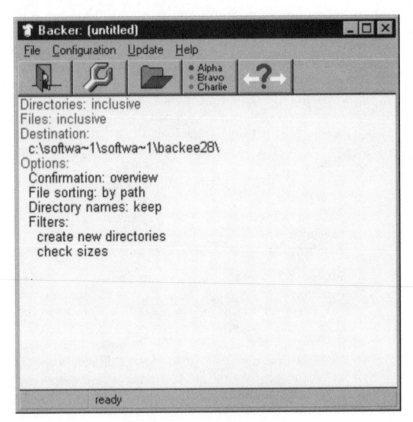

■ **7-1** *The main backup dialog in BACKEE28.*

Backing up system files A backup of your system files can save the day if those files are lost or corrupted. The Backer will copy CONFIG.SYS, AUTOEXEC.BAT, and all .INI files to diskette. For best results, the diskette should be bootable. Open the EXAMPLE.BAC file, insert a bootable diskette in drive A:, and start the update process. Once the backup is complete, try booting the system just to make sure the diskette is working.

Synchronizing files Synchronizing files is an important process for PC users who work on files across several different computers (e.g., a desktop system during the day and a notebook PC at night). One of the major problems with this process is that users often lose track of the latest file version, then wind up accidentally working on an older file. The Backer allows you to select the files to update and copy them to diskette. You can take the diskette to your other machine and update the files on that machine with The Backer.

If your computers are connected to each other (via a network or Interlink), find out which letter the notebook's hard disk is known as by your desktop, or vice versa. Make this drive the destination. Then you can set the directories and documents to be processed as inclusive (under Files). At Options, select "keep" for Directory Names and both "create new directories" and "in both directions" for Filters. The other three filters must be off. You need to run Backer on only one of the two PCs; the other PC is either doing some network task or running the Interlink program. Now start updating, and the latest versions of your documents will be copied from the desktop to the notebook. If your two computers are not connected, you will need floppy disks to transfer the files. The Backer must run on both computers. If necessary, create individual work files for the various subdirectories. The destination must be A:\, and you must update on one machine first, then on the other.

Backing up files to diskette Of course, no user should ignore regular backups of work in progress. As an example, suppose you have created documents with the extension .DOC, located in the directory C:\DOCUMENT\ and its subdirectories. Also suppose that the layout files you've used end in .DOT and are located in the directory C:\WORD\, but not its subdirectories. All these files need to be saved to an empty floppy disk. Under Files, select the named directories and filename extensions (both inclusive). For C:\DOCUMENT\ the option all subdirectories must be checked, but not for C:\WORD\. Under Destination, select the directory A:\. A floppy disk (not necessarily the one designed for backup) must be present in the drive, or this selection will not be accepted. Under Options, check "keep" for Directory Names and "create new directories" for Filters. The other four filters must be off. With the correct floppy disk in the drive, use the Update command. All text documents in C:\DOCUMENT\ (and its subdirectories) and all layouts in C:\WORD\ (without its subdirectories) are copied to disk, provided sufficient disk space. The respective directories (A:\DOCUMENT\ with its subdirectories and A:\WORD\) are created on the disk. This updating can be repeated at any time since you saved the work file and can simply open it again. Then, of course, only the documents and layouts revised since the last backup are copied.

Restoring files from diskette Assuming you have already backed up files to floppy disks, all you have to do now is open the work file created there, select "in both directions" for Filters, and start updating. All files previously saved to floppy disk that do not exist (or exist as an older version) on the hard drive are now copied back into precisely those directories they belong to.

Comparing directory trees Generally, you can use The Backer to compare two directory trees without having to update them. Suppose you want to compare your popular spreadsheet program on hard disk in the directory C:\EXCEL\ to the version on CD-ROM in the directory D:\ (and both directories have several subdirectories). Under Files, select D:\ with all subdirectories, and *.* as the filename and extension (both inclusive). As the destination, choose C:\EXCEL\. Select "overview" for Options, Confirmation, "keep" for Directory Names, and "in both directions" for Filters. The other four filters have to be off. After you start updating, you're shown an overview of all differences in the directory trees. Leave this dialog with Cancel, not with OK. Due to the large number of files, the search might take a while and, if there are a lot of differences, not all of them will be displayed in the overview.

Performance

The Backer is a fairly simple program to use and master, but it takes some practice. One of its significant advantages is compatibility with networks and the DOS Interlink utility. Good Windows help provides hypertext details for all aspects of the program's operation.

Registration

If you continue to use The Backer after a 30-day evaluation period, you must register it with the program author for $25. As a registered user, you will receive a user ID to convert your unregistered version into a registered version. You also have access to technical support by phone, fax, mail, and e-mail. By registering The Backer, you are granted permission to use both the program and documentation on two computers at the same time. If you prefer to register through CompuServe, select GO SWREG and register product 4310. If you install The Backer to a client's PC, you should collect and remit the registration fee, or instruct your client to remit the registration fee directly.

Summary

Technicians and computer users alike will find The Backer to be a simple and inexpensive tool for saving and restoring work, and keeping important files in sync between multiple computers.

CF537D.ZIP

DOS is often criticized for the way it handles files. Through the years, an endless array of third-party file-handling utilities have been developed to help users view file information, review directory trees, launch applications, and perform other file management functions. The File Manager under Windows 3.x (and the current Windows Explorer under Windows 95) illustrate the Microsoft approach to file management. CMFiler (Table 7-3) provides a quick, simple, "one-touch" operating environment for your IBM-compatible 80x86-based computer running under DOS Version 3.0 or later. CMFiler is capable of doing everything your DOS COMMAND.COM processor or other file manager can do, but provides enhanced file management tools. For example, you can display two directories side by side, copy one or more files from one directory to another, back up files in the same directory, delete or rename files and directories, set file and directory attributes, view and edit files, make and remove subdirectories, and launch programs — all with a minimum number of keystrokes.

Installation and configuration

Since CMFiler is intended to serve as a COMMAND.COM supplement, it should be installed to your hard drive. Create a subdirectory for CMFiler on your hard drive. Copy the CF537D.ZIP file from the DLS Diagnostic CD to your new subdirectory, then run PKUNZIP to decompress the archive. Once the archive file is decompressed, make sure the CMFILER.COM and CMFILER.OVY files are present in your new directory. If you want CMFiler to start automatically each time the computer boots, add the CMFiler command line to the end of AUTOEXEC.BAT, such as:

■ Table 7-3 CF537D fact sheet

Program name:	CMFiler
Executable file:	CMFILER.COM
Purpose:	A file/directory management tool
Version:	5.37d (c. 1995)
Operating system:	MS-DOS 3.0 or later
Compressed file:	CF537D.ZIP (archive)
Author:	Charles F. Martin
Address:	NoVaSoft 3239 Riverview Dr. Triangle, VA 22172-1421
Phone:	703-221-1471
CompuServe:	72130,1400
ASP member:	Yes
Registration:	$30
Special notes:	Lengthy documentation

c:\cmfiler\cmfiler

Operation

Once the program boots, you will see a work screen similar to the one shown in Figure 7-2 on the next page. The left panel shows the contents of the current directory on the default drive. Line 1 of this active panel shows the disk volume name (if any) and a prompt area for four display enhancement features. The key combination <Ctrl>–O allows you to select one of nine file-ordering schemes, <Ctrl>–H toggles the Hide mode switch, <Ctrl>–C toggles the Compare mode switch, and <Ctrl>–M allows you to specify a file mask. Line 2 shows the path to the current directory. In a 25-line video display mode, the first 20 entries are displayed: directories first, then files. Line 23 gives vital information about the disk, such as remaining space. Finally, lines 24 and 25 contain an abbreviated help screen. If you do not press any key within about 1½ minutes, the display goes into screen-saver mode; just press any key to return to the main display. You can force the screen-saver mode with <Ctrl>–S.

The two-line help area at the bottom of the screen contains a set of abbreviated cues to remind users of the single-key commands. With no "modifier" keys pressed (<Shift>, <Alt>, and <Ctrl>), the help area shows the operations available. The following are typically the most frequently used operations: C for Copy File, E for Edit File, D for Delete File or Directory, T for Tag File, and 1 for Toggle the File's Read-Only Attribute. If you press a modifier key, the new selections will appear.

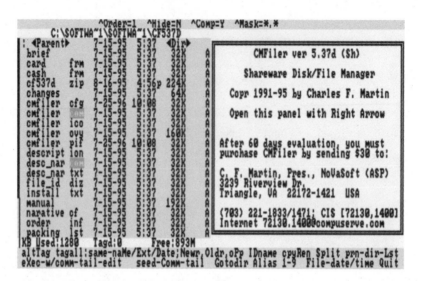

■ **7-2** *The DOS File menu in CF537D.*

Each panel corresponds to a DOS path, so the words *panel* and *path* are used interchangeably. Open the right panel by pressing the right arrow. You will be prompted at the bottom of the screen to specify a drive letter. The bottom lines become the dialog area for information about what CMFiler is doing. Just press the letter corresponding to a valid drive; don't press <Enter>, just a letter key. The current directory of that drive will be shown in the right panel in the same format as the left panel. The bright yellow color of the path specification on line 2 and the blinking cursor now identify the right panel as the source path. The left panel has become the target or destination path for the Copy, Append, and Move operations.

Whenever CMFiler is in Compare mode (and the cursor is on the name of a file in the source panel that also happens to exist anywhere in the target path), the target panel display is adjusted so the file appears in the panel and its date/time signature is set to high intensity to catch your eye. If the date, time, or size of the two files are not the same, the date/time signature of the newer file will blink.

There are a number of other commands you can use with CMFiler, but you should refer to the detailed documentation accompanying the utility for more specific information.

Performance

CMFiler is typically a reliable tool, but there are some cautions and limitations to keep in mind when using the program. First, terminate-and-stay-resident programs (TSRs) should not be launched from CMFiler. At best, you will end up with fragmented memory when you exit CMFiler; at worst, your system will crash. Second, CMFiler requires a minimum of 227KB of free memory to run. This permits adequate memory allocation for the directory listings, a print spooler buffer, and a copy buffer. When an application is launched, however, you can make the resident portion of CMFiler occupy as little as 22KB by using the Small Footprint option of the Kernel command. This is the default selection on initial start-up. Next, the maximum directory size recognized by the main module varies from 300 to 2,400 entries depending on available memory. If the directory size limit is reached, a warning note will be displayed and the rest of the directory will be inaccessible (as though it were hidden).

Also, the algorithms used by the editor module place certain limitations on the module in edit mode that do not apply in view mode. The editor reverts to view mode automatically if the file is too large to fit in available memory in one shot, if the file has more than 16,380 lines, or if the file has lines longer than 8,190 characters (if you're editing in NoWrap mode). The tree module limits the number of entries in a directory tree structure to 1,700 total subdirectories. The limit on number of files is strictly a function of available memory. Finally, the main and tree modules both limit the depth of directory nesting to eight levels (e.g., C:\1\2\3\4\5\6\7\8) and the length of path specifications to 66 characters (this is a DOS limitation).

Registration

If you continue to use CMFiler beyond a 60-day evaluation period, you must register it with the program author for $30. You will receive a copy of the latest registered version, a printed manual, and a set of additional software tools. Registered users also get free technical support for one year. If you install CMFiler to a customer's PC, you should collect and remit the registration fee or instruct your customer to remit the proper registration fee directly.

Summary

For PC users who need powerful file management tools but don't want the complexity and processing overhead associated with File Manager or Windows Explorer, CMFiler offers a worthwhile solution that is worth considering.

DCF49.ZIP

One of the great advantages of diskettes is that they can be copied easily, and DOS readily provides the means for this in commands

259

like COPY and XCOPY. Unfortunately, the classical DOS commands are slow and cumbersome, especially when you're copying a large number of diskettes. The DCF (Disk Copy Fast) utility from DCF Software (Table 7-4) provides a third-party tool for fast, reliable diskette duplication. Version 4.9 is a powerful, one-pass duplicator that uses extended memory to create an image file of the disk to be copied. In actual operation, DCF is rated 42 percent faster than DOS commands. DCF can be run directly from the DOS command line or through a menu (with mouse support). DCF 4.9 also supports diskette formatting, copying, and verification—all in the same pass. DCF supports 360KB, 1.2MB, 720KB, and 1.44MB diskettes.

■ **Table 7-4 DCF49 fact sheet**

Program name:	Disk Copy Fast
Executable file:	DCF.EXE
Purpose:	Utility to copy multiple floppy diskettes
Version:	4.9 (c. 1994)
Operating system:	MS-DOS 3.3 or later
Compressed file:	DCF49.ZIP (archive)
Author:	DCF Software
Address:	P.O. Box 60064
	Palo Alto, CA 94306
ASP member:	No
Registration:	$20 (single user); $40 (commercial)
Special notes:	Faster copying tools than DOS

Installation and configuration

DCF will run from the floppy drive or hard drive, but since you'll be copying floppy disks, it's best to install the program to your hard drive. Create a subdirectory on your hard drive and copy the DCF49.ZIP archive file from your CD to the new subdirectory. Switch to the new subdirectory, then run PKUNZIP to decompress the archive. Once the archive has been decompressed, you can run DCF.EXE from the command line or start DCF as a menu program.

Operation

Once DCF starts, you will see the work screen, as shown in Figure 7-3. There are three windows in Disk Copy Fast: the Resource window, the Option window, and the Information window. The Resource window shows you the resources in your system that can be used for duplicating a diskette. There are several entries in this window: Con Mem shows you the size of free conventional memory, Ext Mem shows you the size of free extended memory, and Cur Dsk shows you the size of free space on the current disk (hard or RAM disk). The Resource window also displays the capacities of available diskette drives. The Option window shows you how the current read/write options are set in DCF. The Information window shows you the status of the loaded source diskette. If it reports 61 out of 80 tracks, for example, it means that the source diskette has 80 tracks but only the first 61 tracks contains useful data and the last 19 tracks are empty. Then it will show you how these 61 tracks are loaded in your system. It might report 34 tracks in conventional memory, 20 in extended memory, and 7 still on the current disk. It will also display other information, such as the time it took to perform the last read or write (in seconds) and how many copies you have made so far. Note that the information window isn't visible until you have a source diskette loaded in your system.

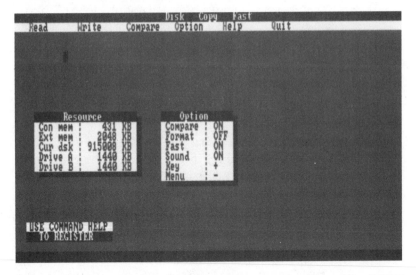

■ **7-3** *The main working menu and configuration settings under DCF49.*

The menu bar at the top of the work screen offers six options: Read, Write, Compare, Option, Help, and Quit. Read loads the source diskette data from a diskette drive (or from an image file created previously by DCF) to conventional memory, then to extended memory if necessary, and finally to the hard disk. Write transfers a loaded source diskette's data to a destination disk drive or an image file. Compare checks the loaded source diskette against another diskette in a disk drive or an image file. Help shows the program's online help file, and Quit exits DCF. Finally, the Option feature includes six subcommands for you to set read/write options, sound, keystrokes, and menu style. These settings are displayed in the Option window, as follows:

Format ON Formats the target diskette before writing.

Format OFF Formats the target diskette only when necessary.

Compare ON Performs a read-back and byte-by-byte comparison immediately after writing a track to the target diskette.

Fast ON Will not work with empty portions of the source and target diskette.

Sound ON Turns the audio signals on.

Key Saves some keystrokes for hot keys.

Menu Gives you a full and faster menu operation.

Performance

You can specify a series of other options for DCF by using command-line arguments. This is particularly useful for "preconfiguring" DCF as the program starts. The command-line options are as follows:

/c [+ or -] Sets the Compare mode. When on, the program performs a read-back and byte-by-byte comparison for every track written to a target diskette. The default is on.

/m [+ or -] Sets the Format mode. When on, the program formats before writing to target diskettes. If off, the program will format only when necessary. The default is off.

/f [+ or -] Sets the Fast mode. When on, the program will read/write only the portion with active data and skip empty portion of diskettes. The default is on.

/s [+ or -] Sets the Sound mode. When on, the program gives an audio signal after reading and writing a diskette (or 20 seconds of inactivity). The default is on.

/k [+ or -] Sets Keystrokes. When +, you need to press the highlighted letter followed by the <Enter> key to execute a command. When –, no <Enter> key is required. The default is +.

/n [+ or -] Sets Menu. Available only when a mouse driver is present. When +, you can see and click at every command to execute. When –, you need to pull the second-level commands down from a level-one command. The default is –.

/d [+ or -] Sets the Delay mode. If your machine is faster than a 4.77-MHz 8088 and you would like to see whether the program can copy at its highest speed on your system, try /d-. The default is on.

/t [+ or -] Sets the density priority. If +, the program tries reading a new disk as a high-density disk in a 1.2MB or 1.44MB drive. If –, low density has higher priority. The default is +.

/o [+ or -] Sets the mono in color mode. In a color system, you can use /o+ to force DCF to run in black and white. The default is –.

/x [+ or -] Sets multiple target on/off. If on, the program reads the source disk once and writes to targets repeatedly. The program quits automatically when you press the <Esc> key. To turn this option on, you also need to specify the source and target on the command line. The default is off.

/b [+ or -] Sets the backup. If on, the program repeatedly reads the source and writes to the target. The program quits automatically when you press the <Esc> key. To turn this option on, you also need to specify the source and target on the command line. The default is off.

/a [+ or -] Sets the analyze mode. If on, the program checks the density before copying to a target diskette. If you copy a low-density disk to a high-density disk (or vice versa), the program will warn you and you can decide to skip, go ahead, or format before writing. The default is on.

/w [+ or -] Sets write protect. If on, the program will not read a diskette that isn't write-protected. This is useful when you are backing up a sequence of diskettes and the source disks are all write-protected. Use this option so you won't read a diskette that should be a target instead of the source. The default is off.

Here are some examples of DCF commands. Suppose you need to run DCF with Format off, Keystrokes on, and Menu off. The command line would appear like this:

DCF /m-k+n-

If you need to run DCF with Format on, Compare on, and Delay off, you'd use the following command:

DCF /m+c+d-

Suppose you wanted to read from the A: drive and write to an image file called ABC. You would use this command:

DCF A: ABC

Finally, if you wanted to read an image file ABC and produce as many target disks as you want to using the A: drive, you'd use a command line like this:

DCF /x+ ABC A:

Registration

If you continue to use DCF beyond a 30-day evaluation period, you must register it with the program author. Registration is $20, and includes a key to convert the shareware version into the registered version. This key also entitles you to free future updates, free telephone support, and special discounts on other DCF Software products. If you install DCF on a client's PC, you should collect and remit the registration fee or instruct your client to remit the registration fee directly.

Summary

DCF 4.9 is an important tool for disk duplication that's simple, fast, inexpensive, and straightforward to use.

DUP59.EXE

Floppy diskettes remain the preferred medium for distributing small amounts of software and files, but the DOS COPY and XCOPY commands are often painfully inefficient and commercial software duplication can be an expensive proposition. This has resulted in the development of streamlined disk duplicator utilities such as DUP59, by Randy MacLean (Table 7-5). Designed primarily for small businesses, DUP59 features an informative user interface and a suite of features, such as an audible disk change signal; one-pass format, write, and verify operation; and serial number increment options. DUP59 can read an entire master disk into a compressed image file, eliminating the need to read the master disk at the beginning of each duplicating session.

Installation and configuration

DCF will run from the floppy drive or hard drive, but since you'll be copying floppy disks, it would be best to install the program to your hard drive. Create a subdirectory on your hard drive and copy the DUP59.EXE self-extracting archive file from your CD to the new subdirectory. Switch to the new subdirectory, then run DUP59.EXE to extract the archive. Once the archive file has been decompressed, you can run DUP.EXE directly.

Program name:	Disk Duplicator
Executable file:	DUP.EXE
Purpose:	A utility for the mass duplication of floppy diskettes
Version:	5.9 (c. 1990)
Operating system:	MS-DOS 3.3 or later
Compressed file:	DUP59.EXE (self-extracting)
Author:	Randy MacLean
Address:	FormGen Corporation 13 Holland Drive Bolton, Ontario L7E 1G4 Canada
Phone:	416-857-0022
ASP member:	Yes
Registration:	$25
Special notes:	Designed for diskettes only

Operation

Once DUP59 starts, the main screen will appear as shown in Figure 7-4. The main screen provides you with all the controls and status information required for disk duplication. The main functions are shown in a menu bar near the top of the screen, and you can select them either by moving the highlight (using the arrow keys or space-bar) and pressing <Enter>, or by typing the first letter of a desired function. You can exit the program by selecting the Quit option.

265

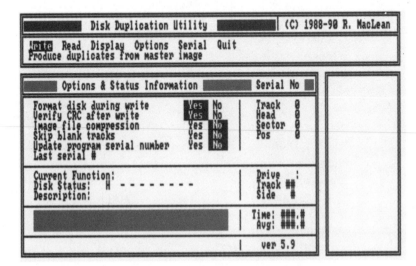

■ **7-4** *The main menu and progress bars for DUP59.*

When you select the Write option, you are creating a duplicate disk. DUP59 will prompt you for the type of disk image to be used (360KB, 720KB, and so on) and the target drive(s), and then display a list of disk images previously read. You select the desired image file by highlighting it and pressing <Enter>. Use the Read option to create an image of an original disk. DUP59 will prompt you for the source drive, and then display a list of disk images previously read. If the disk has not previously been read into the system, select New File and enter an appropriate filename. If a previous version of the disk is already present, simply highlight the name of the older image and press <Enter>. The older image will be updated from the diskette. The Display option allows you to select a serial number. The program will prompt for the source drive and then display a list of disk images previously read. It will then read and display the serial number stored on the disk in the selected drive. This allows you to check the serial number on a produced disk.

The Options feature lets you set the desired options for program operation. When Format is on, DUP59 formats each track prior to writing it, allowing you to use blank diskettes without needing to process them prior to software duplication. When Verify is on, the program verifies the CRC for the track after each write. This is a good check for media flaws, but takes a little more time. If Serial # is on, a serial number is written on each disk that is produced. You must set several parameters before the program will work properly: Data retrieves the standard options stored with each master image, allowing you to modify them, Mode switches the serial number mode between Automatic (where the system assigns an incremental serial number to each disk produced) and Manual (where the operator is prompted to enter each serial number as the disks are produced).

The Serial option allows you to set your serial number parameters for each new diskette. There are several serialization options in DUP59. Data retrieves the serial number parameters stored with each master image, allowing you to modify them. Get S/N searches a master disk for the location of a particular serial number string. Track allows you to set the track where the serial number is to be placed. Cyl (for cylinder) allows you to set the side where the serial number is to be placed. Sector allows you to set the sector where the serial number is to be placed. Position lets you select the serial number's position. Last # allows you to set the last recorded serial number; the serial number of the next disk produced will have a serial number one higher than this.

Performance

You can use several command-line options for DUP59 to optimize the program's operation. In most cases, these options will affect the program's overall speed:

/B Uses BIOS for disk I/O (option for best copy speed, cannot be used with /D)

/D Uses DOS for disk I/O (option for best compatibility, cannot be used with /B)

/R Uses RAM to buffer master image (for 360K disks)

/S Silent option, disables sounds

Registration

If you continue to use DUP59 beyond a reasonable evaluation period, you must register it with the program author. Registration is $25, which gets you a printed manual, the latest registered version of the program, and a $15 credit on CompuServe. If you install DUP59 on a client's PC, you must collect and remit the registration fee or instruct your client to remit the registration fee directly.

Summary

DUP59 is a powerful tool for small businesses that need to duplicate a limited number of diskettes quickly and conveniently.

SUPDIR10.ZIP

While the DOS directory command is useful for diskettes and small directories, it has some serious limitations when you're trying to view large directories, and viewing directory trees is virtually impossible. The Super Directory program (Table 7-6) provides PC technicians and users with a powerful directory listing tool. SuperDIR was originally designed to create directory listings for import into spreadsheets and database programs. The primary use for the program is to make a complete file database of shareware CD-ROMs, to be used by a shareware cataloging/extraction program. Still, SuperDIR is extremely useful in finding duplicate files on a disk, and is an excellent general-purpose DIR replacement with multiple include/exclude capabilities.

Installation and configuration

SuperDIR will run equally well from a floppy disk or hard drive. If you plan to carry SuperDIR in your toolbox, install it to a floppy disk; if you would rather use the program on your PC alone, install

Program name:	Super Directory
Executable file:	SDIR.EXE
Purpose:	A powerful drive directory management utility
Version:	1.0 (c. 1995)
Operating system:	MS-DOS 3.3 or later
Compressed file:	SUPDIR10.ZIP (archive)
Author:	Cottonwood Software
Address:	P.O. Box 6546
	Leawood, KS 66206-0546
Phone:	913-663-3022
CompuServe:	75264,1630
ASP member:	Yes
Registration:	$20
Special notes:	Many different output features

it to your hard drive. Create a subdirectory for SUPDIR10.ZIP or insert a fresh floppy disk to hold the program. Copy the archive file from the DLS Diagnostic CD to your new subdirectory (or a floppy disk), then run PKUNZIP to decompress the archive. Once the archive has been decompressed, you can run SDIR.EXE directly. If you choose to install the program to your hard drive, consider adding the subdirectory to your PATH statement so you can run SDIR.EXE anywhere.

Operation and performance

SuperDIR is driven entirely through the DOS command line, with the following format:

SDIR [*path*] [*switches*]

where the *path* can include drive/directory or a filename mask, like the DOS DIR function. There is also a proliferation of command-line switches that allow you to tailor the program's operation. If you find yourself using complex command lines, you might want to use SuperDIR from batch files. The valid switches are as follows:

/I Includes file filters, up to 10 entries separated by semicolons with no spaces (for example, /I*.c;*.h;x*.*).

/X Excludes file filters, up to 10 entries separated by semicolons with no spaces (for example, /X*.bak;*.obj;temp*.*).

/D Includes directory filters, up to 10 entries separated by semicolons with no spaces (for example, /Dwin*;word).

/E Excludes directory filters, up to 10 entries separated by semicolons with no spaces (for example, /Etemp;tmp;dos;util;bat).

/S Traverses all subdirectory levels.

/. Includes . and .. subdirectories, or you can use /-. to turn it off (the default). .

/A Attribute inclusion; you must give list of attributes to include (for example, /Ahs). Valid attributes are:

h	hidden
s	system
r	read-only
v	volume ID
a	archive
d	subdirectories
n	do not show "normal" files (no attributes)

/O Sorting order specification; you must give sort elements/order. The order of the fields will determine the sorting priority. The elements are:

n	name (without extension)
e	extension
s	size
d	date/time (with seconds)
a	attributes
g	group sorts by subdirectory (default)

(use g- to sort all files regardless of subdirectory)

/F Format specification; you must also provide the format type:

/Ff	Fully formatted output (the default, similar to DIR command output)
/Fq	Quote-delimited output (e.g., "name.c","1234","12:34p")
/Ft	Tab-delimited output (e.g., for Excel text import)
/Fs	Space-delimited output (e.g., for piping to other programs)

Note: /Fq, /Ft, and /Fs must be followed by a list of elements:

p	path (e.g., drive:\dir\subdir . . .)
f	filename with extension
n	name (without extension)
e	extension
s	size (in bytes)
d	date
t	time (in hh:mma format)

m   military time, with seconds (hh:mm:ss)
a   attributes (listed as lowercase letters, like "ahrs")
x   full filename with path (e.g., c:\WINDOWS\WIN.INI)
l   level of subdirectory (root = 1)

/T Tabs (indents) by subdirectory level (doesn't really use tabs).

/B Adds breaks/path names between subdirectories; use /-B to turn off (the default).

/Z Prints size and file totals at the end; use /-Z to turn off (the default).

/P Pauses after 24 lines, or /P*nn* to pause after *nn* lines.

/L Uses all lowercase letters for the path and filename. Uppercase is the default.

/? Displays this help message.

/H Displays this help message.

/R Displays a registration order form (Use SDIR /R > lpt1: to print).

Registration

If you continue to use SuperDIR beyond a 30-day evaluation period, you must register it with the program author. Registration is $20; you will receive the latest registered version, complete source code, a printed manual and quick reference card, and notification of bug fixes and future upgrades. If you install SuperDIR on a client's PC, you should collect and remit the registration fee or instruct your client to remit the registration fee directly.

Summary

SuperDIR provides a suite of features that the DOS DIR command does not, and is an outstanding tool for cataloging and analyzing the contents of your drives, especially large ones such as CD-ROM drives. The output of SuperDIR can be printed or used in database programs.

Boot managers

PCs can be extremely finicky when it comes to supporting different applications and hardware. Not all applications or hardware work together at the same time. This means you might need to boot a PC differently (enabling or disabling different drivers and TSRs as needed) depending on exactly which task needs to be performed. Traditionally, you can accomplish this "selective booting" by using bootable floppy disks containing CONFIG.SYS and AUTOEXEC.BAT files that had been optimized for different configurations, but this can be cumbersome when there are several different configurations. The utilities in this section provide multiple-boot capability.

BOOTSY.ZIP

Users often need to be able to "multiboot" a PC, especially when using games and other demanding applications. The BOOTSY utility (Table 7-7) lets you display one or more menus at bootup time, and execute different parts of CONFIG.SYS and AUTOEXEC.BAT depending on which menu options you select. It is similar to the multiconfiguration feature found in DOS 6.*x*, but BOOTSY goes much further by adding features such as if/then/else decision making and using variables in CONFIG.SYS.

■ Table 7-7 BOOTSY fact sheet

Program name:	Boot Manager
Executable file:	BOOT.SYS
Purpose:	To provide multiple configurations at boot time
Version:	2.0 (c. 1993)
Operating system:	MS-DOS 2.11 or later
Compressed file:	BOOTSY.ZIP (archive)
Author:	Hans Salvisberg
Address:	Salvisberg Software & Consulting Bellevuestr. 18 CH-3095 Berne Switzerland
CompuServe:	73237,3556
ASP member:	Yes
Registration:	$39
Special notes:	Does not run as a TSR

271

Installation and configuration

BOOTSY is intended to provide a service during boot time, so it should be installed to the boot drive, which in most cases is the C: hard drive. The program can be installed to a bootable floppy disk, but you would be better off to copy the program to your bootable floppy from the more permanent installation on the hard drive. Create a temporary subdirectory for BOOTSY. Copy the BOOTSY.ZIP archive file from your DLS Diagnostic CD to the temporary subdirectory, then run PKUNZIP to decompress the archive file.

Once the ZIP file is decompressed, you will find the BOOTINST.EXE program. This is the installation program. Run BOOTINST.EXE. It will ask you for a target directory; this is the final directory that will contain BOOT.SYS. The installer will create the new subdirectory and extract the system files. It will then create sample configuration files that you can use with BOOT.SYS right away. BOOTINST.EXE does *not* make any changes to your CONFIG.SYS and AUTOEXEC.BAT files. The utility relies on you to examine the log file and the sample configuration files first, make sure they look reasonable, and then copy them over your CONFIG.SYS and AUTOEXEC.BAT files and reboot. Before copying anything, however, you should always make a backup copy of your startup files.

Operation

BOOT.SYS first takes control of your CONFIG.SYS file. It passes some commands on to DOS for processing, and hides other commands from DOS. While it has control of your configuration file, BOOT.SYS can display menus, wait for user input, examine your computer's configuration, and perform other tests. It can also create environment variables during CONFIG.SYS processing in all versions of DOS.

The BOOT.EXE companion program (included in the package) extends configuration control to your AUTOEXEC.BAT file and the DOS prompt. In earlier versions of DOS, it creates environment strings to indicate which menu choices you made during CONFIG.SYS processing. It can also signal that it's time to perform periodic activities like making backups and monthly reports, rebooting your computer from any batch file or command line, and instructing BOOT.SYS how to configure your computer automatically.

Unlike other configuration programs, BOOT.SYS doesn't write to your disk, nor does it keep multiple configuration files on your hard disk. BOOT.SYS performs all of its magic in RAM while your computer is processing the CONFIG.SYS file. This eliminates all risks of corrupting the valuable data on your disks. It also lets you use BOOT.SYS on diskless PCs.

After you have created the necessary menus, various users can simply select a configuration with a couple of keystrokes. You never have to worry about managing multiple copies of CONFIG.SYS and AUTOEXEC.BAT; the users can just run their machines using the menus that you and BOOT.SYS provide. You can even set up some spare configurations for your users to tinker with without disturbing the ones you support.

Performance

While the installation process is highly automated, the documentation and specific options provided with BOOT.SYS and BOOT.EXE are very lengthy. You need to read the accompanying documentation very carefully before proceeding.

Registration

If you continue to use BOOTSY after a reasonable evaluation period, you must register it with the program author. Registration is $39, and you will receive a printed manual, the most current registered version, and free technical support for 90 days. If you install BOOTSY on a client's system, you must collect and remit the registration fee or instruct your client to remit the proper fee directly.

Summary

BOOTSY provides technicians with a detailed tool for multiple system configurations, an ideal means of getting your customers out of trouble with incompatible hardware or software.

CCS103.ZIP

Multiple boot options are often the only solution when various incompatible hardware or software exists on the same PC. The Configuration Control System (Table 7-8) allows users to store different options in the CONFIG.SYS and AUTOEXEC.BAT files. At bootup time, they can select the particular options to boot with. As with other multiboot software, developing a menu can be a time-consuming process, but CCS103 offers a relatively simple command structure and detailed documentation to assist you.

Installation and configuration

CCS will run from either a floppy or hard drive, but since most booting occurs from the C: hard drive, you will install CCS to your hard drive in just about all circumstances. Create a subdirectory for CCS. Copy the CCS103.ZIP archive file from your CD to the subdirectory, then run PKUNZIP to decompress the archive file. Once the archive file is extracted, you can edit CONFIG.SYS and AUTOEXEC.BAT to add CCS features to the startup files.

Operation

CCS is executed as a TSR in the CONFIG.SYS file. Once it is loaded, use DEVICE= lines to denote the start and end of various configurations. The CONFIG.SYS file starts by loading CCS.CTL,

■ **Table 7-8 CCS103 fact sheet**

Program name:	Configuration Control System
Executable file:	OPTPICK.COM
Purpose:	Utility to provide multiple boot configurations
Version:	1.02 (c. 1991)
Operating system:	MS-DOS 3.3 or later
Compressed file:	CCS103.ZIP (archive)
Author:	Kok Hong Soh
Address:	Bendix/King Radio Corp.
	400 N. Rogers Road, MD 43
	Olathe, KS 66062
ASP member:	No
Registration:	$0 shareware
Special notes:	Runs as a device driver

then the options begin with OPTION x commands, such as OPTION A, B, or C, and each section ends with an ENDOPT command. You end the CCS "control area" by using DONECCS at the end of CONFIG.SYS. The structure of a typical CONFIG.SYS file using CCS might appear such as this:

```
DEVICE=CCS.CTL [wait] [def]
DEVICE=OPTION B [descriptive text for option B]
[the command lines for "configuration B" would go here_]
DEVICE=ENDOPT
[you might place command lines common to all configurations here_]
DEVICE=OPTION A [descriptive text for option A]
[the command lines for "configuration A" would go here_]
DEVICE=ENDOPT
[you might place additional "common" command lines here_]
DEVICE=OPTION C [descriptive text for option C]
[the command lines for "configuration C" would go here_]
DEVICE=ENDOPT
[you might place a few last "common" command lines here_]
DEVICE=DONECCS
```

Note the optional variables, in brackets. The *wait* variable is the number of seconds to wait for a key to be hit before the default configuration is used to boot up the system. If *wait* is omitted, the menu is put up automatically when the machine boots up. The *def* variable is a single alphabetical character for the default menu item selection. If *def* is too large, too small, or omitted, the default selection will be A. Finally, you can place descriptive text after DEVICE=OPTION x so the menu can display a description of that configuration option. For example, after DEVICE=OPTION B, you might put "Run game mode (maximum CMM)." You will see this text in the startup menu.

For true system startup control, you must also have control over the AUTOEXEC.BAT file. After CCS.CTL is installed as a character device driver, the option selected by the user is stored in its memory. The device sets itself up with the filename CCS103XX. You can then use the OPTPICK.COM program executed in AUTOEXEC.BAT to access the option selected by the user by reading the file CCS103XX. OPTPICK.COM sets the environment variable CCS103 to the letter option selected by the user during the loading of CONFIG.SYS, and can direct the execution of AUTOEXEC.BAT accordingly. The following is an example AUTOEXEC.BAT file using OPTPICK.COM:

```
OPTPICK
if "%CCS103%"=="" goto noconfig
goto config%CCS103%
:noconfig
echo Cannot find configuration. Check AUTOEXEC.BAT and CONFIG.SYS.
goto done
:configA
REM the command lines for "configuration A" would go here
GOTO done
:configB
REM the command lines for "configuration B" would go here
GOTO done
:configC
REM the command lines for "configuration C" would go here
:done
REM you can place common command lines here
```

Performance

Although CCS is a highly configurable package and a bit simpler to use than other boot managers, there are some important limitations that you should be aware of. First, descriptive text in the CONFIG.SYS DEVICE=OPTION x lines is limited to 52 characters. Longer strings are truncated. If you need more characters to be displayed, increase MAXWIDTH in CCS.ASM and recompile the file. Second, CCS can handle 100 lines per option at most, which should be plenty for just about anyone. If you need more lines, increase MAXLINES in CCS.ASM and recompile the file.

Registration

CCS is provided as $0 shareware, so you may use and distribute it freely.

Summary

CCS is a handy (and free) tool for systems that need multiple configurations, yet it's easier to use than other boot managers. What the package lacks is clear documentation and good examples.

Editors

An editor is the kind of tool you never seem to have when you need it. Text editors are always handy for modifying CONFIG.SYS, AUTOEXEC.BAT, and other batch files. For experienced technicians, hexadecimal editors can be invaluable assets for checking and modifying disk files. The programs covered in this section provide shareware versions of both text and hex editors.

HW16V210.ZIP

Hexadecimal (or hex) editors are of particular interest to programmers, but they can also be extremely handy for technicians who are examining disk files or searching files for virus signatures. The Hex Workshop (Table 7-9) is a file and disk editor that allows you to edit, insert, delete, cut, copy, and paste hexadecimal data, all with the ease of a word processor. Additional features include go to, find, replace, compare, and checksum calculation. This version of the program can launch from the File Manager. The Hex Workshop also provides you with a base converter for translating between hex, decimal, and binary, as well as a hex calculator.

■ **Table 7-9 HW16V210 fact sheet**

Program name:	Hex Editor
Executable file:	HWORKS16.EXE
Purpose:	A utility to edit hex files
Version:	2.10 (c. 1996)
Operating system:	Windows 3.1, 95, and NT
Compressed file:	HW16V210.ZIP (archive)
Author:	BreakPoint Software
Address:	P.O. Box 4629
	Stamford, CT 06907-0629
CompuServe:	75554,377
ASP member:	Yes
Registration:	$20
Special notes:	Requires Windows to operate

Installation and configuration

The Hex Workshop will operate from a floppy disk, but hard drive installation is much more common. Create a new subdirectory for the program. Copy the HW16V210.ZIP archive file from your CD to the new subdirectory, then run PKUNZIP to extract the archive. Once the archive file is decompressed, you can run HWORKS16.EXE directly from the Windows File Manager or Windows Explorer. If you prefer, you can create program groups and icons for the program.

Operation and performance

Once you launch The Hex Editor and get past the shareware reminder, you will see the main work screen, shown in Figure 7-5. This area appears almost identical to a word processor, and makes the program very straightforward to use. Cut (<Ctrl>–X), Copy (<Ctrl>–C), and Paste (<Ctrl>–V) operate in a similar manner to other editors. The Paste Special feature allows you to choose from and paste any of the standard Windows clipboard formats currently available into a file. Undo (<Ctrl>–Z) allows you to reverse the most recent editing operation(s). You can set the size of the undo buffer (which determines how many operations are saved) under the Options (Display and General) menu. "Automated inserting" (<Ctrl>–<Ins>) allows you to insert a specified number of bytes at the cursor position with any hex value. Deleting (<Del>) simply deletes the highlighted bytes. You can perform normal editing in either insert or overwrite mode. Insert mode automatically inserts hex values at the cursor position, while overwrite mode overwrites existing bytes at the cursor position with hex values entered. The current mode is shown in the far right pane of the status bar and is toggled with the <Insert> key.

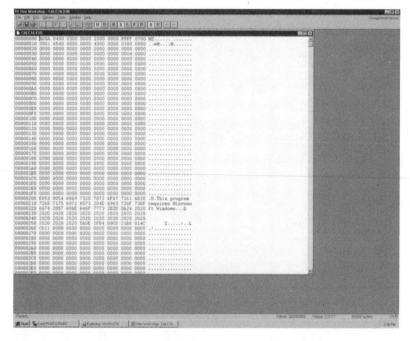

■ **7-5** *Opening a file for review and edit in HW16V210.*

You can edit a file from either the hex or ASCII display. And you can toggle the cursor between hex and ASCII with the <Tab> key, or choose hex/ASCII by clicking the mouse in the particular region. File/Disk Properties (<Alt>–<Enter> or clicking the right mouse button) display information on the current file or disk being edited.

The first pane of the status bar contains information on the current operation (or menu item). The second pane of the status bar contains the cursor position, displayed in either hex or decimal. The third pane contains information on either the data at the cursor position or highlighted data. If no data is highlighted, Hex Workshop interprets the data at the cursor in the specified data format. If data is highlighted, Hex Workshop will interpret the data appropriately, depending on the amount of bytes highlighted (e.g., two bytes as a Short). If an appropriate data type does not exist (if an odd number of bytes is highlighted), Hex Workshop will display the number of bytes being highlighted. The contents of the fourth pane depends on whether a file or disk is being edited. If a file is being edited, the pane contains the file size in bytes, displayed in either hex or decimal (see Options, File Offset, and Data). If a disk is being edited, the pane contains the size in bytes of the sector being edited. The last pane displays whether Hex Workshop is currently in overwrite or insertion mode. If it's in overwrite, it will display an OVR; if it's in insert, it will be blank.

In addition to editing files, you can also use Hex Workshop to edit drive (disk) sectors. By selecting Open Drive from under the Disk menu, you can edit both mounted drives and BIOS disks (INT 13 floppy or fixed disk). In drive mode (default), you can edit PC drives mounted by the operating system. Drives of this type include floppy disks, hard drives, and other external removable disks. You cannot edit CD-ROMs because the operating system mounts these in a different manner than other disks (more like network drives). In raw mode (or disk mode), you can edit BIOS disks. BIOS disks include floppy disks and fixed disks. Available floppy disks are A: and B:, while fixed disks are listed as $0x80$ (first fixed disk), $0x81$ (second fixed disk), and so on.

The difference between the two modes is that drives are accessed as logical volumes through the operating system by letters assigned by the operating system, and can be edited only if the operating system understands the disk format (file system). Disks are accessed as physical media through the BIOS. Raw (disk) mode allows you to edit disks not readable by the operating system, as well as partition information stored on the disk but not residing in a logical volume.

Disk editing information is supplied to the user. The sector number currently being edited and the total number of sectors on the disk are shown in the title bar. The sector size, cursor position (within the sector), and hex data interpretation are shown in the status bar. The current sector and buttons to move forward or backward between sectors are displayed in the toolbar.

You perform drive editing the same way as file editing, with a few exceptions. Since the sector size is fixed, data cannot be inserted or deleted, only overwritten. The Goto utility becomes a Goto Sector utility, allowing movement forward or backward between sectors in the beginning, end, or current sector of the drive/disk. The Find utility operates on a range of sectors specified in the Find dialog, and Replace is disabled for sector editing. Finally, the Compare tool will compare (and wrap) within a sector, but not cross sector boundaries.

Registration

If you continue to use The Hex Workshop beyond a reasonable evaluation period, you must register it with the program author. Registration is $20, and registered users receive the latest versions of both the 16-bit and 32-bit Hex Workshop programs.

Summary

Disk and file editing can be a difficult and dangerous procedure, but reasonably priced tools like the Hex Editor can provide professional technicians with an enormous advantage.

RAVED.ZIP

Technicians often find themselves needing to edit system startup and .INI files, with no text editor handy. The Ravitz Editor (Table 7-10) is an ASCII text editor for DOS. It is a relatively small program (less than 60KB), but it is also a powerful editor with integrated outlining and overview capabilities. The editor includes find/change functions with options such as check case, ignore excluded lines, look only in marked area, and show all. It has block mark functions, including overlay, merge, copy lines, line sort, delete, fill with block pattern, fill with numeric line pattern, shift horizontal, and shift vertical. There are also functions to help in writing documents such as word wrap, flow, flow with right justification, flow into list, center text, and line drawing. You can also configure Ravitz Editor with profiles that are installed in the

.EXE file. You can define keyboard usage, default values, macros, menus, panels, and help text with a profile and assemble it into a new RE.EXE. The macro facility has nestable macros with looping and conditional control.

■ Table 7-10 RAVED fact sheet

Program name:	Ravitz ASCII Editor
Executable file:	RE.EXE
Purpose:	A utility to support the editing of ASCII files
Version:	1.10 (c. 1993)
Operating system:	MS-DOS 3.3 or later
Compressed file:	RAVED.ZIP (archive)
Author:	Cary Ravitz
Address:	Ravitz Software, Inc.
	P.O. Box 25068
	Lexington, KY 40524-5068
BBS:	606-268-0577
CompuServe:	70431,32
ASP member:	No
Registration:	$0 shareware
Special notes:	Use caution when editing files

Installation and configuration

Ravitz Editor will run from a floppy disk or hard drive, but it is more common to install the program to your hard drive first; you can always copy the working file(s) over to a floppy disk later. Create a subdirectory for the editor, then copy the RAVED.ZIP archive file to the new subdirectory. Run PKUNZIP to decompress the archive. Once the archive is decompressed, run REPROF.EXE from the DOS prompt to create RE.EXE. REPROF.EXE is the profile assembler. It assembles a profile to create a new RE.EXE, and can also regenerate the original RE.EXE. The REPROF.1 and REPROF.2 files are profiles you can use as starting points for customizing the editor. You can find the documentation in RE.DOC.

Operation

When you first start the editor, you will have an empty file. If you prefer to start with an old file, type RE and the filename at the DOS prompt. The display must be in 80-column (or greater) mode or RE will not start. If this is not the case, use the DOS MODE command to set it (MODE CO80, MODE BW80, or MODE MONO). To save your data and exit from RE, use the S (Save) and Q (Quit) commands, described later in this section.

There are four ways to interface with RE. The first is through the letter and number keys. The screen and computer memory will echo your input at the cursor location. The cursor is a bright block behind a character or a highlighted underscore character (on a digital monochrome display). The second interface method is through function keys. Function keys perform various often-used functions. They include the cursor movement keys, the <Enter>, <Insert>, and <Delete> keys, and the <Alt> and <Ctrl>-shifted keys. These keys and their functions are described in the accompanying documentation. Some function keys perform two or three functions (sometimes depending on cursor position to distinguish the functions, and sometimes requiring multiple presses to perform a function).

You can also enter commands into the editor at the top line of the editing screen (the command line), and execute them by pressing the <Enter> key. Commands include functions that require the entry of names, numbers, or other options. Some examples are E to edit a file, S to save a file, and Q to quit. The fourth method of working with the editor is through menus. When a menu is displayed, you can move the selection bar to any item with the cursor keys and select the item with the <Enter> key. If one of the letters in an item is capitalized, then you can immediately select that item by pressing the corresponding letter. The <Esc> key will back you out of the current menu, and the <Page Up> and <Page Down> keys display the previous or next menus.

Performance

The Ravitz Editor comes with extensive documentation, so every feature is detailed. Still, there are a few tips that can help you make the most of RE.EXE. For example, if you use the DOS shell often and you have enough memory, put COMMAND.COM on a RAM disk and add the following line to AUTOEXEC.BAT:

```
SET COMSPEC=D:\COMMAND.COM
```

To transfer text between files, edit both files at the same time. Mark an area in one file, press <Alt>–Q to get to the second file, and then move, copy, overlay, or insert (<Alt>–M, <Alt>–C, <Alt>–O, or <Alt>–I) the area mark.

If you have decided where to move a piece of text, but have not marked the text yet, press <Alt>–P to mark your position. Then mark the text and press <Alt>–G to return to that position.

It is rarely necessary to unmark an area. When you get the "Area mark already exists" message, repeat the same function. The area will be unmarked and a new area mark will be started.

For cursor movement, shifting text, inserting new lines, repeat finds, and change functions, the typematic function of the PC keyboard is very useful.

If you accidentally overwrite a file with the Save command, don't forget that the file is still on your disk with the extension .BAK. You can read in the .BAK file and save it to the correct name.

Registration

The Ravitz Editor is provided as $0 shareware, so you may use and distribute it freely.

Summary

Ravitz Editor is a free tool that can come in handy when you need to edit a CONFIG.SYS, AUTOEXEC.BAT, or .INI file.

XEV43.ZIP

Hex editors are a specialized tool that technicians can use to alter disk files or search file contents for such peculiarities as virus strings. While not as sophisticated as other hex editors, HexEdit (Table 7-11) is a DOS-based program that allows you to display or edit the contents of any file. A large number of simple commands makes HexEdit particularly flexible to use.

■ **Table 7-11 XEV43 fact sheet**

Program name:	HexEdit
Executable file:	XE.EXE
Purpose:	A utility to edit disk files
Version:	4.3 (c. 1994)
Operating system:	MS-DOS 3.3 or later
Compressed file:	XEV43.ZIP (archive)
Author:	Robert Stuntz
Address:	2120 Aspen Dr.
	Woodstock, IL 60098
CompuServe:	71043,117
ASP member:	No
Registration:	$0 shareware
Special notes:	Use extreme caution when editing files

Installation and configuration

HexEdit will run from the floppy drive or hard drive. Copy the XEV43.ZIP archive file from the CD to a subdirectory on your hard drive or a floppy disk. Switch to the subdirectory (or floppy drive) and run PKUNZIP to decompress the archive. Once the file is decompressed, you can run XE.EXE directly.

Operation

Once XE.EXE is started, you will see the main display with a list of available files in the current directory, as shown in Figure 7-6. The name of the loaded file (if any) is listed on the top of the screen. On the left side of the display are numbers (in hexadecimal, decimal, or octal) indicating the offset into the file. In the middle are 22 rows of 16 bytes, which are the file's contents. An ASCII character on the right represents each byte in that row. In the ASCII portion of the display, any characters past the EOF (end of file) are shown as a period (ASCII 249). On the bottom is a status word indicating your current operation; a three-letter abbreviation indicating whether the offset display is in hexadecimal, decimal, or octal; the percentage into the file from the top line; and the size of the file in decimal. XE offers a wide range of single-key commands to streamline operation. The list of commands for XE are as follows:

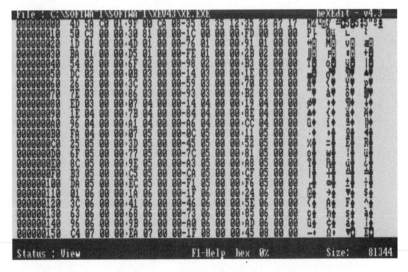

■ **7-6** *Opening a file for review and edit in XEV43.*

F1 Help

A/<Alt>–A ASCII table

B/<Alt>–B Base conversion (decimal-hexadecimal-binary)

C Change colors

D Change offset display to decimal

<Alt>–D Shell out to a DOS prompt or other program

E Edit the file

F Search forward from current position

G Go to offset

H Change offset display to hexadecimal

L Bring up the Load File box

M Push position on marker stack

N Search again (using last search parameters)

O Change offset display to octal

R Retrieve position from marker stack

S Search (from beginning of file)

Z Clear all entries from marker stack

<Alt>–1 through <Alt>–9 Go to marked position

Up/down arrow keys Scroll up and down one line at a time

<Page up>/<Page down> Move up/down one page at a time

<Home> Move to the beginning of the file

<End> Move to the end of the file

<Esc>/<Alt>–X Quit XE

Performance

In addition to a suite of single-key commands, some command-line options are available for HexEdit:

/C Tells XE to use its default color set.

/M Tells XE to use black and white (for monochrome monitors).

/? or /H Either of these two options will display a short message about the start-up syntax.

/Lc[c[c]] The files and directories in the Load File box are sorted, depending on the value of this option. /L is followed by from one to three characters that describe the actual sort options:

U	Unsorted; directory and file entries are listed as they are read from the disk, then the list drive designators
D	Puts directory entries at the top of the list, followed by files and drive designators (the default)

F	Puts file entries at the top of the list, followed by directories and then drive designators
N	Sorts files and directories by name (the default)
E	Sorts files and directories by extension, then name (sorting by extension slows down the speed at which the list is sorted and displayed, more than the other options)
S	Sorts files by size and directories by name (the physical size of directory entry is irrelevant)
T	Sorts files and directories by date/time
A	Sorts files and directories in ascending order (the default)
Z	Sorts files and directories in descending order

HexEdit is provided as $0 shareware, so it may be used and distributed freely.

Summary

HexEdit is a free, DOS-based file editor capable of operating in decimal, hexadecimal, or octal mode. Simple, single-key commands and command-line options make the program very straightforward to operate.

Input devices

Input devices serve a surprisingly important role in PCs; they are the only means of getting commands into the computer. There are three major types of input devices for a PC: the keyboard, the joystick, and the mouse. When problems occur with input devices, PC operation can be erratic and frustrating. Although each type of input device has various features and enhancements, they all work in fundamentally the same way. As a result, you can diagnose problems with just a few general-purpose tools, such as the ones in this section.

CALJOY22.ZIP

Joysticks are used exclusively for games (and occasional VR packages), and are certainly not crucial for proper operation of a PC. Still, when joystick problems arise, it can cause real frustration on the part of the PC user. Joysticks take a lot of abuse—even with the most careful user—and they are prone to failure and intermittent operation with age and wear. Joysticks (and their controllers) can also drift over time and result in erratic joystick operation. Since it is often inconvenient to start a joystick application in order to test the joystick and the controller, diagnostics such as CALJOY22 (Table 7-12) serve an important function. CALJOY22 allows you to calibrate a joystick for a particular controller and test the joystick's operating range.

■ Table 7-12 CALJOY22 fact sheet

Program name:	Joystick Calibration Utility
Executable file:	CALJOY2.EXE
Purpose:	A utility to test the calibration of a standard joystick
Version:	2.2 (c. 1991)
Operating system:	MS-DOS 3.3 or later
Compressed file:	CALJOY22.ZIP (archive)
Author:	EC Systems
ASP member:	No
Registration:	Print registration form for amount and contact information
Special notes:	No related documentation

Installation and configuration

CALJOY22 can be run from a floppy disk or hard drive, but since you'll likely want to have the program in your toolbox, try installing it to a floppy disk. Copy the CALJOY22.ZIP file from your CD to a floppy disk. If you choose to install the program to your hard drive, create a new subdirectory for the program and copy the CALJOY22.ZIP file to the hard drive. Switch to the floppy drive (or subdirectory on the hard drive) and run PKUNZIP to decompress the archive. Once the file is decompressed, you can run CALJOY2.EXE directly.

Operation

Once CALJOY2.EXE starts, you will see a calibration screen, as shown in Figure 7-7 on the next page. There are two calibration grids since the program supports two joysticks on the same standard gameport. If only one joystick is connected to the gameport, the right calibration grid will be unused. A simple-to-follow graphic display will lead you through the calibration process. Once the joystick is calibrated, you can test its range and response, as well as the "fire" buttons. If there is a problem with drift, you can simply let the program run for a while and see if the centered markings move off once the joystick (and especially the controller)warm up.

Performance

In actual operation, the CALJOY2.EXE program ran fine, but they would not print the registration form containing the registration

■ **7-7** *The joystick calibration screen in CALJOY22.*

amount and mailing address for EC Systems. You might have better luck with your own printer.

Registration

Since I was unable to print the registration form, I'm not sure just how much the registration is, but the shareware version is quite complete.

Summary

CALJOY2.EXE is a handy tool for checking joystick operation, and can reveal important details or idiosyncrasies about the joystick or gameport.

JOY2.EXE

While joysticks are certainly not the most important input devices, they are certainly one of the most popular, available with a wide range of styles and features. When trouble occurs with the joystick or its controller, the corresponding application (e.g., a flight simulator) is virtually useless. JOY2.EXE (Table 7-13) is a stand-alone diagnostic you can use to calibrate and test just about any basic joystick.

■ **Table 7-13 JOY2 fact sheet**

Program name:	Joystick Calibration Utility
Executable file:	JOY2.EXE
Purpose:	A utility to calibrate a standard joystick
Version:	1.0 (c. 1994)
Operating system:	MS-DOS 3.3 or later
Compressed file:	None
Author:	Dave Murray
Address:	BioGeoMagnetics 74 Friend St. Adams, MA 01220
Phone:	413-743-5591
ASP member:	No
Registration:	$0 shareware
Special notes:	Works on one joystick only

Installation and configuration

There is nothing to install with JOY2.EXE; the program is provided in an uncompressed form, so you can copy it to a floppy disk or subdirectory on your hard drive and execute it directly.

Operation

When you start JOY2.EXE, you will see a text screen with some brief instructions. Press any key to proceed with calibration. JOY2.EXE calibrates simply by moving the joystick back and to the forth, then pressing the "fire" button to complete the calibration. You can then move the joystick about and see its position move on the display. Both fire buttons can also be detected. Press <Esc> to end the program.

Performance

While the program is simple to run, it is limited to a single joystick and its graphics are somewhat coarse; the joystick pointer leaves "trails" if moved outside the blue box.

Registration

JOY2.EXE is provided as $0 shareware, so you may use and distribute it freely.

Summary

In spite of its limitations, JOY2.EXE can be a useful tool when checking joysticks and gameports.

SCODE22.ZIP

Keyboards are easily the most important—and abused—PC input devices. Not only must a keyboard endure constant pounding, but its openings allow all manner of dust and debris into the key mechanisms. As a result, it is not uncommon for keys to jam, stick, or fail outright. You can use the SCODE22 program from Paul Postuma (Table 7-14) to check the scan codes being received by the CPU. Missing or erratic keycodes almost always indicate a faulty keyboard or keyboard controller.

■ Table 7-14 SCODE22 fact sheet

Program name:	Keyboard Code Scanner
Executable file:	SCODE.COM
Purpose:	Utility to report the make/break codes of each keyboard key pressed
Version:	2.2 (c. 1996)
Operating system:	MS-DOS 3.3 or later
Compressed file:	SCODE22.ZIP (archive)
Author:	Paul Postuma
Address:	16 Fullyer Drive Quispamsis, NB E2G 1Y7 Canada
Phone:	506-849-6967
CompuServe:	74471,1240
Internet:	ppostuma@nbnet.nb.ca
ASP member:	Yes
Registration:	$0 shareware
Special notes:	Program might not recognize very unusual keystrokes

Installation and configuration

SCODE22 can be run from a floppy disk or hard drive, but since you'll likely want to have the program in your toolbox, try installing it to a floppy disk. Copy the SCODE22.ZIP archive file from your DLS Diagnostic CD to a floppy disk. If you choose to install the program to your hard drive, create a new subdirectory for the program and copy the SCODE22.ZIP file to the hard drive. Switch to the floppy drive (or subdirectory on the hard drive) and run PKUNZIP to decompress the archive. Once the file is decompressed, you can run SCODE.COM directly.

Operation

The SCODE.COM program reports scan and ASCII codes returned whenever the INT 16h BIOS function is invoked, as well as the value left in the keyboard BIOS when any valid key combination is used. The calling keystroke is accurately identified (where possible). Scan and ASCII codes are presented in hexadecimal and decimal, their combined AX register value and the BIOS value are shown in hex, and the information is presented in the form of a scrolling display (Figure 7-8) that you can print out at any time. Press <Esc> to exit the program. While SCODE was originally designed to provide key information for programmers, it is also recognized as a tool for technicians.

■ **7-8** *Reviewing the most recent keystrokes with SCODE22.*

Performance

There are some limitations to ScanCode. Some keystrokes might not produce a scan code for INT 16h when you're using a particular keyboard/system combination. For example, pressing F11 should put the value 8500h into AX when INT 16h is called, but it won't on some systems. Examining the BIOS directly, however, shows that F11 can indeed be recognized.

Registration

The ScanCode diagnostic is provided as $0 shareware, so you may use and distribute it freely.

Summary

The ScanCode diagnostic is a good, basic, and free keyboard key checker that's small enough to be used without consuming much memory. It's an easy addition to your collection of toolbox diagnostics.

STKVGA31.ZIP

As analog devices, joysticks tend to misbehave through time and wear, which makes them extremely difficult to use gamed or in other applications relying on the joystick. While there are several diagnostics available to test the operation of a joystick and game-port, few are as detailed as the STKVGA31 package from Rick Horwitz (Table 7-15). The program not only checks for centering and calibration, it also helps technicians measure the joystick's dynamic range. This allows you to objectively compare different joysticks.

■ **Table 7-15 STKVGA31 fact sheet**

Program name:	Joystick Check
Executable file:	STKVGA31.EXE
Purpose:	Program to check the performance of a joystick
Version:	3.1 (c. 1991)
Operating system:	MS-DOS 3.3 or later
Compressed file:	STKVGA31.ZIP (archive)
Author:	Rick Horwitz
Address:	110 Houlton Ct.
	San Jose, CA 85139
ASP member:	No
Registration:	$0 shareware
Special notes:	Good graphic interface

Installation and configuration

STKVGA31 can be run from a floppy disk or hard drive, but since you'll probably want to have the program in your toolbox, try installing it to a floppy disk. Copy the STKVGA31.ZIP archive file from the CD to a floppy disk. If you choose to install the program to your hard drive, create a new subdirectory for the program and copy the STKVGA31.ZIP file to the hard drive. Switch to the floppy drive (or subdirectory on the hard drive) and run PKUNZIP to decompress the archive. Once the file is decompressed, you can run STKVGA31.EXE directly.

Operation

There are three main areas of the STKVGA work screen (Figure 7-9): the calibration grid, the X and Y null values, and the operating menu. As you move the joystick about, you will see the corresponding X and Y cursors. Arrow cursors allow you to trim the nul setting on both axes (the setting is reflected in the X and Y Nul gauges). Finally, you can calibrate the joystick with <F2>,

use the program's help feature with <F3>, or quit the program by
using <F1>.

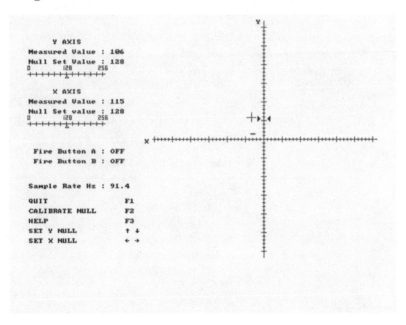

■ **7-9** *A precision joystick calibration screen in STKVGA31.*

Performance

STKVGA31 is probably the cleanest and most informative of the
joystick programs reviewed in this chapter. Its only real limitation
is that it tests only the A joystick, so a second joystick on the same
gameport is not supported.

Registration

The STKVGA diagnostic is provided as $0 shareware, so you may
use and distribute it freely.

Summary

STKVGA is an informative tool for serious technicians trying to
check or compare joystick/gameport performance.

TMTX.EXE

The mouse and trackball (referred to as *pointers*) have become
the premier pointing devices for PCs. Rather than using keyboard commands to run a program, a pointer allows you to select
and manipulate specific icons or screen elements. This, in turn,
makes programs much easier and intuitive to operate. When a
pointer gets old or dirty and begins behaving erratically, users

might have great difficulty operating the corresponding programs. Diagnostics such as TMTX (Table 7-16) provide technicians with a means of checking pointers without having to use Windows or load other pointer-compatible applications (such as text editors).

■ Table 7-16 TMTX fact sheet

Program name:	Mouse/Trackball Testing Utility
Executable file:	TMT.EXE
Purpose:	Tests the operation of a standard mouse
Version:	1.01 (c. 1989)
Operating system:	MS-DOS 3.3 or later
Compressed file:	TMTX.EXE (self-extracting)
Author:	TechStaff Corporation
Address:	64 Carroll St. Watertown, MA 02172
Phone:	617-924-0306
ASP member:	No
Registration:	$30
Special notes:	Requires a mouse driver running in the background

Installation and configuration

You can run TMTX from a floppy disk or hard drive, but you might prefer to keep the diagnostic in your toolbox. Copy the TMTX.EXE self-extracting archive file from your DLS Diagnostic CD to a floppy disk. If you choose to install the program to your hard drive, create a new subdirectory for the program and copy the TMTX.EXE file to the hard drive. Switch to the floppy drive (or subdirectory on the hard drive) and run TMTX to decompress the archive. Once the file is decompressed, you can run the executable file TMT.EXE directly. Keep in mind that, in order to use TMT, you need a mouse driver running in the background that is compatible with the mouse/trackball being used.

Operation

Once TMT starts, you will see a shareware notice, then the main work screen (Figure 7-10). If the mouse is working, you can track the mouse movement in the large center display; this will also show you if the mouse skips or stalls. Version 1.01 provides five options along the top of your display: Help, Sensitivity, Color, Cursor, and Range. The Help feature, <F1>, brings up the help screen for TMT. The help is a bit thin, but it can still be useful. You can adjust the mouse response by checking the Sensitivity settings, <F2>, and adjust mouse colors for easier viewing with the Color function, <F3>. You can set the basic cursor shape by using the Cursor option, <F4>, and use the Range function, <F5>, to set the parameters of mouse motion. The <Esc> key will back you out of menus and exit the program.

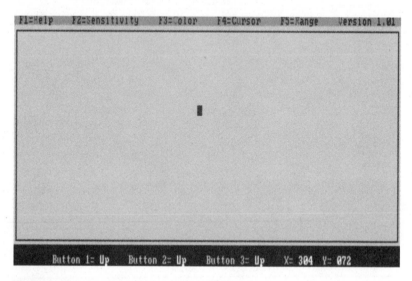

■ 7-10 *The mouse work screen in TMTX.*

Performance

Keep in mind that a suitable mouse driver must be running before you start TMT. If you install TMT to a floppy drive, you might want to place several popular mouse drivers on the disk, and use a boot manager on a bootable floppy to select the proper mouse driver on test system initialization.

Registration

The evaluation period for TMT is limited to only 10 days. If you continue to use TMT after the 10-day evaluation period, you must register the product with the program author. Registration is $30, and registered users receive the latest registered version, a collection of software tools, a printed manual, and two years of technical support.

Summary

TMT.EXE is a good DOS tool for testing the operation of a mouse without having to start Windows, when there are no other mouse-aware DOS utilities handy on the system.

Reference works

In addition to diagnostic tools and utilities, there is a proliferation of reference software that provides cross-references and indexes to assist technicians in setting up and configuring systems. This part of the chapter covers three of the most popular (and frequently updated) reference works available in shareware: Card Guide, Parts Locator, and The Hard Drive Reference.

CARDG2.ZIP

Finding data on I/O cards and other adapters can be a nightmare when there is no documentation (and you can't find the vendor). Collecting and documenting card data—especially jumper settings—has become somewhat of an industry unto itself. The Card Guide program (Table 7-17) is one such shareware "reference utility" that includes a simple menu-driven interface providing a concisely cataloged collection of information (e.g., jumper settings and ANSI diagrams) for various I/O cards. The program concentrates on providing information for "no-name" cards (not made or supported by any stated company) and other cut-rate boards whose documentation is almost impossible to come by.

Installation and configuration

Overall, the Card Guide is small enough to fit on a single 1.44MB floppy disk, but since this is a reference program, you should probably install it to your hard drive. Create a new subdirectory for the

■ **Table 7-17 CARDG2 fact sheet**

Program name:	Card Guide
Executable file:	CARDG.EXE
Purpose:	A reference utility for various I/O card configurations
Version:	2.0 (c. 1995)
Operating system:	MS-DOS 3.3 or later
Compressed file:	CARDG2.ZIP (archive)
Author:	Kevin Noble
Address:	P.O. Box 212
	Regina, Saskatchewan S4P 2Z6
	Canada
CompuServe:	72420,253
Internet:	NOBLE@SIAST.SK.CA
URL:	http://www.siast.sk.ca/~noble/noblpage.htm
ASP member:	No
Registration:	Voluntary contribution
Special notes:	E-mail registration can be tricky

program and copy the CARDG2.ZIP archive file from your CD to the new subdirectory. After the file is copied, switch to the new subdirectory and run PKUNZIP to decompress the archive. You can then start the program by running CARDG.EXE directly.

Operation

Once the Card Guide starts, you will see a main menu, shown in Figure 7-11. The first four selections in the menu allow you to search for different types of I/O and controller cards. Option 5 provides information on cables and connectors. The Card Layout Search in option 6 lets you track down card information based on the general layout of jumpers. The registered version of the Card Guide allows users to enter and recall their own card data (option 7), so the program can actually "grow" with the user's experience. Option 8 provides simple instructions and tips for card installation. Finally, option 9 offers a glossary of terms and abbreviations.

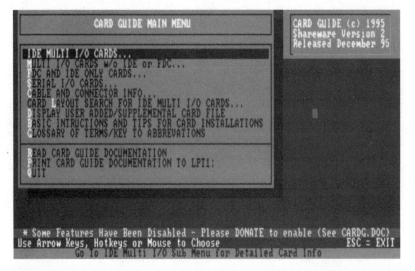

■ **7-11** *The Card Guide main menu options under CARDG2.*

Once you select a search category, a list of available cards for that category are displayed. Simply select the particular card of interest, and the program will provide an ANSI graphic of the board, along with complete jumper settings, such as the example in Figure 7-12. The graphics are very basic, but they do illustrate the position of each jumper and port connection. Press the <Esc> button to back out of a selection or menu, or exit the program.

Performance

The Card Guide is a simple program to use and improve upon, but, like most reference programs, it can quickly become outdated

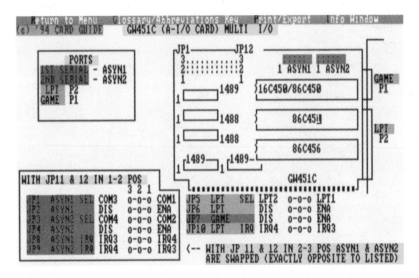

■ **7-12** *A typical page of card data in CARDG2.*

under the constant flood of new I/O and controller boards appearing for PCs. If you find yourself working with many different types of cards, make it a habit to update your copy of the Card Guide yourself, or pass the card data back to the program author so the new information can benefit everyone.

Registration

If you like the Card Guide and continue to use it beyond a reasonable evaluation period, you must register it with the program author. Unlike most shareware, which specifies a certain amount of money for registration, you can register the Card Guide for a voluntary contribution, whatever you think the program is worth. The actual process of registration is also a bit tricky since it is conducted almost entirely by e-mail, so you will need an Internet or CompuServe account. Run the BUYME program included with the CARDG2 package. This generates a code. Note the code and include it in an e-mail message to the program author (don't forget to note the amount you're going to send along). When the program author receives your e-mail, you will get a key that you can use to unlock the full version. You can then mail along your voluntary contribution at your convenience.

Summary

The Card Guide is a particularly useful reference program (especially for no-name I/O and controller cards) that can grow with you as you enter new boards into its database.

LOCATO.ZIP

One of the greatest problems for technicians is locating parts and materials to support repairs. Even if you determine the problem successfully, finding the right component or assembly to finish the repair can often be a hassle. Technicians shopping around for upgrades and new assemblies are also hard-pressed to find manufacturers and distributors. The LOCATO package from Tech Assist, Inc. (Table 7-18) offers a resource for parts and materials—allowing you to search by part, manufacturer, or distributor—along with complete contact information.

■ Table 7-18 LOCATO fact sheet

Program name:	The Electronic Component Locator
Executable file:	OPEN.EXE
Purpose:	To assist in locating sources of parts and materials
Version:	2.2 (c. 1994)
Operating system:	MS-DOS 3.3 or later
Compressed file:	LOCATO.ZIP (archive)
Author:	Daybreak Communication
Address:	Tech Assist, Inc. Ste 105 11350 66th St. Largo, FL 34643
Phone:	813-547-0499
ASP member:	No
Registration:	Contact Tech Assist for current pricing and availability.
Special notes:	Supports printing of contact lists

Installation and configuration

At more than 1MB, the LOCATO package can be installed on a 1.2MB or 1.44MB floppy disk. However, most technicians will choose to install the program on their own workbench system. Create a new subdirectory for LOCATO, then copy the LOCATO.ZIP archive file from the DLS Diagnostic CD to your new subdirectory. Switch to the new subdirectory and run PKUNZIP to decompress the archive. Once the archive is extracted, you can run the working program (OPEN.EXE).

Operation

OPEN.EXE is a DOS program, although the product seems to run just fine through a DOS window in Windows 95. Once the program starts and you sit through several screens of information, the main menu will appear, as shown in Figure 7-13. The main menu allows you to search through manufacturers, distributors, products, and value-added resellers. The lists are cross-referenced, so you can move back and forth among manufacturers, products, and distributors, then print out a contact list. The general process is to select the product you're looking for first. This results in a list of manufacturers who make the product. When you choose a specific manufacturer, a listing of corresponding local distributors appears. You can then contact the distributors to place an order. Fair online help text answers basic operating questions. The <Esc> key backs you out of any list, and allows you to exit the program.

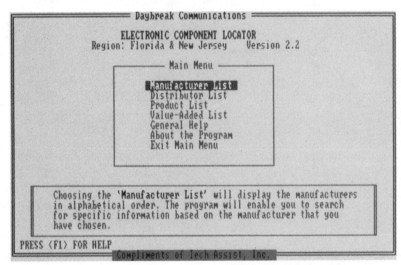

■ 7-13 *The main menu selections available in LOCATO.*

Performance

The program runs quickly and it's easy to navigate its simple, text-based menus, but the shareware version is limited to manufacturers and distributors in Florida and New Jersey. Other regions (and national versions) are available from Tech Assist. The only real disadvantage (as with most reference programs) is the tendency for the information to become dated or obsolete as the industry changes.

Registration

Contact Tech Assist for current pricing and availability of their regional and national part locators.

Summary

If you're having trouble finding parts for your repairs or upgrades, The Electronic Parts Locator is a reference option worth considering.

THEREF43.ZIP

Drive and adapter troubleshooting presents technicians with special problems. Each drive uses its own unique set of parameters (cylinders, heads, sectors per track, and so on) that must be entered into system CMOS in order for the drive to be recognized. Adapters can also be troublesome because of their different jumper settings and configurations. Finding data on a drive or adapter can become quite a challenge, especially for technicians who work with drive systems regularly. THEREF by Robert Falbo (Table 7-19) is a comprehensive directory of hard drives, floppy drives, optical drives, drive controllers, and host adapters. It is designed specifically to help novice and pro alike with integration problems and system setups.

■ **Table 7-19 THEREF43 fact sheet**

Program name:	The Hard Drive Reference
Executable file:	None (printer files only)
Purpose:	To provide an index of drive and controller specifications
Version:	4.3 (c. 1993)
Operating system:	MS-DOS 3.3 or later
Compressed file:	THEREF43.ZIP (archive)
Author:	Robert Falbo
URL:	http://theref.C3D.rl.af.mil
ASP member:	No
Registration:	$0 shareware
Special notes:	No executable software; only printable lists

Installation and configuration

THEREF is simply too big to fit on a single floppy disk, so you have to install it to your hard drive. Create a new subdirectory for THEREF43, then copy the archive file (THEREF43.ZIP) from your CD to the new subdirectory. Switch to the subdirectory and run PKUNZIP to extract the archive. Once the initial archive is decompressed, you have to decompress two additional files (LASERSET.ZIP and LAYOUTS.ZIP) to complete the installation.

Operation

The one major difference between THEREF and other shareware software in this book is that THEREF is not actually a program, but rather a set of documents that can be ported to your printer. When you decompress the archive, the following files are copied to your directory:

CTLREF43.LAN Controller listing (landscape mode)

CTLREF43.POR Controller listing (portrait mode)

FD_REF43.LAN Floppy drive listing (landscape mode)

FD_REF43.POR Floppy drive listing (portrait mode)

OD_REF43.LAN Optical drive listing (landscape mode)

OD_REF43.POR Optical drive listing (portrait mode)

HD_REF43.LAN Hard drive listing (landscape mode)

HD_REF43.POR Hard drive listing (portrait mode)

MFRDIR43.DOC Manufacturer's directory

TITLE43P.AGE Title page for THEREF

INTRO43.DOC Version/revision history for THEREF

DIAGRAMS.DOC A reference guide to connectors, interconnections, etc.

README43.DOC An introductory document

CONTRIBS.DOC The contributors page

LASERSET.ZIP Compressed setup files for LaserJet and PS printers

LAYOUTS.ZIP Compressed setup diagrams for controllers

Performance

Since THEREF is not a program, there are no performance characteristics to report on.

Registration

THEREF is provided as $0 shareware, so you may use and distribute it freely. Check the Internet Web site listed in Table 7-19 to download the latest version of THEREF.

Summary

Few indexes of drive and controller data are as complete as THEREF. Considering it's free and easy to use, consider adding this reference work to your system.

Sound utilities

Sound boards have become almost indispensable in modern PCs; there is hardly a game or application that does not make use of high-quality sound or stereo music. Sound cards are relatively easy to test through CD audio players. However, if an audio CD (or CD-ROM drive) is not available, you can use several of the stand-alone tools in this section to check the sound board alone.

SBBEEP.ZIP

Often, a quick and simple check of a sound board is all that's required in order to determine whether or not the device is working. SBBEEP (Table 7-20) is a basic tool originally intended to replace the PC speaker. When executed, the program emits a single, brief tone from your Sound Blaster (AdLib-compatible) sound board for 500 milliseconds. This allows you to check a sound board without having to load up complex diagnostics or figure out music applications. Casual users sometimes report using SBBEEP in a batch file to produce a tone when a function is completed. The actual tone is a lot louder then a plain speaker beep (about 47 dB).

■ **Table 7-20 SBBEEP fact sheet**

Program name:	Sound Blaster Beep
Executable file:	SBBEEP.COM
Purpose:	To emit a tone from the Sound Blaster or compatible sound board
Version:	1.0 (c. 1994)
Operating system:	MS-DOS 3.3 or later
Compressed file:	SBBEEP.ZIP (archive)
Author:	Travis Gebhardt
Address:	NeoSphere Software 42502 SE Oral Hull Rd. Sandy, OR 97055
America Online:	Trav
ASP member:	No
Registration:	$0 shareware
Special notes:	Emits a single brief beep when executed

Installation and configuration

SBBEEP is a very small utility (under 4KB), so it's perfect for a floppy disk in your toolbox. If you prefer to use SBBEEP as a batch-file marker on your system, install it to your hard drive.

Copy the SBBEEP.ZIP file from your CD to a floppy disk or a subdirectory on your hard drive. Switch to the floppy drive (or the hard drive subdirectory) and run PKUNZIP to decompress the archive file. You can use the utility directly by simply typing SBBEEP from the DOS prompt.

Operation

The program is very simple to operate; just type SBBEEP at the DOS prompt, and the beep will sound. If you don't have an AdLib or Sound Blaster-compatible sound card, you shouldn't hear anything. Run the program again for additional beeps.

Performance

Aside from a short after-tone, th SBBEEP program appears to run just fine (it was tested successfully on an Ensonique SoundScape PnP board). No other problems have been detected.

Registration

The SBBEEP utility is provided as $0 shareware, so you may use and distribute it freely.

Summary

SBBEEP provides a "quick and dirty" tool for testing Sound Blaster/AdLib sound boards, and can be used to provide audible cues in batch files.

SNDST.ZIP

A frequent complaint of most sound board software is that the utilities that set the board's mixer and channel volume settings are not saved once the PC is turned off, which requires users to reset the volume and mixer settings each time the system is initialized. The Sound State program from John Zitterkoph (Table 7-21) is designed to complement the software present in many sound card packages by saving and restoring the mixer settings of Pro Audio Spectrum (PAS), Sound Blaster Pro (SBPro), Sound Blaster 16 (SB16), and Gravis UltraSound (GUSMAX) boards. The program allows you to restore and save the settings of these sound cards to or from disk using batch files, so there is no interaction by the user. It also provides a graphical user interface (GUI) for modifying most mixer and volume settings of these cards.

Installation and configuration

The Sound State program saves and restores sound card settings, so you should install it to the local hard drive. Create a new

■ Table 7-21 SNDST fact sheet

Program name:	Sound Card State Selector
Executable file:	SNDSTATE.EXE
Purpose:	A utility to save and restore the configuration of sound boards
Version:	2.30 (c. 1996)
Operating system:	MS-DOS 3.0 or later
Compressed file:	SNDST.ZIP (archive)
Author:	John Zitterkopf
Address:	ZittWare 7599 Chevy Chase Dr. Suite 106 Austin, TX 78752
URL:	http://www2.msstate.edu/~Ejdz1
ASP member:	No
Registration:	$20
Special notes:	Geared for Sound Blaster, Pro Audio Spectrum, and Gravis boards

subdirectory for Sound State and copy the SNDST.ZIP program from your CD to the new subdirectory. Switch to the subdirectory and run PKUNZIP to decompress the archive. Once the archive has been extracted, you can start SNDSTATE.EXE directly.

Operation and performance

To run the program in its fully interactive mode, simply execute the SNDSTATE.EXE program without any command-line arguments. When the program starts, you can choose to save a file, restore an existing file, view a file, or abort and return to DOS. Next, enter the path and filename to be edited. If you need to restore a file and are not sure of the complete name, type the filename as you know it, along with a wildcard (*) at the point(s) you are unsure of. Sound State will attempt to complete the filename by finding the first file matching what you have entered. Once the desired file is found, the program will ask you to verify the restore operation. If you are saving a settings file, Sound State will ask you to confirm the save operation. When you confirm, the program checks to see if a file with the same name exists. If it determines that a file by that name already exists, Sound State will ask you to verify replacement of the old file. You can force a partial interactive mode by specifying either an -R (restore) or -S (save) switch as the first argument, then entering the filename. If you already know the filename to work with, you can add the name to the command line, for example PROAUDIO/DEFAULT.P16. Then the program will ask you only to verify the filename. The full syntax for Sound State is:

SNDSTATE [-R¦-S¦-V] [*filename*] [/SBP] [/MAX] [/Q] [/M]

The /Q option stands for Quiet mode. When you use this option with an -R or -S option and a filename, the program will run quietly without printing any messages or waiting for input. Use this feature in the AUTOEXEC.BAT to load your custom settings. For example:

SNDSTATE -R C:\PROAUDIO\GENERAL.P16 /Q /M

In this example, Sound State will restore the file named GENERAL.P16 in the directory C:\PROAUDIO with both quiet and smooth options enabled. Provided the file exists, the program will run without error messages or confirmation prompts. If the file does not exist, it will print an error message. The /M switch smoothes the transition when you change the states of the card. Use it if you notice an audible click when executing the program. Note: The /M and /Q features are available only in the registered version.

The /SBP option forces Sound State to run when there is a Sound Blaster Pro in the system but it isn't correctly detected. It will force a SBPro reset that returns the SBPro to a valid state. This will reset the entire SBPro card and attempt to keep your old settings intact. This option is intended to be used *only* if the program does not accurately detect a Sound Blaster Pro in the system. The most common symptom of this problem is when the SBPro is detected as a Sound Blaster 16. If this occurs, just rerun SNDSTATE with the /SBP option.

The /MAX option forces detection of GUSMAX when another sound card is detected. This is particularly useful when there is a GUSMAX and another sound card in the same system.

SNDSTATE GUI is invoked with the command-line switch -V. If your PC has a graphics card capable of 640 × 480 × 16 colors (any VGA/SVGA board) and has a sound board driver, Sound State should come up with an LED digit display with bar graphs showing the current settings of your card. Each display is either a percentage or an error code, with the error code shown as EE (which means that the value retrieved by the program was in error or your sound card does not support this mixer). The GUI also supports a mouse if a suitable mouse driver is installed first.

Registration

If you continue to use Sound State beyond a reasonable evaluation period, you must register the product with the program author.

Registration is $20, and registered users will receive the latest registered version of SNDSTATE with the /Q and /M switches enabled, a printed manual (including a list of error codes), and notification of any updates. If you install Sound State on a client's PC, you must collect and remit the registration fee or instruct your client to remit the registration fee directly.

Summary

Sound State is designed to supplement a sound card when its control settings are not saved properly. For some sound board installations, this program might be the only effective solution.

Speed utilities

Most computer users crave speed; the faster a computer, the better. However, some older applications behave unexpectedly or erratically on very fast machines. To compensate for a very fast PC, you might need a utility that "slows down" the computer to better support a particular application. You should avoid using such a utility unless it is absolutely necessary, and unload the utility (or reboot the computer) after you have finished with it.

SLO23.ZIP

Trying to use older programs (especially games) on new i486 and faster PCs can be extremely difficult; old software was not designed to deal with the blazing speed available on current PCs. SLO23 (Table 7-22) is designed to slow down a faster 386/486 in order to keep pace with older software. There are several advantages to SLO23 that make it particularly appealing for technicians. First, you can select the amount of slowdown, so it is possible to "tweak" the PC for each particular piece of older software. Second, you can disable, reenable, and uninstall SLO23 as necessary without having to reboot the entire PC. Finally, SLO23 is only 1.6KB in size, so it will have minimum effect on free conventional memory.

Installation and configuration

Since SLO.COM is intended to be PC-specific, you should install it to the local hard drive. Create a new subdirectory for the program and copy the SLO23.ZIP file from your CD to the new directory. Switch to the subdirectory and run PKUNZIP to extract the archive. Once the archive is decompressed, you can add SLO.COM to your AUTOEXEC.BAT file (or other batch files).

■ Table 7-22 SLO23 fact sheet

Program name:	PC Slowdown Utility
Executable file:	SLO.COM
Purpose:	To slow fast PCs in order to run older software
Version:	2.3 (c. 1995)
Operating system:	MS-DOS 3.3 or later
Compressed file:	SLO23.ZIP (archive)
Author:	Derek Altamirano
Address:	Granite Mountain Software
	839A Hwy. 20 E.
	Colville, WA 99114
ASP member:	No
Registration:	$5
Special notes:	Can be unloaded from memory

Operation

SLO.COM is run directly from a batch file command line along with a series of switches. The actual command syntax is:

SLO /L:*num* [/D] [/E] [/S] [/U] [/?]

where you need only the /L switch to actually start the program. The remaining switches allow you to control or unload the utility. Keep in mind that you can use only one switch each time SLO.COM is invoked. You can toggle SLO.COM on and off using the <Ctrl>–<Alt>–<left Shift> key combination.

/L:*num* Changes the delay, where *num* is a four-digit hexadecimal number between 0001 and FFFF representing the delay time.

/S Shows a status screen with current settings

/D Temporarily disables the delay

/E Enables the delay

/1, /2, . . . /9 Number of buffers to use

/? Help screen

/U Uninstall

Performance

In actual operation, you might find it easier to use SLO.COM in its own batch file along with the program it is intended for. That way, you can use the batch file to start SLO.COM, call the program you're using SLO.COM for, then unload SLO.COM automatically when the program exits. The following batch file illustrates this process:

```
<\@>echo off
slo /L:7148
[the command line for your program here]
slo /U
```

There are other features of SLO.COM. The program can disable itself during disk access, which allows the computer to slow down without compromising hard disk performance. SLO can also use up to 99 buffers (where each buffer uses the same delay value). This feature could help newer computers that do not have a turbo switch or cannot otherwise change their clock speeds. Finally, it is a simple matter to uninstall SLO.COM. However, it must be the *last* TSR loaded in memory—which is another good reason to use SLO.COM in its own batch file.

Registration

If you continue to use SLO.COM beyond a reasonable evaluation period, you must register it with the program author. Registration is $5, which entitles users to the latest registered version of SLO.COM. If you install SLO.COM on a customer's PC, you must also collect and remit the registration fee or instruct your client to remit the registration fee directly.

Summary

While technicians are rarely (if ever) called upon to slow down a computer, the SLO.COM utility could be an excellent option when you need to establish compatibility between old software and new hardware.

System security

Security is often an after-thought for personal computers because desktop and tower computers aren't generally mobile. However, PCs now rank with televisions and stereos as "quick grab" items for thieves. Mobile PCs such as laptop and notebook systems are particularly vulnerable to theft because they are small and easy to conceal. The shareware utilities shown in this section offer a measure of protection against theft and unauthorized use.

GUARD.ZIP

It is a strange fact of life that the information contained on a disk is often much more valuable than the disk itself, sometimes the whole computer. When a PC is stolen, the hardware can often be replaced with relative ease, but the damage done when the data falls into the wrong hands can be immeasurable. The Guardian (Table 7-23) is a security system designed to protect an entire disk (either hard or floppy) against unauthorized access using an algorithm that logically locks the disk so no files, programs, or directories can be accessed, regardless of whether they are otherwise secured by passwords or encryption schemes. The system consists of two programs: TG.EXE displays a log-on menu and should be the very first entry in an AUTOEXEC.BAT file, and TGM.EXE is the main system support program that provides the ability to unlock a previously locked disk.

■ **Table 7-23 GUARD fact sheet**

Program name:	The Guardian
Executable file:	TG.EXE
Purpose:	A utility that encrypts the contents of your hard drive for data security
Version:	1.5 (c. 1993)
Operating system:	MS-DOS 2.1 or later
Compressed file:	GUARD.ZIP (archive)
Author:	Marcor Enterprises
Address:	8857 Commerce Park Place, Suite D Indianapolis, IN 46268
Phone:	317-876-9376
ASP member:	No
Registration:	$40
Special notes:	A powerful and flexible security tool to protect your data

Installation and configuration

Although The Guardian will work with a floppy disk, you will most likely want to install the program to your hard drive. Note: As with all drive utilities, make a complete backup of your disk before attempting to use The Guardian. Create a new subdirectory for The Guardian and copy the GUARRD.ZIP archive file from your DLS Diagnostic CD to the new subdirectory. Switch to the new subdirectory and run PKUNZIP to extract the archive. Once the main archive is decompressed, you will see a program called GUARDIAN.EXE; this is a self-extracting file containing the main programs used with The Guardian. Run GUARDIAN.EXE to decompress those files.

Before proceeding, copy the program TGM.EXE to a bootable floppy disk and store this disk in a safe place. This is a very important step. If you don't do this and the disk containing TG.EXE and TGM.EXE gets locked, you won't be able to unlock the disk. Next, add the command line for TG.EXE to your AUTOEXEC.BAT file, such as:

c:\guardian\tg

This should be the first entry in the file so the security log-on menu is the first thing that appears. You can use any text editor to edit AUTOEXEC.BAT. Note: In normal operation, The Guardian uses a file called !!!.###, which is stored in the root directory of your disk. Make sure you don't already have a file with this name before running The Guardian.

Operation

When the TG.EXE program is executed, it displays a log-on menu and asks for a valid authorization (password). Any one of six possible passwords will be accepted, and the program simply exits to DOS. As the characters of the password are entered, the system displays block characters to show how many characters have been entered, but not the password itself. If an incorrect password is entered, the computer's speaker will sound, the entry will be erased, and you will be asked to try again. The program provides three opportunities to enter a correct password. After a third incorrect try, the program will automatically lock the disk and sound a warning siren for 10 seconds along with a warning message that the passwords were invalid. At this point, all files are locked and the keyboard is disabled. The only thing you can do is reset (reboot) the computer or turn it off.

Locking the disk Caution: The disk that is locked is the current drive, not necessarily the disk where the sensitive program is located. For example, if the prompt on the screen is C:\> and you enter D:\SECURE\TG (assuming the program TG.EXE is in fact in a subdirectory called SECURE on drive D:), then disk C: will be locked, not drive D:. Make sure to set up your operating configuration so you don't risk locking the wrong disk. When the disk is locked, The Guardian looks for files in the root directory ending with the extension .COM or .SYS. If it finds them, they are left intact. This way, you can still use the disk for starting up DOS. Also, if it finds its own main program (TGM.EXE) in the root directory, it and its master configuration file (GUARDIAN.MRE) are left intact. However, all these files are marked hidden and read-only until the disk is unlocked. While the disk is locked, you cannot make any changes to the installation configuration parameters (e.g., passwords).

To intentionally lock a disk or unlock a previously locked disk, invoke the Master Menu by executing the TGM.EXE program. You can either use the cursor keys to highlight the desired option and press <Enter>, or you can simply press the first letter of the option you want. To return to DOS, press <Esc> and then press either Y or <Enter>. If you press N or <Esc>, you will be returned to the Master Menu. When the Lock Disk Menu is displayed on the screen, enter the drive letter of the disk you want to lock and press <Enter>. The program will then ask you for authorization. Any of six available passwords will be accepted. Remember, if you lock the disk on which The Guardian resides, you might have to use a spare copy of TGM.EXE on a different disk to unlock it. Always keep a spare copy of The Guardian in a separate and secure place.

Any files in the root directory that have a .COM or .SYS extension are not locked, although they are marked as hidden and read-only. This also applies to the main Guardian program and the master configuration file. This way, if your hard drive (e.g., C:) is locked, it is still possible to boot the computer, even though all other files are inaccessible. If you keep TGM.EXE in the root directory, you will be able to use it to unlock the disk. If it is in a subdirectory on the disk, you won't be able to get to it and will have to use a spare copy of the program on another disk. Do not attempt to change any configuration parameters while the disk is locked; the program won't allow it. After the disk has been locked, an unlocked file, READTHIS.MRE, is placed on the disk. You can use the DOS TYPE command to display this file. It contains a message that the disk has been locked by The Guardian and that you should not attempt to add or delete any files on the disk. When the disk is unlocked, this file is removed.

Unlocking the disk When a disk is locked, certain information is recorded that The Guardian uses for unlocking the disk at a later time. Included in this information is the master password and (if the disk was locked intentionally) the password used to authorize the lock. The only way to unlock a disk is to know the master password or the authorization password that was in effect at the time the disk was locked. If the current master password is different from the master password in effect when the disk was locked, the current master password will not work. When you select the Unlock Disk option, the system asks you first for the drive letter of the disk to be unlocked, and then the proper authorization. If the disk was locked as a result of a failed log-on attempt, the only way to unlock it is to enter the master password that was in effect when it was locked. If it was locked intentionally, then either the master password or the password used to authorize the lock can be entered. No other passwords will be accepted. You are given three opportunities to enter the correct password; otherwise, you are returned to the Master Menu.

If disk contents are altered while the disk is locked (e.g., someone saves a new file to the locked disk), The Guardian will find inconsistencies when it tries to unlock the disk. If this happens, it will display a message that it cannot recover the file it is working on and ask you to either press <Enter> to continue or <Esc> to abandon the unlock attempt. Press <Enter> in order to recover (unlock) as many files as possible. If you press <Esc>, the system will abandon its attempt to unlock the disk and return you to the main menu. However, the control information about the locked disk is kept intact, so subsequent unlocking attempts are possible. While this condition exists, however, it is impossible to lock the disk again because The Guardian will tell you the disk is already locked, at least part of it, since it was never completely unlocked. The only way to completely unlock the disk now is to get the DOS file directory back in exactly the same condition it was in immediately after the disk was locked. You might need to use a DOS file recovery program for this.

Performance

When a disk is locked by The Guardian, files on that disk are not physically altered. What *is* altered is the information that tells DOS where those files are. Once a disk has been locked, under no circumstances should you try to add any files to the disk or try to rebuild the files from the raw data recorded in various locations on the disk. Such attempts could result in the permanent loss of files on the disk before it was locked.

Make sure to keep a spare copy of this program on a separate disk. If it exists only on the same disk as the log-on program (and the disk gets locked), you won't be able to execute the program and unlock the disk. If this happens, the only way you could use the disk would be to reformat it, which would destroy all data on it. This program also allows you to intentionally lock any selected disk, select different color combinations, and change installation parameters such as passwords.

The first time a disk is locked, control information is stored in the root directory of that disk. If the root directory is full, The Guardian won't be able to lock the disk. Normally, this should not be a problem because most hard disks can have at least 512 entries in the root directory, so the root directory is almost never full. If it should happen, however, create one or more subdirectories and move some less-used files to those subdirectories.

Registration

If you continue to use The Guardian beyond a 30-day evaluation period, you must register it with the program author. Registration is $40, and registered users receive the latest registered version, a printed manual, and telephone support. If you install The Guardian on a client's PC, you must collect and remit the registration fee or direct your client to remit the appropriate fee.

Summary

The Guardian hides the contents of your sensitive files from DOS without interfering with the boot process or any of your applications — a product worth considering if you need security for your files.

RWARD2.ZIP

Mobile computers are prime targets for thieves because the PCs are small, expensive, and easy to conceal. While you can take steps to protect your notebook or laptop PC, it might also be helpful to "mark" the system with your own special message. The RWARD2 package (Table 7-24) provides a utility that displays a "reward offered" message each time the PC boots up. This might not stop the PC from being stolen, but could help you get it back.

■ Table 7-24 RWARD2 fact sheet

Program name:	Reward Message
Executable file:	REWARD.EXE
Purpose:	Produces a custom "reward" message on the display
Version:	2.01 (c. 1992)
Operating system:	MS-DOS 3.3 or later
Compressed file:	RWARD2.ZIP (archive)
Author:	Les Gainous
CompuServe:	72731,146
America Online:	LesGainous
ASP member:	No
Registration:	Public domain
Special notes:	A simple and straightforward security message

Installation and configuration

RWARD2 should be installed to your local hard drive. Create a new subdirectory for the program, and copy the RWARD2.ZIP archive file from your CD the new subdirectory. Switch to the new subdirectory and run PKUNZIP to decompress the archive. After the archive has been decompressed, you can add the REWARD.EXE program to your AUTOEXEC.BAT file. The following is a typical batch file configuration:

```
<\@>echo off
REM *** all your other AUTOEXEC.BAT entries should go here; put REWARD at the end of
your file
c:
REM *** Switch to the directory containing REWARD.EXE
cd\reward
REM *** Run the REWARD program
reward
REM *** Switch back to the boot drive and directory
c:
cd\
```

Operation

When REWARD.EXE is executed, it displays the contents of REWARD.TXT for about 15 seconds or until a key is pressed. You can edit the REWARD.TXT file in an ordinary text editor to show any message you want. Make sure that each line of text is less than 80 characters. When editing REWARD.TXT, do not use your home address or phone number unless absolutely necessary; remember that the person reading your message is either the one who stole your PC to begin with or someone who bought the stolen property. Keep your own safety in mind.

Performance

The advantage of REWARD.EXE is its simplicity; it alters nothing, is easy to implement, and is easy to customize for each individual user. However, it is also easily disabled by any computer user who has even the vaguest knowledge of batch files. Still, the offer of a reward might be enough to get your PC returned, at least somewhat intact.

Registration

The RWARD2 package has been released to the public domain, so you may use and distribute it freely.

Summary

REWARD.EXE is a simple and free tool that you can easily use as a general deterrent. It is hardly foolproof, but any means of marking a PC can be helpful.

314

MONITORS: the commercial version

8

To successfully test and align a monitor, it is necessary to display a comprehensive set of test patterns and ensure that each image follows a predictable set of criteria or behaviors. Traditionally, specialized hardware tools have been employed as test pattern generators. While signal generators produce clean, precise patterns, the outright cost for such a device is often more than the casual user or electronics enthusiast can justify; even professional service shops are looking for cost-saving options. Since homes and businesses with monitors also have PCs, it makes good sense to use the existing PC as a test instrument. This chapter will introduce you to MONITORS: a complete, commercial, DOS-based monitor/video adapter diagnostic.

All about MONITORS 2.01

MONITORS is a self-contained video board diagnostic and test pattern generator. It is designed to work with MDA, CGA, EGA, VGA, and SVGA video systems, so it's compatible across a variety of hardware (both video adapters and monitors). MONITORS allows you to check a PC's video adapter capabilities and perform a suite of standard test/alignment procedures after a repair is complete. MONITORS has been updated from version 1.0 to include burn-in features (previously a stand-alone utility) and streamline user input and performance. Once the monitor is aligned, the burn-in feature simply works the video system for several hours (or several days) to ensure that no supplemental work needs to be done.

Unlocking your copy of MONITORS

The complete commercial version of MONITORS is included on the DLS Diagnostic CD, in the MONITORS directory. The package has been compressed into the file MONITORS.ZIP, but the file is encrypted so you will need a password (a serial number) in order to unlock and decompress the files. An advertisement and order form for MONITORS (and the companion PRINTERS program) is at the end of this book. Feel free to photocopy the order form (or tear out the page), fill out the required information, and either enclose a check or money order for the proper amount or fill in your credit card information. Please remember that all purchases must be made in U.S. funds. When filling out the order form, note that you may purchase either the software or a one-year subscription to the premier newsletter *The PC Toolbox*, or take advantage of a special rate for both the program and subscription. Subscribers also receive extended access to the Dynamic Learning Systems BBS, which allows you to exchange e-mail with other PC enthusiasts and download hundreds of DOS and Windows PC utilities. Once your order is received, you will be provided with a serial number to unlock the files.

Once you have a serial number to unlock MONITORS.ZIP, copy the file to a subdirectory on your hard drive or a floppy disk. Switch to the subdirectory (or floppy drive) and use PKUNZIP with the following syntax to unlock the files:

C:\MONITORS\> d:\pkunzip monitors.zip -s********** <Enter>

where the asterisks (*) represent the serial number characters. This will decompress the archive into your MONITORS subdirectory. Of course, if your CD-ROM drive uses a drive letter other than D:, substitute the appropriate drive letter (if you copied PKUNZIP to your hard drive, use that drive letter instead). If you are decompressing the file onto a floppy disk, try the following format:

A:\> d:\pkunzip monitors.zip -s********** <Enter>

Once again, if the CD-ROM uses a drive letter other than D:, substitute the proper drive letter (if you copied PKUNZIP to your hard drive, use that drive letter instead). To start the program, simply type MONITORS.

Using MONITORS

When MONITORS is started, you will see a brief initialization text, followed by a disclaimer and media warranty (press any key to clear the disclaimer). You will then see the main menu (Figure 8-1 on the next page). The top portion of the main menu lists the utility name and version. Sixteen selections are available from the main menu (the main menu for version 2.01 is shown, but other versions might appear slightly different). The first two menu selections allow you to test the video adapter and set the appropriate video mode for the monitor in use. The burn-in feature allows you to run your monitor unattended for prolonged periods. If you are done with the program, press <Esc> at the main menu to return to DOS.

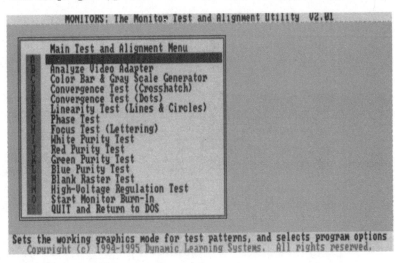

■ **8-1** *The MONITORS main menu.*

Testing your video adapter

MONITORS allows you to test the capabilities of your video adapter by selecting option B from the main menu. The general adapter specifications shown in Figure 8-2 on the next page provide an overview of the adapter's capabilities. Six key pieces of information are provided. The chipset in use is the particular video chipset employed by the adapter. MONITORS is designed to identify the following 16 types of video chipsets:

☐ Ahead Systems

☐ ATI

☐ Avance Logic

☐ Cirrus Logic

☐ Compaq QVision

☐ IBM XGA

☐ NCR

☐ Oak Technologies

☐ Paradise

☐ S3

☐ Trident

☐ Tseng ET3000

☐ Tseng ET4000

☐ VESA (compatible)

☐ Video 7

☐ Weitek

If the chipset cannot be identified, MONITORS will indicate an "unknown chipset." In addition to the type of chipset in use, the chipset revision is also identified wherever possible. If the chipset type is not known and the revision cannot be determined, MONITORS will indicate an "unknown revision."

The total amount of available video memory on the video board is listed next. The specification is given in KB. For VESA-compatible video boards, the VESA version is shown. Otherwise, a "no VESA driver installed" message is shown. If I/O registers are used with the video board, the I/O register base address is listed. Otherwise, an "I/O registers not installed" message is displayed. When a video board with a built-in VESA BIOS is used, the VESA BIOS status is listed last. When VESA BIOS support is not included, a "not installed" message is shown. The last two entries indicate the general video adapter (the generic video system in use) and a recommendation for setting the test display mode (the video mode that should be used for testing and alignment).

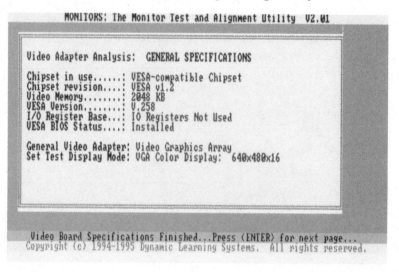

■ 8-2 *Reviewing the general video adapter specifications.*

The next step in adapter analysis identifies each major video mode that the adapter can successfully emulate. A typical listing is shown in Figure 8-3. Available modes are highlighted in green, while incompatible modes are highlighted in red (because it's black and white, the Figure doesn't show these differences clearly). Note the large number of VESA modes that are tested. One important thing to keep in mind when reviewing video mode compatibility is that the available modes don't necessarily mean that the attached monitor is capable of working in every mode. Once you have finished reviewing the available modes, press the <Enter> key to return to the main menu.

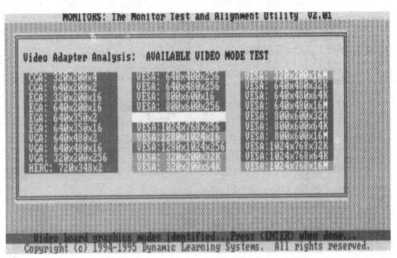

■ 8-3 Reviewing the adapter's compatibility with different popular video modes.

Choosing video test modes

By default, test patterns are generated in VGA at a resolution of $640 \times 480 \times 16$. This automatically accommodates the broad base of VGA and SVGA video systems in service today. Option A from the main menu allows you to override this default and select a different video mode for test pattern displays, as shown in Figure 8-4 on the next page. There are six selections: MDA (for text-only displays), CGA, EGA, VGA, SVGA, and an Auto-Detect mode. If you are not certain what mode is appropriate for your system, the Auto-Detect selection will usually make a reasonable choice. You can also switch back and forth among different screen modes at your discretion. Keep in mind that not all test patterns are available in all screen modes. Table 8-1 shows the availability of test patterns for each screen mode.

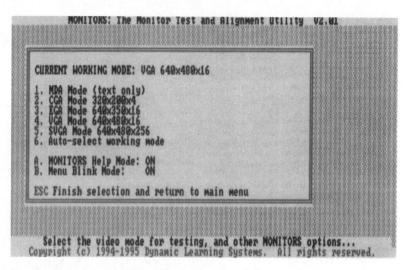

■ 8-4 *The MONITORS Setup dialog.*

■ Table 8-1 Availability of test patterns in every screen mode

Pattern	SVGA	VGA	EGA	CGA	MDA
Color bars	256 colors	16 colors	16 colors	4 colors	n/a
(gray scale)	10 gray	10 gray	n/a	n/a	n/a
Convergence (crosshatch)	graphic	graphic	graphic	graphic	n/a
Convergence (dots)	graphic	graphic	graphic	graphic	n/a
Linearity	graphic	graphic	graphic	graphic	ASCII
Phase	graphic	graphic	graphic	graphic	ASCII
Focus	ASCII	ASCII	ASCII	ASCII	ASCII
White purity	graphic	graphic	graphic	graphic	n/a
Red purity	graphic	graphic	graphic	n/a	n/a
Green purity	graphic	graphic	graphic	n/a	n/a
Blue purity	graphic	graphic	graphic	n/a	n/a
Blank raster	graphic	graphic	graphic	graphic	ASCII
High-voltage	graphic	graphic	graphic	graphic	ASCII

Note the two additional selections marked A and B. The first is MONITORS Help Mode. Normally, the program displays a brief text description of the test before running. If you toggle the help mode off, however, no text information will be displayed; the test pattern will simply start. Novices might find the help mode useful, so it is on by default. The second selection is Menu Blink Mode. This feature was intended to assist visually impaired users by causing the highlighted selection in the main menu to blink. This feature is on by default, but if you find it annoying or otherwise objectionable, just toggle it off. Once you are done selecting a screen mode or features, hit the <Esc> key to return to the main menu.

Color bars

You can access the color bar display by pressing option C from the main menu. In the SVGA mode, a palette of 256 colors is displayed (assuming full SVGA compatibility). In VGA and EGA, 16 colors are shown, as in the VGA display of Figure 8-5 (again, the Figure is in black and white, so it will look different). The CGA mode shows four colors. As you might expect, color bars are unavailable in the MDA mode. Color bars are not used for specific alignment tests, but rather for general quality testing and settings of brightness and contrast. Color bars provide a good overview of monitor quality.

When you are through with the color bars, press any key on the keyboard. Displays in the SVGA and VGA modes will switch from color bars to a set of 10 gray bars, as shown in Figure 8-6 on the next page. Displays in the EGA and CGA modes will return to the main menu. This is a grayscale linearity test, which should produce 10 even graduations of gray (including black and white). As with color bars, grayscale linearity allows you to judge the quality of a monitor's grayscale generation. Press any key on the keyboard to return to the main menu.

■ **8-5** *The color bar display.*

■ **8-6** *The grayscale display.*

Convergence test (crosshatch)

Static convergence is an important test for color monitors of all resolutions. When you select option D from the main menu, a white grid will appear, as shown in Figure 8-7. The use of white is important since all three electron guns are running at equal amplitude. Other colors might be more visually appealing, but only pure white provides useful information. When you observe the convergence grid, there should be no other colors (blue, green, or red) bleeding out from around the grid edges. If there are, you need to perform a static convergence alignment. Pressing the M key will turn the grid color magenta (red and blue electron guns only). This allows you to adjust the magenta convergence magnets. Pressing the W key again returns the grid to white, and you can adjust the white convergence magnets. You can switch back and forth between magenta and white as needed by alternately pressing the M and W keys. Pressing any other key will return you to the main menu. A convergence crosshatch pattern is available in all screen modes except for MDA.

Convergence test (dots)

This is another test for static convergence. When you select option E from the main menu, a pattern of white dots will appear, as shown in Figure 8-8 on page 324. The use of white dots, like the

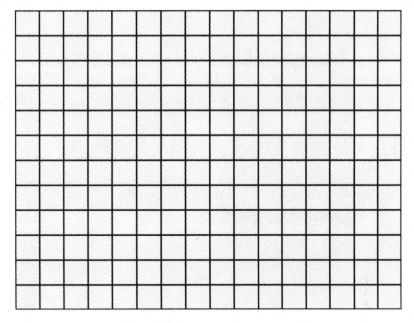

■ **8-7** *The convergence grid adjustment display.*

white crosshatch, is important since all three electron guns must run at equal amplitude. When you observe the convergence dots, there should be no other colors (blue, green, or red) bleeding out from around the individual dots. If there are, you need to perform a static convergence alignment. Pressing the M key will turn the dot color magenta (red and blue electron guns only), which allows you to adjust the magenta convergence magnets. Pressing the W key will return the dots to white, and you can adjust the white convergence magnets. You can switch back and forth between magenta and white by alternately pressing the M and W keys. Pressing any other key will return you to the main menu. The convergence dot pattern is available in all screen modes except for MDA.

Linearity test

Option F from the main menu selects the linearity test pattern, as shown in Figure 8-9 on page 325. By using a series of geometric shapes, linearity tests show the "evenness" of the horizontal and vertical raster. If any portion of the screen image appears compressed or expanded, you need to adjust the linearity. When distortion occurs in the horizontal orientation, horizontal linearity needs to be adjusted; when distortion occurs in the vertical direction, vertical linearity needs to be adjusted. Graphic linearity patterns are available in all screen modes except MDA. An ASCII

■ **8-8** *The convergence dot adjustment display.*

pattern is used to check for MDA display linearity. Press any key on the keyboard to return to the main menu.

Phase test

Option G from the main menu selects the phase test pattern, as shown in Figure 8-10 on page 326. Ideally, an image should be horizontally centered in the raster. You can see the phase of an image by turning up brightness until the raster is visible. The thin white box around the perimeter of the image allows you to adjust horizontal phase until the image is reasonably centered. This allows you to evenly adjust the horizontal width. If the phase is incorrect, widening the image will cause the edge closest to the the raster to "run off" the display. Graphic phase test patterns are available in all screen modes except MDA. An ASCII pattern is used for the MDA mode. Press any key on the keyboard to return to the main menu.

Focus test

The focus test pattern is displayed when you select option H from the main menu. One of the best tests of focus is in the display of ASCII test, so Figure 8-11 on page 327 illustrates the typical focus pattern used for all screen modes. When the text image appears out of focus, you can adjust high-voltage levels to the CRT's focus grid(s) in order to compensate. Older monitors provide a panel-mounted

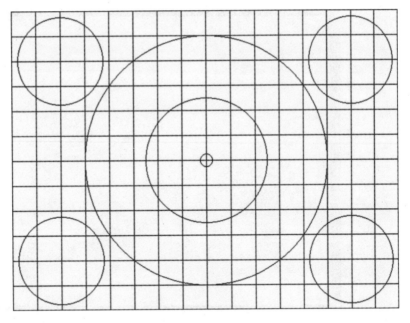

■ **8-9** *The linearity adjustment display.*

focus control, but newer monitor designs place the focus control on the monitor's main PC board. When testing and adjustment are complete, press any key on the keyboard to return to the main menu.

The purity tests

Options I, J, K, and L are color purity selections for checking color gun consistency across the display. The white purity selection (I) is by far the most common and widely used mode. By filling the screen with a pure white image, it is possible to check for discoloration or uneven coloring, which might indicate the need for manual degaussing. When you are done reviewing a purity test pattern, press any key on the keyboard to return to the main menu. Note that the white purity test is available in all screen modes but MDA, and the red, green, and blue purity tests are available in all but the CGA and MDA modes.

Blank raster test

Option M from the main menu starts the blank raster test. Essentially, the blank raster is just a black image. This allows you to increase screen brightness and check the presence of the raster without the distraction of a screen image. Blank raster is available in all screen modes. When you are through, press any key on the keyboard to return to the main menu.

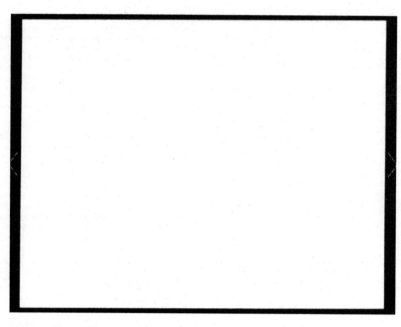

■ **8-10** *The phase adjustment display.*

High-voltage test

Option N from the main menu selects the high-voltage test, as illustrated in Figure 8-12 on page 328. This pattern checks high-voltage regulation by blinking the middle white box on and off. Ideally, the boarder should not flinch significantly. If it does, you might need to make repairs to the high-voltage system. Once the test is complete, press any key on the keyboard to return to the main menu. A graphic image is used to test high-voltage regulation in all screen modes but MDA. An ASCII image is used in the MDA mode.

Monitor burn-In

Once a repair is finished, it is often helpful to let the repaired monitor run for several hours (or even several days) to see that the repair will hold. Unfortunately, when the same image is allowed to remain on the screen for long periods of time at high brightness, there is a small but persistent risk of CRT phosphor burn. Although phosphor burn is almost unheard of today, it is still a wise policy to periodically alternate the screen image. MONITORS offers a burn-in mode (option O from the main menu), which displays a continuously repeating series of test patterns. After the cycle starts, you can walk away from the monitor indefinitely. To stop the cycle and return to the main menu, press the <Esc> key.

■ **8-11** *The focus adjustment display.*

When trouble occurs

The system requirements for MONITORS are very slight, compared to other commercial software in the marketplace today. As a result, the probability of problems with the software should be extremely rare. Make sure that the monitor is connected properly and that it is appropriate for the video board installed in the PC.

Check the screen mode

The most common error is choosing a screen mode that is incompatible with the monitor. When choosing a screen mode, make sure that the monitor is capable of supporting it. For example, choosing an SVGA screen mode for an EGA monitor will result in display problems. However, this should not cause an error in the software. Follow the proper key sequence to return to the main menu and select a more appropriate screen mode.

Not all video boards support the same video mode in the same way, so the SVGA mode might not work properly for all video systems. If the displays in the SVGA mode appear distorted, return to the main menu and select the VGA mode. Virtually all SVGA video boards and SVGA monitors support VGA. Other than the initial color bar display, the VGA and SVGA test patterns are identical.

When problems persist

If problems persist, write your symptoms and system setup on a sheet of paper along with your name, address, and telephone and fax numbers (if possible). Then mail or fax it to:

■ **8-12** *The high-voltage test display.*

Customer Service
Dynamic Learning Systems
P.O. Box 282
Jefferson, MA 01522-0282 USA
Fax: 508-829-6819
BBS: 508-829-6706
CompuServe: 73652,3205
Internet: sbigelow@cerfnet.com
WWW: http://www.dlspubs.com/

Making MONITORS better

Dynamic Learning Systems is committed to providing useful and reliable software tools, so I welcome your comments and suggestions on how to improve MONITORS. Either write or contact the company online through the BBS or CompuServe (addresses in the previous section).

PRINTERS: the commercial version

9

One of the major limitations of printer troubleshooting is testing. Traditionally, technicians were limited to the self-test of each unique printer and printing simple documents from a text editor or other basic application. There are two problems with this haphazard approach. First, self tests and simple printouts do not always test every feature of the printer in a clear fashion. Second, such testing is hardly ever uniform; the quality and range of testing can vary radically from printer to printer. Dynamic Learning Systems has addressed this problem by developing PRINTERS, a PC-based utility designed to provide you with a suite of standardized printer tests. This chapter introduces you to PRINTERS. The program provides you with a reliable platform for testing dot-matrix, ink-jet, and EP printers. PRINTERS not only exercises a printer's main functions (carriage, line feed, print head, and so on), but it also allows you to test printer-specific functions by using escape sequences.

All about PRINTERS

PRINTERS is a stand-alone DOS utility designed to drive virtually any commercial impact, ink-jet, and laser/LED (EP) printer through a series of exercises and test patterns that are specially tailored to reveal faults in the printer's major subassemblies. By reviewing the printed results, you will be able to estimate the source of a printer's problems with a high degree of confidence. Online help and tutorial modes provide additional information about each test, and will help you understand the printed results. A variety of options allow you configure PRINTERS for over 220 unique printers, and tailor performance for speed and print quality. A handy Manual Code section allows you to enter escape code sequences and text to test specific functions of *any* printer.

Unlocking your copy of PRINTERS

The complete commercial version of PRINTERS is included on the DLS Diagnostic CD in the PRINTERS directory, compressed into the file PRINTERS.ZIP. The file is encrypted, however, so you will need a password (a serial number) in order to unlock and decompress the files. An advertisement and order form for PRINTERS (and the companion MONITORS program) is at the end of this book. Feel free to photocopy the order form (or tear out the page), fill out the required information, and either enclose a check or money order for the proper amount or fill in your credit card information. Please remember that all purchases must be made in U.S. funds. When filling out the order form, note that you may purchase either the software or a one-year subscription to the premier newsletter *The PC Toolbox*, or take advantage of a special rate for both the program and subscription. Subscribers also receive extended access to the Dynamic Learning Systems BBS, which allows you to exchange e- mail with other PC enthusiasts and download hundreds of DOS and Windows PC utilities. Once your order is received, you will be provided with a serial number to unlock the files.

Once you have a serial number to unlock the PRINTERS.ZIP file, copy the PRINTERS.ZIP file to either a subdirectory on your hard drive or a floppy disk. Switch to the subdirectory (or floppy drive) and use PKUNZIP with the following syntax to unlock the files:

```
C:\PRINTERS\> d:\pkunzip printers.zip -s********** <Enter>
```

where the asterisks (*) stand for the serial number characters. This command will decompress the archive into your PRINTERS subdirectory. Of course, if your CD-ROM drive uses a drive letter other than D:, substitute the appropriate drive letter (if you copied PKUNZIP to your hard drive, use that drive letter instead). If you are decompressing the file onto a floppy disk, try this command:

```
A:\> d:\pkunzip printers.zip -s********** <Enter>
```

Once again, if the CD-ROM drive uses a drive letter other than D:, substitute the proper drive letter (if you copied PKUNZIP to your hard drive, use that drive letter instead). To start the program, simply type PRINTERS. The title screen and disclaimer for PRINTERS should appear almost immediately. Press any key to pass the title screen and disclaimer, and you will then see the work screen.

After you pass the title screen and disclaimer, you will see the work screen, as illustrated in Figure 9-1. The top of the work screen contains the title bar and main menu bar. The bottom of the work screen contains the message bar and copyright bar. Most of the work screen will be empty when you first start the program. The following six entries are contained in the main menu bar; they are the essential areas you will be concerned with while using PRINTERS:

Configure Allows you to select the program's operating parameters

Impact Allows you to run a selection of tests for impact printers

Ink Jet Allows you to run a selection of tests for ink-jet printers

Laser/LED Allows you to run a selection of tests for EP printers

About Shows you more information about PRINTERS

Quit Leaves PRINTERS and returns to DOS

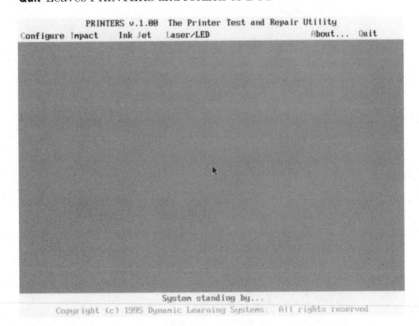

PRINTERS v.1.00 The Printer Test and Repair Utility
Configure Impact   Ink Jet   Laser/LED   About... Quit

System standing by...
Copyright (c) 1995 Dynamic Learning Systems. All rights reserved

■ **9-1** *The PRINTERS main work screen.*

Configuring the program

To configure the various options available in PRINTERS, click on Configure in the main menu bar (or press C). The Configure menu will appear, as shown in Figure 9-2 on the next page. You can return to the work screen at any time by pressing the <Esc> key or right-clicking the mouse anywhere in the display.

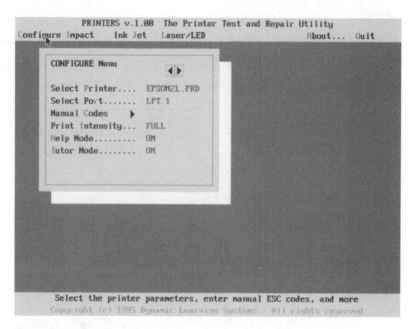

■ **9-2** *The program's Configure menu.*

Selecting the printer

PRINTERS is compatible with the vast majority of Epson, Hewlett-Packard, and compatible printers now in the market, but the utility provides an extensive library of over 220 specific printer drivers. These drivers allow PRINTERS to produce the detailed graphic test patterns used in the program. Table 9-1 shows a comprehensive listing of supported printers and their corresponding driver entries. By default, PRINTERS is set to use the EPSON2L.DRV driver (a generic Epson 24-pin impact printer driver). Refer to Table 9-1 to select the appropriate driver, then scroll through the available printer drivers by left-clicking on Select Printer (or pressing P). As you scroll through each driver, you will see details about each driver in the message bar.

Note: If you accidentally pass the desired driver, you can scroll backward through the driver list by pressing <Shift>–P (a capital P).

Selecting the port

PRINTERS is designed to operate a printer on ports LPT1 through LPT3 or COM1 or COM2. Left-click on Select Port (or press R) to scroll through available ports. Remember to connect your printer to the appropriate port before proceeding. By default, LPT1 is the selected port.

■ Table 9-1 Printer driver index

Manufacture/printer model	Definition	Resolution	B&W/color
Adobe Postscript, all models	PS.PRD	300×300	B&W
Color Postscript, all models	PSC.PRD	30×300	Color
Alps			
ALPS DMX800	EPSON9L.PRD	60×72	B&W
ALPS DMX800	EPSON9M.PRD	120×72	B&W
ALPS DMX800	EPSON9H.PRD	120×216	B&W
ALPS DMX800	EPSON9VH.PRD	240×216	B&W
LSX 1600	HPLSRL.PRD	75×75	B&W
LSX 1600	HPLSRM.PRD	100×100	B&W
LSX 1600	HPLSRH.PRD	150×150	B&W
LSX 1600	HPLSRVH.PRD	300×300	B&W
AMT			
Accel, Office Printer	AMTVL.PRD	60×60	B&W
Accel, Office Printer	AMTL.PRD	120×60	B&W
Accel, Office Printer	AMTLM.PRD	120×120	B&W
Accel, Office Printer	AMTLH.PRD	240×120	B&W
Accel, Office Printer	AMTLVH.PRD	240×240	B&W
Accel, Office Printer	AMTLVVH.PRD	480×240	B&W
Accel, Office Printer	AMTLCVL.PRD	60×60	Color
Accel, Office Printer	AMTLCL.PRD	120×60	Color
Accel, Office Printer	AMTLCM.PRD	120×120	Color
Accel, Office Printer	AMTLCH.PRD	240×120	Color
Accel, Office Printer	AMTLCVH.PRD	240×240	Color
Accel, Office Printer	AMTLCVVH.PRD	480×240	Color
TracJet	HPLSRL.PRD	75×75	B&W
TracJet	HPLSRM.PRD	100×100	B&W
TracJet	HPLSRH.PRD	150×150	B&W
TracJet	HPLSRVH.PRD	300×300	B&W
Anadex			
DP Series	ANDXDPL.PRD	72×72	B&W
DP Series	ANDXDPH.PRD	144×144	B&W
WP Series	ANDXWPL.PRD	72×72	B&W
WP Series	ANDXWPH.PRD	144×144	B&W
WP Series	ANDXWPCL.PRD	72×72	Color
WP Series	ANDXWPCH.PRD	144×144	Color
Anatex Data Systems			
ADS 2000	EPSON9L.PRD	60×72	B&W
ADS 2000	EPSON9M.PRD	120×72	B&W
ADS 2000	EPSON9H.PRD	120×216	B&W
ADS 2000	EPSON9VH.PRD	240×216	B&W
Apple			
Imagewriter II	APPLECL.PRD	60×72	Color
Imagewriter II	APPLECM.PRD	120×72	Color

Manufacture/printer model	Definition	Resolution	B&W/color
Imagewriter II	APPLEL.PRD	60 × 72	B&W
Imagewriter II	APPLEM.PRD	120 × 72	B&W
Laserwriter, IIf, IIg, Personal	PS.PRD	300 × 300	B&W
AT&T			
Model 475	CITOHVL.PRD	80 × 72	B&W
Model 475	CITOHL.PRD	96 × 72	B&W
Model 475	CITOHM.PRD	136 × 72	B&W
Model 475	CITOHH.PRD	160 × 72	B&W
Model 475	CITOHVH.PRD	160 × 144	B&W
Model 570	EPSON9L.PRD	60 × 72	B&W
Model 570	EPSON9M.PRD	120 × 72	B&W
Model 570	EPSON9H.PRD	120 × 216	B&W
Model 570	EPSON9VH.PRD	240 × 216	B&W
Model 583	EPSON2L.PRD	60 × 60	B&W
Model 583	EPSON2M.PRD	120 × 60	B&W
Model 583	EPSON2H.PRD	180 × 180	B&W
Axonix			
LiteWrite, MilWrite	EPSON9L.PRD	60 × 72	B&W
LiteWrite, MilWrite	EPSON9M.PRD	120 × 72	B&W
LiteWrite, MilWrite	EPSON9H.PRD	120 × 216	B&W
LiteWrite, MilWrite	EPSON9VH.PRD	240 × 216	B&W
Bezier			
BP4040	PS.PRD	300 × 300	B&W
Blue Chip			
M 200	EPSON9L.PRD	60 × 72	B&W
M 200	EPSON9M.PRD	120 × 72	B&W
M 200	EPSON9H.PRD	120 × 216	B&W
M 200	EPSON9VH.PRD	240 × 216	B&W
Brother			
1824L, 2024L	BRO24H.PRD	180 × 180	B&W
1550, 1809, HL-8e	BRO9L.PRD	60 × 72	B&W
1550, 1809, HL-8e	BRO9M.PRD	120 × 72	B&W
1550, 1809, HL-8e	BRO9H.PRD	120 × 216	B&W
1550, 1809, HL-8e	BRO9VH.PRD	240 × 216	B&W
Twinriter 5 WP mode	BROTWNL.PRD	60 × 72	B&W
Twinriter 5 WP mode	BROTWNM.PRD	120 × 72	B&W
Twinriter 5 WP mode	BROTWNH.PRD	120 × 216	B&W
Twinriter 5 WP mode	BROTWNVH.PRD	240 × 216	B&W
M-4309A	EPSON9L.PRD	60 × 72	B&W
M-4309A	EPSON9M.PRD	120 × 72	B&W
M-4309A	EPSON9H.PRD	120 × 216	B&W
M-4309A	EPSON9VH.PRD	240 × 216	B&W
HL-8V, -10V, -4Ve	HPLSRL.PRD	75 × 75	B&W
HL-8V, -10V, -4Ve	HPLSRM.PRD	100 × 100	B&W

Manufacture/printer model	Definition	Resolution	B&W/color
HL-8V, -10V, -4Ve	HPLSRH.PRD	150 × 150	B&W
HL-8V, -10V, -4Ve	HPLSRVH.PRD	300 × 300	B&W
HL-4PS, HL-8PS	PS.PRD	300 × 300	B&W
HT-500PS	PSC.PRD	300 × 300	Color
Bull HN Information Systems			
Compuprint 970	EPSON9L.PRD	60 × 72	B&W
Compuprint 970	EPSON9M.PRD	120 × 72	B&W
Compuprint 970	EPSON9H.PRD	120 × 216	B&W
Compuprint 970	EPSON9VH.PRD	240 × 216	B&W
Camintonn			
TurboLaser PS-Plus 3	PS.PRD	300 × 300	B&W
CAL-ABCO			
Legend 1385, CP-VII	EPSON9L.PRD	60 × 72	B&W
Legend 1385, CP-VII	EPSON9M.PRD	120 × 72	B&W
Legend 1385, CP-VII	EPSON9H.PRD	120 × 216	B&W
Legend 1385, CP-VII	EPSON9VH.PRD	240 × 216	B&W
CalComp			
ColorMaster Plus	PSC.PRD	300 × 300	Color
Canon			
BJ 130 Inkjet	CANONBJH.PRD	180 × 180	B&W
BJ 130 Inkjet	CANONBJV.PRD	360 × 360	B&W
LBP-8	CANONLL.PRD	75 × 75	B&W
LBP-8	CANONLM.PRD	100 × 100	B&W
LBP-8	CANONLH.PRD	150 × 150	B&W
LBP-8	CANONLVH.PRD	300 × 300	B&W
PW-1156A	EPSON9L.PRD	60 × 72	B&W
PW-1156A	EPSON9M.PRD	120 × 72	B&W
PW-1156A	EPSON9H.PRD	120 × 216	B&W
PW-1156A	EPSON9VH.PRD	240 × 216	B&W
BJ-800, BJ-830, BJ-20	EPSON2L.PRD	60 × 60	B&W
BJ-800, BJ-830, BJ-20	EPSON2M.PRD	120 × 60	B&W
BJ-800, BJ-830, BJ-20	EPSON2H.PRD	180 × 180	B&W
BJC-800, BJC-830	EPSON2CH.PRD	180 × 180	Color
BJC-800, BJC-830	EPSON2CV.PRD	360 × 360	Color
PJ1080A Inkjet	CANONPJ.PRD	84 × 84	Color
Centronics			
All models	CENTRONL.PRD	60 × 60	B&W
CIE			
CI-250, CI-500	EPSON9L.PRD	60 × 72	B&W
CI-250, CI-500	EPSON9M.PRD	120 × 72	B&W
CI-250, CI-500	EPSON9H.PRD	120 × 216	B&W
CI-250, CI-500	EPSON9VH.PRD	240 × 216	B&W
Citizen			
MSP-10/25, 200GX	CITZN9L.PRD	60 × 72	B&W

335

Manufacture/printer model	Definition	Resolution	B&W/color
MSP-10/25, 200GX	CITZN9M.PRD	120×72	B&W
MSP-10/25, 200GX	CITZN9H.PRD	120×216	B&W
MSP-10/25, 200GX	CITZN9VH.PRD	240×216	B&W
MSP-10/25, 200GX	CITZN9CL.PRD	60×72	Color
MSP-10/25, 200GX	CITZN9CM.PRD	120×72	Color
MSP-10/25, 200GX	CITZN9CH.PRD	120×216	Color
MSP-10/25, 200GX	CITZN9CV.PRD	240×216	Color
GSX-140/130/145/240, PN48	CITZN24L.PRD	60×60	B&W
GSX-140/130/145/240, PN48	CITZN24M.PRD	120×60	B&W
GSX-140/130/145/240, PN48	CITZN24H.PRD	180×180	B&W
GSX-140/130/145/240, PN48	CITZN24V.PRD	360×360	B&W
GSX-140/130/145/240, PN48	CITZ24CH.PRD	180×180	Color
GSX-140/130/145/240, PN48	CITZ24CV.PRD	360×360	Color

Compaq

PageMarq 15/20	HPLSRL.PRD	75×75	B&W
PageMarq 15/20	HPLSRM.PRD	100×100	B&W
PageMarq 15/20	HPLSRH.PRD	150×150	B&W
PageMarq 15/20	HPLSRVH.PRD	300×300	B&W

C.Itoh

8510, 8600, Prowriter	CITOHVL.PRD	80×72	B&W
8510, 8600, Prowriter	CITOHL.PRD	96×72	B&W
8510, 8600, Prowriter	CITOHM.PRD	136×72	B&W
8510, 8600, Prowriter	CITOHH.PRD	160×72	B&W
8510, 8600, Prowriter	CITOHVH.PRD	160×144	B&W
C-310, 5000	EPSON9L.PRD	60×72	B&W
C-310, 5000	EPSON9M.PRD	120×72	B&W
C-310, 5000	EPSON9H.PRD	120×216	B&W
C-310, 5000	EPSON9VH.PRD	240×216	B&W
C-610, C-610II, Prowriter	EPSON2L.PRD	60×60	B&W
C-610 C-610II, Prowriter	EPSON2M.PRD	120×60	B&W
C-610 C-610II, Prowriter	EPSON2H.PRD	180×180	B&W
ProWriter CI-4/CI-8/CI-8e	HPLSRL.PRD	75×75	B&W
ProWriter CI-4/CI-8/CI-8e	HPLSRM.PRD	100×100	B&W
ProWriter CI-4/CI-8/CI-8e	HPLSRH.PRD	150×150	B&W
ProWriter CI-4/CI-8/CI-8e	HPLSRVH.PRD	300×300	B&W

Dataproducts

8050/8070	DATAPM.PRD	168×84	B&W
8050/8070	DATAPCM.PRD	168×84	Color
8052C	IBMCLRL.PRD	60×72	B&W
8052C	IBMCLRM.PRD	120×72	B&W
LX-455	EPSON9L.PRD	60×72	B&W
LX-455	EPSON9M.PRD	120×72	B&W
LX-455	EPSON9H.PRD	120×216	B&W
LX-455	EPSON9VH.PRD	240×216	B&W
LZR 1555/1560	HPLSRL.PRD	75×75	B&W
LZR 1555/1560	HPLSRM.PRD	100×100	B&W

Manufacture/printer model	Definition	Resolution	B&W/color
LZR 1555/1560	HPLSRH.PRD	150×150	B&W
LZR 1555/1560	HPLSRVH.PRD	300×300	B&W
LZR-960	PS.PRD	300×300	B&W
Datasouth			
All models	DATASL.PRD	72×72	B&W
All models	DATASH.PRD	144×144	B&W
XL-300	EPSON9L.PRD	60×72	B&W
XL-300	EPSON9M.PRD	120×72	B&W
XL-300	EPSON9H.PRD	120×216	B&W
XL-300	EPSON9VH.PRD	240×216	B&W
DEC			
LA50, LA100, LN03, DECwriter	DECLAL.PRD	144×72	B&W
LA50, LA100, LN03, DECwriter	DECLAH.PRD	180×72	B&W
LA75+, LA424	IBMGRL.PRD	60×72	B&W
LA75+, LA424	IBMGRM.PRD	120×72	B&W
LA75+, LA424	IBMGRH.PRD	120×216	B&W
LA75+, LA424	IBMGRVH.PRD	240×216	B&W
multiJET 2000	HPLSRL.PRD	75×75	B&W
multiJET 2000	HPLSRM.PRD	100×100	B&W
multiJET 2000	HPLSRH.PRD	150×150	B&W
multiJET 2000	HPLSRVH.PRD	300×300	B&W
DECLaser 1150/2150/2250/3250	PS.PRD	300×300	B&W
Desktop			
Laser Beam	HPLSRL.PRD	75×75	B&W
Laser Beam	HPLSRM.PRD	100×100	B&W
Laser Beam	HPLSRH.PRD	150×150	B&W
Laser Beam	HPLSRVH.PRD	300×300	B&W
Diablo			
S32	DIABLSL.PRD	70×70	B&W
C-150 Inkjet	DIABLCCM.PRD	120×120	Color
P Series, 34LQ	EPSON9L.PRD	60×72	B&W
P Series, 34LQ	EPSON9M.PRD	120×72	B&W
P Series, 34LQ	EPSON9H.PRD	120×216	B&W
P Series, 34LQ	EPSON9VH.PRD	240×216	B&W
Diconix			
150	EPSON9L.PRD	60×72	B&W
150	EPSON9M.PRD	120×72	B&W
150	EPSON9H.PRD	120×216	B&W
150	EPSON9VH.PRD	240×216	B&W
Dynax-Fortis			
DM20, DH45	BROTWNL.PRD	60×72	B&W
DM20, DH45	BROTWNM.PRD	120×72	B&W
DM20, DH45	BROTWNH.PRD	120×216	B&W
DM20, DH45	BROTWNVH.PRD	240×216	B&W
Epson			
LQ, SQ, or Action Printer models	EPSON2L.PRD	60×60	B&W

Manufacture/printer model	Definition	Resolution	B&W/color
LQ, SQ, or Action Printer models	EPSON2M.PRD	120×60	B&W
LQ, SQ, or Action Printer models	EPSON2H.PRD	180×180	B&W
LQ, SQ, or Action Printer models	EPSON2VH.PRD	360×360	B&W
LQ, SQ, or Action Printer models	EPSON2CH.PRD	180×180	Color
LQ, SQ, or Action Printer models	EPSON2CV.PRD	360×360	Color
EPL-6000/7000/7500	EPSON6L.PRD	75×75	B&W
EPL-6000/7000/7500	EPSON6M.PRD	100×100	B&W
EPL-6000/7000/7500	EPSON6H.PRD	150×150	B&W
EPL-6000/7000/7500	EPSON6VH.PRD	300×300	B&W
MX, FX, RX, JX, LX, and DFX	EPSON9L.PRD	60×72	B&W
MX, FX, RX, JX, LX, and DFX	EPSON9M.PRD	120×72	B&W
FX, RX, JX, LX, and DFX	EPSON9H.PRD	120×216	B&W
FX, RX, JX, LX, and DFX	EPSON9VH.PRD	240×216	B&W
MX, FX, RX, JX, LX, and DFX	EPSON9CL.PRD	60×72	Color
MX, FX, RX, JX, LX, and DFX	EPSON9CM.PRD	120×72	Color
FX, RX, JX, LX, and DFX	EPSON9CH.PRD	120×216	Color
FX, RX, JX, LX, and DFX	EPSON9CV.PRD	240×216	Color
GQ 3500 native mode	EPSONGQH.PRD	300×300	B&W
ActionLaser II/EPL-8000	HPLSRL.PRD	75×75	B&W
ActionLaser II/EPL-8000	HPLSRM.PRD	100×100	B&W
ActionLaser II/EPL-8000	HPLSRH.PRD	150×150	B&W
ActionLaser II/EPL-8000	HPLSRVH.PRD	300×300	B&W
Everex			
Laser Script LX	HPLSRL.PRD	75×75	B&W
Laser Script LX	HPLSRM.PRD	100×100	B&W
Laser Script LX	HPLSRH.PRD	150×150	B&W
Laser Script LX	HPLSRVH.PRD	300×300	B&W
Laser Script LX	PS.PRD	300×300	B&W
Facit			
4528	FAC4528L.PRD	60×60	B&W
4542, 4544	FAC4542L.PRD	70×70	B&W
B2400	EPSON2L.PRD	60×60	B&W
B2400	EPSON2M.PRD	120×60	B&W
B2400	EPSON2H.PRD	180×180	B&W
B3550C	EPSON9L.PRD	60×72	B&W
B3550C	EPSON9M.PRD	120×72	B&W
B3550C	EPSON9H.PRD	120×216	B&W
B3550C	EPSON9VH.PRD	240×216	B&W
Fortis			
DP600S	HPLSRL.PRD	75×75	B&W
DP600S	HPLSRM.PRD	100×100	B&W
DP600S	HPLSRH.PRD	150×150	B&W
DP600S	HPLSRVH.PRD	300×300	B&W
DH45	BROTWNL.PRD	60×72	B&W
DH45	BROTWNM.PRD	120×72	B&W
DH45	BROTWNH.PRD	120×216	B&W

Manufacture/printer model	Definition	Resolution	B&W/color
DH45	BROTWNVH.PRD	240×216	B&W
DM2210, DM2215	EPSON9L.PRD	60×72	B&W
DM2210, DM2215	EPSON9M.PRD	120×72	B&W
DM2210, DM2215	EPSON9H.PRD	120×216	B&W
DM2210, DM2215	EPSON9VH.PRD	240×216	B&W
DQ 4110, 4210, 4215	EPSON2L.PRD	60×60	B&W
DQ 4110, 4210, 4215	EPSON2M.PRD	120×60	B&W
DQ 4110, 4210, 4215	EPSON2H.PRD	180×180	B&W
DP600P	PS.PRD	300×300	B&W
Fujitsu			
24C	FUJI24CH.PRD	180×180	B&W
24C	FUJI24CV.PRD	360×180	B&W
24C	FUJ24CCH.PRD	180×180	Color
24C	FUJ24CCV.PRD	360×180	Color
24D	FUJI24DL.PRD	60×60	B&W
24D	FUJI24DM.PRD	90×90	B&W
24D	FUJI24DH.PRD	180×180	B&W
DL 1200/3600/4400/4800/5800	EPSON2L.PRD	60×60	B&W
DL 1200/3600/4400/4800/5800	EPSON2M.PRD	120×60	B&W
DL 1200/3600/4400/4800/5800	EPSON2H.PRD	180×180	B&W
RX 7200/7300E, PrintPartner 10	HPLSRL.PRD	75×75	B&W
RX 7200/7300E, PrintPartner 10	HPLSRM.PRD	100×100	B&W
RX 7200/7300E, PrintPartner 10	HPLSRH.PRD	150×150	B&W
RX 7200/7300E, PrintPartner 10	HPLSRVH.PRD	300×300	B&W
RX 7100PS	PS.PRD	300×300	B&W
GCC			
BLP II(S)	PS.PRD	300×300	B&W
GENICOM			
3180-3404 Series	GENICOML.PRD	72×72	B&W
3410, 3820, 3840	EPSON9L.PRD	60×72	B&W
3410, 3820, 3840	EPSON9M.PRD	120×72	B&W
3410, 3820, 3840	EPSON9H.PRD	120×216	B&W
3410, 3820, 3840	EPSON9VH.PRD	240×216	B&W
1040	EPSON2L.PRD	60×60	B&W
1040	EPSON2M.PRD	120×60	B&W
1040	EPSON2H.PRD	180×180	B&W
4440 XT	IBMGRL.PRD	60×72	B&W
4440 XT	IBMGRM.PRD	120×72	B&W
4440 XT	IBMGRH.PRD	120×216	B&W
4440 XT	IBMGRVH.PRD	240×216	B&W
7170	HPLSRL.PRD	75×75	B&W
7170	HPLSRM.PRD	100×100	B&W
7170	HPLSRH.PRD	150×150	B&W
7170	HPLSRVH.PRD	300×300	B&W
Gorilla			
Banana	GORILLAM.PRD	60×63	B&W

339

Manufacture/printer model	Definition	Resolution	B&W/color
FHermes			
Printer I	EPSON9L.PRD	60×72	B&W
Printer I	EPSON9M.PRD	120×72	B&W
Hewlett-Packard			
7600 Model 355, DesignJet	HP7600M.PRD	102×102	B&W
7600 Model 355, DesignJet	HP7600H.PRD	406×406	B&W
7600 Model 355	HP7600CM.PRD	102×102	Color
7600 Model 355	HP7600CH.PRD	406×406	Color
LaserJet/DeskJet, all models	HPLSRL.PRD	75×75	B&W
LaserJet/DeskJet, all models	HPLSRM.PRD	100×100	B&W
LaserJet/DeskJet, all models	HPLSRH.PRD	150×150	B&W
LaserJet/DeskJet, all models	HPLSRVH.PRD	300×300	B&W
LaserJet 4	HPLSRVVH.PRD	600×600	B&W
DeskJet 500C/550C, PaintJet XL300	HPDSKCL.PRD	75×75	Color
DeskJet 500C/550C, PaintJet XL300	HPDSKCM.PRD	100×100	Color
DeskJet 500C/550C, PaintJet XL300	HPDSKCH.PRD	150×150	Color
DeskJet 500C/550C, PaintJet XL300	HPDSKCVH.PRD	300×300	Color
PaintJet, all models	HPPNTM.PRD	90×90	B&W
PaintJet, all models	HPPNTH.PRD	180×180	B&W
PaintJet, all models	HPPNTCM.PRD	90×90	Color
PaintJet, all models	HPPNTCMT.PRD	90×90	Color
PaintJet, all models	HPPNTCH.PRD	180×180	Color
QuietJet	HPQJTEL.PRD	96×96	B&W
QuietJet	HPQJTEM.PRD	192×96	B&W
QuietJet	HPQJTEH.PRD	192×192	B&W
QuietJet	HPQJTL.PRD	96×96	B&W
QuietJet	HPQJTM.PRD	192×96	B&W
QuietJet	HPQJTH.PRD	192×192	B&W
ThinkJet	HPTNKEM.PRD	192×96	B&W
ThinkJet	HPTNKM.PRD	192×96	B&W
LaserJet 4 (with Postscript)	PS.PRD	300×300	B&W
Hyundai			
HDP-910/920	EPSON9L.PRD	60×72	B&W
HDP-910/920	EPSON9M.PRD	120×72	B&W
IBM			
3852-1 Color Inkjet	IBM381CM.PRD	84×84	Color
3852-2 Color Inkjet	IBM382CM.PRD	100×96	Color
3852 Color Inkjet	IBM38M.PRD	84×63	B&W
Color Printer	IBMCLRL.PRD	60×72	B&W
Color Printer	IBMCLRM.PRD	120×72	B&W
Graphics, Proprinter, 2380 Series	IBMGRL.PRD	60×72	B&W

340

Manufacture/printer model	Definition	Resolution	B&W/color
Graphics, Proprinter, 2380 Series	IBMGRM.PRD	120×72	B&W
Graphics, Proprinter, 2380 Series	IBMGRH.PRD	120×216	B&W
Graphics, Proprinter, 2380 Series	IBMGRVH.PRD	120×216	B&W
Personal Printer 2390, ExecJet	EPSON2L.PRD	60×60	B&W
Personal Printer 2390, ExecJet	EPSON2M.PRD	120×60	B&W
Personal Printer 2390, ExecJet	EPSON2H.PRD	180×180	B&W
LaserPrinter 6p/10p	HPLSRL.PRD	75×75	B&W
LaserPrinter 6p/10p	HPLSRM.PRD	100×100	B&W
LaserPrinter 6p/10p	HPLSRH.PRD	150×150	B&W
LaserPrinter 6p/10p	HPLSRVH.PRD	300×300	B&W

IDS

440	IDS440L.PRD	64×64	B&W
Prism, 560, 480, P132, P80	IDSM.PRD	84×84	B&W
Prism, 560, 480, P132, P80	IDSCM.PRD	84×84	Color

Integrex

Colour Jet 132	INTE132L.PRD	60×60	B&W

JDL

750	JDL750L.PRD	60×60	B&W
750	JDL750M.PRD	90×90	B&W
750	JDL750H.PRD	180×180	B&W
750	JDL750CL.PRD	60×60	Color
750	JDL750CM.PRD	90×90	Color
750	JDL750CH.PRD	180×180	Color

Kentek

K30D	HPLSRL.PRD	75×75	B&W
K30D	HPLSRM.PRD	100×100	B&W
K30D	HPLSRH.PRD	150×150	B&W
K30D	HPLSRVH.PRD	300×300	B&W

Kodak Diconix

150	EPSON9L.PRD	60×72	B&W
150	EPSON9M.PRD	120×72	B&W
150	EPSON9H.PRD	120×216	B&W
150	EPSON9VH.PRD	240×216	B&W
Ektaplus 7008	HPLSRL.PRD	75×75	B&W
Ektaplus 7008	HPLSRM.PRD	100×100	B&W
Ektaplus 7008	HPLSRH.PRD	150×150	B&W
Ektaplus 7008	HPLSRVH.PRD	300×300	B&W
Color 4	HPPNTM.PRD	90×90	B&W
Color 4	HPPNTH.PRD	180×180	B&W
Color 4	HPPNTCM.PRD	90×90	Color
Color 4	HPPNTCMT.PRD	90×90	Color
Color 4	HPPNTCH.PRD	180×180	Color

Kyocera

Ecosys a-SiFS-1500A	HPLSRL.PRD	75×75	B&W
Ecosys a-SiFS-1500A	HPLSRM.PRD	100×100	B&W

Manufacture/printer model	Definition	Resolution	B&W/color
Ecosys a-Si FS-1500A	HPLSRH.PRD	150 × 150	B&W
Ecosys a-Si FS-1500A	HPLSRVH.PRD	300 × 300	B&W
Laser Computer			
190E, 240	EPSON9L.PRD	60 × 72	B&W
190E, 240	EPSON9M.PRD	120 × 72	B&W
190E, 240	EPSON9H.PRD	120 × 216	B&W
190E, 240	EPSON9VH.PRD	240 × 216	B&W
Laser Master			
Unity 1000/1200XL, WinPrinter 800	HPLSRL.PRD	75 × 75	B&W
Unity 1000/1200XL, WinPrinter 800	HPLSRM.PRD	100 × 100	B&W
Unity 1000/1200XL, WinPrinter 800	HPLSRH.PRD	150 × 150	B&W
Unity 1000/1200XL, WinPrinter 800	HPLSRVH.PRD	300 × 300	B&W
TrueTech 800/1000	PS.PRD	300 × 300	B&W
Malibu			
All models	MALIBUL.PRD	60 × 60	B&W
Mannesmann Tally			
160	MAN160L.PRD	50 × 64	B&W
160	MAN160M.PRD	100 × 64	B&W
160	MAN160H.PRD	133 × 64	B&W
420, 440	MAN420L.PRD	60 × 60	B&W
Spirit 80, 81	MANSPRTL.PRD	80 × 72	B&W
Spirit 80, 81	MANSPRTM.PRD	160 × 72	B&W
Spirit 80, 81	MANSPRTH.PRD	160 × 216	B&W
905, 908, 910, 661, 735	HPLSRL.PRD	75 × 75	B&W
905, 908, 910, 661, 735	HPLSRM.PRD	100 × 100	B&W
905, 908, 910, 661, 735	HPLSRH.PRD	150 × 150	B&W
905, 908, 910, 661, 735	HPLSRVH.PRD	300 × 300	B&W
MT150/9,MT151/9	EPSON9L.PRD	60 × 72	B&W
MT150/9,MT151/9	EPSON9M.PRD	120 × 72	B&W
MT150/9,MT151/9	EPSON9H.PRD	120 × 216	B&W
MT150/9,MT151/9	EPSON9VH.PRD	240 × 216	B&W
MT150/24,151/24, 82	EPSON2L.PRD	60 × 60	B&W
MT150/24,151/24, 82	EPSON2M.PRD	120 × 60	B&W
MT150/24,151/24, 82	EPSON2H.PRD	180 × 180	B&W
All Postscript models	PS.PRD	300 × 300	B&W
Microtek			
TrueLaser	PS.PRD	300 × 300	B&W
Mitsubishi			
DiamondColor Print 300PS	PSC.PRD	300 × 300	Color
CHC-S446i ColorStream/DS	PSC.PRD	300 × 300	Color

342

Manufacture/printer model	Definition	Resolution	B&W/color
MPI			
All models	MPIL.PRD	60×72	B&W
All models	MPIM.PRD	120×72	B&W
All models	MPIH.PRD	120×144	B&W
NEC			
P2200/3200/3300/5300/9300 models	NEC24L.PRD	60×60	B&W
P2200/3200/3300/5300/9300 models	NEC24M.PRD	120×60	B&W
P2200/3200/3300/5300/9300 models	NEC24H.PRD	180×180	B&W
P2200/3200/3300/5300/9300 models	NEC24VH.PRD	360×360	B&W
P2200, P5300, 24-pin models	NEC24CH.PRD	180×180	Color
P2200, P5300, 24-pin models	NEC24CVH.PRD	360×360	Color
8023	NEC8023L.PRD	72×72	B&W
8027A	NEC8027L.PRD	80×72	B&W
P2, P3, CP2, CP3, 9-pin models	NEC9L.PRD	60×60	B&W
P2, P3, CP2, CP3, 9-pin models	NEC9M.PRD	120×60	B&W
P2, P3, CP2, CP3, 9-pin models	NEC9H.PRD	120×120	B&W
P2, P3, CP2, CP3, 9-pin models	NEC9VH.PRD	240×240	B&W
P2, P3, CP2, CP3, 9-pin models	NEC9CL.PRD	60×60	Color
P2, P3, CP2, CP3, 9-pin models	NEC9CM.PRD	120×60	Color
P2, P3, CP2, CP3, 9-pin models	NEC9CH.PRD	120×120	Color
P2, P3, CP2, CP3, 9-pin models	NEC9CVH.PRD	240×240	Color
LC 890XL, SilentWriter 95	HPLSRL.PRD	75×75	B&W
LC 890XL, SilentWriter 95	HPLSRM.PRD	100×100	B&W
LC 890XL, SilentWriter 95	HPLSRH.PRD	150×150	B&W
LC 890XL, SilentWriter 95	HPLSRVH.PRD	300×300	B&W
All Postscript models	PS.PRD	300×300	B&W
NewGen			
TurboPS/400p/630En/660/840e/880	HPLSRL.PRD	75×75	B&W
TurboPS/400p/630En/660/840e/880	HPLSRM.PRD	100×100	B&W
TurboPS/400p/630En/660/840e/880	HPLSRH.PRD	150×150	B&W
TurboPS/400p/630En/660/840e/880	HPLSRVH.PRD	300×300	B&W
TurboPS/1200T	HPLSRL.PRD	75×75	B&W
TurboPS/1200T	HPLSRM.PRD	100×100	B&W
TurboPS/1200T	HPLSRH.PRD	150×150	B&W
TurboPS/1200T	HPLSRVH.PRD	300×300	B&W
North Atlantic Quantex			
All models	NORTHL.PRD	72×72	B&W
All models	NORTHM.PRD	120×72	B&W
All models	NORTHH.PRD	144×72	B&W
Okidata			
Okimate 20	OKI20L.PRD	60×72	Color
2410, 2350	OKI2410L.PRD	72×72	B&W
2410, 2350, 24-pin models	OKI24L.PRD	60×60	B&W

Manufacture/printer model	Definition	Resolution	B&W/color
2410, 2350, 24-pin models	OKI24M.PRD	120×60	B&W
2410, 2350, 24-pin models	OKI24H.PRD	180×180	B&W
2410, 2350, 24-pin models	OKI24VH.PRD	363×363	B&W
2410, 2350, 24-pin models	OKI24CH.PRD	180×180	Color
ML-92,ML-93,ML-82,ML-83 (w/o P&P)	OKI9L.PRD	72×72	B&W
ML-92,ML-93,ML-82,ML-83 (w/o P&P)	OKI9M.PRD	144×72	B&W
ML-92,ML-93,ML-82,ML-83 (w/o P&P)	OKI9H.PRD	144×144	B&W
Above models (w/ Plug & Play)	EPSON9L.PRD	60×72	B&W
Above models (w/ Plug & Play)	EPSON9M.PRD	120×72	B&W
Above models (w/ Plug & Play)	EPSON9H.PRD	120×216	B&W
Above models (w/ Plug & Play)	EPSON9VH.PRD	240×216	B&W
Laserline (HP)	HPLSRL.PRD	75×75	B&W
Laserline (HP)	HPLSRM.PRD	100×100	B&W
Laserline (HP)	HPLSRH.PRD	150×150	B&W
Laserline (HP)	HPLSRVH.PRD	300×300	B&W
Pacemark 3410	EPSON9L.PRD	60×72	B&W
Pacemark 3410	EPSON9M.PRD	120×72	B&W
Pacemark 3410	EPSON9H.PRD	120×216	B&W
Pacemark 3410	EPSON9VH.PRD	240×216	B&W
Microline 184 Turbo	IBMGRL.PRD	60×72	B&W
Microline 184 Turbo	IBMGRM.PRD	120×72	B&W
Microline 184 Turbo	IBMGRH.PRD	120×216	B&W
Microline 184 Turbo	IBMGRVH.PRD	240×216	B&W
OL 810 LED	HPLSRL.PRD	75×75	B&W
OL 810 LED	HPLSRM.PRD	100×100	B&W
OL 810 LED	HPLSRH.PRD	150×150	B&W
OL 810 LED	HPLSRVH.PRD	300×300	B&W
OL 830	PS.PRD	300×300	B&W
Olympia			
NP	EPSON9L.PRD	60×72	B&W
NP	EPSON9M.PRD	120×72	B&W
NP	EPSON9H.PRD	120×216	B&W
NP	EPSON9VH.PRD	240×216	B&W
Output Technology			
All models	EPSON9L.PRD	60×72	B&W
All models	EPSON9M.PRD	120×72	B&W
All models	EPSON9H.PRD	120×216	B&W
All models	EPSON9VH.PRD	240×216	B&W
LaserMatrix 1000 Model 5	HPLSRL.PRD	75×75	B&W
LaserMatrix 1000 Model 5	HPLSRM.PRD	100×100	B&W
LaserMatrix 1000 Model 5	HPLSRH.PRD	150×150	B&W
LaserMatrix 1000 Model 5	HPLSRVH.PRD	300×300	B&W

344

Manufacture/printer model	Definition	Resolution	B&W/color
PMC			
DMP-85	NEC8027L.PRD	80 × 72	B&W
Panasonic			
All models (9-pin printers)	PANASL.PRD	60 × 72	B&W
All models (9-pin printers)	PANASM.PRD	120 × 72	B&W
All models (9-pin printers)	PANASH.PRD	120 × 216	B&W
All models (9-pin printers)	PANASVH.PRD	240 × 216	B&W
All models (24-pin printers)	EPSON2L.PRD	60 × 60	B&W
All models (24-pin printers)	EPSON2M.PRD	120 × 60	B&W
All models (24-pin printers)	EPSON2H.PRD	180 × 180	B&W
KX-P4410/4430	HPLSRL.PRD	75 × 75	B&W
KX-P4410/4430	HPLSRM.PRD	100 × 100	B&W
KX-P4410/4430	HPLSRH.PRD	150 × 150	B&W
KX-P4410/4430	HPLSRVH.PRD	300 × 300	B&W
All Postscript models	PS.PRD	300 × 300	B&W
Postscript			
All models	PS.PRD	300 × 300	B&W
Printronix			
L2324	HPLSRL.PRD	75 × 75	B&W
L2324	HPLSRM.PRD	100 × 100	B&W
L2324	HPLSRH.PRD	150 × 150	B&W
L2324	HPLSRVH.PRD	300 × 300	B&W
QMS			
All Postscript models	PS.PRD	300 × 300	B&W
Quadram			
Quadjet	QUADRL.PRD	80 × 80	B&W
Quadjet	QUADRCL.PRD	70 × 72	Color
Qume			
All Postscript models	PS.PRD	300 × 300	B&W
Raster devices			
All Postscript models	PS.PRD	300 × 300	B&W
Ricoh			
All Postscript models	PS.PRD	300 × 300	B&W
Riteman			
All models	EPSON9L.PRD	60 × 72	B&W
All models	EPSON9M.PRD	120 × 72	B&W
All models	EPSON9H.PRD	120 × 216	B&W
All models	EPSON9VH.PRD	240 × 216	B&W
Royal			
CJP 450	HPLSRL.PRD	75 × 75	B&W
CJP 450	HPLSRM.PRD	100 × 100	B&W
CJP 450	HPLSRH.PRD	150 × 150	B&W
CJP 450	HPLSRVH.PRD	300 × 300	B&W

Manufacture/printer model	Definition	Resolution	B&W/color
Samsung			
Finale' 8000	HPLSRL.PRD	75 × 75	B&W
Finale' 8000	HPLSRM.PRD	100 × 100	B&W
Finale' 8000	HPLSRH.PRD	150 × 150	B&W
Finale' 8000	HPLSRVH.PRD	300 × 300	B&W
Seikosha			
GP-100A	SEIKOL.PRD	60 × 63	B&W
SP-180AI/1600AI/2400/2415, BP-5460	EPSON9L.PRD	60 × 72	B&W
SP-180AI/1600AI/2400/2415, BP-5460	EPSON9M.PRD	120 × 72	B&W
SP-180AI/1600AI/2400/2415, BP-5460	EPSON9H.PRD	120 × 216	B&W
SP-180AI/1600AI/2400/2415, BP-5460	EPSON9VH.PRD	240 × 216	B&W
SL-230AI, LT-20	EPSON2L.PRD	60 × 60	B&W
SL-230AI, LT-20	EPSON2M.PRD	120 × 60	B&W
SL-230AI, LT-20	EPSON2H.PRD	180 × 180	B&W
Sharp			
JX 720	SHARPCM.PRD	60 × 63	B&W
JX-9500H	HPLSRL.PRD	75 × 75	B&W
JX-9500H	HPLSRM.PRD	100 × 100	B&W
JX-9500H	HPLSRH.PRD	150 × 150	B&W
JX-9500H	HPLSRVH.PRD	300 × 300	B&W
JX-9500PS	PS.PRD	300 × 300	B&W
Siemens			
PT90, PT88S	EPSON9L.PRD	60 × 72	B&W
PT90, PT88S	EPSON9M.PRD	120 × 72	B&W
PT90, PT88S	EPSON9H.PRD	120 × 216	B&W
PT90, PT88S	EPSON9VH.PRD	240 × 216	B&W
Smith-Corona			
D-200, D-300	EPSON9L.PRD	60 × 72	B&W
D-200, D-300	EPSON9M.PRD	120 × 72	B&W
D-200, D-300	EPSON9H.PRD	120 × 216	B&W
D-200, D-300	EPSON9VH.PRD	240 × 216	B&W
Star Micronics			
Delta,Radix,Gemini,SD,SR,NX,XR	STAR9L.PRD	60 × 72	B&W
Delta,Radix,Gemini,SD,SR,NX,XR	STAR9M.PRD	120 × 72	B&W
NX, and XR Series	STAR9H.PRD	120 × 144	B&W
NX, and XR Series	STAR9VH.PRD	240 × 144	B&W
SB-10 STAR24H.PRD	180 × 240	B&W	
NB24-15,XB24-10/15,SJ-48, NX-2430	EPSON2L.PRD	60 × 60	B&W
NB24-15,XB24-10/15,SJ-48, NX-2430	EPSON2M.PRD	120 × 60	B&W

PRINTERS: the commercial version

Manufacture/printer model	Definition	Resolution	B&W/color
NB24-15,XB24-10/15,SJ-48, NX-2430	EPSON2H.PRD	180 × 180	B&W
LaserPrinter 4	HPLSRL.PRD	75 × 75	B&W
LaserPrinter 4	HPLSRM.PRD	100 × 100	B&W
LaserPrinter 4	HPLSRH.PRD	150 × 150	B&W
LaserPrinter 4	HPLSRVH.PRD	300 × 300	B&W
LaserPrinter 4 Star Script	PS.PRD	300 × 300	B&W
Synergystex			
CF1000	HPLSRL.PRD	75 × 75	B&W
CF1000	HPLSRM.PRD	100 × 100	B&W
CF1000	HPLSRH.PRD	150 × 150	B&W
CF1000	HPLSRVH.PRD	300 × 300	B&W
Talaris			
1590-T Printstation	HPLSRL.PRD	75 × 75	B&W
1590-T Printstation	HPLSRM.PRD	100 × 100	B&W
1590-T Printstation	HPLSRH.PRD	150 × 150	B&W
1590-T Printstation	HPLSRVH.PRD	300 × 300	B&W
Tandy (Radio Shack)			
2100 Series	TAN2100L.PRD	60 × 60	B&W
2100 Series	TAN2100H.PRD	180 × 180	B&W
DMP-430/440	TAN430M.PRD	120 × 144	B&W
CGP-220	TANCGPCL.PRD	70 × 72	Color
CGP-220	TANCGPL.PRD	80 × 80	B&W
Most Tandy printers	TANDYL.PRD	60 × 72	B&W
Most Tandy printers	TANDYM.PRD	60 × 144	B&W
IBM emulation	TANIBML.PRD	60 × 72	B&W
IBM emulation	TANIBMM.PRD	120 × 72	B&W
IBM emulation	TANIBMH.PRD	120 × 216	B&W
IBM emulation	TANIBMVH.PRD	240 × 216	B&W
DMP-310	EPSON9L.PRD	60 × 72	B&W
DMP-310	EPSON9M.PRD	120 × 72	B&W
DMP-310	EPSON9H.PRD	120 × 216	B&W
DMP-310	EPSON9VH.PRD	240 × 216	B&W
LP 950	HPLSRL.PRD	75 × 75	B&W
LP 950	HPLSRM.PRD	100 × 100	B&W
LP 950	HPLSRH.PRD	150 × 150	B&W
LP 950	HPLSRVH.PRD	300 × 300	B&W
Tektronix			
PhaserII PXe/IIsd/III PXi	PSC.PRD	300 × 300	Color
Texas Instruments			
855/857/865	TI855CL.PRD	60 × 72	Color
855/857/865	TI855CM.PRD	120 × 72	Color
855/857/865	TI855CH.PRD	120 × 144	Color
855/857/865	TI855CVH.PRD	120 × 144	Color
855/857/865	TI855L.PRD	60 × 72	B&W
855/857/865	TI855M.PRD	120 × 72	B&W

347

Manufacture/printer model	Definition	Resolution	B&W/color
855/857/865	TI855H.PRD	120 × 144	B&W
855/857/865	TI855VH.PRD	144 × 144	B&W
850	EPSON9L.PRD	60 × 72	B&W
850	EPSON9M.PRD	120 × 72	B&W
TI MicroLaser Turbo/XL Turbo	HPLSRL.PRD	75 × 75	B&W
TI MicroLaser Turbo/XL Turbo	HPLSRM.PRD	100 × 100	B&W
TI MicroLaser Turbo/XL Turbo	HPLSRH.PRD	150 × 150	B&W
TI MicroLaser Turbo/XL Turbo	HPLSRVH.PRD	300 × 300	B&W
Toshiba			
1350	TOSH1350.PRD	180 × 180	B&W
24-pin models	TOSH24CE.PRD	360 × 360	Color
24-pin models	TOSH24CH.PRD	180 × 180	Color
24-pin models	TOSH24CV.PRD	360 × 180	Color
24-pin models	TOSH24H.PRD	180 × 180	B&W
24-pin models	TOSH24VH.PRD	360 × 180	B&W
24-pin models	TOSH24EH.PRD	360 × 360	B&W
Express Writer 301/311	EPSON2L.PRD	60 × 60	B&W
Express Writer 301/311	EPSON2M.PRD	120 × 60	B&W
Express Writer 301/311	EPSON2H.PRD	180 × 180	B&W
PageLaser GX200/GSX400	HPLSRL.PRD	75 × 75	B&W
PageLaser GX200/GSX400	HPLSRM.PRD	100 × 100	B&W
PageLaser GX200/GSX400	HPLSRH.PRD	150 × 150	B&W
PageLaser GX200/GSX400	HPLSRVH.PRD	300 × 300	B&W
Unisys			
AP 1327/9 Mod5, 1371, 115, 37	EPSON9L.PRD	60 × 72	B&W
AP 1327/9 Mod5, 1371, 115, 37	EPSON9M.PRD	120 × 72	B&W
AP 1327/9 Mod5, 1371, 115, 37	EPSON9H.PRD	120 × 216	B&W
AP 1327/9 Mod5, 1371, 115, 37	EPSON9VH.PRD	240 × 216	B&W
AP 1234	EPSON2L.PRD	60 × 60	B&W
AP 1234	EPSON2M.PRD	120 × 60	B&W
AP 1234	EPSON2H.PRD	180 × 180	B&W
AP 92/94 Mod 37 (HP)	HPLSRL.PRD	75 × 75	B&W
AP 92/94 Mod 37 (HP)	HPLSRM.PRD	100 × 100	B&W
AP 92/94 Mod 37 (HP)	HPLSRH.PRD	150 × 150	B&W
AP 92/94 Mod 37 (HP)	HPLSRVH.PRD	300 × 300	B&W
AP 94 (Postscript)	PS.PRD	300 × 300	B&W
Xante			
Accel-a-Writer 8000	HPLSRL.PRD	75 × 75	B&W
Accel-a-Writer 8000	HPLSRM.PRD	100 × 100	B&W
Accel-a-Writer 8000	HPLSRH.PRD	150 × 150	B&W
Accel-a-Writer 8000	HPLSRVH.PRD	300 × 300	B&W
Xerox			
2700/4045	XER2700L.PRD	77 × 77	B&W
2700/4045	XER2700H.PRD	154 × 154	B&W
4020 Inkjet	XER4020C.PRD	120 × 120	Color

PRINTERS: the commercial version

Manual codes

Most printers provide a suite of printer-specific functions and features (bold print, underlining, double-width print, double-height print, and so on). While it's virtually impossible for any diagnostic to test each of these functions for every available printer, PRINTERS provides a means for you to test your printer's functions manually using printer codes (also referred to as *escape sequences* or *escape codes*). The Manual Codes feature provides printer technicians with almost unlimited versatility for checking and verifying the most subtle features of a printer's operation.

Note: In order to enter an escape code, you need the user's manual for your particular printer. The diskette's documentation lists escape codes for several popular printer models, but to test printer-specific functions you need printer- specific documentation.

To enter an escape code, left click on Manual Codes (or press C) in the Configure menu. A text entry window will appear below the Configure menu, as shown in Figure 9-3. You can enter up to 50 characters per line. Pressing the <Tab> key or right- clicking anywhere on the display will abort the text entry routine. If you make a mistake in typing, simply backspace over the error and retype the entry.

349

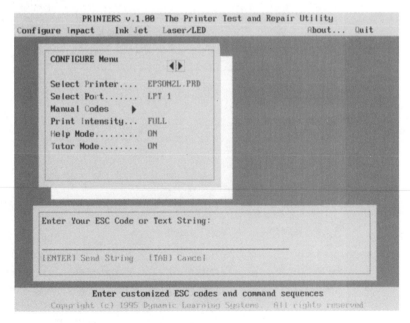

■ **9-3** *The text entry window for manual control codes.*

Example 1: setting the Panasonic KX-P1124 to underline mode

With the text entry routine running, reset the printer (by turning it off and on), then enter the following text:

This is a test of default text <Enter>

Your printer should print this text string in its default font and pitch. Now let's set the printer to its underline mode using the code <Esc> - 1 (from the PRINTERS documentation). Type the three keystrokes and press <Enter>. Keep in mind that when you press the <Esc> key, a backspace arrow will appear in that space. The printer should now be in underline mode, so type the following text:

This is the printer's underline mode <Enter>

The printer should produce the text underlined. To turn the underline mode off, enter the code <Esc> - 0 (from PRINTERS documentation). Type the three keystrokes and press <Enter>. Keep in mind that when you press the <Esc> key, a backspace arrow will appear in that space. Now type the following text:

The underline mode is off <Enter>

The type should no longer be underlined. To leave the text entry routine, press <Tab> or right-click anywhere on the display.

Example 2: Setting the Panasonic KX-P1124 to letter quality (LQ) mode

With the text entry routine running, reset the printer (by turning it off and on), then enter the following text:

This is the printer's default text <Enter>

Your printer should print this text string in its default font and pitch. Now let's set the printer to its LQ mode using the code <Esc> x 1 (from PRINTERS documentation). Type the three keystrokes and press <Enter>. Keep in mind that when you press the <Esc> key, a backspace arrow will appear in that space. The printer should now be in letter quality mode, so type the following text:

This is the printer's LQ mode <Enter>

The printer should produce this text in higher quality than the default. To turn the LQ mode off, enter the code <Esc> x 0 (from PRINTERS documentation). Type the three keystrokes and press <Enter>. Keep in mind that when you press the <Esc> key, a backspace arrow will appear in that space. Now type the following text:

The letter quality mode is off <Enter>

The type should be back in its draft form. To leave the text entry routine, press <Tab> or right-click anywhere in the display.

Print intensity

The print intensity setting allows you to set the overall darkness and lightness (i.e., contrast) of your test images. There are two choices: Half and Full. By default, all images are printed at Full intensity (maximum contrast). At Half intensity, the shading is lightened to reduce the image's contrast. You can toggle between Full and Half intensity by clicking on Print Intensity (or pressing I). For low-resolution devices (e.g., impact printers at 75 dpi or less), Full intensity will typically yield superior results. For medium-to-high resolution devices (e.g., ink-jet and almost all EP printers), Half intensity is often better. Of course, you will probably want to experiment to find the best settings for your particular printer.

Help mode

PRINTERS is designed with two online documentation sources, intended to provide instruction and guidance before and after a test is conducted. The Help screens appear before the selected test starts, providing insight into the purpose and objectives of the selected test. You can toggle the Help mode on and off by left-clicking on Help Mode (or pressing H). By default, the Help mode is on. If you turn the Help mode off, the selected test will start immediately.

Tutor mode

The second online documentation source intended to provide instruction and guidance before and after running PRINTERS is the Tutor. The Tutor screens appear after the selected test is complete, and provide advise on how to interpret the printed results. You can toggle the Tutor mode on and off by left clicking on Tutor Mode (or pressing T). By default, the Tutor mode is on. If you turn the Tutor mode off, there no instruction will be provided when the test is finished.

Running the impact tests

The impact tests allow you to check the operations of almost any impact dot-matrix printer (impact DMP), as well as any 9-pin or 24-pin printer capable of Epson emulation. From the main menu bar, left-click on Impact (or press I). The Impact DMP Test menu will appear, as shown in Figure 9-4 on the next page. You can return to the main menu at any time by pressing the <Esc> key or right-clicking anywhere in the display. There are seven functions available from the Impact DMP Test menu:

Preliminary Setup Information Supplies initial information to help you set up and operate the printer safely

Carriage Transport Test Allows you to test the impact DMP carriage transport system

Paper Transport Test Allows you to test the impact DMP paper transport system

Paper Walk Test Allows you to check friction feed paper transport systems in impact DMPs

Print Head Test Allows you to test the impact DMP print head assembly

Clean Rollers Allows you to check and clean the paper handling rollers

Print Test Page Provides a uniform test pattern for initial or final printer inspection

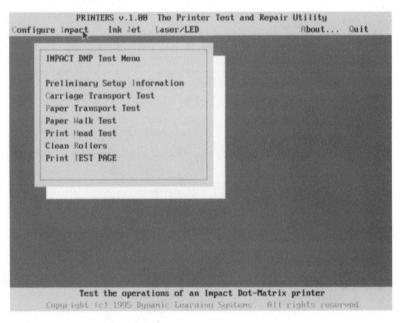

■ **9-4** *The Impact DMP Test menu.*

Preliminary Setup Information

You can access the Preliminary Setup Information screen by left-clicking on Preliminary Setup Information (or pressing I). This is not a test *per se*, but an information screen intended to provide helpful setup information. Novice troubleshooters will find it helpful to review this information before attempting any of the test sequences. Experienced troubleshooters might find it to be a handy reminder. To leave the information screen, press <Esc> or right-click anywhere in the display.

Carriage Transport Test

Impact printers are moving-carriage devices, meaning the print head is carried back and forth across the page surface. This movement is handled by the carriage transport mechanism. Proper printing of text and graphics demands that the print head be positioned precisely in both its left-to-right and right-to-left movement. The Carriage Transport Test is designed to test carriage alignment by generating a series of vertical lines, as shown in Figure 9-5 on the next page. The print head sweeps from left to right, producing a series of vertical tic marks, then reverses direction and produces a right-to-left series of tic marks. Similarly, each line of tic marks is the result of two independent passes. Using this approach, you can check carriage alignment not just between lines, but within the same line.

If the tic marks are not aligned precisely, there might be some mechanical slop in the carriage mechanics. Badly or erratically placed tic marks might indicate a fault in the carriage motor driver circuitry or the carriage home sensor. If marks within the same line are aligned precisely at the edges (but not elsewhere in the line), there might be wiring problems in the print head or print head cable. Start this test by left-clicking on Carriage Transport Test (or pressing C).

Paper Transport Test

There are two traditional means of moving paper through a printer: pulling the paper with a tractor feed or pushing the paper with a friction feed. Regardless of the means, the paper must be carried through a printer evenly and consistently, otherwise the print will overlap and cause distortion. The Paper Transport Test is designed to check the paper transport system's operation. While the Paper Transport Test works with any transport type, it is intended primarily for tractor feed systems that pull the paper through. The test pattern counts off a number of marked passes. You must check each pass to see that they are spaced apart evenly. If not, there might be a problem with the transport mechanics, motor, or driving circuitry. Start this test by left-clicking on Paper Transport Test (or pressing P).

353

PRINTERS: The Printer Test and Alignment Utility V.1.00
IMPACT CARRIAGE REGISTRATION Test Pattern

■ **9-5** *The carriage transport test.*

Paper Walk Test

Like the last test, the Paper Walk Test is designed to check the paper transport system's operation. While the Paper Transport Test is best used with tractor feed paper transports, the Paper Walk Test is intended primarily for friction feed systems that push the paper through. The test pattern generates a series of evenly spaced horizontal lines. You must check each pass to see that they are spaced evenly apart. If not, there might be a problem with the transport mechanics, motor, or driving circuitry.

Another problem particular to friction feed paper transports is the tendency to "walk the page." Proper friction feed operation depends on roller pressure applied evenly across the entire page surface. Any damage, obstructions, or wear could cause excessive roller pressure, allowing the page to spin clockwise or counterclockwise. If you notice lines closer together on the left or right side of the image, the roller assembly might need adjustment or replacement or there might be an obstruction in the paper path. Start this test by left-clicking on Paper Walk Test (or pressing W).

Print Head Test

Ideally, every pin on the print head should fire reliably. In actual practice, however, age, lack of routine maintenance, and heat buildup can affect firing reliability. This often results in horizontal white lines in the text where the corresponding print wires fail. The best way to stress-test an impact print head and detect problems is by printing a dense graphic. The Print Head Test produces a large black rectangle, as shown in Figure 9-6; this demands the proper operation of all print wires, and will often reveal any age, damage, or heat and maintenance-related issues. You can adjust the speed and density of printing by adjusting print intensity and driver resolution under the Configure menu.

PRINTERS: The printer Test and Alignment Utility V.1.00
IMPACT PRINT HEAD Test Pattern

■ **9-6** *The print head test.*

Examine the black rectangle for horizontal white lines. Consistent white lines indicates that a print wire is not firing. Check and clean the face of the print head to remove any accumulations of debris that might be jamming the print wire(s). If the problem persists, there might be a fault in the print head or print wire driver circuitry. If white lines appear only briefly or intermittently, there might be wiring problems with the print head cable or within the print head itself. There might also be an intermittent problem in the corresponding print wire driver circuit. Finally, print intensity should be relatively consistent throughout each pass. Light (faded) printing might indicate trouble with print head wear or spacing, ribbon quality, or the power supply. Start this test by left-clicking on Print Head Test (or pressing H).

Clean Rollers

To combat the dust and debris that naturally accumulate in a printer's mechanics, it is customary to periodically clean the main rollers that handle paper, usually the platen and other major rollers. This is especially important for friction feed paper transports where age and any foreign matter on the rollers can interfere with the paper path and "walk the page." While it is possible (and sometimes more convenient) to rotate the rollers by hand (using the platen knob), the Clean Rollers function provides a paper advance that allows you to streamline the routine cleaning/rejuvenation of roller assemblies. Note that paper must be present in the printer to use this function.

The typical cleaning procedure involves rotating the rollers while wiping them gently with a clean cloth lightly dampened with water. You can use a bit of very mild household detergent to remove "gunk" that resists water alone, but avoid using detergent regularly since chemicals applied to rubber and other synthetic roller materials can reduce their pliability. *Never* use harsh detergents or solvents—ever! If you choose to try rejuvenating the rollers with a roller cleaning solvent, use extreme caution. First, work in a well-ventilated area (solvent fumes are dangerous). Second, it is impossible to predict how cleaning solvents will affect every possible roller material, so always try the solvent on a small patch of the roller in advance. Start this procedure by left-clicking on Clean Rollers (or pressing R). A single cycle will advance the paper transport by two pages.

Print Test Page

The test page is typically the first and last test to be run on any printer. Initially, the test page will reveal problems with the print head, paper transport, or carriage transport. You can then proceed with more detailed tests to further isolate and correct the problem(s). When the repair is complete, the test page is proof of the printer's operation that you can either keep for your records or provide to your customer. The moving-head test page pattern is illustrated in Figure 9-7. You can start this test by left-clicking on Print Test Page (or pressing T).

PRINTERS: The Printer Test and Alignment Utility V.1.00
IMPACT TEST PAGE Pattern

```
A B C D E F G H I J K L M N O P Q R S T U V W X Y Z
A B C D E F G H I J K L M N O P Q R S T U V W X Y Z
a b c d e f g h i j k l m n o p q r s t u v w x y z
a b c d e f g h i j k l m n o p q r s t u v w x y z
'  ~ ! @ # $  % ^ & * ( )  - _ = + / . > , <
'  ~ ! @ # $  % ^ & * ( )  - _ = + / . > , <
```

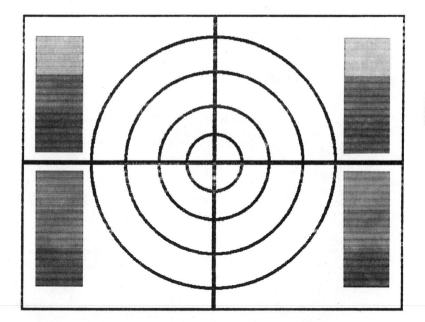

■ 9-7 *The impact test page.*

Running the ink jet tests

The ink-jet tests allow you to check the operation of almost any ink-jet dot-matrix printer (and any printer capable of HP DeskJet emulation). From the main menu bar, left click on Ink Jet (or press J).

The Ink Jet DMP Test menu will appear, as shown in Figure 9-8. You can return to the main menu at any time by pressing the <Esc> key or right-clicking anywhere in the display. There are seven functions available from the Ink Jet DMP Test menu:

Preliminary Setup Information Supplies initial information to help you setup and operate the ink-jet printer safely.

Carriage Transport Test Allows you to test the ink-jet DMP carriage transport system.

Paper Transport Test Allows you to test the ink-jet DMP paper transport system.

Paper Walk Test Allows you to check friction feed paper transport systems in ink-jet DMPs.

Print Head Test Allows you to test the ink-jet DMP print head assembly.

Clean Rollers Allows you to check and clean the paper handling rollers.

Print Test Page Provides a uniform test pattern for initial or final printer inspection.

358

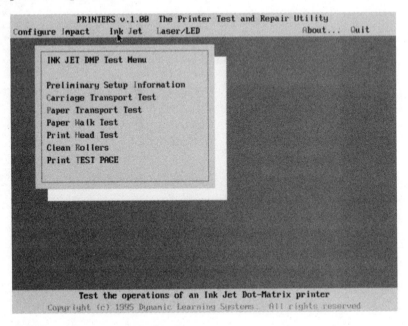

■ **9-8** The Ink Jet DMP Test menu.

Preliminary Setup Information

You can access the Preliminary Setup Information screen by left-clicking on Preliminary Setup Information (or pressing I). This is not actually a test, but an information screen intended to provide helpful setup information. Novice troubleshooters should review this information before attempting any of the ink-jet test sequence, and experienced troubleshooters might find it a handy reminder. To leave the information screen, press <Esc> or right-click anywhere in the display.

Carriage Transport Test

Like impact printers, ink-jet printers are moving-carriage devices; the print head is carried across the page surface. This movement is handled by the carriage transport mechanism. Proper printing of text and graphics demands that the print head be positioned precisely in both its left-to-right and right-to-left movement. The Carriage Transport Test is designed to test carriage alignment by generating a series of vertical lines (refer back to Figure 9-5). The print head sweeps from left to right, producing a series of vertical tic marks, then reverses direction and produces a right to left series of tic marks. Each line of tic marks is the result of two independent passes, and allows you to check carriage alignment not just between lines, but within the same line.

If the tic marks are not aligned precisely, there might be some mechanical slop in the carriage mechanics. Badly or erratically placed tic marks might indicate a fault in the carriage motor driver circuitry, the mechanical home sensor, or the optical position encoder. If marks within the same line are aligned precisely at the edges (but not elsewhere in the line), there might be wiring problems in the ink-jet print cartridge or print head cable. Start this test by left-clicking on Carriage Transport Test (or pressing C).

Paper Transport Test

Regardless of whether it's pushed or pulled, paper must be carried through a printer evenly and consistently, otherwise the print will overlap and cause distortion. The Paper Transport Test is designed to check the paper transport system's operation. While the Paper Transport Test works with any transport type, it is intended primarily for tractor feed systems that pull the paper through. The test pattern counts off a number of marked passes. You must check each pass to see that they are spaced apart evenly. If not, there might be a problem with the transport mechanics, motor, or driving circuitry. You can start this test by left-clicking on Paper Transport Test (or pressing P).

Paper Walk Test

Like the Paper Transport Test, the Paper Walk Test checks the paper transport system's operation. While the Paper Transport Test is designed tractor feed paper transports, the Paper Walk Test is intended primarily for friction feed systems that push the paper through. Today's ink-jet printers use friction feed systems almost entirely. The test pattern generates a series of evenly spaced horizontal lines. You must check each pass to see that they are spaced apart evenly. If not, there might be a problem with the transport mechanics, motor, or driving circuitry.

Another problem with friction feed paper transports is the tendency to "walk the page." Proper friction feed operation depends on roller pressure applied evenly to the entire page surface. Any damage, obstructions, or wear can cause excessive roller pressure, which allows the page to spin clockwise or counter-clockwise. This is especially evident in inexpensive ink-jet systems. If you notice lines closer together on the left or right side of the image, the roller assembly might need adjustment or replacement or there could be an obstruction in the paper path. Start this test by left-clicking on Paper Walk Test (or pressing W).

Print Head Test

Every nozzle on the ink cartridge should fire reliably, but cartridge age, lack of routine maintenance, low ink levels, and circuit defects can affect firing reliability. This often results in horizontal white lines in the text where the corresponding print nozzles fail. The best way to stress-test an ink-jet print head and detect problems is by printing a dense graphic. The ink jet print head test produces a large black rectangle (refer back to Figure 9-6); this demands the proper operation of all print nozzles, and will often reveal any age, damage, or maintenance-related issues. You can adjust the speed and density of printing by adjusting print intensity and driver resolution in the Configure menu. Remember that this is a very dark image and requires a substantial amount of ink to form. If the current ink cartridge is marginal, you might need to insert a new ink cartridge before proceeding.

Examine the black rectangle for horizontal white lines. Consistent white lines indicates that a print nozzle is not firing (or possibly that the ink level is low). Check and clean the face of the print cartridge to remove any accumulations of dried ink or debris that might be jamming the print nozzle(s). If the problem persists, there might be a fault in the print cartridge or print nozzle driver circuitry. If white lines appear only briefly or intermittently, there might be wiring problems with the print head cable or within the print cartridge itself. There might also be an intermittent problem in the corresponding print nozzle driver circuit. Finally, print intensity should be relatively consistent throughout each pass. Light (faded) printing could indicate poor paper selection, low ink levels, or trouble with the print nozzle power supply. Start this test by left-clicking on Print Head Test (or pressing H).

Clean Rollers

To combat the debris that accumulates in a printer's mechanics, you must periodically clean the main rollers that handle paper, usually the platen and other major rollers. This is especially important for delicate ink-jet friction feed paper transports where age and any foreign matter on the rollers can interfere with the paper path and "walk the page." Few contemporary ink-jet printers allow you to rotate the rollers by hand (using a platen knob), so the Clean Rollers function provides a paper advance, allowing you to streamline the routine cleaning/rejuvenation of roller assemblies. Note that paper must be present in the printer to use this function.

The cleaning procedure involves rotating the rollers while wiping them gently with a clean cloth lightly dampened with water. You can use a bit of very mild household detergent to remove accumulation that resists water alone, but don't use detergent regularly since chemicals applied to rubber and other synthetic roller materials can reduce their pliability. *Never* use harsh detergents or solvents. If you choose to clean the rollers with a roller cleaning solvent, use *extreme* caution. Work in a well-ventilated area (solvent fumes are dangerous), and always try the solvent on a small patch to the edge of the roller in advance since it's impossible to predict how cleaning solvents will affect every possible roller material. You can start this procedure by left-clicking on Clean Rollers (or pressing R). A single cycle will advance the paper transport by two pages.

Print Test Page

The test page (such as the one shown in Figure 9-7, earlier in the chapter) is typically the first and last test to be run on any printer. The test page will initially reveal problems with the print cartridge, paper transport, or carriage transport. You can then proceed with more detailed tests to further isolate and correct the problem(s).

When the repair is complete, the test page is proof of the printer's operation; you can either keep it for your records or give it to your customer. Start this test by left-clicking on Print Test Page (or pressing T).

Running the laser/LED tests

The Laser/LED (EP) tests allow you to check the operation of almost any electrophotographic (EP) printer, and any printer capable of HP LaserJet emulation. From the main menu bar, left-click on Laser/LED (or press L). The Laser/LED Test menu will appear, as shown in Figure 9-9 on the next page. You can return to the main menu at any time by pressing the <Esc> key or right-clicking anywhere in the display. There are seven functions available from the Laser/LED Test menu:

Preliminary Setup Information Supplies initial information to help you set up and operate the EP printer safely

Toner Test Allows you to check the effects of low/expired toner or poor toner distribution

Corona Test Allows you to quickly identify the location of fouling on the primary or transfer corona wires

Drum and Roller Test Allows you to identify the source of repetitive defects in the printer

Fuser Test Allows you to check for low or inconsistent fusing

Paper Transport Test Allows you to quickly and conveniently check the paper transport without wasting time or toner

Print Test Page Provides a uniform test pattern for initial or final printer inspection

Preliminary Setup Information

You can access the Preliminary Setup Information screen by left-clicking on Preliminary Setup Information (or pressing I). This is not a test *per se*, but an information screen that provides helpful setup information for EP testing. Novice troubleshooters will find it helpful to review this information before attempting any of the test sequences, and experienced troubleshooters might find it a handy reminder. To leave the information screen, press <Esc> or right-click anywhere in the display.

Toner Test

Toner is the raw material (media) used to form printed images, the "ink" of the EP printer. As a consequence, low, expired, poor

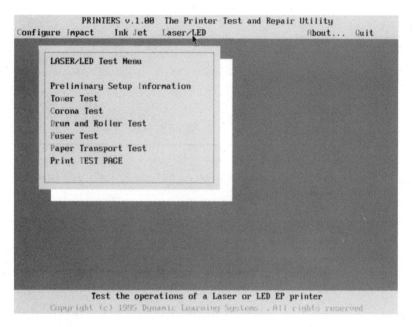

■ **9-9** *The Laser/LED Test menu.*

quality, and badly distributed toner will affect print quality. The Toner Test is designed to test the toner condition by printing a full-page black graphic, as shown in Figure 9-10 on the next page. Light streaks appearing vertically along the page (usually on either side of the image) are typical of low toner. You might be able to correct an overall light image by increasing the print intensity wheel (on the printer itself), but such a condition might also suggest a poor-quality toner cartridge or expired toner. If a fresh toner cartridge fails to correct the problem and print intensity is already set high, the fault could be in the printer's high-voltage power supply. Remember that EP printing technology is heavily dependent on paper type and quality. Light splotches might result from damp or coated paper. Try a supply of fresh, dry, 20-pound, xerography-grade paper. You can start this test by left-clicking on Toner Test (or pressing N).

Corona Test

EP technology relies on high voltages to produce the electrostatic fields that charge the EP drum and attract toner off the drum to the page. These fields are established by a primary corona and a transfer corona, respectively. A *corona* is really nothing more than a length of thin wire, but it has a crucial impact on the evenness of the electric field it produces. Later EP engines replaced corona wires with charge rollers, but the effect is the same as corona wires.

363

PRINTERS: The Printer Test and Alignment Utility V.1.00
TONER Cartridge Test

■ **9-10** *The toner test printout.*

The Corona Test pattern shown in Figure 9-11 on the next page is designed to highlight corona problems.

The dust and paper particles in the air tend to be attracted to high-voltage sources such as corona wires. Over time, an accumulation of foreign matter will weaken the field distribution and affect the resulting image. Fouling at one or more points on the primary corona will cause toner to always be attracted to those corresponding points on the drum, which results in black vertical streaks that can be seen against a white background. Conversely, fouling at one or more points on the transfer corona will prevent toner at those corresponding points from being attracted off the

PRINTERS: The Printer Test and Alignment Utility V.1.00
PRIMARY and TRANSFER CORONA Test Pattern

Transfer Corona:

Primary Corona:

■ **9-11** *The corona test printout.*

drum and onto the page, which results in white vertical streaks that can be seen against a black background. You can start this test by left-clicking on Corona Test (or pressing C).

Drum and Roller Test

In spite of the high level of refinement in today's EP printers, image formation is still a delicate physical process. Paper must traverse a torturous course through a series of roller assemblies in order to acquire a final, permanent image. With age, wear, and accidental damage, the various rotating elements of an EP printer can succumb to marks or other slight damage. While such damage is incidental, the results can be seen in the printed output.

Consider the EP drum itself. It has a circumference of about 3.75 inches. This means that any one point on the drum approaches every page surface at least twice. If a nick were to occur on the drum surface, it would appear in the final page at least twice, separated by about 3.75 inches. Since each of the major roller assemblies have a slightly different circumference, it is possible to quickly identify the source of a repetitive defect simply by measuring the distance between instances. The Drum and Roller Test pattern shown in Figure 9-12 on the next page is designed to help you correlate measured distances to problem areas. For example, a defect that occurs every 3.75 inches can be traced to the EP drum, an error that occurs every 3 inches or so can be traced to the fusing rollers, and a defect that occurs every 2 inches is often related to the development roller. Start this test by left-clicking on Drum and Roller Test (or pressing D).

Fuser Test

Fusing is a vital part of the image formation process; it uses heat and pressure to literally melt toner into the paper fibers. To ensure proper fusing, the upper fusing roller must reach a particular temperature, then stay within a fairly narrow range of temperatures. When temperature is marginally low, fusing might not complete. The Fuser Test checks the stability of a fusing system's temperature control by running a series of full-page test graphics. You can then run your thumb briskly over each page. Low or inadequate fusing will result in toner smudging (you can see toner on your thumb). You can then take the appropriate steps to optimize fusing temperature or troubleshoot the fusing system.

Note that this test is intended to detect marginal or inconsistent fusing performance. It will not catch a serious or complete fusing system failure because the printer will generate an error message and halt if the fusing assembly either fails to reach the proper fusing temperature in 90 seconds or so or falls below a minimum temperature for a prolonged amount of time. You can start this test by left-clicking on Fuser Test (or pressing F).

Transport Test

The paper transport system of an EP printer is a highly modified friction feed system designed to carry paper through the entire image formation system. There are also a series of time-sensitive sensors that track each page as it passes (and detect jam conditions). When you work on any aspect of the printer's mechanics, you affect the paper transport. The Paper Transport Test ejects five sheets of blank paper (saving toner and printing time). You

PRINTERS: The Printer Test and Alignment Utility V.1.00
DRUM and Roller Test

0.5" (13mm) Registration transfer roller defect

1.5" (38mm) Upper registration roller defect
1.75" (44mm) Lower registration roller defect
2.0" (51mm) EP developer roller defect

2.56" (65mm) Lower fusing roller defect

1.5" (38mm)

3.16" (80mm) Upper fusing roller defect

1.75" (44mm)

3.75" (95mm) EP drum defect

2.0" (51mm)

1.5" (38mm)

2.56" (65mm)

1.75" (44mm)

1.5" (38mm) 2.0" (51mm)

3.16" (80mm)

1.75" (44mm)

1.5" (38mm) 3.75" (95mm)

2.56" (65mm)

2.0" (51mm)

■ **9-12** *The drum/roller test printout.*

can use this test to either troubleshoot problems in the paper path or verify that any repairs you've made do not obstruct the paper path. Once a repair is complete, it's a good idea to verify the paper path before running test patterns. You can start this test by left- clicking on Paper Transport Test (or pressing P).

Print Test Page

The test page is typically the first and last test to be run on any Laser/LED printer. Initially, the Laser/LED test page (shown in Figure 9-13 on the next page) will reveal problems with the toner cartridge, paper transport, fusing system, coronas, or writing mechanism. You can then proceed with more detailed tests to further isolate and correct the problem(s). When the repair is complete, the test page is proof of the printer's operation, which you can either keep for your records or provide to your customer. Start this test by left-clicking on Print Test Page (or pressing T).

PRINTERS: The Printer Test and Alignment Utility V.1.00
LASER/LED (EP) Test Page Pattern

Testing Line Widths

1 pix
2 pix
3 pix
4 pix
5 pix
7 pix
9 pix

Testing Dither Patterns

Testing Light and Dark Patterns

Copyright (c) 1995 by Dynamic Learning Systems. All rights reserved worldwide.
Dynamic Learning Systems P.O. Box 805, Marlboro, MA 01752 USA
Tel: 508-366-9487 Fax: 508-898-9995 BBS: 508-366-7683 CIS: 73652,3205

■ **9-13** *The laser/LED test page.*

About PRINTERS

To learn about the PRINTERS program, click on About in the main menu bar (or press A). An information box will appear in the middle of the display. To clear the information box, press the <Esc> key or click the right mouse button anywhere in the display.

Quitting PRINTERS

To quit the PRINTERS program and return to DOS, click on Quit in the main menu bar (or press Q). After a moment, the DOS prompt will appear.

Making PRINTERS better

Dynamic Learning Systems is dedicated to providing high-quality, low-cost diagnostic utilities. As a result, the company is always interested in ways to improve the quality and performance of their products. Please send any comments, questions, or criticisms to:

Dynamic Learning Systems
P.O. Box 282
Jefferson, MA 01522-0282
Phone: 508-829-6744
Fax: 508-829-6819
BBS: 508-829-6706
CompuServe: 73652,3205
Internet: sbigelow@cerfnet.com
WWW: http://www.dlspubs.com/home.htm

369

Shareware author contacts (alphabetical by product) A

486TST.ZIP (burn-in/stress test)

No contact information listed

486TEST.ZIP (memory/cache test)

No contact information listed

ASQ0315.ZIP (general system test)

Qualitas, Inc.
7101 Wisconsin Ave.
Bethesda, MD 20814
Phone: 301-907-6700

ATMEM10.ZIP (video ID/BIOS tool)

Charles Vachon
170 DeBray
BerniSres, Quebec G7A 1T3
Canada
Internet: CVACHON@VM1.ULAVAL.CA

AUTOTEST.ZIP (floppy drive tool)

No contact information listed

BACKEE28.ZIP (backup utility and organizer)

Bernd Cordes
Wiesingerweg 34
20253 Hamburg
Germany
Phone/fax: 49 (40) 494370
CompuServe: 100334,375

BBX201.ZIP (port/data analyzer)

FoleyHi-Tech Systems
185 Berry St.
San Francisco, CA 94107
Phone: 415-826-6084
Fax: 415-826-1706
BBS: 415-826-1707 (8N1)

BIOS.ZIP (BIOS ID/reporting utility)

No contact information listed

BIOSR11.ZIP (BIOS ID/reporting utility)

Paul Postuma
16 Fullyer Dr.
Quispamsis, New Brunswick E2G 1Y7
Canada
Phone: 506-849-6967
Compuserve: 74471,1240
Internet: ppostuma@nbnet.nb.ca

BOOTRX.ZIP (hard drive tool)

Jack A. Orman
Box 858
Southaven, MS 38671
CompuServe: 72261,677

BOOTSY.ZIP (boot manager)

Hans Salvisberg
Bellevuestr. 18
CH-3095 Berne
Switzerland
CompuServe: 73237,3556

CACHECHK.ZIP (memory/cache test)

Ray Van Tassle
1020 Fox Run Ln.
Alqonuin, IL 60102
Phone: 708-658-4941

CALJOY22.ZIP (input device)

No contact information available

CARDG2.ZIP (reference work)

Kevin Noble
1210 McNeill Crescent
Regina, Saskatchewan S4N 5Z4
Canada
CompuServe: 72420,253
Internet: NOBLE@SIAST.SK.CA
WWW: http://www.siast.sk.ca/~noble/noblpage.htm

CCS103.ZIP (boot manager)

Kok Hong Soh
Bendix/King Radio Corp.
400 N. Rogers Road, MD 43
Olathe, KS 66062

CDCP10.ZIP (CD-ROM drive tool)

Ray Polczynski
133 Hickory Rd.
Lake in the Hills, IL 60102

CDQCK120.ZIP (CD-ROM drive tool)

Peter Volpa
Circuit Systems
418 Church Rd.
Sicklerville, NJ 08081-1727

CDSPEED.ZIP (CD-ROM drive tool)

No contact information listed

CDTA.ZIP (CD-ROM drive tool)

Eric Balkan
14704 Seneca Castle Ct.
Gaithersburg, MD 20878
BBS: 301-294-0756

CF537D.ZIP (backup utility and organizer)

Charles F. Martin
NoVaSoft
3239 Riverview Dr.
Triangle, VA 22172-1421
Phone: 703-221-1471
CompuServe: 72130,1400

CHECK136.ZIP (general system test)

Public domain; no contact information listed

CHKDRV.ZIP (floppy drive tool)

Douglas S. Parman
Software Specialists
300D Versailles Dr.
Melbourne Beach, FL 32951
Phone: 407-984-0219

CHKIO.ZIP (I/O, IRQ, and DMA test)

No contact information listed

CLEAN4.ZIP (floppy drive tool)

Randy Stack
6222 Brookhill Circle
Orlando, FL 32810

CMOS.ZIP (CMOS utility)

Scott Alan Hoopes
62 Plaza Drive
New Albany, IN 47150
Phone: 812-948-8521
CompuServe: 73304,274

CMOSRAM2.ZIP (CMOS utility)

Thomas Mosteller
1872 Rampart Ln.
Lansdale, PA 19446-5051
CompuServe: 72637,173

CNVRGE.ZIP (alignment tool and diagnostic)

Brent Turner
P.O. Box 3612
Fullerton, CA 92634-3612

CONF810E.ZIP (general system test)

Michael Holin
P.O. Box 1147
65432 Florsheim
Germany
Phone: 49 6145 941888
Fax: 49 6145 941889
CompuServe: 100441.1366
WWW: http://ourworld.compuserve.com/homepages/holin

COMPRT25.ZIP (port/data analyzer)

Open Systems Resources (OSR), Inc.
105 Route 101A, #19
Amherst, NH 03031-2244

COMRESET.ZIP (port/data analyzer)

FBN Productions
917 W. Columbia Ave.
Champaign, IL 61821
BBS: 217-359-2874

COMTAP21.ZIP (port/data analyzer)

Paladin Software, Inc.
3945 Kenosha Ave.
San Diego, CA 92117
Phone: 619-490-0368
Fax: 619-490-0177

COMTEST.ZIP (port/data analyzer)

No contact information listed

CRTAT2.ZIP (alignment tool and diagnostic)

Stephen Jenkins
1310 S. Taylor St. #22
Arlington, VA 22204-3718
CompuServe: 76666,1066
Internet: stephenj@ix.netcom.com

CSCTEST2.ZIP (hard drive tool)

Corporate Systems Center (CSC)
730 N. Pastoria Ave.
Sunnyvale, CA 94086
Phone: 408-737-7312
Fax: 408-737-1017

CTSSPU22.EXE (port/data analyzer)

John Jerrim
Computer Telecommunication Systems (CTS), Inc.
3847 Foxwood Road, Suite 1000
Duluth, GA 30136-6100
Phone: 404-263-8623
Fax: 404-263-0124
CompuServe: 76662,2315

DA7.ZIP (CD-ROM drive tool)

T. Roscoe
AVIXIVA Reflective Systems
11367 Wright Rd., #3
Lynwood, CA 90262

DAAG310.ZIP (general drive tool)

Steve Leonard
212 Green Springs Ln.
Madison, AL 35758
CompuServe: 73557,203

DATA_REC.ZIP (general drive tool)

Uwe Gissemann
Plug 'n Play
Crellestr. 6
D-10827 Berlin
Germany
Phone: 49-30-782 95 06
Fax: 49-30-788 52 31
CompuServe: 101457.1447
WWW:http://ourworld.compuserve.com/homepages/data_recovery

DCF49.ZIP (backup utility and organizer)

> DCF Software
> P.O. Box 60064
> Palo Alto, CA 94306

DDARP_13.ZIP (general drive tool)

> Robert Stuntz
> 2120 Aspen Dr.
> Woodstock, IL 60098
> CompuServe: 71043,117

DFR.ZIP (floppy drive tool)

> No contact information listed

DISKUTIL.ZIP (general drive tool)

> Rich Belgard
> AOL: RICHB89600

DKI191.ZIP (general drive tool)

> Philippe Duby
> 7 rue Jules VallSs
> 69100 Villeurbanne
> France
> CompuServe: 73551,1561
> Internet: duby@lanpc1.univ-lyon1.fr

DUGIDE.ZIP (hard drive tool)

> Doug Merrett
> P.O. Box 432
> Stones Corner, Q 4120
> Australia
> Internet: dcm@mincom.oz.au

DUP59.EXE (backup utility and organizer)

> Randy MacLean
> FormGen Corporation
> 13 Holland Dr.
> Bolton, Ontario L7E 1G4
> Canada
> Phone: 416-857-0022

EZSET.ZIP (parallel port utility)

McAdams Associates
P.O. Box 835505
Richardson, TX 75083-5505

FIPS10.ZIP (hard drive tool)

Arno Schaefer
Internet: schaefer@rbg.informatik.th-darmstadt.de

FIXCLOCK.ZIP (general system test)

Irving Maron
CompuServe: 76614.2666

GUARD.ZIP (system security)

Marcor Enterprises
8857 Commerce Park Pl., Suite D
Indianapolis, IN 46268

HDCP.ZIP (hard drive tool)

Chang Ping Lee
DCF Software
P.O. Box 60064
Palo Alto, CA 94306

HDINFO.ZIP (hard drive tool)

Shane Gilbert
AOL: ShaneG7108

HISCAN.ZIP (screen/palette tool)

Joerg H. Arnu
CompuServe: 100326,564
WWW: http://ourworld.compuserve.com/homepages/joerg

HW16V210.ZIP (editor)

BreakPoint Software
P.O. Box 4629
Stamford, CT 06907-0629

IDATA.ZIP (hard drive tool)

Brian Ryan
CompuServe: 103043,357

IRQINFO.ZIP (I/O, IRQ, and DMA test)

John Jerrim
Computer Telecommunication Systems (CTS), Inc.
3847 Foxwood Road, Suite 1000
Duluth, GA 30136-6100
Phone: 770-263-8623
Fax: 770-263-0124
CompuServe: 76662,2315
Internet: jjerrim@comminfo.com
WWW: http://www.comminfo.com/

IS_VID.EXE (video ID/BIOS tool)

Barry St. John
CompuServe: 76247,264

JCBENCH.EXE (benchmarking utility)

Jesse Bize
15 Yerba Buena Ave.
San Francisco, CA 94127

JOY2.EXE (input device)

Dave Murray
74 Friend St.
Adams, MA 01220
Phone: 413-743-5591

LASERTST.ZIP (printer maintenance utility)

Michael Bruss
569 Villanova Dr.
Davis, CA 95616

LASMAN.ZIP (printing utility)

MicroMetric
98 Dade Avenue
Sarasota, FL 34232-1609
Phone: 813-377-2515
Fax: 813-377-2091
BBS: 813-371-2490

LISTEN10.ZIP (modem utility)

No Preservatives Software
5135 E. Evergreen St. #1272
Mesa, AZ 85205
Phone: 602-924-4878

LOCATO.ZIP (reference work)

Tech Assist, Inc.
11350 66th St., Suite 105
Largo, FL 34643
Phone: 813-547-0499

LZC26.ZIP (printer maintenance utility)

Spacebook Consulting
17 Skylark Drive #32
Larkspur, CA 94939

MAXSPEED.EXE (CPU utility)

Maxim Computers
Phone: 212-505-0909

MEMSCAN.ZIP (memory/cache test)

James B. Penny
Coastal Computer Consulting
415 East Beach Dr., Suite 506
Galveston, TX 77550

OVERHEAD.ZIP (general system test)

Ed Ross
CompuServe: 75776,151

PALU15.ZIP (screen/palette tool)

Harold Holmes
Lincoln Beach Software
P.O. Box 1554
Ballwin, MO 63022-1554
Phone: 314-861-1500
CompuServe: 70700,630

PARAMO.ZIP (parallel port utility)

Jean-Georges Marcotte
145 Grenier
Ste-Anne de Bellevue, Quebec H9X 3L2
Canada
CompuServe: 70065,1220
Internet: JGM.Dorval@XCI.Xerox.Com

PARTITV1.ZIP (hard drive tool)

Bill Holt
430 Morningside Rd.
Ridgewood, NJ 07450
AOL: KayakRBill

PCM140.EXE (BIOS ID/reporting utility)

MicroSystems Development, Inc.
4100 Moorpark Ave., Suite 104
San Jose, CA 95117
Phone: 408-296-4000
Fax: 408-296-5877

PORT11.ZIP (I/O, IRQ, and DMA test)

John De Armond
Rapid Deployment Systems, Inc.
P.O. Box 670386
Marietta, GA 30066
Phone: 404-578 9547
Internet: jgd@dixie.com

PRINTGF.ZIP (printing utility)

Ravitz Software Inc.
P.O. Box 25068
Lexington, KY 40524-5068
BBS: 606-268-0577
CompuServe: 70431,32

PRINTGL.ZIP (printing utility)

Ravitz Software Inc.
P.O. Box 25068
Lexington, KY 40524-5068
BBS: 606-268-0577
CompuServe: 70431,32

PRN-TEST.ZIP (printer maintenance utility)

Harry P. Calevas
P.O. Box 830
Trenton, GA 30752
Phone: 404-657-5484

PSPS30.ZIP (screen/palette tool)

A.N.D. Technologies
P.O. Box 64811
Los Angeles, CA 90064
Phone: 213-467-8688
CompuServe: 71011,3570
Internet: andtech@netcom.com

PSV10.ZIP (video ID/BIOS tool)

Patrick Swayne
28 Cauthen Ct.
Ellenwood, GA 30049-2919

RAMMAP.ZIP (memory/cache test)

Computer Tyme
411 North Sherman, Suite 300
Springfield, MO 65802
Phone: 417-866-1222
Fax: 417-866-1665

RAVED.ZIP (editor)

Ravitz Software Inc.
P.O. Box 25068
Lexington, KY 40524-5068
BBS: 606-268-0577
CompuServe: 70431,32

READBI.EXE (BIOS ID/reporting utility)

Markus Klama
Carl-Maria-von-Weber Weg 8
82538 Geretsried
Germany
CompuServe: 100115,2167

RESOUR11.ZIP (general system test)

Chet Williams
1737 Peyton Ave. K
Burbank, CA 91504
Phone: 818-954-9128

RITM25.ZIP (general system test)

Air System Technologies, Inc.
14232 Marsh Ln., Suite 339
Dallas, TX 75234-3899

RWARD2.ZIP (system security)

Les Gainous
Phone: 212-734-1599
CompuServe: 72731,146
AOL: LesGainous

SBBEEP.ZIP (sound utility)

Travis Gebhardt
42502 SE Oral Hull Rd.
Sandy, OR 97055
AOL: Trav

SCODE22.ZIP (input device)

Paul Postuma
16 Fullyer Dr.
Quispamsis, New Brunswick E2G 1Y7
Canada
Phone: 506-849-6967
Compuserve: 74471,1240
Internet: ppostuma@nbnet.nb.ca

SHADTEST.ZIP (memory/cache test)

No contact information listed

SHOWS174.ZIP (BIOS ID/reporting utility)

Micro Firmware Inc.
1430 W. Lindsey St.
Norman, OK 73069-4314
Phone: 405-321-8333
Fax: 405-321-8342
BBS: 405-321-2616

SIMTRM.ZIP (port/data analyzer)

Rick Hardy
B&B Electronics Mfg. Co.
P.O. Box 1040
Ottawa, IL 61350
Phone: 815-434-0846

SLO23.ZIP (speed utility)

Derek Altamirano
Granite Mountain Software
839A Hwy. 20 E.
Colville, WA 99114

SNDST.ZIP (sound utility)

Zittware Support
7599 Chevy Chase Dr. #106
Austin, TX 78752
WWW: http://www2.msstate.edu/~jdz1

SNOOP330.ZIP (general system test)

Vias and Associates
P.O. Box 470805
San Francisco, CA 94147-0805
Phone: 415-921-6262
Fax: 415-922-3197
CompuServe: 72260,1601

SPC.ZIP (general system test)

Bob Eyer
1100 Bloor Street West, Suite 16

Toronto, M6H 1M8
Canada
CompuServe: 73230,2620

SPYDOS.ZIP (I/O, IRQ, and DMA test)

Wolfgang Heck
CompuServe: 71730,2657

SREP.ZIP (general drive tool)

Scott Alan Hoopes
62 Plaza Dr.
New Albany, IN 47150
Phone: 812-948-8521
CompuServe: 73304,274

SRXTEST.EXE (CPU utility)

No contact information listed

STKVGA31.ZIP (input device)

Rick Horwitz
110 Houlton Ct.
San Jose, CA 85139

SUPDIR10.ZIP (backup utility and organizer)

Cottonwood Software
P.O. Box 6546
Leawood, KS 66206-0546

SWAPIRQ.ZIP (I/O, IRQ, and DMA test)

John Jerrim
Computer Telecommunication Systems, Inc.
3847 Foxwood Road, Suite 1000
Duluth, GA 30136-6100
Phone: 770-263-8623
Fax: 770-263-0124
CompuServe: 76662,2315
Internet: jjerrim@comminfo.com
WWW: http://www.comminfo.com/

SYSCHK40.ZIP (general system test)

Paul Griffith
Advanced Personal Systems
105 Serra Way, Suite 418
Milpitas, CA 95035

SYSINF.ZIP (general system test)

Tobin Fricke
25271 Arion Way
Mission Viejo, CA 92691-3702
CompuServe: 76660,3110

THEREF43.ZIP (reference work)

Robert Falbo
WWW: http://theref.C3D.rl.af.mil

TMTX.EXE (input device)

TechStaff Corp.
64 Carroll St.
Watertown, MA 02172
Phone: 617-924-0306

UARTTS.ZIP (port/data analyzer)

No contact information listed

VGAHUE.ZIP (screen/palette tool)

GMH Code
P.O. Box 2117
Lowell, MA 01851

VIDEO.EXE (alignment tool and diagnostic)

Abri Technologies, Inc.
HC 62 Box 100K
Great Cacapon, WV 25422

VIDEOT.ZIP (alignment tool and diagnostic)

No contact information listed

VIDSPD40.ZIP (alignment tool and diagnostic)

No contact information listed

XEV43.ZIP (editor)

Robert Stuntz
2120 Aspen Dr.
Woodstock, IL 60098
CompuServe: 71043,117

ZC33.ZIP (printing utility)

Morton Utilities
81-887 Tournament Way
Indio, CA 92201

Using the Dynamic Learning Systems BBS

Technicians today face an information problem. With the proliferation of PCs and peripherals, keeping pace with changes can be a real challenge. Sometimes it seems that just when you've got one concept or standard figured out, it's abandoned in favor of something new. Dynamic Learning Systems is dedicated to helping you stay in touch with the latest PC technical information via access to its BBS. The BBS is set up to provide the very best in shareware, freeware, and public-domain diagnostic and business utility software. You can also exchange e-mail with other professionals and PC enthusiasts.

Connecting to the BBS

The DLS BBS operates a single node 24 hours a day, 7 days a week, and is available at 508-829-6706 (toll charges apply). The resident modem can handle from 300 bps to 28.8 Kbps and uses a data configuration of 8 data bits, no parity bit, and 1 stop bit (set your communication software for 8/N/1). Be sure to adjust the configuration of your modem to accommodate this data frame. New users are allowed on the system up to 30 minutes per day. Professional subscribers (see our newsletter offer at the back of this book) are allotted 60 minutes per day and have access to an extensive file area. First-time users are asked to fill out a brief online questionnaire to identify their names, choose passwords, and provide address/phone number information. When filling out the questionnaire, be sure to provide complete answers; incomplete questionnaires are automatically erased.

Getting started

The BBS is menu- and keyboard-driven. You will find that selecting options and navigating from menu to menu is fast and convenient. Menu entries that are "blued out" are not available to your current level of access. Once you've logged onto the BBS for the first time and completed the new user questionnaire, please take a moment to review the Newsletter file and the various bulletins on the system. These files are updated regularly, and will keep you informed of changes and additions to the BBS resources.

Notes on downloading

The DLS BBS is primarily an electronic information service. Shareware and public-domain utilities and applications are downloaded by users for their private use. The BBS is approved by the Association of Shareware Professionals (ASP) and we are fortunate to receive regular mailings of the latest and best available shareware. Most common file-transfer protocols are supported, but Zmodem provides best performance. When signing on for the first time, you can select a default transfer protocol, or you can elect to choose the protocol during each download session—which is the preferred setting if you're new to downloading or want to try different settings to find the optimum transfer technique.

Notes on uploading

New files and documents are also welcome, and the BBS often receives new files as online uploads. However, since each file must be sorted and checked for viruses, you can upload files only to several limited areas. When uploading from the File menu, you will be asked to enter the DOS-compatible filename, along with a brief text description of the file. We encourage you to password-protect your file(s). When uploading, you are also encouraged to compress the various file(s) comprising your upload using the PKZIP compression utility from PKWARE.

Security and operation policy

You will see a disclaimer in the initial log on screen. Please read and understand the disclaimer completely before logging onto the BBS. If you do not understand the disclaimer or do not agree to its terms, disconnect from TechNet *immediately* without logging on. We are proud of our BBS's high-quality reputation. As a professional BBS devoted to technical enthusiasts, technicians, and designers, no profane, pornographic, insulting, degrading, or otherwise unprofessional material is allowed on the BBS at any time under any circumstances. Dynamic Learning Systems reserves the right to decide whether or not an upload falls into one or more of these categories. Continued attempts to upload undesirable material is considered to be an abuse of the system. Repeated abusers will be permanently restricted from system access. As a BBS user, remember to change your password frequently.

When problems occur

Due to drastic variations in telecommunication quality around the world, as well as differences in modem setups and configurations, Dynamic Learning Systems cannot guarantee the integrity of serial communication for any length of time. Serial communication is intrinsically prone to problems, such as initial connect failures and dropped carrier, and any other random occurrence that accidentally disconnects you from the system.

If you consistently encounter problems connecting to or dropping off the BBS, check your modem's initialization and setup strings in your communications software. Altering an operating parameter can often radically improve the modem's integrity. If new settings do not work, try slowing down the communications speed. Although the BBS will work with error-correcting modems up to 28.8 Kbps, you might want to try connecting at 2400, 4800, or 9600 bps, which is much less demanding of a typical telephone voice channel.

Index

A

A.N.D. Technologies, 120
Abrash, Michael, 92
Abri Technologies, Inc., 129
Access Time Test Utility (*see* AUTOTEST.ZIP)
Air System Technologies, Inc., 62
Altamirano, Derek, 307
Amu, Joerg H., 115
Apogee Games, 6
ASCII files, RAVED.ZIP ASCII file editor, 279–282
ASQ Qualitas (*see* ASQ0315.ZIP)
ASQ0315.ZIP memory management utility, 44–48, **46**, **47**
Association of Shareware Professionals (ASP), 8, **8**
ATMEM10.ZIP identify video board in system, 104–106
AUTOEXEC.BAT (*see* boot managers; system configuration)
AUTOTEST.ZIP access-time test, 208–210

B

B&B Electronics Mfg. Co., 183
BACKEE28.ZIP backup, restore, sync files, 252–256, **253**
Backer, The (*see* BACKEE28.ZIP)
backup (*see also* file management; recovery/restore), 250–270

backup, *continued*
BACKEE28.ZIP backup, restore, sync files, 252–256, **253**
CF537D.ZIP file/directory manager, 256–259, **258**
CMOSRAM2.ZIP CMOS backup and restore, 38–41, **40**
CMOS.ZIP CMOS backup and restore, 36–38
DATA_REC.ZIP data recovery, 194–197, **196**
DCF49.ZIP copy multiple diskettes, 259–264, **261**
DUP59.EXE mass duplication of diskettes, 264–267, **265**
HDCP.ZIP copy hard disk contents by sector, 226–229, **228**
SUPDIR10.ZIP drive directory manager, 267–270
Balkan, Eric, 245
BBX201.ZIP serial port debugger/breakout box, 164–166
benchmarking, 15, 17–19
CONF810E.ZIP system info/benchmarking, 51–54
CSCTEST2.ZIP hard drive performance test, 217–219
486TEST.ZIP write-time benchmark, 91–93

Bendix/King Radio Corp., 274
BioGeoMagnetics, 288
BIOS, 19–32
486TST.ZIP system burn-in, 33–35, **34**
ATMEM10.ZIP video board identification, ATMEM10.ZIP 104–106
BIOS.ZIP BIOS age/date extraction, 19–21
BIOSR11.ZIP data area reader, 21–24, **22**, **23**
CHECK136.ZIP command-line system descriptor, 48–51
READBI.EXE drive type-recorder/burn-in, 26–30
video ID/BIOS tools, 104–113
BIOS.ZIP BIOS age/date extraction, 19–21
BIOSR11.ZIP data area reader, 21–24, **22**, **23**
Bize, Jesse, 17
Boot Manager (*see* BOOTSY.ZIP)
boot managers
BOOTRX.ZIP boot record parameters displayed, 216–217
BOOTSY.ZIP multiple configuration at boot, 271–273
CCS103.ZIP multiple configuration at boot, 273–275

Illustrations are indicated in **boldface**.

393

boot managers, *continued*
  DDARP_13.ZIP ID/rename device drivers, 197–200
Boot Record Reporter (*see* BOOTRX.ZIP)
BOOTRX.ZIP boot record parameters displayed, 216–217
BOOTSY.ZIP multiple configuration at boot, 271–273
Boshears, John, 20
Breakout Box (*see* BBX201.ZIP)
BreakPoint Software, 276
Bridges, John, 134
Bruss, Michael, 158
BUFFER.EXE FIFO buffer control, serial port tests, 179
bulletin board systems (BBS), DLS support/help, 14
burn-in/stress tests, 32–35
  READBI.EXE drive type-recorder/burn-in, 26–30

C
cache, 91–102
  486TST.ZIP system burn-in, 33–35, **34**
  CACHCK.ZIP performance test, 93–96
  CDQCK120.ZIP CD-ROM cache performance enhancer, 238–242
  SREP.ZIP SmartDrive cache perform monitor, 207–208
Cache Check (*see* CACHECHK.ZIP)
CACHECHK.ZIP cache performance test, 93–96
Calevas, Harry P., 161
CALJOY2.ZIP joystick calibrator, 285–287, **287**
Card Guide (*see* CARDG2.ZIP)
CARDG2.ZIP I/O card configuration list, 295–297, **296**, **297**

CCS103.ZIP multiple configuration at boot, 273–275
CD Control Panel (*see* CDC10.ZIP)
CD Quick Cache (*see* CDQCK120.ZIP)
CD Speed Test (*see* CDSPEED.ZIP)
CD-ROM, 236–249
  CDCP10.ZIP play audio CDs, 236–238
  CDQCK120.ZIP CD-ROM cache performance enhancer, 238–242
  CDSPEED.ZIP measure data transfer rate, 242–245
  CDTA.ZIP measure data throughput, 245–246
  DA7.ZIP play audio CDs, 247–249, **249**
  DISKUTIL.ZIP info on all drives, 200–203
  DKI101.ZIP info on all drives, 203–206
CD-ROM Timing Analyzer (*see* CDTA.ZIP)
CDCP10.ZIP play audio CDs, 236–238
CDQCK120.ZIP CD-ROM cache performance enhancer, 238–242
CDSPEED.ZIP measure data transfer rate of CD-ROM, 242–245
CDTA.ZIP measure data throughput of CD-ROM, 245–246
central processing unit (CPU), 41–44
  486TST.ZIP system burn-in, 33–35, **34**
  CHECK136.ZIP command-line system descriptor, 48–50
  JCBENCH.EXE, 17–19, **18**
  MAXSPEED.EXE clock speed test, 41–43, **42**

central processing unit (CPU), *continued*
  SHOWS174.ZIP identifier for system chipset, 30
  SPYDOS.ZIP interrupt line analyzer, 86–88
  SRXTEXT.EXE Cyrix upgrade CPU test, 43–44
CF537D.ZIP file/directory manager, 256–259, **258**
Changeline Check Utility (*see* CHKDRV.ZIP)
Check I/O Ports (*see* CHKIO.ZIP)
CHECK136.ZIP command-line system descriptor, 48–51
chipset identifier, SHOWS174.ZIP 30–32
CHKDRV.ZIP change-line signal check, 210–212
Circuit Systems, 239
CLEAN4.ZIP clean read/write heads, 212–214
clock
  BIOS.ZIP age/date extraction, 19–21
  FIXCLOCK.ZIP clock set, 54–56
  IDLE.EXE idle timer setting, 201–202
  MAXSPEED.EXE clock speed test, 41–43, **42**
  RITM25.ZIP clock set, ZIP 61–65
  STANDBY.EXE power-down hard drive, 202–203
CMFiler (*see* CF537D.ZIP)
CMOS utilities, 35–41
  CMOS.ZIP backup and restore, 36–38
  CMOSRAM2.ZIP backup and restore, 38–41, **40**
  HDINFO.ZIP hard drive geometry info, 229–231
  IDATA.ZIP ATA drive geometry info, 231–232

CMOS utilities, *continued*
RITM25.ZIP clock set, 61–65
CMOS.ZIP backup and restore, 36–38
CMOSRAM2.ZIP backup and restore, 38–41, **40**
CNVRGE.ZIP monitor color convergence test, 124–126
Color Master utility, VGA/SVGA support suite, 109
Color Protector (CP) utility, VGA/SVGA support suite, 110
COLOR utility, VGA/SVGA support suite, 113
COM Port Reset (*see* COMRESET.ZIP)
Command Line Diagnostic (*see* CHECK136.ZIP)
communications/modems (*see also* port management), 163–188
    BBX201.ZIP serial port debug/breakout box, 164–166
    BUFFER.EXE FIFO buffer control, serial port, 179
    COMPRT25.ZIP COM and LPT port info, 166–169
    COMRESET.ZIP reset stuck COM ports, 169–171
    COMTAP21.ZIP serial protocol analyzer, 171–173, **173**
    COMTEST.ZIP test serial port/devices, 173–176, **175**
    COM_BPS.EXE port data-rate setting, serial port, 179
    COM_FMT.EXE port character-format set, serial port, 180
    CTSSPU22.EXE serial port tests, 176–182

communications/modems, *continued*
    DOS_COM.EXE DOS BIOS serial port insertion, 180
    DOS_SWAP.EXE serial port swap, 180
    DTR.EXE data term ready (DTR) command line control, 180
    IRQ.EXE serial port interrupt disable, 181
    LISTEN10.ZIP test for incoming signals, 186–188
    modem utilities, 186–188
    PORTINFO.EXE serial port info, 177
    RESETCOM.EXE serial port reset, 181
    RTS.EXE request to send (RTS) command control, 181
    SIMTRM.ZIP serial port troubleshooter, 182–185, **184**
    UARTTS.ZIP COM port hardware info, 185–186
COMPort (*see* COMPRT25.ZIP)
compressed files, decompression, 9–10
COMPRT25.ZIP COM and LPT port info, 166–169
Computer Telecommunication Systems, Inc., 82, 89, 176
Computer Tyme, 98
COMRESET.ZIP reset stuck COM ports, 169–171
ComTAP (*see* COMTAP21.ZIP)
ComTest (*see* COMTEST.ZIP)
COMTEST.ZIP test serial port/devices, 173–176, **175**
COM_BPS.EXE port data-rate setting, 179–180
COM_FMT.EXE port character-format set, 180

CONF810E.ZIP system info/benchmarking, 51–54, **53**
CONFIG.SYS (*see* boot managers; system configuration)
configuration (*see* system configuration)
Configuration Control System (*see* CCS103.ZIP)
Convergence Test (*see* CNVRGE.ZIP)
copy files (*see* backup procedures; file management)
Cordes, Bernd, 252
Corporate Systems Center, 218
Cottonwood Software, 268
CPU (*see* central processing unit)
Crosshatch Utility (HATCH) utility, 112
CRT Alignment Tool (*see* CRTAT2.ZIP)
CRTAT2.ZIP align/test color CRTs, 126–128, **128**
CSCTEST2.ZIP hard drive performance test, 217–219, **218**
CTSSPU22.EXE serial port tests, 176–182
Cyrix upgrade CPU test, SRXTEXT, 43–44

D
DA7.ZIP play audio CDs, 247–249, **249**
DAAG310.ZIP tree of disk contents, 191–194, **192**, **194**
DATA_REC.ZIP data recovery, 194–197, **196**
Daybreak Communication, 298
DCF Software, 260
DCF49.ZIP copy multiple diskettes, 259–264, **261**
DDARP_13.ZIP ID/rename device drivers, 197–200

395

De Armond, John, 84
diagnostics, 2–4
    benchmarking, 15, 17–19
    BIOS ID/reporting, 19–32
    burn-in/stress tests, 32–35
    choosing correct diagnos-
        tics, 3
    commercial product vs.
        shareware, 4–5
    CD-ROM tools, 236–249
    CMOS, 35–41
    CPU, 41–44
    DLS Diagnostic CD, 8–14
    DOS vs. Windows versions,
        4
    drive tools (see CD-ROM
        tools; floppy drive;
        hard disk)
    general system tests, 44–78
    general-purpose/core
        processing
        diagnostics, 16
    port management tools,
        137–162
    printer tools, 137–162
    reference works, 295–301
    updates, versional
        differences, 3
    video tools, 103–136
Digital Audio CD Player (see
    DA7.ZIP)
direct memory access (DMA)
    channel tests, 78–91
directories (see file
    management)
Disk at a Glance (see
    DAAG310.ZIP)
Disk Copy Fast (see
    DCF49.ZIP)
Disk Duplicator (see
    DUP59.EXE)
Disk Information Utility (see
    DISKUTIL.ZIP;
    DKI101.ZIP)
Disk Recovery Utility (see
    DRF.ZIP)
DISKTYPE.EXE drive
    geometry listing, 201
DISKUTIL.ZIP info on all
    drives, 200–203
DKI101.ZIP info on all drives,
    203–206

DLS Diagnostic CD, 8–14,
    103
    bulletin board support/
        help, 14
    caring for the CD, 13–14
    compressed files, decom-
        pression, 9–10
    installation, 10–13
    MONITORS diagnostic
        program, 13
    PRINTERS diagnostic
        program, 13
    registration, 13
    subdirectories and files of
        CD, 9
DOS
    diagnostics and utilities, 4
    DOS_COM.EXE DOS BIOS
        serial port insertion,
        180
    DOS_SWAP.EXE serial port
        swap, 180
    PALU15.ZIP palette ad-
        juster, 117–119, **118**
    DOS_COM.EXE DOS BIOS
        serial port insertion,
        180
    DOS_SWAP.EXE serial port
        swap, 180
DRF.ZIP recover erased
    diskette data, 214–215
drive tools (see CD-ROM
    tools; floppy drive;
    hard disk)
Driver Display and Rename
    (see DDARP_13.ZIP)
drivers (see also boot
    managers; system
    configuration)
    DDARP_13.ZIP ID/rename
        device drivers,
        197–200
DTR.EXE data term ready
    (DTR) command line
    control, 180
Duby, Philippe, 200, 203
DUGIDE.ZIP IDE drive
    information, 219–220
DUP59.EXE mass
    duplication of
    diskettes, 264–267,
    265

Dynamic Learning Systems,
    13, 328, 369

E

EC Systems, 286
editors, 276–285
    HW16V210.ZIP hex file
        editor, 276–279,
        277
    RAVED.ZIP ASCII file
        editor, 279–282
    XEV43.ZIP disk file editor,
        282–285, **283**
Electronic Component Loca-
    tor (see LOCATO.ZIP)
encryption, GUARD.ZIP
    encrypt files,
    308–313
energy savings
    IDLE.EXE idle timer
        setting, 201–202
    STANDBY.EXE power-
        down hard drive,
        202–203
Eyer, Bob, 69–70
EZSET.ZIP printer control,
    141–143, **142**

F

486 System Burnin (see
    486TST.ZIP)
486TEST.ZIP memory write-
    time benchmark,
    91–93
486TST.ZIP system burn-in,
    33–35, **34**
Fade-to-Clear (CLF),
    VGA/SVGA support
    suite, 113
FBN Productions, 170
file management (see also
    backup procedures;
    recovery/restore)
    CF537D.ZIP file/directory
        manager, 256–259,
        258
    DAAG310.ZIP tree of disk
        contents, 191–194,
        192, **194**
    DATA_REC.ZIP data
        recovery, 194–197,
        196

file management, *continued*
DCF49.ZIP copy multiple
diskettes, 259–264,
261
DRF.ZIP recover erased
diskette data,
214–215
DUP59.EXE mass
duplication of
diskettes, 264–267,
265
editors, 276–285
GUARD.ZIP encrypt files,
308–313
HDCP.ZIP copy hard disk
contents by sector,
226–229, **228**
HW16V210.ZIP hex file
editor, 276–279,
277
PARTITV1.ZIP hard drive
cluster analyzer,
232–235, **235**
RAVED.ZIP ASCII file
editor, 279–282
SUPDIR10.ZIP drive
directory manager,
267–270
XEV43.ZIP disk file editor,
282–285, **283**
FIPS10.ZIP partition splitter,
220–226
First Interactive Partition
Splitting Program (*see*
FIPS10.ZIP)
Fix Clock (*see*
FIXCLOCK.ZIP)
FIXCLOCK.ZIP clock setting,
54–56
floppy drive, 208–215
AUTOTEST.ZIP access-
time test, 208–210
CHKDRV.ZIP change-line
signal check,
210–212
CLEAN4.ZIP clean read/
write heads,
212–214
DISKUTIL.ZIP info on all
drives, 200–203
DKI101.ZIP info on all
drives, 203–206

floppy drive, *continued*
DRF.ZIP recover erased
diskette data,
214–215
Floppy Drive Cleaning Utility
(*see* CLEAN4.ZIP)
Foley, David R., 165
Free System Resources (*see*
RESOUR11.ZIP)
Fricke, Tobin, 77

G
Gainous, Les, 313
Gebhardt, Travis, 302
general support tools, chart,
251
Gilbert, Shane, 230
Gissemann, Uwe, 195
global heaps, 60
Granite Mountain Software,
307
graphics file printing,
PRINTGF.ZIP,
146–151, **149**
Green, Rodey, 185
Griffith, Paul, 73–74
GUARD.ZIP encrypt files,
308–313
Guardian, The (*see*
GUARD.ZIP)

H
hard disk, 215–235
AUTOTEST.ZIP access-
time test, 208–210
BOOTRX.ZIP boot record
parameters
displayed, 216–217
CSCTEST2.ZIP hard drive
performance test,
217–219, **218**
DAAG310.ZIP tree of disk
contents, 191–194,
192, **194**
DATA_REC.ZIP data
recovery, 194–197,
196
DDARP_13.ZIP ID/rename
device drivers,
197–200
DISKTYPE.EXE drive
geometry listing, 201

hard disk, *continued*
DISKUTIL.ZIP info on all
drives, 200–203
DKI101.ZIP info on all
drives, 203–206
DUGIDE.ZIP IDE drive
information,
219–220
FIPS10.ZIP partition
splitter, 220–226
HDCP.ZIP copy hard disk
contents by sector,
226–229, **228**
HDINFO.ZIP hard drive
geometry info,
229–231
IDATA.ZIP ATA drive
geometry info,
231–232
IDLE.EXE idle timer set-
ting, 201–202
JCBENCH.EXE 17–19, **18**
PARTITV1.ZIP hard drive
cluster analyzer,
232–235, **235**
READBI.EXE drive type-
recorder/burn-in,
26–30
SPC.ZIP system info, **72**
SREP.ZIP SmartDrive
cache perform
monitor, 207–208
STANDBY.EXE power-
down hard drive,
202–203
THEREF43.ZIP drive/
controller spec.
index, 300–301
Hard Disk Copy Program
(*see* HDCP)
Hard Drive Benchmark (*see*
CSCTEST2.ZIP)
Hard Drive Information Utility
(*see* HDINFO.ZIP)
Hard Drive Reference (*see*
THEREF43.ZIP)
hardware diagnostics, 15–102
486TEST.ZIP memory
write-time
benchmark, 91–93
486TST.ZIP system burn-in,
33–35, **34**

hardware diagnostics,
  continued
  ASQ0315.ZIP memory
    management,
    44–48, **46**, **47**
  benchmarking utilities, 15,
    17–19
  BIOS ID/reporting utilities,
    19–32
  BIOS.ZIP BIOS age/date
    extraction, 19–21
  BIOSR11.ZIP data area
    reader, 21–24, **22**,
    23
  burn-in/stress tests, 32–35
  CACHECHK.ZIP cache
    performance test,
    93–96
  CHECK136.ZIP command-
    line system
    descriptor, 48–51
  CHKIO.ZIP I/O port assign-
    ment test, 79–81
  CMOS utilities, 35–41
  CMOS.ZIP backup and
    restore, 36–38
  CMOSRAM2.ZIP backup
    and restore, 38–41,
    40
  CONF810E.ZIP system
    info/benchmarking,
    51–54, **53**
  CPU utilities, 41–44
  direct memory access
    (DMA) channel
    tests, 78–91
  FIXCLOCK.ZIP clock
    setting, 54–56
  general system tests, 44–78
  input/output (I/O)
    management, 78–91
  interrupt (IRQ) line tests,
    78–91
  IRQINFO.ZIP interrupt
    (IRQ) assignment
    test, 81–84
  JCBENCH.EXE 17–19, **18**
  MAXSPEED.EXE clock
    speed test, 41–43,
    42
  memory/cache tests,
    91–102

hardware diagnostics,
  continued
  MEMSCAN.ZIP check
    contents of RAM
    1MB, 96–98, **97**
  OVERHEAD.ZIP system
    "overhead" test,
    57–58
  PCM140.EXE POST code
    cross-reference
    master, 24–26, **25**
  port tests, 78–91
  PORT11.ZIP port reassign-
    ment, 84–86
  RAMMAP.ZIP map active
    software in RAM,
    98–100
  READBI.EXE drive type-
    recorder/burn-in,
    26–30
  RESOUR11.ZIP free up
    system resources,
    58–61
  RITM25.ZIP clock setting,
    61–65
  SHADTEST.ZIP shadow
    RAM test, 100–102
  SHOWS174.ZIP system
    chip-set identifier,
    30–32
  SNOOP330.ZIP system
    info, 65–69, **67**, **68**
  SPC.ZIP system info,
    69–73, **72**
  SPYDOS.ZIP interrupt
    analyzer, 86–88
  SRXTEXT, Cyrix upgrade
    CPU test, 43–44
  SWAPIRQ.ZIP interrupt-
    swapping, commun-
    ications, 88–91
  SYSCHK40.ZIP system info,
    73–77, **74**
  SYSINF.ZIP system info,
    77–78
Hardy, Rick, 183
HATCH.EXE 112
HDCP.ZIP copy hard disk by
    sector, 226–229, **228**
HDINFO.ZIP hard drive geo-
    metry info, 229–231
Heck, Wolfgang, 87

Hex Editor (*see*
    HW16V210.ZIP)
hex files
  HW16V210.ZIP hex file
    editor, 276–279, **277**
  XEV43.ZIP disk file editor,
    282–285, **283**
HexEdit (*see* XEV43.ZIP)
HISCAN.ZIP scan-rate
    optimizer, 114–117
Holin, Michael, 51
Holt, Bill, 233
Hoopes, Scott A., 36, 206
Horwitz, Rick, 291
HP Self-Test Utility (*see*
    LASERTST.ZIP)
HW16V210.ZIP hex file editor,
    276–279, **277**

I

IDATA.ZIP ATA drive
    geometry info,
    231–232
IDE Drive Information Utility
    (*see* DUGIDE.ZIP)
Identify ATA (*see* IDATA.ZIP)
IDLE.EXE idle timer setting,
    201–202
input devices, 285–294
  CALJOY2.ZIP joystick
    calibrator, 285–287,
    287
  JOY2.EXE joystick
    calibrator, 287–288
  SCODE22.ZIP make/break
    keyboard code re-
    porter, 289–290, **290**
  STKVGA31.ZIP joystick
    performance test,
    291–292, **292**
  TMTX.EXE mouse
    operation test,
    292–294, **294**
input/output (I/O), 78–91
  CARDG2.ZIP I/O card
    configuration list,
    295–297
  CHKIO.ZIP I/O port assign-
    ment test, 79–81
  PORT11.ZIP port
    reassignment,
    84–86

Integrated System Utility (*see* SPC.ZIP)

interrupt (IRQ) lines, 78–91
   SPYDOS.ZIP analyzer, 86–88
   SWAPIRQ.ZIP interrupt-swapping, communications, 88–91
   IRQ.EXE serial port interrupt disable, 181
   IRQINFO.ZIP line-assignment test, 81–84, **83**

IRQ.EXE serial port interrupt disable, 181

IRQInfo (*see* IRQINFO.ZIP)

IRQINFO.ZIP interrupt (IRQ) line assignment test, 81–84, **83**

IS_VID.EXE identify/characterize video system, 106–108

J

JC-DBench (*see* JCBENCH.EXE)

JCBENCH.EXE 17–19, **18**

Jenkins, Stephen, 126

Jerrim, John, 176

Johnson, Aaron, 131

JOY2.EXE joystick calibrator, 287–288

Joystick Calibration Utility (*see* CALJOY2.ZIP; JOY2.EXE)

Joystick Check (*see* STKVGA31.ZIP)

K

KayakR Software, 233

Keyboard Code Scanner (*see* SCODE22.ZIP)

keyboards (*see* input devices)

Klama, Markus, 26

L

Laser Manager (*see* LASMAN.ZIP)

laser printers (*see* printers)

LaserClean (*see* LZC26.ZIP)

LASERTST.ZIP laser printer self-test, 158–159

LASMAN.ZIP laser printer ASCII file printing, 144–146, **145**

Lee, Chang P., 227

Lee, Paul, 129

Leonard, Steve, 191

Levey, Richard, 33

Lincoln Beach Software, 117

Lines utility, VGA/SVGA support suite, 111–112

LISTEN10.ZIP test for incoming signals, 186–188

LOCATO.ZIP parts/materials locator index, 298–299, **299**

locks (*see* security)

LZC26.ZIP clean laser printer, 159–161

M

MacLean, Randy, 264

map active software, RAMMAP.ZIP, 98–100

Marcor Enterprises, 309

Marcotte, Jean-Georges, 139

Maron, Irving, 55

Martin, Charles F., 257

math coprocessor, 486TST.ZIP system burn-in, 33–35, **34**

MAXSPEED.EXE clock speed test, 41–43, **42**

Maxum Computers, 41–43, **42**

McAdams, T.C., 141

McAfee Associates, 6

memory
   486TEST.ZIP write-time benchmark, 91–93
   ASQ0315.ZIP memory management, 44–48, **46**, **47**
   CACHCHK.ZIP cache performance test, 93–96
   direct memory access (DMA) channel tests, 78–91
   global heaps, 60
   hardware diagnostics, 91–102
   MEMSCAN.ZIP first MB of RAM test, 96–98, **97**

memory, *continued*
   OVERHEAD.ZIP "overhead" or "overload" test, 57–58
   RAMMAP.ZIP map active software, 98–100
   RESOUR11.ZIP free up system resources, 58–61
   RITM25.ZIP clock set, 61–65
   SHADTEST.ZIP shadow RAM test, 100–102
   SREP.ZIP SmartDrive cache perform monitor, 207–208
   virtual memory management, 60

Memory Scan (*see* MEMSCAN.ZIP)

Memory Write Test (*see* 486TEST.ZIP)

MEMSCAN.ZIP check contents of RAM 1MB, 96–98, **97**

Merrett, Doug, 220

mice (*see* input devices)

MicroFirmware, Inc., 30

MicroMetric, 144

MicroSystems Development, 24

Modem Listen Utility (*see* LISTEN10.ZIP)

MONITORS 2.01 program, 103, 315–328
   blank raster test, 325
   burn-in process, 326
   color bars, 321, **321**, **322**
   convergence tests (crosshatch/dots), 322–323, **323**, **324**
   DDARP_13.ZIP ID/rename device drivers, 197–200
   focus test, 324–325, **327**
   high-voltage test, 326, **328**
   improving MONITORS, 328
   linearity test, 323–324, **325**
   main menu, 316–317, **317**
   phase test, 324, **326**
   purity tests, 325

399

MONITORS 2.01 program, *continued*
  screen mode selection errors, 327
  serial number, 316
  test patterns, 320
  troubleshooting, 327
  unlocking MONITORS program files, 315–316
  video adapter test, 317–319, **318**, **319**
  video test mode selector, 319–321, **320**
monitors (*see also* MONITORS 2.01; video tools)
  CNVRGE.ZIP color convergence test, 124–126
  CRTAT2.ZIP align/test color CRT, C126–128, **128**
  HISCAN.ZIP scan-rate optimizer, 114–117
  PSPS30.ZIP capture-and-dump screen, 119–121
  screen mode selection errors, 327
  troubleshooting, 327
  VIDEO.ZIP video board mode test, 131–134
  VIDEO.EXE video mode check/set, 128–131, **130**
  VIDSPD40.ZIP video read/write speed test, 134–136
Morton, Robert L., 155
Mosteller, Thomas, 38
motherboard
  486TST.ZIP system burn-in, 33–35, **34**
  SHOWS174.ZIP identifier for system chipset, 30–32
Mouse/Trackball Testing Utility (*see* TMTX.EXE)
Murray, Dave, 288
MVP Software, 7

N
NeoSphere Software, 302
Netscape, 6
No Preservatives Software, 187
Noble, Kevin, 295
notebook monitor scan-rate optimizer, HISCAN.ZIP 114–117
NoVaSoft, 257

O
Orman, Jack A., 216
OSR Open Systems Resources, Inc., 167
OVERHEAD.ZIP system "overhead" test, 57–58

P
Paladin Software, Inc., 171
Palette Adjuster (*see* PALU15.ZIP)
palette tools, 114–124
PALU15.ZIP palette adjuster for DOS, 117–119, **118**
parallel ports (*see* port management)
PARAMO.ZIP LPT1 port data capture, 138–141, **140**
Parman, Douglas S., 211
Partition Cluster Analyzer (*see* PARTITV1.ZIP)
partitioning, FIPS10.ZIP partition splitter, 220–226
PARTITV1.ZIP hard drive cluster analyzer, 232–235, **235**
parts (*see* reference works)
PC Slowdown Utility (*see* SLO23.ZIP)
PC-Config (*see* CONF810E.ZIP)
PCM140.EXE POST code cross-reference master, 24–26, **25**
pen plotter printing, PRNTGL.ZIP 151–155, **153**
Penny, James B., 96
Perkel, Marc, 98
PhG, 79

PKWare, 6
Plug 'n' Play, 195
Polczynski, Ray, 236
PORT.EXE (*see* PORT11.ZIP)
port management (*see also* communications/modems), 78–91, 137–162
  BBX201.ZIP serial port debugger/breakout box, 164–166
  BUFFER.EXE FIFO buffer control, serial port tests, 179
  CHKIO.ZIP I/O port assignment test, 79–81
  COMPRT25.ZIP COM and LPT port info, 166–169
  COMRESET.ZIP reset stuck COM ports, 169–171
  COMTAP21.ZIP serial protocol analyzer, 171–173, **173**
  COMTEST.ZIP test serial port/devices, 173–176, **175**
  COM_BPS.EXE port data-rate setting, 179
  COM_FMT.EXE port character-format set, 180
  CTSSPU22.EXE serial port tests, 176–182
  DDARP_13.ZIP ID/rename device drivers, 197–200
  DOS_COM.EXE DOS BIOS serial port insertion, 180
  DOS_SWAP.EXE serial port swap, 180
  DTR.EXE data term ready (DTR) command line control, 180
  IRQ.EXE serial port interrupt disable, 181
  LISTEN10.ZIP test for incoming signals, 186–188
  modem utilities, 186–188

port management, *continued*
  PARAMO.ZIP LPT1 port
    data capture,
    138–141, **140**
  PORT11.ZIP port reassign-
    ment, 84–86
  PORTINFO.EXE serial port
    info, 177–179
  PRINTERS program, 332
  RESETCOM.EXE serial
    port reset, 181
  RTS.EXE request to send
    (RTS) command
    control, 181
  SIMTRM.ZIP serial port
    troubleshooter,
    182–185, **184**
  SWAPIRQ.ZIP interrupt-
    swapping, commun-
    ications, 88–91
  UARTTS.ZIP COM port
    hardware info,
    185–186
PORT11.ZIP port reassign-
  ment, 84–86
PORTINFO.EXE serial port
  info, 177–179
POST Code Master (*see*
  PCM140.EXE)
postcard-ware (*see*
  shareware)
PostScript Print Screen (*see*
  PSPS30.ZIP)
Postuma, Paul, 21, 289
Printer Capture Utility (*see*
  PARAMO.ZIP)
Printer Test Utilities (*see*
  PRN-TEST.ZIP)
printers (*see also* PRINTERS
  program)
  DDARP_13.ZIP ID/rename
    device drivers,
    197–200
  EZSET.ZIP printer control,
    141–143, **142**
  LASERTST.ZIP laser
    printer self-test,
    158–159
  LASMAN.ZIP laser printer
    ASCII file printing,
    144–146, **145**

printers, *continued*
  LZC26.ZIP clean laser
    printer, 159–161
  maintenance utilities,
    158–162
  PARAMO.ZIP LPT1 port
    data capture,
    138–141, **140**
  PRINTERS program,
    329–369
  PRINTGF.ZIP graphics file
    printing, 146–151,
    149
  PRN-TEST.ZIP impact
    printer tests,
    161–162
  PRNTGL.ZIP pen plotter
    printing, 151–155,
    153
  PSPS30.ZIP capture-and-
    dump screen,
    119–121
  ZC33.ZIP printer codes con-
    trol, 155–158, **156**
PRINTERS program, 329–369
  carriage transport test, 352,
    353, **354**, 358, 359
  clean rollers, 352, 356, 358,
    361
  compatible printers/drivers,
    332, **333–348**
  corona test, 362, 363–365,
    365
  description of program,
    368–369
  drum and roller test, 362,
    365–366, **367**
  escape sequences/escape
    codes, 349–351, **349**
  exiting or quitting, 369
  fuser test, 362, 366
  help mode, 351
  impact tests, 351–352, **352**
  improving PRINTERS
    program, 369
  ink jet tests, 357–362, **358**
  laser/LED printer tests,
    362–368, **363**
  manual codes, 349
  paper transport test, 352,
    353, 358, 359, 362

PRINTERS program,
  continued
  paper walk test, 352,
    354–355, 358, 360
  port selection, 332
  preliminary setup inform-
    ation, 352–353, 358,
    362
  print head test, 352,
    355–356, **355**, 358,
    360–361
  print intensity setting, 351
  serial number, 330
  startup and configure
    menus, 331, **332**
  test page printing, 352,
    356–357, **357**, 358,
    361–362, **368**
  toner test, 362–363, **364**
  transport test, 366–367
  tutor mode, 351
  unlocking PRINTERS
    program files, 330
PRINTGF.ZIP graphics file
  printing, 146–151, **149**
PRN-TEST.ZIP impact printer
  tests, 161–162
PRNTGL.ZIP pen plotter
  printing, 151–155, **153**
PSPS30.ZIP capture-and-
  dump screen, 119–121
PSV10.ZIP VGA/SVGA sup-
  port utilities, 108–113
public domain products, 6

Q
Qualitas, 44–48, **46**, **47**

R
RAM (*see* cache; CMOS;
  memory)
RAMMAP.ZIP map active
  software in RAM,
  98–100
Rapid Deployment Systems,
  Inc., 84
RAVED.ZIP ASCII file editor,
  279–282
Ravitz Editor (*see*
  RAVED.ZIP)
Ravitz, Cary, 148, 152, 280

READBI.EXE drive type-recorder/burn-in, 26–30
Record BIOS Utility (*see* READBI.EXE)
recovery/restore (*see also* backup)
    BACKEE28.ZIP backup, restore, sync files, 252–256, **253**
    CMOSRAM2.ZIP CMOS backup and restore, 38–41, **40**
    CMOS.ZIP CMOS backup and restore, 36–38
    DATA_REC.ZIP data recovery, 194–197, **196**
    DRF.ZIP recover erased diskette data, 214–215
reference works, 295–301
    CARDG2.ZIP I/O card configuration list, 295–297, **296**, **297**
    LOCATO.ZIP parts/materials locator index, 298–299, **299**
    THEREF43.ZIP drive/control spec. index, 300–301
registration of products, 6, 7, 13
RESETCOM.EXE serial port reset, 181
RESOUR11.ZIP free up system resources, 58–61
Reward Message (*see* RWARD2.ZIP)
RighTime (*see* RITM25.ZIP)
RITM25.ZIP clock setting, 61–65
Roscoe, T., 248
Ross, Ed, 57
RTS.EXE request to send (RTS) command control, 181
RWARD2.ZIP reward message on display, 313–314
Ryan, Brian, 231

S
Salvisberg, Hans, 271
SAVCOLOR, save color, VGA/SVGA support suite, 110
SBBEEP.ZIP tone generator, 302–303
Schaefer, Arno, 222
SCODE22.ZIP make/break keyboard code reporter, 289–290, **290**
Screen Color (COLOR), VGA/SVGA support suite, 113
screen tools, 114–124
security, 308–314
    GUARD.ZIP encrypt files, 308–313
    RWARD2.ZIP reward message on display, 313–314
Serial Port Utilities (*see* CTSSPU22.EXE)
serial ports (*see* port management)
SHADTEST.ZIP shadow RAM test, 100–102
shareware, 1–14
    Association of Shareware Professionals (ASP), 8, **8**
    cost, 5
    distributing shareware, 5–6
    "limited functionality" blockers, 7
    postcard-ware, 6
    problems, 6–8
    public domain products vs., 6
    registration, 6, 7
    selection, 5
    try-it-out first concept, 5–6
    updates/versional differences, 8
    zero-dollar ware, 6
Shearer, Dan, 49
Show System Chipset (*see* SHOWS174.ZIP)
SHOWS174.ZIP system chipset identifier, 30–32

Simple Terminal Emulator (*see* SIMTRM.ZIP)
SIMTRM.ZIP serial port troubleshooter, 182–185, **184**
SLO23.ZIP slow down PC, 306–308
SmartDrive Monitor (*see* SREP.ZIP)
SNDST.ZIP save/restore sound card configuration, 303–306
SNOOP330.ZIP system info, 65–69, **67**, **68**
Snooper (*see* SNOOP330.ZIP)
Software Interrupt Analyzer (*see* SPYDOS.ZIP)
Software Specialists, 211
Soh, Kok Hong, 274
Sound Blaster Beep (*see* SBBEEP.ZIP)
Sound Card State Selector (*see* SNDST.ZIP)
sound utilities, 302–306
    CDCP10.ZIP play audio CDs, 236–238
    DA7.ZIP play audio CDs, 247–249, **249**
    SBBEEP.ZIP tone generator, 302–303
    SNDST.ZIP save/restore sound card configuration, 303–306
SPC.ZIP system info, 69–73, **72**
speed utilities, 306–308
    CDSPEED.ZIP measure data transfer rate of CD-ROM, 242–245
    CDTA.ZIP measure data throughput of CD-ROM, 245–246
    MAXSPEED.EXE clock speed test, 41–43, **42**
    SLO23.ZIP slow down PC, 306–308
    VIDSPD40.ZIP video read/write speed test, 134–136

SPYDOS.ZIP interrupt analyzer, 86–88

SREP.ZIP SmartDrive cache perform monitor, 207–208

SRXTEXT, Cyrix upgrade CPU test, 43–44

Stack, Randy, 213

STANDBY.EXE power-down hard drive, 202–203

STKVGA31.ZIP joystick performance test, 291–292, **292**

stress tests, 32–35

Stuntz, Robert, 198

subdirectories (*see* file management)

SUPDIR10.ZIP drive directory manager, 267–270

Super Directory (*see* SUPDIR10.ZIP)

SWAPIRQ.ZIP interrupt-swapping, 88–91

Swayne, Patrick, 108

SYSCHK40.ZIP system info, 73–77, **74**

SYSINF.ZIP system info, 77–78

SysInfo (*see* SYSINF.ZIP)

System Checker (*see* SYSCHK40.ZIP)

system configuration (*see also* boot managers; hard disks)

486TST.ZIP system burn-in, 33–35, **34**

ASQ0315.ZIP memory management, 44–48, **46**, **47**

backing up existing config, 15, 104, 138, 164, 189

benchmarking utilities, 15, 17–19

BOOTSY.ZIP multiple configuration at boot, 271–273

CCS103.ZIP multiple configuration at boot, 273–275

system configuration, *continued*

CHECK136.ZIP describe system, command-line descriptor, 48

CMOS.ZIP CMOS backup and restore, 36–38

CMOSRAM2.ZIP CMOS backup and restore, 38–41, **40**

CMOS utilities, 35–41

CONF8103.ZIP system info/benchmarking, 51–54, **53**

DATA.ZIP ATA drive geometry info, 231–232

DDARP_13.ZIP ID/rename device drivers, 197–200

DISKTYPE.EXE drive geometry listing, 201

FIXCLOCK.ZIP clock setting, 54–56

general system tests, 44–78

HDINFO.ZIP hard drive geometry info, 229–231

IDLE.EXE idle timer setting, 201–202

OVERHEAD.ZIP "overhead" or "overload" test, 57–58

RESOUR11.ZIP free up system resources, 58–61

RITM25.ZIP clock set, 61–65

SHOWS174.ZIP system chipset identifier, 30–32

SNOOP330.ZIP system info, 65–69, **67**, **68**

SPC.ZIP system info, 69–73, **72**

STANDBY.EXE power-down hard drive, 202–203

SYSINF.ZIP system info, 77–78

System Overhead Checker (*see* OVERHEAD.ZIP)

T

TCOLORS, Color Text Mode, VGA/SVGA support suite, 110

Tech Assist, Inc., 298

TechStaff Corp., 293

THEREF43.ZIP drive/control spec. index, 300–301

Tiramisu Data Recovery (*see* DATA_REC.ZIP)

TMTX.EXE mouse operation test, 292–294, **294**

trackballs (*see* input devices)

tree display, disk contents, DAAG310.ZIP, 191–194, **192**, **194**

Turner, Brent, 124

U

UART Port Identifier (*see* UARTTS.ZIP)

UARTTS.ZIP COM port hardware info, 185–186

utilities, 2–4

backup utilities, 252–270

benchmarking utilities, 15, 17–19

BIOS ID/reporting utilities, 19–32

boot managers, 270–275

burn-in/stress tests, 32–35

CD-ROM tools, 236–249

CMOS utilities, 35–41

CPU utilities, 41–44

DOS vs. Windows versions, 4

editors, 276–285

floppy drive tools, 208–215

general system tests, 44–78

hard disk tools, 215–235

input devices, 285–294

modem utilities, 186–188

port management tools, 137–162

printer tools, 137–162

reference, 295–301

sound utilities, 302–306

utilities, *continued*
  speed utilities, 306–308
  video alignment tools,
    124–136
  video tools, 103–136

V
Vachon, Charles, 105
Van Tassle, Ray, 93
VESA list (VL) utility, 110,
  111
VGA Color Display
  (VCOLORS), 112
VGA/SVGA support suite
  (PSV10.ZIP), 108–113
  Color Master utility, 109
  Color Protector (CP) utility,
    110
  Crosshatch Utility
    (HATCH) utility, 112
  Fade-to-Clear (CLF) utility,
    113
  Lines utility, 111–112
  SAVCOLOR, save color,
    110
  Screen Color (COLOR)
    utility, 113
  TCOLORS, Color Text
    Mode, 110
  VESA list (VL) utility, 110,
    111
  VGA Color Display
    (VCOLORS) utility,
    112
  VGAHUE.ZIP VGA color
    adjustment,
    122–124, **123**
  Video Mode Disabler
    (VMD) utility, 111
  Video Mode Selector (VM)
    utility, 110–111
  Video Speed Test
    (VTEST_T,
    VTEST_G), 112
VGAHUE.ZIP VGA color
  adjustment, 122–124,
  123
Vias, John, 65

Video Adapter Test Program
  (*see* VIDEO.ZIP)
Video Board Detector (*see*
  ATMEM10.ZIP)
Video Detector Utility (*see*
  IS_VID.EXE)
Video Mode Controller (*see*
  VIDEO.EXE)
Video Mode Disabler (VMD)
  utility, 111
Video Mode Selector (VM)
  utility, 110–111
Video Speed Analyzer (*see*
  VIDSPD40.ZIP)
Video Speed Test (VTEST_T,
  VTEST_G), 112
video tools (*see also*
  monitors; MONITORS
  program), 103–136
  486TST.ZIP system burn-
    in, 33–35, **34**
  alignment tools/diagnostics,
    124–136
  ATMEM10.ZIP identify
    video board in
    system, 104–106
  CNVRGE.ZIP monitor
    color convergence
    test, 124–126
  Color Master utility, 109
  Color Protector (CP) utility,
    110
  Crosshatch Utility
    (HATCH) utility, 112
  CRTAT2.ZIP align/test
    color CRTs,
    126–128, **128**
  Fade-to-Clear (CLF)
    utility, 113
  HISCAN.ZIP scan-rate
    optimizer, 114–117
  IS_VID.EXE identify/
    characterize video
    system, 106–108
  JCBENCH.EXE 17–19, **18**
  Lines utility, 111–112
  MONITORS 2.01 program,
    315–328

video tools, *continued*
  palette tools, 114–124
  PALU15.ZIP palette
    adjuster for DOS,
    117–119, **118**
  PSPS30.ZIP capture-and-
    dump screen,
    119–121
  PSV10.ZIP VGA/SVGA
    support utilities,
    108–113
  SAVCOLOR, save color,
    110
  Screen Color (COLOR)
    utility, 113
  screen tools, 114–124
  TCOLORS, Color Text
    Mode, 110
  VESA list (VL) utility, 110,
    111
  VGA Color Display
    (VCOLORS), 112
  VGAHUE.ZIP VGA color
    adjustment,
    122–124, **123**
  video ID/BIOS tools,
    104–113
  Video Mode Disabler
    (VMD) utility, 111
  Video Mode Selector
    (VM) utility,
    110–111
  Video Speed Test
    (VTEST_T,
    VTEST_G), 112
  VIDEO.EXE, video mode
    check/set, 128–131,
    130
  VIDEO.ZIP video board
    mode test, 131–134
  VIDSPD40.ZIP video
    read/write speed
    test, 134–136
  VIDEO.EXE, video mode
    check/set, 128–131,
    130
  VIDEO.ZIP video board mode
    test, 131–134

VIDSPD40.ZIP video read/write speed test, 134–136

virtual memory management, 60

viruses, 15, 36, 104, 138, 164, 189, 250

Vitt, Mark, 214

Volpa, Peter, 239

W

Whetstone, Bert, 174

Williams, Chet, 59

Windows/Windows 95, 4

Witt, David, 160

X

XEV43.ZIP disk file editor, 282–285, **283**

Z

ZapCode (*see* ZC33.ZIP)

ZC33.ZIP printer codes control, 155–158, **156**

zero-dollar ware (*see* shareware)

Zitterkopf, John, 304

ZittWare, 304

405

About the Author

Stephen J. Bigelow is the founder and President of Dynamic Learning Systems, a technical writing and research company specializing in electronics and PC servicing. The electrical engineer has written nine books, including *Troubleshooting, Maintaining, and Repairing PCs*, *Troubleshooting and Repairing Computer Printers, Second Edition*, and *Troubleshooting and Repairing Computer Monitors*, and nearly 100 feature articles for both mainstream magazines and technical journals. He also edits and publishes *The PC Toolbox*, a popular newsletter for PC repair technicians.